Guilt

Guilt

THE BITE OF CONSCIENCE

Herant Katchadourian

STANFORD GENERAL BOOKS
An Imprint of Stanford University Press
Stanford, California

Stanford University Press
Stanford, California

©2010 by the Board of Trustees of the Leland Stanford Junior University.
All rights reserved.

Printed in the United States of America on acid-free, archival-quality paper

Library of Congress Cataloging-in-Publication Data
Katchadourian, Herant A.
  Guilt : the bite of conscience / Herant Katchadourian.
      p. cm.
  Includes bibliographical references and index.
  ISBN 978-0-8047-6361-5 (cloth : alk. paper)
  1. Guilt. 2. Guilt—Religious aspects. I. Title.
  BF575.G8K38 2009
  152.4'4—dc22
                          2008053323

Typeset by Bruce Lundquist in 10/14 Minion

For Stina

CONTENTS

PREFACE

"FOR I CAN TELL YOU," wrote Cervantes in the introduction to *Don Quixote*, "that although it cost me some effort to compose [this book], none seemed greater than creating the preface you are now reading. I picked up my pen many times to write it, and many times I put it down again because I did not know what to write."[1]

Many an author has shared Cervantes's experience, as I do now. Why should writing an introduction be so hard?

To begin with, there is a general feeling, be it true or not, that people do not read introductions. Like the prefatory remarks to a speech or mail addressed to Resident, they seem generic, and hence of no personal interest. For the author, another problem is deciding what to say. Would revealing the highlights of the book whet the reader's appetite or dull it like a lump of sugar before a meal? In order to entice the reader, should one give away the goods before they are carefully unwrapped?

Much depends on what the material sets out to do. To be properly called an "introduction" it should delve into the subject matter itself, like a short chapter. A preface, on the other hand, is an introduction to the book; it tells the reader what to expect. What I have here is a preface aimed at three objectives: to tell the reader why I have written the book; to propose reasons for reading it; and to provide a road map to the contents.

My reasons for writing this book are similar to those that led me to teach an undergraduate seminar on guilt and shame at Stanford University for a decade. I told my students that I had two main interests in teaching the course: one was professional, the other personal. With respect to the first, most of the courses I had taught over four decades were very large classes (enrolling over twenty thousand students). Now I wanted to teach a small seminar that would allow me to know my students better. Moreover, my courses approached their topics from a multidisciplinary perspective. I was a professor of psychiatry with wider intellectual interests and I considered a multidisciplinary approach to be the best way to learn about human behavior. The topic of guilt and shame fit that mold very well.

As for personal reasons, when I was at the age of my students, I felt unduly burdened with feelings of guilt. There were no good reasons for it; as young men go, I had no more reason to feel guilty than my peers. I was like a man who was paying income tax on money he was not making. When I asked my students to write down their reasons for taking my course, their answers more or less replicated my own concerns. About half said they had an academic interest in the subject—they were majoring in psychology or were intellectually intrigued by the topic. Others had personal issues with guilt because they were Jewish/Catholic/evangelical Christians or belonged to some other group presumed to be guilt prone, or they had parents who made them feel guilty, or felt guilty and did not know why.

I expect similar considerations to apply to many readers of this book. If you have an intellectual interest in the subject of guilt, you will find this book to be a rich source of material. No other book I know of covers as many facets of guilt. This is a bold claim but I make it for good reasons: I searched in vain for such a book to use in my course. It took half a dozen specialists, in addition to me, with my own areas of competence in psychiatry and the behavioral sciences, to teach the course. Their topics, also represented in this book, range over evolutionary psychology and anthropology, six major religious traditions (Judaism, Christianity, Islam, Hinduism, Buddhism, and Confucianism), moral philosophers (Aristotle, Kant, John Stuart Mill, Nietzsche), and legal conceptions of guilt.

A great deal has been written about guilt (and shame) from various academic perspectives. Modern knowledge is organized into specialized disciplines. That is necessary if our knowledge is to expand, but it results in books with a lot of depth in one particular aspect of guilt but not much else about what is outside it.

The primary intellectual merit of this book is in bringing together various disciplinary viewpoints in one volume. I wish I could claim that I have achieved an integrated synthesis of all these views, but I cannot. The differences in methodology, language, conceptions, and assumptions of various specialists that would make the denizens of the Tower of Babel proud, preclude that. Consequently, what you find here is not a real dialogue but "parallel monologues" (as an academic friend called it). However, these disparate voices are at least now speaking in the same room, even if not to each other. I hope hearing these different views may convince you that the best way to understand a topic such as guilt is to look at it from diverse points of view. Similar sentiments are expressed by William Miller in the preface to his fascinating book on disgust:

> I see this book as an homage to a time when, in a strange way, psychology was less constricted than it is now. In that time it was about virtues and vices, narratives both fictional and historical, about how one stood with others as much as how one stood with oneself. The psychological was not yet divorced from either the moral or the social. The book is thus methodologically promiscuous as a methodological commitment, drawing from history, literature, moral philosophy, and psychology.[2]

Moreover, readers who have a professional interest in one or another of the fields represented here may also find the book useful. They are not likely to find much that they do not know within their own fields but a good deal that is new to them in a half dozen fields outside their own.

This book, however, is neither a textbook nor a research monograph. It is academically sound but intended for a general and a broader than purely academic audience. Within these pages, you will hear not only the voices of experts and literary figures, but also those of ordinary people relating the experiences of guilt in their everyday lives. Each chapter opens with a case history based on a personal account or a work of literature. Within each chapter there are shorter accounts and examples that illustrate the issues being discussed.

The matter of a more personal interest in guilt is harder to address. Like my students and myself, many readers, I expect, may have faced concerns over guilt, or to be struggling with them now. If you are one of these people, what can you expect by way of help from this book? As I said above, this is an academically sound but non-academic book; similarly, this not a self-help book but nonetheless it tries earnestly to be helpful. Reading this book should help you understand not only what guilt is and is not, and what it should and should not be in general terms, but also within your own life experiences. Knowing about guilt will provide you with greater insight into who you are as well as equip you to exercise greater control over your own life and actions. It will help you understand how guilt works as a currency of exchange in your relationships with others, particularly with those close to you. It will help you protect yourself when someone uses guilt to manipulate you.

It is particularly important for you to know when guilt is excessive, as well as inadequate, in your life. Its excess will suck the joy out of your life, while its deficiency will ruin your relationships and pit you against society. When you clash with the expectations of your social group, you will ultimately lose. This book may help you to avoid both pitfalls. It is also my hope that reading this book will provide you with greater insight into religious and philosophical views on guilt, and by extension, into your own moral sentiments and ethical convictions.[3]

At the outset, I was reluctant to provide advice to readers on how to deal with guilt. Unsolicited advice is intrusive and ineffective since it does not respond to an expressed need. Moreover, advice has to be compatible with a person's moral values and psychological concerns. Generic advice is like junk mail. To be useful, you have to customize it—one size does not fit all. To that end, there is a section at the end of each chapter on the issue of dealing with guilt from the particular vantage point of that chapter.

There are, however, limits to how helpful a book can be in dealing with deep moral dilemmas. A friend of mine who was keen on reading a draft copy of this book turned out to have a personal agenda. He was in a relationship that troubled his conscience. What he was really looking for was a way out of his dilemma—a vindication of sorts. It is no wonder that he was disappointed by what he read since he did not find specific answers to his problem. Such specific answers may require counseling or therapy that goes beyond the reading of books.

Looking at guilt in broader cultural terms, how relevant or important is it in our modern world? In the Victorian period, moral zealots clobbered people with guilt. Consider the lament of a divorced Catholic woman involved in a surreptitious affair with a Protestant man in Evelyn Waugh's *Brideshead Revisited*:

> *Living in sin with sin*, by sin, for sin, every hour, every day, year in, year out. Waking up with sin in the morning, seeing the curtains drawn on sin, bathing in it, dressing it, clipping diamonds to it, feeding it, showing it around, giving it a good time, putting it to sleep at night with a tablet of Dial [a barbiturate] if it's fretful.[4]

Does anyone lose sleep anymore over this sort of thing? It seems that many people are now more likely to nurse a sense of entitlement rather than guilt.[5] They are more concerned with what others owe them than with taking responsibility for what they owe to others. Even the very basis of traditional moral judgments, hence the need to feel guilty, seems under assault. Consider, for instance a recent book entitled *In Defense of Sin* whose contributors purport to provide a defense for: idolatry, blasphemy, dismissing mother and father, murder, adultery, deceit, greed, breaking the Golden Rule, refusing to forgive, pride, gossip, lust, promiscuity, prostitution, despair, and suicide. Yet, despite the provocative (and rather misleading) title and chapter headings, the book is not a wholesale rejection of traditional morality but a critique of its excesses and irrationalities. We have, of course, heard all this before and no one has said it better than Nietzsche did a hundred years ago. Consequently, guilt is alive and well, and very much with us.

To state it at the outset, the basic thesis of this book is as follows: The capacity for guilt is innate—we are born with it hard-wired into our brain through evolution. Guilt serves a variety of functions in connection with social control, hence its experiences are subject to cultural variation. Like other emotions, guilt is neutral in itself, neither good nor bad as such. It becomes pathological when it is excessive or deficient. Guilt is an integral part of moral reasoning and closely tied with the monotheistic religions, and to a lesser extent with Asian religions. It is an important part of philosophical discourse on morality and a key concept of legal systems. We shall deal with each of these issues in subsequent chapters.

You already may have some sense of what this book is about, but a road map to its contents will provide a more concrete idea of what to expect. The table of contents does not make it explicit, but there are two main parts to this book. The first (Chapters 1 to 6) deals with our individual experiences of guilt, primarily from a psychological perspective. The second part (Chapters 7 to 11) addresses guilt in a broader societal context by looking at guilt through the lenses of evolutionary psychology, anthropology, religion, philosophy, and the law. The first part provides a micro-, the second a macro-perspective.

Chapter 1 lays the groundwork by mapping out the geography of guilt and its neighbors—regret, embarrassment, shame, and disgust. Chapter 2 looks at the behaviors that have been typically associated with guilt. It relies on the Ten Commandments and the seven Cardinal Sins to provide a framework for guilt-inducing behaviors. The Ten Commandments (the heart of Judeo-Christian ethics) focus on specific behaviors; the Cardinal Sins (a legacy of the Christian Middle Ages) go to the heart of human motivation by pointing to those proclivities that lead to guilt-inducing behaviors.

Chapter 3 probably comes closest to what most readers expect to find in a book of this sort. It addresses the crucial question of how guilt works in our personal and intimate relationships. Chapter 4 is unusual in that it deals with several types of guilt that do not entail personal wrongdoing: survivor guilt, collective guilt, and existential guilt. Chapter 5 tackles the difficult problem of pathological guilt: the difference between guilt that is healthy and helps regulate our moral behavior, and guilt that becomes pathological through excess or deficiency.

Chapters 6 and 7 address how the capacity for moral judgment (hence the prospect of feeling guilty) develops. Chapter 6 examines this process within the lifetime of individuals; Chapter 7 looks at it at the level of the human species. By addressing the role of the evolution of guilt, Chapter 7 acts as a bridge between the individual and the societal perspectives that divide the book.

Chapters 8 and 9 look at the vast ancient traditions of guilt in six major religions of the world: Judaism, Christianity, and Islam in the West; Hinduism, Buddhism, and Confucianism in the East. These are perhaps the most challenging chapters (they were certainly the hardest to write), but they are crucial to our understanding of guilt—whether we are religious or not. More than any other approach, religions have shaped the moral consciousness of most people, and they still do. Hence it is important for us to be familiar with them, whether we adhere to their teachings or not.

Chapter 10 is the secular counterpart of the chapters on religion. It presents three key philosophical approaches to guilt: Aristotle's ethics of virtue, Kant's ethics of duty, and John Stuart Mill's ethics of utility. It also presents Nietzsche's scathing critique of Western morality. Finally, Chapter 11 again shifts the ground from what is elective in our experience of guilt to what is obligatory in legal terms. We may choose to accept or reject all of the other approaches to guilt, but we have no choice about being under the rule of law. Hence the need to know how the law determines legal culpability.

A distinguished philosopher and friend told me that if this was going to be a book on guilt, then guilt should be on stage at all times. Should other characters make an appearance, they too should be speaking about guilt.[6] I have tried but may not have succeeded in heeding this excellent advice consistently, and I ask for the reader's indulgence when I occasionally digress. I have also made an earnest effort to keep my own opinions and prejudices out of this book, so far as humanly possible, relegating such personal comments to the Epilogue.

Writing this book has been an enormously challenging and enriching experience for me. I have learned from it more than I have from any comparable effort. Moreover, this has been more than a purely intellectual exercise; it has changed the way I feel and behave. I hope that similar benefits will be passed on to readers of the book as well.

Finally, you can of course read this book any way you wish, but my suggestion is that you read the chapters in sequence. It may be tempting to go directly to what may look more interesting to you. That is fine, if it will help you get what you are looking for. However, it may mean losing sight of the logic that underlies the organization of the book. Therefore, if you think a chapter may not interest you, at least skim over it. Keep in mind that this book is not an encyclopedia with freestanding entries—the chapters build on each other and are intended to provide you with a sense of continuity to make sense out of the whole.

ACKNOWLEDGMENTS

THE IDEA OF THIS BOOK originated from a multidisciplinary seminar on guilt and shame that I taught at Stanford University for about a decade. A number of colleagues served as guest lecturers on topics that fell outside my areas of competence. I owe them a world of thanks for introducing me to the perspectives on guilt of their respective disciplines. Their ideas are reflected throughout this book. These colleagues are cited at the beginning of the appropriate chapters.

Some of these colleagues, along with others at Stanford or other institutions, also provided invaluable help with the preparation of this book. Sanford Gifford, Ernlé Young, Nancy McGaraghan, and Dan Bernstein read the entire manuscript and offered thoughtful comments and most helpful suggestions with respect to their areas of expertise and interest, and as general readers. Others critiqued specific chapters from their particular disciplinary perspectives: Anne Fernald, Cendri Hutcherson, and Mark Gross (psychology); John Racy (psychiatry); David Hamburg and Ulla Morris Carter (collective guilt); Esther Hewlett (philanthropy); Robert Sapolsky (evolution); Arnold Eisen and Estelle Halevi (Judaism); Mark Mancall (who provided extensive help on Judaism, Hinduism, and Buddhism); Robert Gregg (monotheism; particularly extensive help with Christianity); Scotty McLennan (monotheism and Asian religions); Ebrahim Moosa, Shahzad Bashir, and Hank Edson (Islam); Raka Ray, Shireen Pasha, Smita Singh, and Zulfiqar Ahmad (Hinduism); Mark Berkson (Buddhism, and particularly Confucianism); Lee Yearley, Sheila Melvin, Jindong Cai, and Rachel Zhu (Confucianism); Robert Audi and Lanier Anderson, who reviewed several drafts (philosophy); Robert

Weisberg, Paul Brest, and Steve Toben (law). Without their help this book could not have been written.

I am most appreciative of Michael Keller's initial interest in this book and for his ongoing support throughout the publication process. I would like to thank the staff of Stanford University Press: Alan Harvey, Emily-Jane Cohen, Jeffrey Wyneken, and Judith Hibbard; as well as all those who worked behind the scenes. Richard Gunde did outstanding work in editing the manuscript, and he did far more than correcting my grammar. Donald Lamm was most generous with his time and provided helpful advice for making this book more readily accessible to a general audience. David Lyon was also helpful in this regard.

I am most grateful to the Hewlett Foundation, and its president, Paul Brest, for providing me with a superb office as a resident scholar and the companionship and support of the foundation's staff, including Denise Robichau, Brian Hendrickson, Chuck Ferreira, and Marc Greenfield, who provided ongoing help with my endless struggles with the word processor.

I have a special debt of gratitude to my wife, Stina, to whom this book is dedicated. She read the entire manuscript several times. Her keen judgment as a writer and translator was most helpful with improving the style and content. Our many discussions helped clarify many an obscure phrase and idea. Her support and patience made it possible for me to spend the time and effort it took to bring this book to a successful completion. My daughter Nina brought her discerning artist's eye to the choice and design of the cover illustration. Sina Najafi, my son-in-law, helped to procure the image for publication. My son Kai was most forgiving for my closeting myself in my study summer after summer at our island home in Finland, instead of going windsurfing with him.

All my colleagues, family members, and friends who became engaged with the arduous process of producing this book deserve much of the credit for what may be good about the book. I am solely responsible for what is not.

Herant Katchadourian

Guilt

1 GUILT AND ITS NEIGHBORS

When I was in college, I fashioned in my imagination an idealized image of a woman who would one day fulfill all my yearnings. During my last year at architecture school, I met that woman—at least, I thought I did. Cynthia seemed to embody all that I wanted. She was beautiful, intelligent, and gifted; a strong-willed woman with enormous self-confidence. If I could have her, there was nothing more I could ask of the Lord. Men far more mature and better established than me courted her. Yet, to my amazement, I was the one who won her heart—at least, I thought I did.

By the time we got married, I knew it was an awful mistake. Yet, I felt trapped and went ahead with it out of a misguided sense of commitment, the fear of losing face, and the crumbling residues of my insane passion for her. Soon enough, our lives became mired in a gloomy discontent that did not even have the cleansing relief of emotional outbursts. Feelings of guilt permeated my life as I blamed myself for making Cynthia feel miserable, condemning myself to a bleak future and most of all, for failing God, who had granted me what I wanted so desperately. As our marriage dragged on, and I tried to lose myself in my work, my feelings of guilt became blunted and gave way to resignation and resentment. Since Cynthia was as unhappy as I was, I tried to persuade her that we would be better off going our separate ways. Yet, the prospect of losing me made her tighten her grip for reasons I could not fathom. Finally, I left her.

I am grateful to Anne Fernald, Cendri Hutcherson, and Mark Gross for their comments and helpful suggestions for this and the next two chapters. Cendri Hutcherson also provided help with the identification of valuable sources in the psychological literature.

Some months after our separation, I met with Cynthia with the hope of getting a handle on our stalled relationship. Our encounter was surprisingly amicable but we made no headway. As I was leaving, Cynthia broke down and begged me to let her come back to me. I was stunned. She had never—not once—expressed the slightest regret or ever admitted guilt for anything that concerned me. Since I knew she had a conscience, she must have been stubbornly proud to admit such feelings or contemptuous to express them. Yet here she was pleading with me in abject humility. As I looked into her tearful emerald eyes, my arms yearned to embrace her but my legs urged me to run. With a wan smile, I turned around and walked to my car.

As I drove on, an overwhelming sense of guilt washed over me. How could I cause so much pain? How could my hopes for a happier life be purchased at the cost of so much suffering? I wanted to turn back, but I pressed on like a prey running from a predator. Cynthia's remorse was no doubt genuine and I could forgive her but I could not imagine living with her for the rest of my life.

It took a couple of years before my lingering sense of guilt allowed me to file for divorce. When it became clear that I was determined to go through with it, Cynthia became vindictive. That, more than anything else, hardened my heart enough to break free. As our divorce became public, my lingering guilt became replaced by a mounting sense of shame. For the first time I had failed in a big way. It was hard to know which hurt more—the guilt or the shame.[1]

PHILIP K. is a brilliant young architect and Cynthia is a gifted painter. One may wonder how two attractive, intelligent, and decent individuals could blunder into such a mismatched relationship. However, what concerns us here is not that intriguing issue but the role that guilt plays in such human dramas. How are we to understand Philip's struggle with guilt? Is he a merely a man with a sensitive audience or excessive, pathological guilt? Is guilt the reflection of his guilt-prone character or the result of his troubled relationship with Cynthia? If Philip had married someone else, would he have been free of the guilt that burdened his life? Had Cynthia married someone more mature, would she have been as inclined, or as successful, in inducing guilt in her husband? We do not have Cynthia's side of the story to better understand her, but does she come across to you as the villain or the victim of this sorry tale? Should there always be villains and victims or could the relationship itself be at fault? In that case, does guilt help or hinder intimate relationships? Does it enhance love or fuel hatred?

We have so far addressed these matters in psychological and relational terms. However, guilt has equally significant social and cultural components. Philip came from a traditional and conservative background. In his community, divorce was rare and disgraceful. Given his family's social prominence and his own reputation as an exemplary young man, it was particularly galling for Philip to get branded with the shame of his divorce. It also raised the question of whether Philip had correctly understood God's will or substituted his own desires for it. Philip's sense of personal failure and the prospect of public condemnation of his divorce enhanced each other in generating Philip's raging feelings of guilt and shame.

Even if most of us have not have suffered through the same experiences that Philip did, there must have been other occasions for us to know what it is like to feel guilty or ashamed. Philip refers to these emotions as distinct feelings that troubled him at different times in different ways. That is the way most of us think too. However, guilt and shame, as well as regret and embarrassment, were tangled up in Philip's experience (as they often are in ours).

When we do something wrong, or shameful, we "feel bad." Usually, we do not stop to tease apart and label what these feelings consist of. It is only when we reflect on them, or try to convey them to others, that we attach labels to them, saying we feel guilty or ashamed. Such labels are readily understood since the feelings they convey are widely shared. However, as often as not, these feelings are neither discrete nor sharply defined in our minds. Even those who study them do not always agree on what they represent.

It is also worth noting that lay and scientific usage of the terminology for emotions often differ quite a bit. In other words, when we use terms like shame and guilt in everyday use, what we mean is not necessarily what psychologists mean by these terms. This may explain why some of the fine distinctions made in formal studies may not seem to fit our experiences. This might account for some of the discrepancies between what psychologists claim differentiates these emotions, and what they find in surveys of ordinary people whose perceptions of what constitutes guilt and shame may not be as sharply defined.

Although this book is primarily about guilt, we cannot discuss guilt without some reference to its "neighbors"—regret, embarrassment, shame, and disgust.[2] These emotions serve *self-evaluative* functions. They reflect our judgments of our actions and the kind of person we think we are. In experiencing them, we put ourselves on trial within our own hearts and minds. These judgments are tied up with how we think others judge us and the consequences of those judgments for our social standing and sense of self-esteem. Consequently, the fear of retribution and anxiety over the loss of our social standing inevitably color our experiences of guilt and shame.

The pain and discomfort caused by guilt and shame may range from mild uneasiness to deep anguish. Most of the time they merely ruffle the emotional surface of our lives, but they can also turn into raging storms. Since they are unpleasant, we try to avoid them. However, not everything that hurts is bad. The pain caused by my twisted ankle stops me from stepping on it and causing further damage. Similarly, painful feelings like guilt and shame alert us that there is something amiss in our lives and relationships that must be set right.

WHAT ARE EMOTIONS?

The word emotion is associated with psychological excitement (from the Latin "I was moved"; "I got upset").[3] The more informal term for emotion—feeling—may be used both as a noun ("I have a guilty feeling") as well as a verb ("I feel guilty").[4] Emotions are states of heightened psychological arousal accompanied by physical manifestations, like the pounding heart of fear and the blush of embarrassment. They play a crucial role in motivating and guiding our thoughts and actions, and their facial and bodily expressions communicate our inner feelings to others. Emotions solve problems important to social relationships in the context of ongoing interactions. Theorists, however, have different assumptions about the origins, defining characteristics, and consequences of emotions.[5]

Early studies of emotion tended to focus on its "*intra*personal" aspects as experienced by individuals. More recently, they have shifted more to the "*inter*personal" functions of emotions that deal with human interactions, such as between parents and children and romantic partners.[6]

Emotions are at the core of human nature. They are universal and part of our evolutionary heritage, hence shared with higher animals; but they are also shaped by culture in ways that are distinctively human. People have both cherished and feared emotions. They add spice to life and make us feel ecstatic ("I'm so excited!"). They also imply loss of control ("I was swept off my feet") and interfere with our ability to act rationally ("I was so angry, I lost my head").

Natural as they are, emotions do not just happen—they occur for some reason.[7] They are neither good nor bad in and of themselves; their impact depends on how and why they are used. Traditionally, philosophers have been suspicious of emotions because they cloud our judgment and psychologists have considered feelings to be too vague for empirical study. However, we now view emotions as integral to all human experience. Instead of being antagonistic to reason, they are interconnected with and inseparable from it; thinking and feeling are complementary and inseparable—we cannot experience one without the other.[8]

Earlier investigators focused on *primary emotions* such as anger and fear (as well as sadness, happiness, disgust, and surprise). These core emotions have a biological basis (hence they are shared with higher animals) and distinctive physiological manifestations. They are present in all cultures and have universally recognized facial expressions. For instance, we can usually tell if a person is angry, anywhere in the world, even by simply looking at the photograph of an angry face. These emotions have evolved (and been culturally modified) by serving important survival and reproductive functions.

The subjective experiences of guilt, shame, regret, embarrassment, and pride place them squarely in the emotional ballpark. However, they lack some of the universal components of the primary emotions, and hence are called *secondary emotions*. It is easier to tell if a person is angry or afraid than if a person feels guilty or ashamed. Secondary emotions are more subject to social conditioning, and thus show greater cultural differences in their experience and expression. For example, the way the French and the Chinese would experience anger or sadness would be closer than the way they would experience guilt or shame. However, secondary does not mean of secondary importance. These secondary emotions play a central role in regulating our thoughts, feelings, and behaviors.

Until recently, neuroscientists could not tap directly into the brain mechanisms that control emotions. A commonly used method in earlier neurological studies was to electrically stimulate various parts of the brain and observe the resulting behavioral manifestations, thus localizing the brain centers controlling those functions. Currently, more sophisticated tools like positron emission tomography (PET) and functional magnetic resonance imaging (fMRI) are used with remarkable results. Although we are still far from a full understanding of the neuroscience of guilt and shame, there are studies that have profound implications for our understanding of how these emotions work normally and under pathological conditions.

Neuroscientists are currently focusing on how and where the subjective experiences of emotions are localized in the brain. Functional magnetic resonance imaging detects subtle increases in blood flow associated with activation of parts of the brain. Image processing techniques then convert these blood flow changes into images that can be photographed. Thus when experimental subjects are induced to experience feelings of guilt or shame by having them imagine to have done something wrong, particular parts of the brain "light up" in response.

What are the implications of these findings? How are we to interpret the linkage of thoughts and feelings with their underlying neural mechanisms? Consider the following example. When we speak on the phone, the sound of our voice is converted to electrical impulses which travel along telephone cables and are then reconverted to sound waves that can be heard as speech. This process explains the transmission of the sound of the voice but it tells us nothing about the meaning of our words. Similarly, when we detect what is happening in the brain when we experience guilt, is the brain simply acting as a telephone? Or, is it also involved in conveying the "meaning" of the emotion of guilt itself?

No one is claiming to have located the seat of the conscience in the brain. Nonetheless, knowing about what specific parts of the brain are associated with the experience of guilt helps us to establish the neural geography of emotions. That is a good start since it shows not only what part of the brain is transmitting emotion-bearing messages but distinguishes between, for instance, guilt and embarrassment.[9] We shall have more to say about these issues when we discuss the impact of brain dysfunction on moral judgment.

In studying morality, psychologists take a secular and nonjudgmental approach. They are primarily interested in the issue of how individuals make moral judgments and how the capacity for such judgments develop. They are generally less concerned with the sort of moral questions that preoccupy those who approach morality from religious or philosophical perspectives. They generally take a culturally relativistic view. Nonetheless, some psychologists have attempted to find the basic ways in which various ethical systems inform moral standards. One such approach addresses three major components (the "Big Three"): The "ethic of autonomy" focuses on individual rights and justice, with particular attention to rules against harming others. The "ethic of community" is concerned with shared social conventions that determine moral rules. The "ethic of divinity" addresses religious beliefs and practices, including concerns over purity. Standards of behavior emanating from the ethic of autonomy (such as prohibitions against murder) are generally more universal than those dictated by the ethic of community (as in rules of sexual conduct) or by divinity (as in religious obligations).[10]

SELF-CONSCIOUS EMOTIONS

Psychologists call guilt, shame, embarrassment, and pride *social emotions* because they are heavily dependent on social interactions. They are considered *moral emotions* because they involve social judgments about how one should and should not behave. These emotions are linked to the welfare of others and society as a whole. They provide the moral force to do good and to avoid doing evil. Not all moral emotions are self-judgmental and negative. There are also positive moral emotions like pride (in a positive sense) as well as feelings like admiration and gratitude for the good deeds of others.[11]

Psychologists now generally refer to guilt, shame, embarrassment, and pride as *self-conscious emotions*. This is a rather awkward term since emotions cannot be self-conscious, only people can. What the term is meant to convey is that such emotions reflect the evaluations of the self by others. In that case, it would be more correct to refer to them as "other-oriented" emotions since they reflect people's perceptions of how others feel about them.[12] To call them *emotions of self-assessment* would be even less cryptic, but that term is far less commonly used.[13] Regret and disgust are usually not included in this group of emotions, but they share a number of important connections with them and we will discuss them briefly further on.

Self-conscious emotions share a number of basic characteristics. They require self-awareness—a sense of who we are with respect to others. They emerge later in childhood than the basic emotions and require a certain degree of cognitive maturation and reasoning. Unlike primary emotions, such as anger, that are present earlier in life, embarrassment, shame, and guilt do not emerge until about age three. They do not have discrete and universally recognized facial expressions, unlike fear, anger, and joy (except for blushing, which reflects embarrassment or shame). Self-conscious emotions facilitate the attainment of complex social goals. Whereas an emotion like fear may help deal with danger, as fleeing from a predator, self-conscious emotions depend on more complex social roles involving the attainment and maintenance of social status and the prevention of rejection by the group.[14] Finally, self-conscious emotions can be both a blessing as well as a curse, an issue we will return to.

Embarrassment used to be thought of as an integral part of shame. Now it is considered to be an independent emotion. The distinction between guilt and shame is more complex and uncertain. Some investigators consider guilt and shame to be two aspects of the same emotion; others see them as quite distinct from each other (how distinct varies). Those who overemphasize their commonalities lose sight of their important differences, making guilt and shame look like amorphous banks of clouds merging into each other. Those who take the opposite view engage in a fruitless search for guilt and shame in "pure" forms that may not exist. The more sensible approach is to view regret, embarrassment, shame, and guilt as distinct emotions that nonetheless overlap and flow into each other.

For example, suppose that my elderly mother complains about visual changes in her left eye. She does not seem unduly distressed (and I am very busy), so I do nothing about it. A week later her eye goes blind. I rush her to the hospital, but it is too late. I feel guilty and regret having been negligent. When it comes to explaining what happened, I feel ashamed and embarrassed for not having known better. Or, at a dinner party, when engaged in an animated discussion, I spill red wine on the tablecloth. I am acutely embarrassed (especially as my wife glares at me); and when it turns out that the tablecloth was a family heirloom, I feel guilty.

In such daily experiences, it is often hard to tell where guilt ends and shame begins, and vice versa. Even researchers, as we have noted, vary in how they conceive of these entities. Moreover, their definitions may change over time. For instance, over the past two decades, a new conception of shame and guilt has emerged that challenges the conventional views of these entities, as we shall discuss shortly. However, before we get into these more controversial matters, we need to clarify what the various components of the self-conscious emotions are.

REGRET

Regret is usually not listed among the self-conscious emotions as such. However, it is an important component of all of these emotions, as well being important in and of itself. Regret is a ubiquitous part of our lives and one of the most common topics married couples talk about. As the origin of the word suggests (Old French, "to sob"), regret conveys a sense of disappointment and sadness over what one has lost or failed to attain. It has been characterized as a form of "counterfactual thinking" that pits the realities of life against the "what-ifs" and the "if-onlys" of what could have been. Regret usually serves no useful purpose ("crying over spilled milk"), but it can sometimes provide valuable lessons from our failures. It is useful in consoling and commiserating with others, but it is not useful when we turn it into an instrument of self-flagellation over what cannot be changed.[15]

People are more likely to regret their actions than inactions—to regret what we did rather than what we did not do. This is perhaps because the former entails more personal responsibility. Yet there are some of us who dwell more on what we failed to do than what we did do (I am one of them). Some forms of regret have a rational basis (for example, regret for not having gotten a better education); other forms are less rational. For instance, failing to win the lottery by one number causes more regret than if the ticket was off by several digits. Missing a flight at the airport by a few minutes is more aggravating than being late by half an hour. Although the narrowness of the margins does not change the outcome, the closer we came to it, the more it troubles us.

President Harry Truman considered regret a total waste of time. Woody Allen claims his only regret in life is that he was not someone else. We may dismiss regret or make light of it, but it can have a powerful effect on us, even overriding guilt. For instance, splurging on a vacation or a pair of shoes may result in buyer's remorse, but when we think about it years later the regret of what we missed doing tends to replace the guilt.[16]

Regret often follows simple misjudgment ("I should not have bought those shoes"). It may express a formulaic refusal ("We regret to inform you that your application has been denied"), or a more genuine sentiment ("I am so sorry I cannot make it to your birthday party"). Expressions of regret act as a casual form of apology (like saying "sorry" for bumping into someone). Or they may be a more serious acknowledgment of responsibility ("I truly regret I hurt your feelings").

Much of the time, regret follows trivial choices but it can also follow momentous decisions ("I picked the wrong career"; "I married the wrong person"). As an integral part of guilt and shame, regret compounds one's sense of failure. However, regret is free of moral taint as is embarrassment, to which we turn next.

EMBARRASSMENT

Embarrassment is a reaction to unsettling, unpredictable, and uncontrollable events. It is a feeling of awkwardness, being flustered, abashed, and at worse, mortified ("I thought I would die"). Embarrassment is caused typically by a breach of social convention or etiquette (what the French call *faux pas* or *gaucherie*). It represents a "category violation" where a social boundary is trespassed. This is also true for shame and guilt, except that in embarrassment no moral or ethical rules are violated. The breach is merely one of custom, convention. This amoral quality of embarrassment is one of its key characteristics. Consider the following examples.

> When having dinner at my boyfriend's house, his father asked me where I planned to live after graduation. I said I hoped to get into graduate housing on campus although preference was given to married students. My boyfriend set down his wine glass and said, "This is why we are sleeping in the same bed, so she can get better housing next year." My jaw dropped and my face burned. I stared down at my plate of pasta wanting to bury my face in the noodles to avoid his parents' eyes and kicked my boyfriend under the table.[17]

Several factors are at play here. One is the element of surprise. The revelation, or at least the claim that the couple is sleeping in the same bed, comes out of the blue and is totally out of place. It has the same effect as exposing the young woman, like undressing her in public. The sexual innuendo is obviously another important component; they are not just sleeping in the same bed but "sleeping together." However, despite the discomfiture it causes, there is no harm intended and no cause for guilt or shame. It is a joke and the parents are presumably amused. Otherwise, the young woman would have felt insulted and her boyfriend gotten scolded.

> I dread going to large parties because I run into people that I have met before but cannot remember their name; its gets especially embarrassing when I have to introduce them to my wife.

> I was sitting on the toilet and thought I had locked the door. When someone opened it I got flustered.

The situation in these cases is different. The failure to remember names implies that the people are unimportant—"forgettable." Though unintended, it puts people, and oneself, in a poor light. Sitting on the toilet is nothing to be ashamed of, as long as it is private; when it becomes public, even accidentally, one is "caught with one's pants down."

We can also be embarrassed by what others do, especially if their conduct reflects negatively on who we are:

> My mom and dad wear old-fashioned clothes and listen to outdated music. I find it embarrassing to have friends over and hear that old music playing on the stereo.

> My husband and I were visiting another couple. We were sitting on the couch and he decided to rest his feet on top of their fine coffee table. It was so inconsiderate and I felt awful.[18]

Another key element in embarrassing situations is the sense of *incongruity.* For instance, we feel awkward when we are overdressed or underdressed at a party. We feel out of place—as if we do not belong there because we have been ignorant or have failed to conform to the social code that defines membership in the in-group:

> Shortly after I came to America, I was taken to a party at a prominent lawyer's home in Washington. As I walked in, I realized that every man in the room was wearing an almost identical dark suit, very different from my more informal blazer. I felt like a soldier in a parade out of uniform.

In this case, since the person was a recent arrival in the country he could be forgiven. Otherwise, the disparagement would be worse. Expectations of formality in dress have become more relaxed in recent years but rules of conformity have not. If you now go formally dressed to a gathering where everyone else is not, it would be just as bad.

This sense of incongruity can also follow a clumsy action that that makes one look ridiculous:

> I was carrying a basket overloaded with groceries when I stumbled and scattered everything around. As potatoes tumbled and oranges rolled away, someone asked me if I was alright, and another tried to help, which made me feel even more self-conscious.

Slapstick comedy exploits this sort of thing to make us laugh. There is an element of glee at someone's discomfiture (what Germans call *Schadenfreude*), reflecting our ambivalence particularly toward authority figures. We take no notice if a child drops something and there is nothing funny when a handicapped person falls out of a wheelchair; it is hilarious, however, when a waiter spills champagne on the boss at the office party.

Of all the self-conscious emotions, embarrassment has the most distinctive physical manifestations. People avert their gaze, look down, suppress their smiling or break into a sheepish grin. However, its quintessential sign is *blushing*. Traditionally, blushing was considered a sign of modesty, hence particularly welcome among young women. Juliet tells Romeo,

> Thou know'st the mask of night is on my face;
> Else would a maiden blush bepaint my cheek,
> For that which thou hast heard me speak tonight.[19]

In Milton's *Paradise Lost*, even the angel Raphael blushes when questioned about the love life of angels:

> To whom the angel with a smile that glowed
> Celestial rosy red, love's proper hue,
> Answered. Let it suffice thee that thou know'st
> Us happy, and without love no happiness.
> Whatever pure thou in the body enjoy'st
> (And pure thou wert created) we enjoy
> In eminence, and obstacle find none
> Of membrane, joint, or limb, exclusive bars.[20]

Darwin considered blushing to be universal and the most human of all expressions. It is already present in childhood but not shared with animals:

> Blushing is not only involuntary but the wish to restrain it makes it worse. The young blush more than the old. . . . Women blush more than men. . . . The blind do not escape . . . as well as the completely deaf.
>
> In most cases the face, ears and the neck are the sole parts which redden; but many persons, whilst blushing intensely, feel that their whole bodies grow hot and tingle. . . .
>
> The reddening of the skin is succeeded by a slight pallor, which shows that the capillary vessels contract after dilating. . . .
>
> . . . Most persons, whilst blushing intensely, have their mental powers confused. . . . They are often much distressed, stammer, and make awkward movements or strange grimaces. . . . The mental states which induce blushing

. . . consist of shyness, shame and modesty; the essential element in all being self-attention. . . . It is not the simple act of reflecting on our own appearance, but the thinking of what others think of us, which excites a blush.[21]

Embarrassment requires an audience. It is hard to imagine how one could be embarrassed in private. This is because the basic determinant in embarrassment is the feeling of unwanted *exposure*. This is reflected in the traditional association of embarrassment with nudity; more specifically, exposure of those parts of the body that must be hidden from public view—especially the genitals. Much depends, however, on the circumstances under which exposure occurs. For instance, men and women are embarrassed by exposure to each other but not to members of their own sex, as in public baths and showers. Near nudity at the beach is not embarrassing. We reveal our bodies to our lovers and doctors, but not to strangers.[22] Western attitudes toward nudity are now much more relaxed, especially among the young. In some college dorms men and women take showers together, ostensibly to "demystify" nudity.

The shame of nudity, and by extension the exposure of undergarments, applies to both sexes ("Your slip is showing"; "Your zipper is open"), but it has been more closely associated with women. The old medical term for female (but not male) genitals is *pudendum*, meaning, "a thing of shame." In most cultures, female genitals are considered arousing while male genitals are threatening, which is why men pay to see female nudity but male exhibitionists go to jail. The female body is more objectified than that of the male and subject to the "male gaze." This is why women are much more attentive to how they sit, cross their legs, or otherwise expose themselves to others.

These considerations extend to the public display of certain bodily functions in both sexes. It is embarrassing to be seen ("caught") urinating, defecating, masturbating, or having sexual intercourse. To a lesser extant, this is also true for belching, farting, spitting, vomiting, and picking one's nose. (It may be embarrassing to some to even hear these terms.) We get embarrassed by things that would be disgusting to others.

Girls learn early to conceal all signs of menstruation and are highly embarrassed if they fail to do so. Various religious traditions have menstrual taboos where a woman is "unclean" and must undergo a ritual cleansing after her menstrual period is over. Similar restrictions applied to pollution by semen in men but are far less strictly enforced.[23]

Embarrassment veers into the more negative emotion of shame when it is caused by who we *are*, not just what we *do*. This is often a reaction to how our bodies look, how others make us feel, and how we feel about ourselves. Those with physical handicaps may be more vulnerable to such feelings, cruel as that may be. However, such feelings are more often simply based on thinking that one is too short, tall, thin, or fat ("My fat buttocks and potbelly repulse me and I assume others feel the same way about me"). Even a blemish that others may hardly notice can make us self-conscious. Nor is it always a matter of physical appearance. The way we talk, walk, laugh, tell jokes—in short, anything that makes us feel different, foreign, inferior will make us embarrassed.

Moreover, the causes of embarrassment are not only physical. We are embarrassed when our vulnerable selves are exposed to social scrutiny. This may involve personal inadequacies—real or imagined—that make us appear stupid, ignorant, or lacking in talent, social graces, athletic prowess, or attractiveness. The same is true for perceived shortcomings based on family connections—such as social class or ethnic origin—as reflected in the clothing we wear, the food we eat, the accents we speak with, and all else that represents our public face. The infliction of shame and embarrassment is one of the nastier tools of prejudice and discrimination.

Nonetheless, more appropriate forms of embarrassment serve useful social functions. Its universality and physical features point to its evolutionary origins and cultural variations. Embarrassment acts as a conciliatory gesture to get us out of awkward situations. It is a form of apology and its submissive posture acknowledges that one has committed a social misstep and regrets it, thereby deflecting the irritation caused by our clumsiness. It implies taking responsibility for one's clumsiness. (Think how irritated we feel at those who do something embarrassing but then act as if nothing untoward has happened.) Moreover, embarrassment may be induced by positive comments about one's accomplishments, for instance, when parents brag about their children, or a person's achievements are celebrated at a retirement party.

If embarrassment occurs too readily or excessively, it becomes a social handicap. Individuals who suffer from *social anxiety* are more subject to it. Those who are shy, introverted, self-conscious, and overly dependent on social approval are more vulnerable to it. We must differentiate, however, between *situational* shyness, which is virtually universal (who would not feel some tension addressing a crowd?), and shyness as a *personality trait* that hangs like a millstone around the neck.[24] People who carry that weight live in constant fear that they will disgrace themselves, as if they were on stage being observed by an audience ready to laugh at them. Like pathological shyness, embarrassment erodes self-confidence, belittles our selves, and leads to withdrawal from social interactions.[25]

Finally, although most embarrassment is unintentional and self-inflicted, there is an intentional variety, called *strategic embarrassment,* that is used to discredit, compromise, or tarnish another's image.[26] Also called *shaming,* it is done through criticism, accusation, rumor, innuendo, and lies. For instance, it occurs by leaking embarrassing information to damage a political opponent's reputation and public image.

SHAME

The word *shame* is derived from the Old German term *skew* ("to cover"). This points to the association of shaming with exposure, which we described as the essential element in embarrassment. The defense against exposure is concealment. When children are embarrassed, they bury their faces in their parent's lap. This same tendency persists in adulthood when we wish to hide, shrink, or vanish altogether when we are ashamed. Darwin's description of shame is hard to distinguish from embarrassment:

> Under the keen sense of shame there is a strong desire for concealment. We turn away the whole body, more especially the face, which we endeavour in some manner to hide. An ashamed person can hardly endure to meet the gaze of those present, so that he almost invariably casts down his eyes or looks askant.[27]

Is the overlap between the two emotions the residue of the traditional view of embarrassment as an essential part of shame? Should we therefore eliminate all manifestations of embarrassment from our current definition of shame? What is then left of shame after we take embarrassment out it? Does it stand naked staring at guilt? How can we then tell it apart from guilt?[28]

There are as yet no definitive answers to these questions. We must therefore assume that shame continues to share with embarrassment certain features, such as the desire for concealment and blushing as well as the other physical expressions we described above. On the other hand, some of the other psychological and social characteristics of shame and embarrassment are quite different. For instance, there is a clear difference between someone stumbling on a slippery sidewalk and a ballet dancer falling down during a performance. The first is merely embarrassing; the second reflects ineptitude and incompetence, and is thus shameful. An embarrassing act induces laughter (which the victim may join in), but the reaction to a shameful act is disapproval and disgust (which leads to self-loathing). Shame is not only more painful but it has deeper psychological and social implications than embarrassment. We could say that shame always implies embarrassment but not vice versa—one can be embarrassed without being ashamed. However, embarrassment is not simply a milder version of shame. The difference between the two emotions is not only a matter of intensity but is qualitative as well.

One key difference is in their ethical burden. Shame might, or might not, have ethical implications; embarrassment never does. There are actually two types of shame: *Moral* and *non-moral*. Non-moral shame results from public exposure of defects that lead to loss of social status; in that sense, it may overlap with embarrassment. Moreover, non-moral shame also entails a sense of personal inadequacy, incompetence, and failure that are socially more damning and lead to loss of respect. For example, non-moral shame may result from a student failing a course, an employee being fired, a surgeon bungling an operation, a lawyer losing a lawsuit, or a marriage ending in divorce. Nonetheless, such failings may still fall short of moral shame since there is no intent to harm another person nor the violation of a moral code. These boundaries, however, are not rigid. Depending on the circumstances, some of these·events, as in the above examples, may also reflect moral shame or guilt.

Another key distinction is that moral shame—or shame more generally—leads to a global negative evaluation of the self, whereas embarrassment and guilt are focused on a specific act, thus leaving the person's self intact. This is an important new distinction that differentiates between shame and guilt—an issue we will discuss in more detail.

Shame has important social and cultural aspects. In Western cultures, shame has occupied a position secondary to guilt as a moral emotion, whereas the opposite is true in Asian cultures. This is reflected in the terms used in various languages to refer to guilt and shame. For instance, English has only one word while Chinese has over one hundred words for shame. Since there is but one English word for shame, one can make no distinction between its moral and non-moral components. Yet this distinction is nicely captured in French, which has two terms: *Pudeur* is shame as embarrassment associated with nudity (derived from "covering up"); it implies modesty and has no direct moral connotations. By contrast, *honte* refers to the loss of honor and disgrace, with the implication of moral failure. The French also differentiate between "good shame" (*la bonne honte*) of modesty and the "bad shame" (*la mauvaise honte*) of dishonor.

The same distinction holds true in Greek, where *aidos* stands for modesty (derived from *aidoia*—the word for genitals—hence nudity). For instance, when the Olympian goddesses refrained from joining the gods in laughing at Aphrodite and Ares caught in bed, it was because of *aidoi*—their sense of shame or modesty. The context can also be asexual. Odysseus is ashamed to have his hosts see him cry.

A second word for shame is *aischune*, which refers more directly to moral shame, implying disgrace and ignominy. During the Trojan war, Ajax uses shame as a battle cry urging the men to fight—not to do so would be dishonorable. *Aidos* arises within the self; *aischune* is externally induced: but the distinction is not sharp and *aischune* may also imply embarrassment. Individuals have both a sense of their honor and the honor of others; they can feel indignation when either their or someone else's honor is violated.[29] The reaction in Homer to someone who has done something shameful is *nemesis*—a sense of indignation that leads to retribution. (Nemesis was the goddess who meted out divine punishment for wrongdoing and presumption. The term now refers more generally to an implacable agent of someone's downfall.)

Most of us are not aware of these fine distinctions. Moreover, many people would find it difficult to distinguish between moral shame and guilt. The quotes that follow were offered as examples of shame but could have just as easily been cited as examples of guilt. (As you read them, consider how you would label them.)

I am suffering some degree of shame over my divorce proceedings. After twenty years of marriage, my husband admitted to having four affairs over the years. I'm sure I contributed to our marital problems but cannot excuse his bad behavior. Nonetheless, I still feel shame that my marriage failed though I don't know why I am so hard on myself about this.

This incident is probably the most awkward one in my life. My mother asked me if I had started to engage in any type of sexual behavior; the usual talk about sex and protection. I denied having done anything sexual—I lied. I felt both ashamed and guilty because I had let my parents down. The fact that it was always such a sensitive subject made me feel even more guilty about lying to them than for what I actually had done. I was always open to my parents about everything, but now I was hiding things from them.

I got involved in a silly affair with a co-worker. When my wife became suspicious, I lied to her. What I am really ashamed of is not the infidelity (though that bothers me too) but the fact that I lied to a person who has always trusted me.

In the first instance, the woman is ashamed for getting divorced. Her husband has been unfaithful to her, but she blames herself for contributing to their marital problems and feels guilty over it. Unlike her husband, she has not violated the marital trust yet she does not feel blameless. In the next two instances, there is a sexual transgression, but the actual trigger for the ensuing feeling of shame is the lie that has followed it. Had lying been interpreted as a violation of a moral code, it is likely that these individuals would have labeled their feeling as guilt. As it is, the transgression is seen as a form of disloyalty to a significant other, hence the occasion for shame (although the young woman also refers to it as guilt).

Moral shame has traditionally been associated with dishonor rather than guilt. Honor has a long history as a code of behavior. The twin virtues for Homeric heroes were honor (*timê*) and fame (*kleos*). For many centuries, European men fought duels over slights to their honor. Shame plays an even more central role in Asian cultures. Moreover, there is an important cultural distinction between having a *sense of shame* and being *ashamed*. The ability to feel shame, or modesty, is a virtue, particularly in Asian cultures. Being ashamed implies failure. To be free of shame is a good thing—to be shameless is not (in contrast, to be guiltless means being innocent).

It has been long maintained that guilt results from the violation of a moral code that entails *crossing* a line—a trespass. Shame, by contrast, results from *falling short* of a line by failing to measure up to a personal and social standard. In psychoanalytic terms, guilt is associated with the failure to obey the dictates of the *superego*, shame with failing to fulfill the expectations of the *ego-ideal*. Wrongdoing elicits guilt; shortcomings elicit shame. Guilt makes the person feel bad ("I'm no good"); shame makes the person feel inadequate ("I'm not good enough").[30]

From this perspective, guilt and shame would be typically associated with particular antecedents whereby some actions would typically lead to shame and others to guilt. Another common view, going back to Darwin, distinguishes between shame and guilt based on their relationship to public exposure. Shame is considered to be the more *public* emotion, linked as it is to the exposure of a defect, failure, or transgression that damages one's public standing. Guilt, on the other hand, arises within the self, is rooted in the conscience, and is associated with *private* feelings of remorse and self-reproach.

Many psychologists have come to challenge some of the traditional aspects of shame and its relationship to guilt, based on empirical studies. The key concept in this new perspective is that shame engulfs the whole self while guilt is felt in reaction to specific transgressions that leave the global self intact. This makes shame rather than guilt the more damaging emotion. We will return to this issue after we have presented the more conventional view of guilt.

PRIDE

Psychologists view pride as the quintessentially positive self-conscious emotion, a view currently shared by people more generally. This is in sharp contrast to the earlier, more traditional view of pride as a moral blemish and liability to be condemned and rejected rather than celebrated and embraced. This represents a cultural shift that we will discuss in the next chapter when we take up the older, religious-based negative view of pride.

It is also a linguistic artifact of English that it has only one word for the two different emotional expressions—one positive and one negative—of pride. Other languages differentiate between them. For instance, French has *fierté*, which refers to good or healthy pride, and *orgueil*, which is bad or unhealthy pride.[31] Are we dealing here with two separate emotions, or a single emotion with positive and negative aspects? In either case, the two must be considered separately. In this chapter we will deal with pride as a positive emotion then take up its darker side in the next chapter.

Pride is the feeling of pleasure and satisfaction that we take in our accomplishments and good deeds, as well as in the achievements of those that we care about. It promotes prosocial behavior and motivates us to excel. Pride is the backbone of our sense of self-esteem ("I feel good about myself"). Pride is also part of our individualism—a core psychological virtue in Western culture. To be able to stand on one's own two feet, to be dependent on no one else, fills us with the pride of our independence. Its failure leads to shame. In that sense pride and shame are closely connected, with pride being the antithesis of shame. Its association with guilt is less direct. Hence we will not dwell on it here.

Although pride has so far received relatively little research attention, it fully qualifies as a self-conscious emotion. It has readily recognized facial and bodily expressions: The person stands erect with hands on the hips, the head tilted back or raised high, and the face wreathed in a self-satisfied smile. Darwin thought that of all of the emotions, pride was the most clearly expressed. Pride has evolutionary roots and is recognized in virtually all cultures, although it is subject to cultural modifications.[32]

DISGUST

Disgust, like regret, is usually not included with the self-conscious emotions and relatively little has been written on it in the psychological literature. Perhaps this is because disgust is a reaction we have toward others; it is less "self-conscious." In that sense, it is more like anger. However, disgust has close linkages with shame and guilt, and can be experienced toward the self as well. When we experience strong feelings of guilt, shame, and embarrassment, we may also feel disgusted with ourselves. Thus it represents the ultimate in self-condemnation.

We typically experience disgust in reaction to offensive physical conditions; things we consider slimy and filthy that offend our senses based on how they look, feel, smell, or taste. Often these are associated with certain bodily functions and products. As we discussed above, we feel embarrassed if what we do is disgusting to others. However, this form of disgust does not usually have moral connotations. As a moral sentiment, disgust is elicited by hypocrisy, betrayal, cruelty, and various forms of unctuousness (like fawning and cringing servility), and character failings that offend and irritate us (such as being overly fastidious, picky, and boorishly stupid).[33]

Disgust is a positive emotion we can be proud of if its object is, for instance, cruelty. Our condemnation of what is unjust and unfair attests to our moral sensibility. However, when the objects of our disgust are stigmatized individuals—the deformed, disabled, obese, the odd, and the unattractive—it may (or should) make us subject to social disapproval.

In harsher times, people could openly laugh at all who were "abnormal" in one fashion or another. They attended public executions or visited mental hospitals for entertainment. Medieval moralists tried to induce disgust as a weapon against lust. Thus when you looked lustfully at a beautiful woman, you were to think of all the gore that was inside her lovely body—the disgust with that was certain to extinguish any desire to touch her.

Now we feel awkward and self-conscious by merely noting another person's stigma. We try to stifle our feelings of disgust by invoking our conscience. But we also feel somehow polluted by the experience. Unlike contempt, which has a purifying effect, disgust admits our own vulnerability and leaves us somehow tainted by the feeling.

GUILT

The word guilt is used in two senses. The first is the state of *being* guilty of a transgression; it entails moral or legal *culpability* in an *objective*, factual sense. The second is the *subjective* emotion of *feeling* guilty that follows committing a moral offence. It is the painful internal tension due to the awareness of having done wrong, or having failed to carry out a moral obligation. Feeling guilty is also expressed by the term *remorse* (from the Latin), which hints at the metaphor of the bite or sting of conscience. Thus, if I steal a car, I *am* guilty of theft and I *feel* guilty for having committed theft.

Guilty action and guilty feeling do not always go together. It is possible to be guilty but not feel guilty, or feel guilty without having done anything wrong. For instance, killing is a legal and moral offence but if I kill someone in self-defense my action may be justified—I am not guilty and I need not feel guilty. Conversely, even if I was not responsible for the accidental death of someone, I may still feel guilty over it.

It may come as a surprise that the word "guilt" does not exist in the Hebrew Old Testament. However, there are significant differences in the way it is used in the Greek New Testament. This gives some clues to the way guilt has been conceptualized in Christianity, which has greatly influenced Western beliefs and attitudes toward guilt. For instance, ancient Greek has no word for guilt in the sense of "feeling guilty." The closest term for being guilty of sin is *hamartia*, which means making a mistake (literally, "missing the mark"). Other terms that also refer to guilt as culpability (from the Latin *culpa*, "guilt" or "fault") include being "under judgment" or "held in bondage" (Hab. 2:15).

The idea of *debt* is central to guilt. Guilt is actually derived from the Old English word for *debt*.[34] (In German, *Schuld* means both guilt and debt.) The association between guilt and debt goes back to ancient religious codes and continues to color our legal and moral views. Retribution ("an eye for an eye") is a key foundation of justice in the Old Testament which relies on the idea of paying back a debt. We will discuss guilt as culpability more fully in subsequent chapters that deal with religious, philosophical, and legal views on guilt. We will be concerned here mainly with the subjective feeling of guilt as exemplified in the following accounts:

> My deepest sense of guilt concerns my mother's last year of life. I did not spend enough time with her. I left her with the sweet nursing aids when she wanted me. I was at a lecture when she went to the hospital. I was on the phone when she died. I feel deep regret and guilt over this—more than anything else in my life.

> I had an accident when driving home from a party under the influence of alcohol. My wife was killed. I feel I incurred a debt through the loss of her life.

> I hated my stepmother since I first met her at the age of five. When I was home during Christmas break, I made a thoughtless remark about her health. My father was upset and told me later that night that my stepmother had almost died of cancer when I was young. I felt profoundly guilty.

What is it that qualifies these experiences as guilt? Several are framed as transgressions against persons in valued relationships, rather than in terms of abstract moral rules. A daughter's neglect of a dying mother elicits deep regret. Causing the accidental death of the spouse is an obvious reason for feeling guilty, but drunk driving could have also elicited a sense of shame. Hating the stepmother does not seem to have been an issue until the person makes a thoughtless comment about her health, not knowing her past struggles with cancer.

Guilt, perhaps more so than shame, may be *retrospective*—felt after having done wrong, or it can be *prospective* in contemplating doing what would be wrong. It may result from acts of *commission* (doing the wrong thing) or *omission* (failing to do the right thing). Either way, guilt is part of the "currency" we use carrying out our personal transactions with others. It is a powerful influence technique (laying "guilt trips") to change the behavior of others, as we will take up in the next chapter.

The extent to which guilt figures in our lives varies widely. Some people seem hardly bothered by it while the lives of others revolve around it. One study claims that people spend about two hours each day "feeling guilty." If that sounds excessive, perhaps it includes all the thoughts that go through our minds that have the potential of making us feel guilty.[35] As with shame, guilt has strong cultural associations. Historically, guilt seems to have been more significant to human lives within Western cultures than at present.

Nonetheless, guilt remains a common source of distress in the modern world. The *New York Times* "Ethicist" claims to hear from a lot of people who are struggling with ethical dilemmas. The questions asked most often are in the "Do you tell?" category: Do you report the infidelity of a spouse to a friend; the kickbacks extorted by a coworker to management; a grandmother shoplifting in a grocery store? These situations pose a dilemma between minding your own business and ignoring wrongdoing. Either choice carries the prospect of guilt.[36]

There is an important element of intentionality in determining personal responsibility ("attribution of agency"). Hurting someone intentionally and without justification is much more likely to result in feeling guilty than merely causing damage. Most everyday experiences of guilt are mild and transient.[37] They result from the feeling that we have hurt someone, which we can do in countless ways: we take advantage of others; we neglect our responsibilities; we act in ways that are selfish and allow us to reap disproportionate benefits; we aspire to wield power over others or fail to provide assistance to those in need. Most often we hurt the feelings of those who are dear to us by being thoughtless and neglectful. Yet, most of us are not big-time offenders. So we have to calibrate when, why, and how guilty we should feel commensurate to the offence we have committed.

In existential terms, guilt ties us down to the past, making it difficult for us to live in an authentic present. It undermines the trust we have in the adequacy of our selves and leads to a loss of self-esteem and self-confidence. We feel diminished in our own eyes and the eyes of others. Under the weight of guilt, we feel at a loss to know how to behave in public and to show ourselves as we are.

Guilt is a good thing to the extent that it helps us protect our relationships and enhance our social ties. It leads us to take cognizance of our shortcomings, admit our faults, and make amends. Such corrective action repairs the damage to our social ties and our valued relationships. It helps us to get back on track. However, *excessive* guilt robs life of its joys and leads to social paralysis. It may damage our relationships and weaken our bonds and create a breach between ourselves and others. It alienates us from society, making us feel isolated and vulnerable to punishment and exclusion.

There are no reliable physical manifestations of "looking guilty," despite Darwin's claim that the expression of guilt could be recognized across cultures.[38] Studies based on photographic expressions of self-conscious emotions have so far failed to find distinctive features of guilt. It is possible that the facial and bodily expressions of guilt are more subtle than for embarrassment and shame, or depend more on movement than static expressions reflected in photographs. Or, perhaps guilt is a more complex emotion that cannot be adequately communicated nonverbally but requires verbal expression.[39]

NEW PERSPECTIVES ON GUILT AND SHAME

Historically, guilt has been the dominant moral emotion in Western cultures. Religion and philosophy have been largely concerned with guilt rather than shame. Guilt has also been the primary focus within psychiatry under the influence of psychoanalytic theory over the past century. The same is largely true for literature, where people suffer the torment of guilt rather than shame. In short, guilt has been the big-time, heavy-duty emotion of moral judgment.

There is now a significant move within psychology to reinterpret this historically established view of guilt and shame and revise its conceptual underpinnings.[40] As some skeptical psychologists have put it, "In the scientific and popular media of the past two decades, shame has gripped center stage as the emotional source of psychological and interpersonal woe, and is often branded a 'dark' emotion contrasting starkly with the nobler feeling of guilt."[41] This novel view has now become the dominant conceptual model among psychologists who study self-conscious emotions and has generated an extensive literature.[42]

Psychologists who espouse this new view take a *functionalist* approach that focuses on the *social purposes* that emotions serve.[43] The key concept, in the new view of shame and guilt, as already noted, is that guilt entails a specific act ("I *did* that horrible *thing*") whereas shame involves the whole self ("*I* did that horrible thing"). Hence, guilt has a more circumscribed effect on the person's sense of self while shame has a broader impact, engulfing the whole self ("I'm ashamed of who *I am*").[44]

The theoretical roots of this position are traced back to the work of psychiatrist Helen Block Lewis, who integrated clinical insights from psychoanalytic theory with ego psychology and experimental work on cognitive styles.[45] Actually, Helen Lynd expressed the central idea earlier, in 1958:

> Shame is an experience that affects and is affected by the whole self. This whole-self involvement is one of its distinguishing characteristics. . . . One does not, as in guilt, choose to engage in a specific act. . . .
>
> Because of this over-all character, an experience of shame can be altered or transcended only in so far as there is some change in the whole self. . . .

It is not an isolated act that can be detached from the self. . . . The thing that has been exposed is what I am.[46]

These key differences between shame and guilt are elaborated by psychologist June Price Tangney, one of the leading investigators in this area:

> In shame, the focus of the negative evaluation is on the entire self. Following some transgression or failure, the entire self is painfully scrutinized and found lacking. With this painful self-scrutiny comes a sense of shrinking, a feeling of being small, and a sense of worthlessness and powerlessness. Shame also involves the imagery of being exposed before a real or imagined disapproving audience. Although empirical findings indicate that shame can be experienced when a person is alone . . . shame typically involves an awareness of how the defective self may appear to others. Not surprisingly, the shame experience is often accompanied by a desire to hide—to sink into the floor and disappear. And . . . shame can engender a hostile, defensive type of anger . . . presumably aimed at a real or imagined disapproving other.
>
> Guilt, in contrast, is a bad feeling, but it is a less global and devastating emotion than shame. Guilt arises from a negative evaluation of a specific behavior, somewhat apart from the global self; this specific behavior is found to be immoral, lacking, or otherwise defective. The global self, however, remains intact. With this focus on a behavior (rather than the self) comes a sense of tension, remorse, and regret. The person in the midst of a guilt experience often feels a press to confess, apologize, or make amends for the bad deed that was done. This is, without question, an unpleasant emotion. But because a behavior—not the self—is the object of approbation, the self remains mobilized and ready to take reparative action to the extent that circumstances allow.[47]

A number of other commonly accepted aspects of guilt and shame are also called into question by these researchers, such as the view that shame is a public emotion while guilt is more private. Or that shame is a reaction to what others think about a person, while guilt pertains to what one thinks of one's own self. Yet, empirical studies have shown that this private/public distinction does not reliably distinguish between these emotions. Both shame and guilt may have internal and external components. They are often felt in public situations but can also be experienced privately.

Another common view called into question is linking guilt, shame, and embarrassment to specific events that trigger them. Here too, a number of

studies have found no evidence for predictable connections between antecedent events and the emotions they elicit. What embarrasses one person may
make another feel ashamed or guilty. The same event may trigger either shame
or guilt. For example, lying, cheating, failing to help others, or disobeying
parents are cited by some people as eliciting shame and by others as inducing
guilt, depending on how a given situation is interpreted.[48]

Another interesting distinction is based on the emotional signals from
the individual who has been wronged. We typically feel shame when our actions cause sadness, anger, or contempt in others; we feel guilt when our actions have caused pain, suffering, fear, and disappointment.[49]

The studies that now challenge the established views are in turn challenged by yet other studies which, for instance, show that there are, in fact,
distinct situations that are more likely to elicit guilt or shame. They reaffirm
that guilt is typically associated with situations that entail moral transgressions, whereas shame results from the public exposure of moral or non-moral
offences. The list of antecedents shows that embarrassment is most commonly
associated with physical pratfalls, conspicuousness, poor performance, and
loss of control over the body; shame results from poor performance and hurting others; guilt results from failure of duties, lying, cheating, neglecting others, and infidelity.[50]

This is not to say that any given behavior must by necessity result in a particular emotion. Rather, it is a matter of greater or lesser likelihood. For example, poor performance may be a cause for shame, embarrassment, and guilt
in a decreasing order of frequency, whereas for infidelity, the order is guilt,
shame, and embarrassment. There is some validity, therefore, to both claims
that specific events are, or are not, associated with particular emotions.[51]

Such ambiguities and contradictions may make us feel like throwing up
our hands. However, it is in the nature of science that everything is subject to
revision when more compelling evidence becomes available. (And we should
bear in mind that it is more realistic to view human behavior in shades of gray
than in black and white.)

The most significant and consequential claim of the new functionalist approach is that shame is more damaging than guilt. This is an important shift
from how guilt and shame were generally seen in clinical theory and practice.
Instead, from being the culprit guilt becomes the vehicle for prosocial behaviors like empathy and altruism, and shame is cast as an "ugly" feeling that is
largely detrimental to the person's psychological and moral well-being.[52] This

is an issue we will return to in more detail when we discuss the pathology of guilt in Chapter 5.

WE HAVE LOOKED, in this chapter, at the general characteristics of embarrassment, shame, and guilt, considered their similarities and differences and the problems in differentiating between them. This is essentially the perspective of the behavioral sciences, which will continue to inform our discussion in the next six chapters. This approach focuses on the experience of guilt from a psychological perspective that looks at the subjective sense of guilt. It is not primarily concerned with issues of morality in a religious or philosophical sense.

As we go through this book, you will become increasingly aware of a tension between the empirical, scientific, and experimental methods of psychology as against clinical and humanistic fields that bring cultural, historical, literary, philosophical, and religious perspectives to bear on issues of guilt and shame. We must avoid a forced choice between these two camps since they both contribute to our understanding in different ways. They have different assumptions, methods, and rules of evidence. The scientific approach aspires to the creation of a mosaic where each component piece comes from a specific study. The clinical and humanistic approaches generate more of an impressionist painting where it is not the individual pieces but the integrated image that conveys their meaning. They are two different ways of representing reality and one is no more real than the other.

As I pointed out in the Preface, my central purpose in this book is to bring together these various and disparate approaches to guilt. We need to do this if we are to avoid the limited perceptions exemplified in the proverbial elephant and the blind men. This is a difficult, if not impossible, task. I may not be able to make these different voices speak to each other, but I have at least put them together between the covers of one book.

2 COMMANDMENTS AND SINS

THE SORRY TALE OF HUMAN TRANSGRESSIONS is long and dreary. What we will be concerned with in this chapter are those behaviors that have long been viewed as the more serious moral failings that render offenders guilty—both in making them morally culpable as well as remorseful. Murder, in that sense, is the prototypical crime. The first death in the Bible is the murder of Abel by his brother Cain: "And the Lord had regard for Abel and his offering, but for Cain and his offering, he had no regard. So Cain was very angry . . . [and] rose up against his brother Abel, and killed him" (Gen. 4:4–8).

Shakespeare's *Macbeth* is a tale of murder leading to a ferocious sense of guilt that drives Macbeth to his doom and Lady Macbeth to insanity and suicide. Hence, it is a fitting example with which to open this chapter. The plot is well known. Macbeth is returning home with his companion Banquo after subduing a rebellion on behalf of Duncan, the king of Scotland. They encounter three witches who hail Macbeth as the future king. This hatches in his mind the idea of killing Duncan and seizing the throne. Lady Macbeth, his "dearest partner of greatness," fuels his ambitions yet she fears that Macbeth lacks the resolve to carry out the bloody deed.[1] When Duncan comes to spend the night in Macbeth's castle, Lady Macbeth gives vent to her raging ambition:

> Come, you spirits
> That tend on mortal thoughts, unsex me here,
> And fill me, from the crown to the toe, top-full
> Of direst cruelty! make thick my blood,
> Stop up th' access and passage to remorse,

That no compunctious visitings of nature
Shake my fell purpose, nor keep peace between
Th' effect and it! Come to my woman's breasts,
And take my milk for gall, you murdering ministers.[2]

Lady Macbeth will stifle her womanly conscience and act like a man ("unsex me here"), but Macbeth hesitates. Why not wait for the witch's prediction to come true in good time; why murder the king? Duncan is his cousin, a guest in his house. He is a good and beloved king who has been most generous to him. Lady Macbeth will have none of it. She berates Macbeth and challenges his manhood for failing in his resolve. Nothing will deter her:

. . . I have given suck, and know
How tender 'tis to love the babe that milks me:
I would, while it was smiling in my face,
Have plucked my nipple from his boneless gums,
And dash'd the brains out, had I sworn as you
Have done to do this.[3]

Macbeth still hesitates: What if they fail? We shall not fail, says Lady Macbeth. She will drug the grooms attending the king, then kill Duncan and smear his blood on the sleeping grooms to make it look like they have killed him. However, Lady Macbeth cannot carry out the act because the sleeping Duncan reminds her of her father. Macbeth ends up committing the murder and is crowned king of Scotland. He is overcome with remorse ("Will all great Neptune's ocean wash this blood clean from my hand?"), but not for long. He kills Banquo, who suspects him of Duncan's death. And when Banquo's ghost begins to haunt him, Macbeth becomes unhinged.

Lady Macbeth has to take charge. She makes light of the murder ("A little water clears us of this deed"); tells Macbeth to let go of what has no remedy ("What's done is done"); she pretends that all is well, acting bright and jovial among the guests. Ultimately, however, she is undone as the awesome power of her guilt is unleashed. The change is rapid and unexplained. She walks in her sleep speaking in enigmatic phrases that hint at her misdeeds. She rubs her hands in a futile attempt to get them clean:

. . . here's a spot.

. . .

Out, damned spot! out, I say!

. . .

. . . Yet who would have thought the old man
to have so much blood in him?

. . .

What, will these hands ne'er be clean?

. . .

Here's the smell of blood still: all the
perfumes of Arabia will not sweeten this little
hand.[4]

Lady Macbeth's guilt allows no redemption and she hangs herself. Macbeth's famous soliloquy is an epitaph to their lives and to human existence:

Life's but a walking shadow, a poor player
That struts and frets his hour upon the stage
And then is heard no more: it is a tale
Told by an idiot, full of sound and fury,
Signifying nothing.[5]

Macbeth is Shakespeare's most sharply focused study of evil with guilt as its central theme. Ostensibly it is a story of unbridled ambition that, once kindled, leads the protagonists to their doom. Nevertheless, the play raises many baffling questions. Did the predictions of the witches foretell a future that could not be altered by Macbeth? Or was he hearing the voice of his own repressed ambitions that would transform him into a murderer? If Macbeth and Lady Macbeth were an honorable couple, as they seem, what brought about their sinister transformation? Would Macbeth have carried out his misdeeds without the prodding of his wife? Does it take two to stifle a conscience? Was it something in their relationship rather than in their individual natures that pushed them over the edge? Was Macbeth's ferocity a reaction to the challenge posed by his wife to his manhood? How does Lady Macbeth's iron will, which stifled her conscience at the outset, turn into a raging guilt that led to her disintegration? As with all great tragedies, there are no ready answers to these questions, although many have been offered.[6] Here is Freud's interpretation, which delves into deeper psychological motives to explain these events.[7]

Freud starts by asking why is it that people will occasionally fall apart after a long-cherished wish is fulfilled. After the Macbeths had achieved their ambitions, why were they wrecked by success? When an *external* obstacle is taken out of our way, we are delighted. However, when the obstacle to the fulfillment of our wish is *internal*, put up by our conscience, and that obstacle is over-come, that is when we get into trouble. The trigger for the confrontation with the internal obstacle is often the resolution of an external wish.

How does this fit into the Macbeth case? Lady Macbeth has no scruples in pressing her husband into killing Duncan. After the murder, as Macbeth begins to fall apart, it is Lady Macbeth who shores him up. Yet, when she reappears on stage, she is in the grip of an overwhelming sense of guilt that drives her to hang herself. What was it, asks Freud, "that broke this character which seemed forged from the toughest metal"?

The way events unfold in the play is so fast that it makes them hard to understand. Freud fashions an explanation that requires that we alter the time frame within which events unfold. In Holingshed's *Chronicle*, from which Shakespeare took the plot of *Macbeth*, ten years pass between Macbeth's ascending the throne after Duncan's murder and the couple's disintegration depicted in the play. The key event during this period is the failure of the couple to have children. Why should that have mattered?

When the witches predicted that Macbeth would be king, they also told Banquo that his children will succeed to the crown. The only way that Macbeth could have his reign extended beyond his own rule would be to have children, as he tells Lady Macbeth:

Bring forth men-children only!
For thy undaunted mettle should compose
Nothing but males.

However, the couple remains barren and Macbeth's dreams of establishing a dynasty crumble. Lady Macbeth blames herself for it. And she is the key to understanding the tragedy. The external wish that is fulfilled for the Macbeths is their ascending to the throne and the price is the murder of Duncan. However, the deeper unconscious wish for Lady Macbeth is parricide, the murder of her own father. Her explanation why she could not murder Duncan is a denial and concealment of that repressed wish. Her conscience is stifled as long as there is the prospect of their establishing a dynasty. When that fails to materialize, Lady Macbeth's defenses crumble and her conscience bites back, punishing her with death.

There are other layers to Freud's convoluted analysis that we need not go into. Nor is it pertinent for our purposes whether or not Freud's interpretations are correct. The question here is whether we can identify psychological factors that explain crimes rather then ascribing them to evil. Does one explanation preclude the other, or should we look at them as complementary? A purely psychological explanation will lead to an amoral universe, and to fall back on evil will render human actions fatalistic.

What does the tragedy of Macbeth have to do with our own lives? Very few of us are murderers, but murder is not the only instance when we stifle our conscience to further our ambitions. When we tell ourselves that we will do good after we have achieved power, no matter how, do we enter into a Faustian bargain with the devil that we cannot retreat from?

Most experiences of guilt are not the stuff of tragedy but part of our everyday lives. Far more pervasive are violations of trust and the breach of obligations. They are not the things that keep theologians, philosophers, and clinicians awake at night, who are not concerned with the small moral lapses of the many but the larger lapses of the few.

The moral and legal codes intended to restrain such behaviors are meant for everyone, but in reality they have not been enforced uniformly. Double standards have applied to men and women, to rulers and the ruled, and to some extent they still are. The more power one has, the greater the freedom to act with impunity. As the Roman emperor Caracalla put it, "Remember that I can do anything I want to anyone."

To make sense of the bewildering variety of crimes and misdemeanors that have rendered people morally and legally culpable, we need some organizing principles. To that end, we will first consider the biblical Ten Commandments—the most widely used ethical code in Western culture. We will then turn to the Cardinal Sins, which have represented since medieval Christianity the human inclinations that lead to moral failings. Whereas the Ten Commandments relate to specific behaviors (such as murder and adultery), the Cardinal Sins (such as anger and lust) lead to such behaviors.

THE TEN COMMANDMENTS

Moral and legal codes originated as religious prohibitions. The oldest known is the Babylonian Code of Hammurabi (eighteenth century BCE). Inscribed on a stele, it shows the sun god Shamash transmitting the legal ordinances to the king. Similarly, Moses received the Ten Commandments from the Lord during the Exodus from Egypt (Exod. 20:1–18; Deut. 5:6–12). Such commandments are stated in the negative: "You shall not," rather than "You shall." The primary concern of the Ten Commandments as well as the Cardinal Sins is with guilty behavior, not guilty feelings. However, it is quite evident in both cases that feelings of guilt and remorse (and quite often shame) are their natural and expected outcomes, and essential for repentance and redemption.

The Torah (the first five books of the Hebrew scriptures) contains 613 commandments but it is the Ten Commandments that constitute the basic framework of Judaic law and ethics. They are called the Ten Words (*asaret ha-devarim* in Hebrew; *dekalogos* in Greek).[8] Originally intended for the use of Israelites, the Ten Commandments became central to Christian ethics as well through the Old Testament. Jesus referred to the "commandments" and listed some of the sins they cover: "For out of the heart come evil thoughts, murder, adultery, fornication, theft, false witness, slander" (Matt 15:19–20). Subsequently, these commandments attained a universality unmatched by any other moral code in the Western world. The moral codes of non-Western religious traditions also reflect some of the same basic moral and social concerns.

In religious terms, the Ten Commandments represent the will of God transmitted to human beings. Their understanding and interpretations have evolved over the centuries to fit changing social circumstances, but their basic meanings remain the same. Their religious significance may have faded for secular minds, but they continue to exert a strong moral influence. In secular terms, they represent the distillation of human experience over the millennia with the regulation of human relationships and the effective functioning of society. They still "work." For example, the "Big Three" ethical concerns postulated by psychologists, as referred to earlier, are encompassed within them. They address issues of justice and individual rights through prohibitions against hurting others (do not kill, do not steal, do not bear false witness); they protect social conventions shared by the community (honor your parents; do not commit adultery; do not covet what belongs to your neighbor); and they define the relationship of human beings to God.

Since the Ten Commandments are well known, our purpose in discussing them is not to belabor their religious, legal, and historical significance. Rather, it is to examine how they relate to our experience of guilt. How does their violation make us culpable? What was the original intent of these commandments and what should they mean to us today?

The Ten Commandments are apodictic statements that are categorical and allow no qualification. However, they have always been subject to reinterpretation. "You shall not commit adultery" still stands, but what was meant by "adultery" is not how we understand the term today, as we will discuss later.

That does not make the commandment obsolete, but requires that we understand it in its original as well as its current cultural context.

The first three commandments deal with the relationship of people with the Lord. They can therefore be better understood in their religious contexts. Briefly, Judaism was the first religion to make the worship of one God preeminent over other gods ("You shall have no other gods before me"). Thus, what started as henotheism developed into monotheism or the exclusive worship of one God.

Idolatry is the worship of "graven images" (not just the representations) of the divine in any form. It is the paramount sin in Judaism, as it is in Christianity and Islam. The worship of idols is no longer an issue in the modern world for which anyone need feel guilty. However, idolatry may go beyond idol worship in a literal sense. Anything that takes precedence over God is a form of idolatry. Even the best things in life—family, friends, career, enjoyments, and any other attachments, good or bad—represent "idolatrous ultimate concerns," says Protestant theologian Paul Tillich, if they take precedence over God.

The Third Commandment forbids taking the name of the Lord in vain. Orthodox Judaism forbids using the name of God altogether. He is referred to as Lord (Adonai, Elohim). The name of God is transliterated from the Hebrew consonants YHVH, as Jahveh or Jehovah. Christians and Muslims will use the name of God but only with reverence.[9] In popular usage it is denigrated into a swear word.

How do these commandments relate to the experience of guilt? If one does not believe in God, they obviously do not matter. However, if one does believe in God, then offences against God generate the most profound feelings of guilt. If one's relationship with God is right, all else will follow; if it is not, then nothing else matters.

The next seven commandments have a more direct interpersonal focus. Our discussion will address their original intent as well as their modern relevance to our experience of guilt.

You Shall Keep the Sabbath Holy
The commandment to keep the Sabbath holy is in celebration of the Lord's resting on the seventh day of creation. Those who observe the Sabbath diligently abstain from all work and spend the day in religious observance and spiritual reflection: Jews go to the synagogue, and Seventh-Day Adventists to

church, on Saturdays, other Christians attend church on Sundays; and Muslims gather for congregational prayer on Fridays.

The failure to observe the Sabbath used to make many people guilty. This may no longer be the case but it still troubles some people:

> It was Sunday morning. I was hiding under my covers as my family was getting ready for church. My mom opened the door and I coughed pitifully. "Maybe you should stay home from church," she said. "I will if I have to," I replied, my sinful little heart singing. The next day guilt hit. I was sure God was out to get me. I didn't skip church again for three and a half months, and at that time, I really was sick. Honest.

Religion aside, the prospect of working on weekends can be problematic. This does not typically trouble those with a fixed work schedule. However, it can be problematic for career-driven professionals whose responsibilities do not end on Friday afternoon. The occasional need to work on a weekend may elicit no more than some regret, but doing so repeatedly pits it against family obligations, making it a rife source of conflict and guilt. The mother of two young children says of her husband,

> I don't mind staying home and taking care of the kids during the week but I really need a break over the weekend. So if Bob heads for the office Saturday morning, I really get upset. I understand he is working for the family, but he needs to spend time with his children if he wants to be a real father to them. When I tell him this, he says he is sorry and feels bad for neglecting his kids (let alone me) but I suppose not bad enough. If I make enough of a fuss, he will stay home, but what is the use if his head is going to be at the office.

When it is the mother who works over the weekend, she may feel even worse and the husband may resent it even more. Such situations bring to a head the thorny issue of who should be doing what when it comes to the division of responsibility between men and women with respect to career and family obligations. It represents a new source of guilt that the framers of the commandment could hardly have envisaged.

Honor Your Father and Mother

The relationship between parents and children is arguably the single most important source of feeling guilty. The failure to honor one's obligations to one's parents—understood broadly—is a big component of this. (In my class surveys, interactions with parents represented by far the single largest category for feeling guilty.) There are several reasons for this. Obviously, everyone has (or has had) a parent; no other human relationship is as universal. Parent-child relationships are indissoluble; once a parent, always a parent. Even if parents and children disown each other, they will always be part of each other's lives at some level. Since these relationships include the vulnerable years of childhood, the hurts people suffer and inflict, and the guilt that follows them, are particularly potent. No other intimate relationship—be it between spouses, lovers, friends, or foes—can match it.

A basic reason for feeling guilty is the failure to repay the debt we owe parents for bringing us into the world and raising us. Even when parents fail in their responsibilities, it does not cancel the debt. We fail to honor our parents when we are rude, ungrateful, and unappreciative; when we are insensitive to their feelings and needs. Even when these failures involve relatively trivial issues, their effect can be sharp:

> I was having an awful week, so when my mom called on the phone, I snapped at her and blamed her for basically all my life's problems. I was so mean that I made her cry.

> I am now old enough to be the father of two grown-up children, but I still cannot stop being annoyed by my father. I get frustrated and end our conversation abruptly. Then I feel guilty for being such a jerk even after all these years.

> I told my mother that she cared more about my sister than me. After my wave of anger subsided, I felt horribly guilty for making her look like a bad mother.

Mothers are cited more often than fathers in inducing guilt in their children. This is because mothers interact with their children more than fathers, especially in childhood, but also because mothers may be more prone to make their children feel guilty. Traditionally, fathers have had direct ways of controlling their children whereas mothers have had to appeal to their children's feelings to influence them. Interactions with parents remain a potent source of guilt even for older adults as the guilt over the love we did not express and the anger we did not suppress linger on long after our parents are gone.

Filial obligations have been particularly strong in non-Western cultures. The Qur'an says we should not utter the slightest murmur of irritation at our parents for as long as they live. In traditional Chinese society, parents were

revered and ancestors worshipped. The obligation to honor parents has traditionally extended to the respect for elders, a practice that seems to have de-
clined in the modern world.

Some parents are hard to honor. They are intrusive, controlling, disap-
proving, and belittling. Nonetheless, the failure to honor them still fills us
with guilt. This may also extend to grandparents:

> I don't like my grandparents. They're tactless, insensitive, and go out of their
> way to make people feel bad. They accuse people of things they never did and
> don't apologize when they realize their mistake. They make racist, sexist com-
> ments that border on the ridiculous. They have their favorite grandkids and
> make very little attempt to hide their preferences. And then they wonder why
> I don't visit them, even though they say they are getting old and are not going
> to be around much longer. I feel guilty because I think they actually really love
> me and at some level I love them because they are family. It bothers me they
> may think I don't love them.

> I had a lot of anger at my father because he was so critical of me. Nothing I did
> was good enough. I desperately wanted his approval but never got it. During
> his last illness, I was tempted to let him know how I had felt about him, but I
> am glad I kept my mouth shut.

We could readily cite as many examples where parents feel guilty for their
interactions with their children. We feel responsible for our own children and
feel guilty when things go wrong in their lives, even if it is their own doing. It
is hard to imagine parents who have never asked themselves, "What did we
do wrong?"

> When my son dropped out of high school, my husband and I felt terrible. We
> blamed ourselves for not sending him to a better school, for not hiring tutors
> to help him, and for all else that we could and should have done to keep him
> in school.

> My daughter's divorce hit me hard. I was divorced myself when she was fifteen
> and wondered if that was somehow responsible for what happened to her.

> I succeeded my father in the family business and expected my son to do the
> same. He had no interest in running a clothing store and even less interest in
> working for me. However, I more or less forced him into it. For a couple of
> years he put up with it, but finally he quit. He says it is too late now, too late to

start over and to do what he wanted. He looks like a deflated tire and my wife and I don't know what to do with him. She blames me for what happened, but I did what I thought was best for him. I suppose I was wrong, but all I can do now is to feel bad over it.

While it is natural to feel responsible for one's children, the extent to which parents shape their lives may be much less than they tend to imagine. Parents do matter, but gender, birth order, and the family circumstances under which one grows up are also significant, along with other important influences that determine how one turns out. That is one reason why two children growing up in the same family can be so different. Therefore, the extent to which parents feel guilty about what happens to their children should be commensurate with their level of responsibility for determining the outcome. Moreover, once the die is cast, guilt is not going to change anything.

You Shall Not Kill

Killing is the general term for the taking of life, but in Hebrew the word (*ratsah*) typically meant committing murder, which is unjustified killing.[10] There are occasions, such as self-defense, when killing is legally permitted. Such justification extends to "just wars," which is an idea that is easily abused. However justified, killing in combat or in self-defense may still entail a certain burden of guilt.

The United States is one of the few countries in the Western world that imposes the death penalty (its opponents consider it "judicial murder"). Presumably, anyone involved in its administration, from the judge to the executioner, would have qualms over it. Yet, many do not seem troubled by it. The Catholic church and evangelical Christians extend the commandment not to kill to abortion, claiming the unborn fetus to be a "person" with the right to life. Similar considerations may also apply to euthanasia or assisted suicide.

Abortion generally does not have serious psychological consequences (the dominant feeling is one of relief). However, some women and men still feel burdened by the moral responsibility of terminating a pregnancy.

I had an abortion nineteen years ago. I feel guilty, not because of the abortion but because I felt no guilt. It wasn't easy to go through the procedure and I was not cavalier about it. My husband and I did not want another child. Yet I know I would have loved the child and been a good mother to it. But I took the pragmatic approach.

> There was no doubt in my mind that I had to have the abortion. But when I started having contractions during the procedure, I felt guilty because I was reminded of the birth of my children.

Some pro-life groups try to instill guilt by holding memorial services for the fetus. And protesters at abortion clinics display pictures of aborted fetuses. Yet those who bomb clinics (almost always men) do not seem to be troubled by putting the lives of others at risk.

In some religious traditions, such as Buddhism, the taking of all life is prohibited, be it human or animal. However, in much of the world the line between killing and murder remains hazy and allowances are made that would render the perpetrator free of blame. When we discuss the legal aspects of guilt, we will have more to say about this issue. However, given that the taking of human life is the most grievous and irreparable harm one can inflict on another, it is hard to imagine how such an act can be entirely free of guilt for a person of conscience, whatever the circumstances.

You Shall Not Commit Adultery

Adultery is voluntary sexual intercourse between a married person and someone other than the spouse. We now equate it with extramarital sex with anyone, but the prohibition in the Old Testament defined it more narrowly as having sexual intercourse with one's *neighbor's* spouse—not just anyone other than the spouse. Moreover the Bible does not condemn patriarchs and kings like Solomon for having concubines. The problem in adultery therefore appears to have been not sex as such, but the betrayal of trust—taking what belongs to the neighbor (which usually meant one's kin). This distinction is important; we are not splitting hairs. The biblical punishment for adultery was death by stoning, but since it required four adult male witnesses to the act, convictions were rare and difficult to obtain (Lev. 21:10).

Jesus reiterated the commandment against adultery, but in his encounter with the woman caught in adultery he took a more forgiving attitude. Jesus shamed her accusers ("Let him who is without sin among you be the first to throw a stone at her"). And when all of her accusers no longer condemned her, Jesus told the woman, "Neither do I condemn you; go and sin no more" (John 8:7–11).

Adultery has been a prime cause for feeling guilty, and still is, for many people. It is a common theme in literature, especially in Victorian novels, where it usually ends badly, especially for the woman. Flaubert's Emma Bovary and Tolstoy's Anna Karenina stray from their marriages and come to grief: Emma poisons herself; Anna throws herself in front of a train. (Their lovers get on with their lives.) A notable exception is the Reverend Dimmesdale in Hawthorne's *Scarlet Letter*, where it is the man rather than his lover, Hester Prynne, who carries the burden of guilt. His overwrought confession bursts from him:

> "People of New England!" cried he with a voice that rose over them, high, solemn, and majestic—yet had always a tremor through it, and sometimes a shriek, struggling up out of a fathomless depth of remorse and woe—"ye, that have loved me—ye that have deemed me holy!—behold me here, the one sinner of the world! At last—at last!—I stand upon the spot where, seven years since, I should have stood; here, with this woman, whose arm sustains me . . . from groveling down upon my face."[11]

The traditional condemnation of adultery, and its attendant guilt, was challenged during the 1960s but the alternative of "open marriage" did not quite make it into the mainstream. This idea was based on the premise that what makes extramarital sex morally objectionable is the element of deception and disloyalty to the spouse, rather than the sexual act itself. If a couple freely agreed to it, there was no infidelity, hence no reason to feel guilty. This turned out to be hard to do (especially for women), although some seemed able to make it work.

Despite the failure to institutionalize open marriages, quite a few men and women continue to engage in extramarital sex; 30–50 percent of men and 20–40 percent of women are estimated to have had at least one extramarital affair.[12] At the same time, close to 80 percent of Americans consider extramarital sex to be always wrong.[13] Consequently, those who engage in it are apt to feel guilty—fleetingly or deeply—and the spouse to feel betrayed:

> I was having an affair but denied it to my wife when challenged. I feel like a good-for-nothing. Like I owe my wife something.

> I know these things happen, but I felt betrayed and angry when I found out about my husband's affair. It's true, I have done the same thing but it was in reaction to what he had done.

> While I can justify it by the fact that I didn't know it at the time, I felt horribly guilty to know I had kissed another girl's boyfriend. Since I knew the girl, it made it worse. I had disregarded my morals and beliefs. I never wanted to

come in between a relationship and felt like the proverbial "other woman." It was wrong. I was an awful person for doing it.

Religious guilt over adultery does not allow for mitigating factors. However, in other cases, whether one feels guilty, or is judged as guilty by others, may depend on a variety of factors. For instance, if marital sex is lacking or unfulfilling (be it due to absence of the spouse, lack of interest, illness, or conflict), then the spouse who is sexually deprived may feel justified in seeking sexual satisfaction elsewhere. Whether the sexual "indiscretion" is sporadic or habitual, undertaken casually or within a romantic attachment, along with a variety of other considerations may make a difference. These considerations depend on whether one follows an absolute or relativistic moral standard—an issue we will take up shortly.

Since marital infidelity often leads to divorce, the disruption of the family and the negative impact on children are additional sources of guilt. When adultery involves a public figure, the ensuing scandal can seriously damage the person's political career. President Clinton was almost impeached over the Monica Lewinsky affair; New York governor Eliot Spitzer resigned after having had sex with a prostitute. Both of them made public admissions of regret and guilt. However, beyond the sex, it is the lying to the public, and the hypocrisy, that may have been more damaging. Perhaps that is why Gavin Newsom, who promptly confessed to having had an affair with the wife of his colleague and friend, was handily reelected mayor of San Francisco.

Adultery and premarital sex share a common element in involving sex outside of marriage; but premarital sex does not involve infidelity to a spouse. Nonetheless, like adultery, premarital sex used to be roundly condemned and provided a rife source of guilt. Public attitudes have changed dramatically since the 1960s and currently sex between consenting single adults has become virtually normative in large segments of the population. When there is guilt attached to it, it is usually due to the special circumstance under which it takes place:

> Last year I met someone at a frat party. We had been both drinking. We started flirting and ended up going home and becoming physically involved. It was not the sex that makes me feel ashamed; rather because I let it go much farther than I would under sober circumstances.

The prevailing sexual ethic is that sex is morally acceptable within committed relationships, or at least in a relational context; but casual sex remains potentially more problematic. Actually, about a third of the American population still considers premarital sex to be always wrong.[14]

The latest installment of this issue is the practice of "hooking up"—guilt-free sexual engagement of some sort without a relational component—particularly among college youth. Men generally have always been more willing to engage in casual sex than women; what is new is the apparent willingness of women to do likewise. The same claims were made in the 1960s when the rates of premarital sex for women skyrocketed, but time has shown that female reticence to forgo sex outside of a relationship (even a tenuous one) tends to persist. And detractors of hooking up caution women not to pursue sex, delay love, and lose at both.[15] Moreover, even those who purport to speak for the guilt-free casual sex indulged in by their generation conclude that "we might dally in the land of easy sex and stilted text-message flirtation, but deep down we crave the warm embrace of all-consuming love."[16]

You Shall Not Steal

Who can honestly claim to have never taken anything that belonged to someone else? Few of us burglarize houses, but many more fudge on our tax returns. We are reluctant to defraud a friend, but institutions are fair game. Shoplifting is a sport for some and a compulsion for others. Yet, when something is stolen from us, we react with indignation.

Guilt is commonly associated with stealing; even when done in childhood, it may linger on. St. Augustine never got over the guilt of stealing some pears from a neighbor's tree when he was a boy. We feel particularly guilty when we steal from someone who is close to us.

> I feel guilty about stealing stuff. One time I switched my hair drier, which had broken down, with my friend's identical model and felt bad about it.

> When I was nine, I thought my mother wouldn't mind so I took five dollars from her purse. My father discovered it and insisted to know who had done it. I denied it at first but then I was overwhelmed with guilt and confessed.

> I was 3 years old when I brought home one of my older friend's toys; when my mother asked me about it, I told her my friend gave it to me. My mother called to thank him for the gift and I was discovered. The fear of punishment inspired the lie, and it was the lie that inspired the guilt.

Stealing and lying are particularly important in childhood since they are the common ways in which children may act unethically; there is not much else they can do. Parents are concerned over them because it may lead to more serious offences as the child grows up. It is important, however, not to over-react. The father of a six-year-old boy became very upset when his son had taken a few coins from a cup where he kept his small change. He reprimanded and lectured the boy on why it was so important never to steal. The child, however, was quite confused. He thought the father was angry because he had taken what belonged to him, like the toy of a friend. He had no conception of the moral principle of not stealing that the father was expounding. Therefore, he learned little from the experience.

The material consequences of stealing may be quite trivial. Yet, even if no real harm is done, they induce guilt because stealing results in a violation of trust to a valued person or principle. It implies selfishness, lack of caring and respect, a hostile act that leads to loss of trust and alienation. We experience it as a personal violation, an invasion of our private space—a trespass. The symbolic, rather than materiel, motivations for stealing are particularly salient in behaviors like shoplifting and compulsive theft. The excitement and guilt they induce are part of their conscious or unconscious appeal.

We usually associate stealing with theft or burglary, but these involve small change compared with the breathtaking amounts swindled in the corporate world. Enron became the emblem of corporate greed and fraud. However, nothing in recent times has caused as much of a sensation and righteous indignation as the Ponzi scheme of Bernard Madoff, which will be easier to deal with in our discussion of psychopathic characters. Most of us are not thieves, yet we are fascinated by accounts and movies of ingenious and daring heists presumably because of the vicarious pleasure we get from them.

Slavery, forced prostitution, and kidnapping are particularly egregious forms of theft since they rob their victims of their humanity by treating them as objects. Theft of intellectual property is more subtle. While every book, piece of art, or musical composition has antecedents that it draws from, there is a difference (albeit a gray area) between the legitimate transmission of knowledge and plagiarizing.

Is stealing always wrong? The commandment sounds absolute but, like the prohibition against killing, it is often qualified. Many of us would make allowances for stealing food to feed our starving children and not feel guilty. Later on we will see how this issue is dealt with in religious and philosophical traditions and the workings of the law.

You Shall Not Bear False Witness

The Ten Commandments do not refer to lying as such, but it may be sub-sumed under bearing false witness, or *perjury* (lying under oath). Perjury is the most serious form of lying since it can send the accused to jail. Aside from that, lying as such is not a criminal offence (otherwise, prisons would be even more congested than they are).

Lying would be virtually universal if we expand it to include myriad forms of deceitfulness (expressed in 112 English words).[17] Even more than stealing, lying is subject to mitigating circumstances. The gold standard of veracity is telling the truth, the whole truth, and nothing but the truth. However, if we apply that standard strictly, everyday life would be impossibly difficult and the outcome not necessarily desirable. In her insightful book on lying, Sissela Bok poses a set of questions that highlight the moral complexities in always telling the truth:

> Should physicians lie to dying patients so as to delay the fear and anxiety which the truth may bring them? Should professors exaggerate the excellence of their students on recommendations in order to give them a better chance in a tight job market? Should parents conceal from children the fact that they were adopted? Should social scientists send investigators masquerading as patients to physicians in order to learn about racial and sexual biases in diagnosis and treatment? Should government lawyers lie to members of Congress who might otherwise oppose a much-needed welfare bill? And should journalists lie to those from whom they seek information in order to expose corruption?[18]

Honest and thoughtful people may answer these questions differently, as have theologians and philosophers. St. Augustine and Immanuel Kant represent the always-tell-the-truth position. St. Thomas Aquinas had a more qualified view and subsumed lies under three categories: lies that serve a good purpose; lies told in jest; and lies that are malicious and do harm. Only the last consti-tuted a mortal sin; the first two could be pardoned. A similar latitude exists in Judaism, where the Talmud allows lies to maintain peace in the household. Martin Luther also took the more tolerant view: "What harm would it do, if a man told a good strong lie for the sake of the good and for the Christian church . . . a lie out of necessity, a useful lie, a helpful lie, such lies would not be against God, he would accept them."[19]

Most lies do not have momentous consequences. A person may not even regret the action that led to the lie, yet lying about it may still induce guilt because it entails a betrayal of trust:

> I was 15 years old in boarding school and instead of going home for spring break, I went to New York with my boyfriend and told my parents I would be working on a community project. Then I felt guilty towards my parents, and most of all towards God.

As people get older, practical realities intrude on the need for absolute honesty. A middle-aged man speaking of his dying mother said,

> When it became clear that her cancer had spread, I thought my mother should be told about it. But it looked like she did not really want to know, so I told her she was going to be fine and let her doctor deal with the truth, if necessary.

> My husband does not know that I am a transsexual and have had sex surgery. Why should I upset him by telling him about something that happened before I met him?

The last statement was made by a panelist in one of my classes in human sexuality. The students were taken aback. One of them asked, how could she be married to a man who did not know about such an important aspect of who she was? She said to him, "Does your father know everything about your mother?"

You Shall Not Covet

To covet means to desire eagerly what belongs to another. The commandment specifically refers to coveting what belongs to a neighbor, the same condition we discussed in connection with adultery. The rabbis made a distinction between what one may legitimately wish for and other desires that had to be kept in check.[20] The things listed in the commandment that one should not covet move from a neighbor's wife to his house, manservant, maidservant, ox, ass; in short anything that belongs to a neighbor. Does that mean that a man could covet things that belonged to someone other than a neighbor?

The idea of the "neighbor" is important in defining the scope of moral responsibility and raises difficult questions. It suggests that what matters is not *what* you do but *whom* you do it to. This conflicts with religious and philosophical claims that actions are right or wrong in and of themselves, irrespective of whom they involve. Moreover, who is my neighbor? Judaism arose within tightly knit tribal communities based on kinship. The neighbor was actually one's brother, cousin, or some other relative. Beyond such kin, the primary responsibility of a Jew was to other Jews. In the parable of the Good Samaritan, Jesus extended the scope of caring to include even a member of a despised group, thereby aspiring to a much wider sense of moral responsibility. Nonetheless, followers of virtually all religions have in practice, if not in principle, favored their co-religionists over others.

Following the murder of Abel by Cain, the Lord asked, "Cain, where is Abel your brother?" He answered, "I do not know; am I my brother's keeper?" Indeed, whose keeper are we? The answers to this question range from the evolutionary to the religious, philosophical, and legal.

THE CARDINAL SINS

The Ten Commandments are concerned with what people should and should not do, not with *why* they do it. The Cardinal Sins point to the impulses that lead to moral violations: For instance, greed may lead to stealing, anger to murder, and lust to adultery.

Plato attributed three elements to the soul: the capacity to reason and two impulses (shared with animals)—*irascibility* as expressed in anger, and *concupiscence*, or strong desire, as expressed in sexuality. Moral behavior requires the control of these impulses by reason. Over time, these impulses became linked with planets: Venus generated lust, Mars aggression. Early Christian writers purged these notions of their pagan associations and focused on a series of sins, designated as *capital sins*, as the sources of all other sins.[21]

In the sixth century, Pope Gregory the Great singled out seven sins and ranked them in terms of their gravity, with pride at the top and lust at the bottom. St. Thomas Aquinas in the thirteenth century renamed them the *Cardinal Sins*. Andrew Greeley characterizes them as follows:

> The so-called Cardinal Sins are not sins at all but seven disorderly propensities in our personality that lead us to sinful behavior . . . sound and healthy human proclivities gone askew. . . . The Cardinal Sins result not from fundamental evil but from fundamental goodness running out of control, from human love that is confused and frightened and not trusting enough of love. . . . Traditional Catholic spirituality has contended that all of us have a "dominant fault," the cardinal sin that is strongest in our personality.[22]

The Cardinal Sins consist of pride, envy, anger, sloth, avarice, gluttony, and lust. Thomas Aquinas, following Plato, subsumed lust, gluttony, avarice, and sloth under concupiscence; anger, envy, and pride under irascibility. This fitted nicely with Aristotle's basic ethical principle that vices are the result of the excess or deficiency of virtues.[23]

In the late Middle Ages, Dante in the *Divine Comedy* used the Cardinal Sins as the organizing scheme of Purgatory—the mid-station between Hell and Paradise. He based them on the idea that all human actions are motivated by love; good love leading to good outcomes, perverse love to bad outcomes. The Cardinal Sins represent various forms of perverse love: Pride, envy, and anger are associated with *bad* love; sloth, with *too little* love; avarice, gluttony, and lust with *immoderate* love.[24] The notion of the Cardinal Sins may now sound quaint to our ears, but if we convert them to their modern equivalents, they sparkle with relevance.[25]

In the *Inferno*, Dante condemns sinners to nine concentric circles in Hell with a number of subdivisons (*bolge*) corresponding to increasing levels of wickedness. Although there is considerable overlap between the stations of Purgatory and the circles of Hell, there are additional and more detailed categories of sinners in Hell and their offences are far more grievous. Moreover, those in Purgatory have sinned but prayed for forgiveness before their deaths, hence they are laboring to be free of their sins; those in Hell died unrepentant and are doomed forever.[26]

Pride (L., *superbia*)

In the preceding chapter, we discussed the positive view of pride that is currently dominant in psychology and in mainstream Western cultures. The older and negative view of pride is reflected in its standing at the top of the Cardinal Sins and being their primary source.

Pride is the ultimate offence because it challenges God's greatness and mercy. Lack of humility takes the credit for accomplishments that are God's gifts. In the first station (cornice) of Purgatory, Dante encountered the souls of the proud crawling about bearing enormous slabs of stone. The proud soul could not raise itself because of the weight of its worldliness.

It may come as a surprise that the prideful do not appear as a separate category among sinners in Dante's Hell. This may be because pride is reflected in the offences of many sinners. Moreover, at the bottom of Hell, in the ninth circle, is Lucifer himself, the mightiest of angels whose pride led to his downfall. His companions are traitors, such as those who have betrayed their kindred (starting with Cain), their cities and countries, their guests, lords, and benefactors, and worst of all is Judas—the betrayer of Jesus. They are all encased in a frozen lake of ice fanned by the six bat-like wings of Lucifer. Betrayal is the worst sin because it destroys the trust that binds humanity.[27]

The ancient Greeks had a special term—*hubris*—to refer to overweening pride and unbridled ambition. The hubris of the high and the mighty challenged the prerogatives of the gods. Gods could act as they pleased, but when humans tried to imitate them, they were crushed by Nemesis on their behalf.

Philosophers took a more balanced view by attributing to pride both positive and negative qualities. Aristotle equated the excessive desire for honor with *vanity* and its lack with *pusillanimity* (being "small minded"). David Hume saw pride as part of a robust sense of self that refuses to subordinate itself to another's will. The distinction is between having a healthy sense of one's worth and bragging about it or lording it over others.[28]

This negative view of pride is primarily, if not exclusively, of religious origin. Psychologists also recognize it and differentiate *authentic* from *hubristic* pride. Authentic pride promotes the person's long-term social status by enhancing relationships ("getting along"); hubristic pride aims for short term gain ("getting ahead") and generates resentment. Excessive self-regard merges into narcissism, or self-absorbed love, a strident sense of self-worth that leads to arrogance and alienates others:

> My boyfriend is stuck on himself. It's always, me, me, me. It would not be so bad if he didn't constantly put other people down. It doesn't seem to bother him because he thinks people are stupid. I'd feel embarrassed if not guilty in his place. I don't know how much longer I can put up with him.

Guilt has a complex relationship with pride. Feelings of superiority, at the expense of others, make us feel bad. The sense of guilt is especially acute when we are contemptuous toward those who are close to us. On the other hand, when we act in a servile manner, we feel humiliated and diminished. The very feeling of guilt—for whatever reason—may be injurious to our pride, which is why some people feel reluctant to admit or submit to it.

Rather than pitting the religious/negative against the psychological/positive aspects of pride, we need to acknowledge that pride has a problematic side in psychology as well and the religious condemnation is aimed mainly at the element of *vainglory* in pride.

The negative medieval view of pride fitted well with the conception of human beings as born in Original Sin and predestined to sin thereafter. This made them unworthy. The Protestant Reformation further fostered the view that people could be saved only through the grace of God and had no moral merits of their own to be proud of. Therefore, what was required was abject humility rather than prideful self-satisfaction.

The Renaissance and the Enlightenment changed all this. Human beings took center stage as rational, autonomous, self-sufficient individuals. They had much to be proud of in their conquest of nature and the creation of a world in their own image. Recent attitudes have further enhanced a "feel good" mentality based on enhancement of self-esteem and a sense of entitlement. It is no wonder that in this mind-set pride occupies pride of place.

Envy (L., *invidia*)

Envy is the feeling of resentment over another person's success, qualities, or possessions. In the second station of Purgatory, Dante heard voices of the great love of others; virtue opposed to envy. These voices lashed out at the guilty souls of the envious whose eyes were shut because they were offended by all the good they saw in others. A disembodied voice lamented its being cut off forever from humanity—it was the voice of Cain, who killed Abel out of envy.

No matter how common it may be, envy has no redeeming features; no one has a kind word for it. People find it easier to admit being greedy than to being envious. It implies being inferior and is damaging to one's self-esteem.[29]

Envy may result from a sense of injustice rooted in long-forgotten sibling rivalries. The people we generally envy are those close to us—not some remote figure. Thus, I may envy my friend wearing a nice jacket from Brooks Brothers but not Prince Charles for his exquisite custom-made Savile Row suits.

Envy is often confused with *jealousy*; some languages actually do not have separate words for them. There is, however, an important distinction. Jealousy involves the fear of *losing* something we have (such as a lover being courted by a rival), whereas envy is wanting to have what belongs to someone else. Feeling envious may make us feel guilty. Or we may feel guilty by being the object of another person's envy.

My relationship with my brother is a major source of guilt in my life. I think the main reason is that he compares himself to me and then feels like I am trying to outdo everything he does. Now that we are both at college, my parents want me to reach out to him. But it just seems overwhelming to try to make up for eighteen years. Then my lack of willingness to make the effort makes me feel even guiltier.

The philosopher John Rawls observes, "a rational individual is not subject to envy, at least when the differences between himself and others are not thought to be the result of injustice and do not exceed certain limits."[30] Rawls differentiates between *general envy*, such as the envy of the poor for the rich, and *particular envy*, which arises from the rivalry between individuals where someone loses out in a quest for jobs, honor, or the affection of another person. Guilt is more likely to be attached to particular envy than to general envy. We should also not confuse envy with the resentment that arises from attributing the differences in our fortunes to unjust institutions or the wrongful conduct of others. Since such resentment may be justified, it need not lead to guilt. When those who can hardly feed their children look at the self-indulgences of the rich, the indignation and sense of helplessness they feel could hardly qualify as a sin.

There is also *benign envy*, where we wish we had attained what someone else has, but harbor no ill will; hence, the object may perceive it as a compliment rather than an expression of hostility. *Emulative envy* may even become an incentive to achieve what others have. There is no guilt attached to it either.

People who are objects of envy may fear its consequences. Various cultures have ways of fending off such a danger in symbolic ways, for instance by protections against the *evil eye*. We can also deflect envy by playing down our privileges and accomplishments ("It was just luck") or by sharing our good fortune by being generous and charitable.

Anger (L., *ira*)

Anger is a primary emotion with deep evolutionary roots. It is the most dangerous of all emotions and has the greatest potential for causing harm. Jesus condemned anger ("everyone who is angry with his brother shall be liable to judgment"), but he also vented his righteous indignation on the money changers in the temple courtyard. St. Paul admonished "be angry . . . but do not let the sun go down on your anger," thus allowing for its expression as well as limiting it (Matt 5:22; Eph. 4:26).

Feelings of anger, especially accompanied by acts of aggression, are particularly potent sources of guilt and appear quite early in life. This is especially true if the person the anger is directed at is someone close to us.

> I was about 12 years old. My mom, sister, and I had gotten off the airplane. We had all our luggage on this cart which (much to my dismay) I was forced to push by myself. My sister was "kissing up" to mom; holding her hand, skip-

ping around, looking all cute. Suddenly, I was overwhelmed with jealousy, rage, fury, and just couldn't take it anymore. So I accelerated my pace and very purposefully ran into my sister from behind, causing her to fall. To this day, I feel like this is the most awful, evil thing I have ever done to anyone.

Anger is a serious problem when it is out of control. Intemperate anger expressed as fury and rage can lead to murder and mayhem.[31] Thus the Cardinal Sin of *ira* is more properly rendered as *wrath*—such as the wrath of Achilles at Agamemnon for taking Briseis, his captive girl, from him. Had Athena not restrained him, he would surely have killed him:

> . . . anguish gripped Achilles.
> The heart in his rugged chest was pounding, torn . . .
> Should he draw the long sharp sword slung at his hip, . . .
> . . . and kill Agamemnon now?— . . .
> or check his rage and beat his fury down?[32]

Athena's intervention is masterful. She knows that confronting Achilles would infuriate him further. So she uses soft words to calm him down. Athena says that Hera has sent her to stop the quarrel for she loves both Achilles and Agamemnon equally. Achilles can abuse Agamemnon verbally ("Lash him with threats of the price that he will face") but he may not kill him. One day glittering gifts will pay three times over for all his outrage. The message is clear: You can feel and express your anger but you cannot act on it.

Dante encountered the souls of the wrathful at the third station of Purgatory in an acrid and blinding cloud of smoke, corrosive to the body as anger is to the spirit. The Whip of Wrath extolled the virtue of meekness toward kin, friends, and even enemies.

In Hell, the wrathful appear in the fifth circle, fighting each other on the surface of the river Styx. The souls of the violent are in a separate category, placed in the outer ring of the seventh circle, where they are immersed in a river of boiling blood, at a level commensurate to their sins. In the middle ring of this circle are those who have committed suicide—violence toward one's own self. In the inner circle are the blasphemers who are guilty of violence against God. Finally, there are those who have been violent against nature (sodomites) and those violent against order (usurers).

Moral philosophers have been particularly concerned with anger. Joseph Butler described three forms. "Hasty and sudden" anger is manifested by humans and animals as an instinctive response to threat. "Settled and deliberate" anger is in reaction to the perception of wrongful feelings, intentions, and actions of others toward us. These two forms of anger are episodic. The third form refers to a more fixed angry disposition, or character trait, expressed as irritability and churlishness.[33]

The first two varieties of anger need not necessarily elicit feelings of guilt because they feel necessary or justified. The third variety of anger is more likely to cause guilt since it lacks such justification and feels needless and excessive. Those who lose their temper and lash out at others usually regret it, yet guilt is usually insufficient to restrain them from doing it again.

Psychologists distinguish between proneness to anger as a personality trait and anger that occurs sporadically in response to various circumstances, the sort of anger we all experience. The latter occurs as a response to threats to our integrity (when we are insulted or falsely accused), to aggression (when we are threatened), to inequity (when we are cheated), to the frustration of our aims (when we cannot get what we want), and to ineptness and incompetence that exhaust our patience. Ultimately, whether we feel guilty or not will depend largely on how justified we feel our anger is and who it is we are venting our anger at. Fair-minded persons will feel bad even if the object of their anger is of no particular significance to them; on the other hand, we are more likely to feel guilty if we express our anger at someone we love.

Sloth (L., *accidie*)

The word "sloth," derived from the Middle English, implies laziness and indifference. (The animal of the same name is a New World mammal, hence no one in Europe had ever seen one when the Cardinal Sins were formulated.)

Lethargy and idleness are no virtues but neither would they qualify as grave sins. Yet, how would you feel being married to an indolent, work-shy goof-off? Or how would you like to be the parent of adult children who refuse to grow up and take care of themselves? Put in these terms, sloth begins to look bad. The slothful are particularly exasperating when they seem untroubled by their indolence. Actually, looked at more closely, there may be a great deal of guilt experienced by those who fail in their responsibilities to others and to themselves. Consequently, the failure to live up to parental and spousal expectations is a rife source of guilt, particularly in competitive cultures like the United States where self-reliance is highly valued.

There is an even deeper meaning to sloth. In its original sense, sloth stood for spiritual aridity ("dryness of the heart"), condemned by Dante as indifference to God. In the fourth circle of Purgatory, the souls of the slothful ran about frantically trying to make up for all the opportunities they had missed in their life for doing good. Their position in Hell is puzzling. They lie gurgling beneath the surface of the river Styx in the fifth circle, below the wrathful.

A profound form of sloth is *tedium vitae*—a sense of being sick of life and full of despair and ennui. This is not the self-conscious posturing of pseudo-intellectuals but a paralyzing disgust with life manifested by the refusal or inability to care, indifference to the suffering of others and to injustice, and the failure to stand up and be counted.[34]

Sloth may be also be a reaction to a dehumanizing and joyless world of work. Here is how Irina, in Chekov's *Three Sisters*, expresses it: "I can't work, I won't work. I have had enough of it. . . . I'm almost twenty-four. I have been working for ages. My brains are drying up. . . . I'm losing my looks, I'm aging and for what? Nothing."[35]

The listlessness of sloth may also be a symptom of depression. Early writers were quite aware of this element of sadness (*tristitia*), yet they still condemned it because it paralyzed the will and impaired moral action.

Avarice (L., *avaritia*)

Avarice—the sibling of greed—is the excessive desire for gain. If greed is acquisitiveness, avarice is hoarding. What makes them objectionable, and guilt-inducing, is that by accumulating more than we need, we deprive others of their fair share. In a zero-sum world of limited resources, when some get more, others get less.

Dante found the fifth station of Purgatory crowded with the souls of Hoarders and Wasters. The Whip of Avarice praised the blessed Mary who gave birth to Jesus in a manger, achieving a blessedness surpassing all the riches of the world. Another example is the honorable poverty of Roman consul Fabricius Luscinus, who spurned the bribes and gifts that were the perquisites of his office and died so poor that the state had to bury him. (Pagans could be virtuous too.)

The avaricious and miserly who hoarded possessions end up in the third circle of Hell, as do their opposites—the prodigal who squandered them. The two mobs push boulder-like weights crashing against each other, then they push them apart to begin over again.

St. Ambrose, a great Roman aristocrat who became bishop of Milan in the fourth century (and mentor of St. Augustine), exclaimed,

> How far, O rich, do you extend your senseless avarice? So you intend to be the sole inhabitants of the earth? Why do you drive out fellow sharers of nature, and claim it all for yourselves? The earth was made for all, rich and poor, in common. Why do you rich claim it as your exclusive right?[36]

We must be careful not to equate avarice with wealth as such—the poor can be avaricious too and it is possible to be rich without being avaricious. In a free and fair society, people are entitled to what they have rightly earned or inherited. To be hardworking, thrifty, and frugal is what Max Weber called the *Protestant Ethic*—the moral backbone of the spirit of capitalism (although Protestants do not have a monopoly on it).[37]

Avarice is especially aggravating when it is combined with miserliness. It is not hard to understand why the rich may be self-indulgent; but why would anyone accumulate wealth to just sit on it? Does hoarding money assuage the guilt for having it? Does money become an idol to be worshipped? Is hoarding a symptom of anal retentiveness?

There is a special form of guilt called *positive inequity* that is associated with privilege. Some affluent people assuage their guilt by being charitable, but one can also be charitable out of compassion, a sense of moral obligation and social responsibility. Furthermore, there is a distinction between making money and keeping it. Philanthropist Andrew Carnegie, who was immensely rich, thought it was "a disgrace to die rich," and John Wesley, cofounder of Methodism, preached, "Earn all you can. Save all you can. Give all you can." However, no matter how charitable some people may be, they appear self-indulgent when they lavish hundreds of millions of dollars on yachts and airplanes. And when they do so without lifting a finger to help those in need, it makes one's blood boil. It then hardly matters if they feel guilty or not.

Gluttony (L., *gula*)

Food and drink are among the great pleasures in life. The French distinguish between those with a refined palate (*gourmet*) and gluttons (*gourmand*). Yet the line is hard to draw since those who like to eat well also tend to eat a lot.

Overindulgence in food and drink is bad for one's health. And it implies selfishness and insensitivity to the needs of others. In a world where so many went hungry, it is easy to see why gluttony was singled out for condemnation.

The antidote to gluttony is fasting: Christians fast during Lent and Muslims during the Ramadan. Hindu ascetics and Buddhist monks beg for their food. The pangs of hunger make us empathize with the plight of the poor, as well as encourage spiritual self-examination. Romans raised gluttony to lofty heights. They would vomit so they could eat more. The banquet of Trimalchio in the *Satyricon* by Petronius is a wonderful parody of gluttony; unfortunately it is too long to reproduce here.[38]

Dante encountered the souls of gluttons at the sixth station of Purgatory. Their emaciated souls went around an enormous tree laden with fruit that was denied to them. They reminded Dante of Erysichthon, who offended Ceres, the goddess of plenty. Ceres induced an insatiable hunger that forced him to eat all he had, sell his daughter so he could buy more food, and finally devour his own limbs.

The gluttons in Hell are consigned to the third circle, where they lived in a vile slush of stinking snow and freezing rain. The gluttons—and the lustful— are guilty of sins of incontinence: abusers of food and sex, which are good in moderation.

Obesity in Western cultures has now acquired a special moral taint, particularly in the United States. Since the metabolism of some people predisposes them toward it, obesity can be a form of illness, yet some obese persons still feel guilty. Corpulence used to be a mark of high social status—now, it is the opposite. Even if we do not feel guilt, many of us feel shame over being overweight—it shows a lack of self-discipline, a weakness of character. The specter of being fat especially haunts young women from middle class or more privileged backgrounds.

I feel guilty for eating. It is a very consuming guilt and it takes over all my thoughts and actions. To make things worse, I usually feel guilty that I felt guilty because I know I shouldn't be feeling that way.

The preoccupation with being fat takes an especially troublesome form in anorexia and bulimia. These eating disorders are attempts to deal with emotional problems and guilt plays a prominent part in these conditions. A middle-aged woman recalls:

By the middle of my freshman year, my guilt consumed me. I felt I deserved to suffer; food became my weapon of choice. I ate less and less at each meal. Soon I was just pushing the food around my plate. Eventually I missed meals altogether. . . . My last two years of college, I became a different kind of sick. I gorged on massive amounts of food until my belly was so distended I was unable to get out of bed. . . . [Now] I am a whole person. I have gained self-respect, and my mind and body are healthy and strong.[39]

The idea that fat is "ugly" has generated the reaction that "fat is beautiful." Some obese individuals let their weight go where it might by refusing to accept the cultural stereotype of attractiveness:

> When I was in junior high, I would feel very guilty after eating something fattening. I wanted to be thin and fit like the girls in *Seventeen* magazine. I also wanted the taste of chocolate in my mouth and savor the flavor of sin sliding down my throat. Things are different now. I will weigh my feelings of guilt with my desire to pig out before actually eating so that once I swallow the sinful goodness of chocolate cake I savor each bite as a guiltless gift to myself and my beautiful, womanly, perfectly un-thin body.

The guilt of gluttony can also be associated with excessive drinking, smoking, and drug use. The pleasure one gets from these substances may be spoiled by the guilt they induce but usually not enough to act as a deterrent. Even though we now treat alcoholism as an illness, it too still induces guilt. The remarkable change in smoking habits over the past several decades may have been at least partly due to guilt. For those of us old enough to remember the glamour of smoking, the sight of people furtively smoking in solitude is quite remarkable.

Lust (L., *luxuria*)

Lust is the last but not the least of the Cardinal Sins, and it has carried a disproportionate burden of guilt. The very notion of lust may sound antiquated. We now talk instead about sexual desire or erotic attraction. Lust is not an exclusively sexual term—it simply means an intense desire or yearning for anything. In the original Latin, *luxuria* connoted sensuality.[40]

Dante encountered the lustful ("carnal") on his ascent to the seventh and last cornice of Purgatory. The souls of the lustful were covered in sheets of flame (the "fire" of lust). In Hell itself, the lustful got off relatively lightly. Dante placed them in the second circle. (The only ones better off in the first circle—or *Limbo*—are virtuous pagans who lived before Christ and hence had no opportunity to become Christians.) The souls of the lustful were caught in a great turbulence like their passion. Included among them were the most celebrated lovers of history: Helen and Paris, Paolo and Francesca, Dido and Cleopatra. (So much for great love worth dying for.)[41]

Far from the struggles of medieval ascetics with lust and its condemnation through the Victorian era down to modern times, lust that is expressed through legitimate sexual channels has now become fully rehabilitated. Even conservative evangelical Christians praise the virtues of marital sex and the Catholic church endorses its fulfillment in the conjugal bed. The sexual revolution of the 1960s unleashed an avalanche of books that have described, illustrated, endorsed, and instructed couples in the delights and intricacies of sex. Such books, magazines, and films continue to pour out, while the internet is awash in pornography. Not only sexologists and would-be experts, but some ordinary married couples have contributed to the celebration of sex through sexual marathons by making love 101 days straight or even every day for a whole year.[42] Western societies have evolved into the most sexually permissible cultures where sex seems to have cast off its mantle of guilt, but it is not entirely off the hook. Sex that is out of control or heedlessly seeking satisfaction irrespective of its consequences to others, as well as to oneself, remains a serious problem.

Lust at its simplest may take the form of sexual fantasies. Erotic thoughts and feelings are virtually ubiquitous and hard to control. Christianity has traditionally imposed a moral judgment on sexual fantasies alone (lusting in one's heart), whereas Judaism and Islam mainly judge actual conduct. In our discussion of guilt in Judaism, Christianity, and Islam, we will deal with the broader question of sexual morality. What we will address here is an extension of our earlier discussion of adultery and premarital sex. Specifically, we will consider masturbation and homosexuality, both of which have been potent sources of guilt but no longer are, at least to the same extent. We will also look at behaviors that are still considered deviant, as well as sexual violence and child sexual abuse, which represent very serious problems.

Since it can be socially disruptive, it is not hard to understand why adultery would be morally objectionable. However, why was masturbation considered to be a vice? Masturbation is commonly accompanied by erotic fantasies that in themselves may be guilt-inducing, so it is not always clear which of these elements one is responding to with guilt—erotic feelings and thoughts or the actual sexual activity they elicit through the act of masturbation itself.

> I think I started masturbating when I was five years old, but I don't recall feeling guilty about it until my youth pastor gave a sermon about sexual sin and

the one sexual outlet I thought God had left open became yet another damnable sin. It was awful. I was in such pain—I thought I was an evil person, a failure. Every time I touched myself, I had allowed Satan to gain a foothold in my life. I tortured myself wondering how many times God would be willing to acquit me of the same crime.

We have come a long way from the absurd theories of masturbatory insanity that captured the Victorian imagination.[43] Masturbation is now widely accepted as a common and harmless practice, even though the official position of the Catholic church still finds it morally objectionable (possibly on the same grounds that it opposes contraception). However, this is not only a religious concern. Even those who are quite open about their sexual experiences still conceal the fact that they masturbate, probably more out of shame than guilt. It makes them look immature, or lacking what it takes to attract a partner for "real sex."[44]

Homosexuality is another instance where social attitudes have undergone dramatic changes. Same-sex relationships were long considered to be a psychological disorder, a moral blemish, and illegal; consequently, homosexual desires and behaviors often led to feeling guilty. By the mid-1970s it had ceased to carry these burdens: The American Psychiatric Association took it off its list of mental disorders and there are now state laws that protect gay men and lesbians against discrimination. However, homosexuals have yet to attain parity with heterosexuals in matters like marriage. And some people still associate homosexuality with guilt.

I feel somewhat guilty that my youngest son is gay. I realize that genetics play a major role. However, I feel that I may have contributed to his homosexuality because I focused on him to an extreme when he was a boy. He was the center of my life and we had such a wonderful mother-son relationship that in many ways he took the place of my husband, although not in a physical sense, due to the fact that my marriage was so unhappy.

Same-sex relationships may be more prone to induce guilt because of, among other things, the higher prevalence of AIDS among homosexuals than among heterosexuals (exclusive of drug users). People tend to think of illness as a form of punishment (such as smoking and lung cancer). However, sexually transmitted diseases tend to carry an additional, special moral taint. This was the case in the nineteenth century with syphilis and now the same may be true for AIDS. If a sexual partner infects another, it is not hard to see why one would feel guilty. If one partner gets the disease and the other does not, then there is a sense of survivor guilt. Such considerations, of course, fuel prejudice. While we must take responsibility for safeguarding our own and our sexual partner's health, it makes no sense to view illness as a punishment; what are children born with congenital diseases being punished for?

Other forms of sexual behavior remain socially problematic. Conditions that used to carry pejorative labels like "deviations" are now called *paraphilias* in psychiatry and *sexual offences* in the law. Some of these behaviors, like sado-masochistic acts between consenting adults, need not victimize others. Yet others, like voyeurism and exhibitionism are intrusive and clearly objectionable. Nonetheless, the perpetrators of such socially problematic conduct are often lumped with other antisocial characters and treated as criminals by the law.

Rape and other forms of sexual violence, as well as the sexual abuse of children, are particularly serious problems both in terms of the number of victims and the damage done to them. These too could be seen as perversions of lust, but other factors, such as the drive for dominance and violence, often complicate the picture.

Ironically, those who are victimized are the ones who may feel guilty in these situations, rather than the perpetrators. Women are generally more subject to this unwarranted self-attribution of responsibility.

> I went to the party because my friend was so eager to go. Once we got there we got separated. I started drinking with some of the guys and one of them more or less dragged me to his room and forced me to have sex. My friend found me asleep on the sofa and took me back to the dorm. The next morning, I felt angry but also responsible for what happened. I knew I should not have gotten drunk but that did not justify what that guy did to me. Yet I somehow felt guilty and decided to keep my mouth shut.

Sometimes, the physical and the psychological reactions to sexual arousal become disconnected. When this happens, the victim may feel sexually aroused no matter how appalled and horrified she, or he, may feel otherwise. That leads to more guilt. (This is why men who are forced into sex may get erections, which negates the idea that men cannot be raped.)

At the end of the day, are the Cardinal Sins still relevant to our lives? The discussion above argues that they are. Some may object, however, that these ancient sins have been superseded by more modern concerns. In 1973, Konrad Lorenz, the great Austrian ethologist, wrote a book called *Civilized Man's Eight Deadly Sins*. They included none of the traditional Cardinal Sins; instead, the list consists of overpopulation; devastation of our natural environment; the blinding of people by technology to real human values; intolerance of everything that interferes with pleasure; the failure to preserve instinctive norms of social behavior; the break with tradition; increased ideological indoctrination; and proliferation of nuclear weapons.[45]

More recently, Bishop Gianfranco Girotti of the Vatican came out with a similar list of new deadly sins that include ruining the environment, eco-abuse, genetic manipulation, and consumerism.[46] In such cases, however, "deadly sins" is being used as a rhetorical device to get people's attention to more modern concerns. Actually these problems are not predispositions like the Cardinal Sins but rather undesirable behaviors, whose prohibitions would fit better with the Ten Commandments. They do not replace older moral concerns but complement them through expanding them into new areas.

DEALING WITH GUILT

Since guilt is a painful emotion, we need to deal with it. If we shove it under the carpet, it will not go away. We usually try to deal with guilt in the privacy of our conscience; less often, by approaching the person we have offended. Talking to family members, friends, or reading self-help books may help. Those who are religious can speak to their clergy. Catholics are most likely to take advantage of the practice of confession. It is only when guilt cannot be resolved through such means, or becomes too hard to bear, that we seek help from psychiatrists, psychologists, or other professionals.

When I set out to write this book, giving advice on how to deal with guilt was not part of my agenda. Unsolicited advice, as noted in the Preface, is intrusive and ineffective since it does not respond to an expressed need or a person's specific concerns. Generic advice is like junk mail. To be useful, advice must be customized—one size does not fit all.

Nonetheless, virtually everyone I spoke to about this book told me that I had to discuss the issue of dealing with guilt. A book written for a general audience had to be helpful beyond being informative. I could not just lay it all out and expect readers to sort out what they could apply to their personal lives. Even if this was not to be a self-help book, it still needed to be helpful. So I wrote a final chapter to address the issue of dealing with guilt. Then I was told that readers would not want to wait to the end to hear what I had to say. So we shall deal with the issue in installments, as they relate to the subject matter of each chapter.

The various ways of dealing with guilt may be characterized as positive: effective, adaptive, or healthy; or as negative: ineffective, maladaptive, and unhealthy. Psychologist Roger Brooke characterizes these two paths as the *authentic* and the *inauthentic* modes of dealing with guilt.[47] Derived from existentialist philosophy, these terms focus on the uniqueness of the individual. To be authentic means to be true to oneself, free from conventional expectations of personal responsibility that involve "bad faith." By contrast, to be inauthentic means to be untrue to oneself and to drift along in stereotypical roles, thereby losing our ability to define our own lives.[48]

The key element underlying the resolution of guilt is the acceptance of responsibility. All else flows from it. The authentic way of dealing with guilt heals the rupture in damaged relationships caused by wrongdoing, and it removes the sense of isolation that guilt produces. The inauthentic way perpetuates and deepens the rupture, leading to further isolation and alienation of the person feeling guilty. The underlying dynamic in inauthentic resolutions is denial of responsibility. This leads to various tactics to get out of facing the consequences of our actions rather than dealing with them in a fair and positive manner. We will apply these principles when we consider how to deal with guilt in the context of personal relationships in the next chapter.

3 GUILT AND RELATIONSHIPS

ANN K. IS A PARTNER in a prestigious law firm in Boston. She is married to a surgeon and is the mother of two bright teenagers. Ann is in her late forties. Her sister, Debbie, five years older, is a divorced high school teacher with no children and lives at home with her widowed mother.

The two sisters grew up in a small Midwestern town under modest circumstances. Ann went to Amherst, on a scholarship, and then to Yale Law School. She married a surgeon and settled in Boston. Debbie became a teacher and never strayed far from home. After their father died, she continued living at home until she married a fellow teacher. The marriage did not last (it is not clear why) and Debbie moved back to live with her mother.

The two sisters got along well but were not close. Debbie lived in the shadow of her smarter, ambitious, and more attractive sister. She was proud of Ann's accomplishments, but also envied her. It seemed unfair that Ann should be so much more successful in her professional and personal life. Debbie felt ashamed for these feelings, but she could not help it. On her part, Ann felt vaguely guilty for her more fortunate life. She told herself she had worked harder, so she deserved what she had. Yet a nagging sense of inequity lingered in her mind.

One evening Ann got a frantic call from Debbie: Their mother had suffered a stroke and was in the hospital. Ann was in the middle of a trial but said she would come as soon as possible. Three days later, they met at the hospital. The doctor told them their mother would survive but she would need constant care for the rest of her life.

That evening, Debbie and Ann sat at the kitchen table to sort things out. There was not much Ann could do other than provide financial help, if necessary. On the other hand, she could hardly suggest that Debbie give up her job and stay home to care for their mother. When Ann raised the prospect of placing their mother in a nursing home, Debbie rejected it: that would make their mother miserable—it would be like burying her alive.

Ann's lawyerly mind searched for a rational solution, but her feelings clouded her judgment. She felt guilty, not only for the situation they now faced, but for having had so little to do with her mother and sister all these years. Her visits home had been few and far between. The past suddenly caught up with her and she felt trapped. Debbie realized that Ann was entitled to live her own life. If she herself did not have much of a life, that was surely not Ann's fault. Now it seemed she was about to lose what little independence and leisure she enjoyed. She had to take care of her mother because she always had taken care of her mother, and that did not seem fair.

The following day, when Ann was visiting their mother, Debbie went to see her friend Julia for advice. Julia told Debbie that putting her mother in a nursing home or quitting her job to take care of her were not the only options. They could hire people to help look after their mother and Ann would pay for it. Moreover, there would come a time when it would no longer be possible to care for her mother at home. When that time came, their mother would understand and Debbie and Ann would have the satisfaction of having done all they could for her.

Debbie conveyed all this to Ann, and she accepted it with relief. Of course she would pay for it. Moreover, when their mother died, the house and their mother's assets would go to Debbie so that she would have more than her pension to live on when she retired. Once in place, the solution seemed obvious; why then had they not figured it out by themselves? Focusing on *how* best to take care of their mother would have addressed the realities of the situation; delving into the issue of *who* should take responsibility for their mother dredged up feelings of all sorts, including guilt, that muddied up their minds.

IN PREVIOUS CHAPTERS, we have been mainly concerned with guilt-inducing behaviors at the personal level, rather than the role of guilt in personal relationships. The two are, of course, inseparable: two sides of the same coin. After all, most of our behaviors involve other people—either in fact or in our minds: When we lie, we lie to someone; when we steal, we steal from someone.

It takes two to play the guilt game. However, studies of guilt within human relationships are relatively new.[1] This is partly due to the Freudian heritage of emphasizing the *intra-psychic* rather than the *interpersonal* aspects of psychological conflicts.[2]

Is guilt limited to our dealings with those that we care about such as family members and friends? Do we always hurt the ones we love? To what extent does the prospect of guilt extend to the colleagues we work with and the clients we serve? How about others we may encounter fleetingly, or who live on the other side of the globe? We need some way of categorizing such relationships. The following model will provide us with useful handles to understand our own personal relationships.[3]

COMMUNAL AND EXCHANGE RELATIONSHIPS

Let us start by clarifying some key terms, even if they may seem self-evident. *Personal* relationships are typically based on family connections and long-standing friendships. They require a high degree of emotional investment.[4] *Intimate* relationships suggest even closer ties, with hints of romantic and sexual involvement. *Impersonal* associations apply to professional relationships with colleagues and business partners including service providers (be they doctors or housekeepers) and the clients we ourselves serve. The more important impersonal relationships may share some of the characteristics of personal relationships in terms of length and intensity. They may become even more important. Think of the relationship between a woman suffering from cancer and her doctor, or that of a man on trial for murder and his lawyer. In such cases, we may depend more heavily on relative strangers than on kith and kin. We also cross paths with countless strangers with whom we share only, at best, a vague sense of fellow-feeling. However, some transient encounters can leave stronger impressions on us than longer-term relationships. Have you ever shared intimate details of your life with the passenger sitting next to you on an airplane, someone you will never see again?

Interpersonal relationship is the term that refers to all forms of relationships between people. These have been categorized into two types: *communal* and *exchange* relationships, each of which has a special bearing on the experience of guilt.[5] Communal relationships are exemplified by the way family members relate to each other. They may vary in their level of closeness, but share a general sense of belonging. The implicit rule governing communal relationships is that we need to be concerned with each other's well-being without the expectation of reciprocal benefits. This applies not only to material concerns but emotional needs as well. Communally related individuals are there for each other. Their basic, albeit not only, reward is in the satisfaction of caring for those they care about.

Communal relationships involve what we commonly think of as close relationships. Compared to exchange relationships, their emotional connections are more intense and durable. They are the source of the most blissful as well as the must hurtful feelings we experience in our relationships.[6] How we feel at a given time is largely dependent on how others we care about feel toward us.

Exchange relationships are more impersonal, shallow, and short-term. They have a contractual basis, as exemplified in our professional interactions. The principles governing these interactions are *equity* and *trust*. We expect to give and to receive a fair deal or good value for our money. While we want respect and civility in exchange relationships as well, there is no expectation of real intimacy or affection. (When you say, "I love my gardener," you usually do not mean it literally.)

The differences between communal and exchange relationships are real but not sharply defined. Communal relationships often have an exchange component and exchange relationships may include some features of communal relationships. For instance, your doctor or lawyer may also be your friend; you may even fall in love and marry one of them (at which point you will need a new doctor or lawyer). We may relate to our neighbors in a communal manner, but only up to a point ("Good fences make good neighbors"). We may respond to an exchange partner in a communal manner with the hope of fostering a more personal relationship, either out of genuine interest or to gain some advantage. (Who would not want to be friends with the boss?) These distinctions have subtle boundaries and it takes social skills to navigate them.

Transgressions within communal relationships are more often associated with guilt than in exchange relationships. Typically, guilt results when we neglect our partners, fail to fulfill our obligations to them, or act selfishly. The primary purpose of guilt in these contexts is to deter wrongdoing and to repair the damage to the relationship. In exchange relationships, the prospect of guilt is to insure that the relationship continues to serve the mutual needs and expectations of all concerned.[7]

The reasons that guilt serves a more important role in communal than exchange relationships are not hard to fathom. Damaging a close personal relationship obviously hurts more and is more detrimental to our lives than damaging an impersonal one. This, however, is not always the case. For instance, some people are so heavily invested in their work that it may seem less disruptive to get a divorce than to compromise their career. (One man left his wife after he became head of the company because she could no longer "handle her social obligations.")

HOW DOES GUILT WORK (OR NOT WORK)
IN INTERPERSONAL RELATIONSHIPS?

The association of guilt with the notion of debt suggests an economic model where guilt functions as a currency of exchange in the business of dealing with each other. Like money, guilt can be used effectively, but also abused or debased. It may be used to pay an honest debt, or it may be contrived. If you feel obligated to a relationship partner over a past transgression, it may work like a line of credit, or money in the bank. Or it may be used to blackmail and control you. Is inducing guilt an effective or appropriate way of profiting from our partner's vulnerability? What are its costs and benefits? Does guilt operate in a zero-sum system where my gain is someone else's loss? Or is it a non-zero-sum game where we both stand to gain or lose together? Is guilt a good investment in maintaining a valued relationship or simply a way of propping up a relationship that is falling apart, or has simply run its course? (Some psychologists refer to failed relationships as having been "completed.")

There are two emotional sources for feeling guilty within relationships. The first is *empathic distress*, where we share another person's pain. However, if we have not caused the pain, we are less likely to feel guilty, even though we may empathize with the other person's suffering. The second source of guilt is associated with *exclusion anxiety*, which results from the sense of alienation from the relationship partner we have hurt. Guilt acts like a thick curtain that comes between people.[8]

The fact that guilt makes us feel bad helps to make things better by achieving three positive purposes: It enhances the relationship, it redresses the power imbalance between the partners, and it redistributes emotional distress by making the victim feel better through making the perpetrator feel worse.

In enhancing the relationship, guilt performs both a *prospective* function when it stops us from harming the relationship partner and a *retrospective* function when it kicks in after the bad deed is done. In the first instance it prevents damage to the relationship; in the second it repairs the damage. Since guilt serves these positive functions, does it mean we should deliberately precipitate it as a way of strengthening our relationships? That would be like breaking a piece of furniture in order to fix it. Guilt is a remedy for natural breaks, not contrived ones. Guilt always exacts a price; like surgery, it leaves residual damage in the form of emotional scars. Better a scar than a wound, but better yet is having neither.

The need to redress power imbalances arises from the fact that couples are rarely matched evenly in assets and liabilities, which means that we do not wield equivalent power within our relationships. Yes, true love should make considerations of power irrelevant. Unfortunately, that is not the way things generally work, and it is better to face reality than deny it.

There is usually some parity between couples with respect to things like physical attractiveness ("Swans fly with swans and ducks with ducks") as well as psychological and social characteristics like education and social class. However, these features do not match each other exactly. Instead, partners typically bring into their relationship a roughly equivalent mix of assets and liabilities. For example, one person's higher income may be matched by the other's looks; intelligence by social status; education by warmth of character. Although feelings supplement (and can overwhelm) reason, we rely on our heads and our hearts in ascertaining the "worth" of the person we wish to associate with. Feelings in themselves are influenced by value considerations, and vice versa. The more valuable we think the person is, the more we are likely to like and love him or her; and the more we like and love, the more valuable that person will appear to us.[9]

Guilt acts as an equalizer when disparities in power within a relationship become problematic. The person wielding less power relies on guilt to even the balance. In that sense, guilt is a weapon of the weak. To the extent that women have wielded less influence, they have been more likely to induce guilt. Age is another variable and one that works both ways. For example, a child is dependent on its parents and subject to their authority. Yet, that authority is quite limited. When a child misbehaves, parents could punish the child or withdraw their love, but those moves are emotionally costly. A more cost effective way is to make the child feel guilty. A 32-year-old man recalls:

> I was sick as a child for almost a year and spent a lot of time with my mother at home. One day, I really got fed up being cooped up and refused to take my pills. My mother tried patiently to reason with me but I kept whining until she began to cry softly. I felt awful and swallowed the damn pills without another word. I will never forget her tear-stained face.

Finally, guilt can redress power imbalances in a relationship through the redistribution of distress. When we are subjected to harsh words or hurtful acts, or distressed by our partner's indifference or neglect, we feel disappointed, hurt, angry, and sad. If the offending partner shows neither regret nor remorse, it aggravates the emotional pain. If, on the other hand, there is a genuine expression of remorse, we feel better by our partner feeling worse. The distress is easier to bear when it is more evenly distributed.

INDUCING GUILT

Whether inducing guilt is a good or a bad thing depends on the circumstances under which it is done. A single mother with small children trying to induce guilt in a deadbeat dad is in a different situation than a spoiled young man trying to extract money from his parents. The guilt-inducer may be acting out of desperation to elicit empathy from an uncaring partner, or exploiting the other's guilt for all it is worth.

When someone offends us, we are entitled to let the person know about it. If the offender is unrepentant, we have to express our feelings more emphatically. In these cases, we are simply letting guilt do its work. That is quite different from when someone "lays a guilt trip" as an influence tactic. The objective may be to induce the other person to be more attentive ("How could you forget my birthday?"), or to comply with one's wishes ("We haven't slept together for two weeks—don't you care for me any more?"), or to pursue some other agenda. The provocation for inducing guilt may be trivial or serious, real or fabricated, justified or unjustified.

The particular techniques of inducing guilt vary from the subtle ("You must have been too busy to call me") to the theatrical ("I'm dying here and you don't give a damn"). They include reminding others of their obligations ("Remember, I'm your friend"), pointing to services one has rendered ("I took care of you when you were sick"), and comparing the person to someone else ("Jim would have lent me the money"). The elderly play up the fact that they do not have much time left to live ("You'll be sorry for this after I'm dead and gone").

The sick, disabled, disadvantaged, unfortunate, and unhappy deserve our sympathy and help. However, they may also play up their infirmities to soften us up by the "wounded puppy" ploy, where one pretends to be helpless. The "secondary gain" people derive from these tactics is usually short-lived. Those subjected to it became aware of it soon enough and harden their hearts. However, these encounters should not be seen as a contest of wills but difficult situations that need to be dealt with. If you have cared for someone who has an incurable illness, is chronically depressed, or is struggling with alcoholism and addiction, then you know how difficult that is, how guilty you should feel and for how long. While it is usually parents who induce guilt in their children, children too can use it to devastating effect:

> My 8-year-old daughter, Tracy, is one of our two adopted children. We have loved and provided her with all the advantages that she could not have possibly received from her single, teenage mother, who had put her up for adoption. Tracy turned out to be a difficult child who, after my husband and I separated, became increasingly demanding and manipulative.
>
> One day she came from school all excited about getting a puppy. I explained to her that I could hardly keep up with my job and taking care of her and her sister; there was no way I could also look after a dog in the small apartment we lived in. But Tracy would not give up and kept at it day after day. . . . Finally, I became exasperated and told her we were not going to get a puppy or talk about it ever again. She went to her room and then came back with a tear-stained face and said to me, "Mommy, I know you don't want me to talk about this but can I say just one thing?" I told her, "Go ahead. What is it?" And she said, "I am sure my birth mother would have gotten me a puppy."

The mother was stunned, then furious; filled with doubts about her adequacy as a mother and regret over having adopted the child in the first place; and then tormented by guilt over all these feelings. On her part, the daughter exacted her revenge, but at what cost? When older, would she perhaps remember these words and be filled with remorse? Heartrending encounters like these show the power of guilt in seeking out vulnerable spots and striking where it hurts most.

The most common means to induce guilt is to reproach the offender directly ("You tried to humiliate me"). Such confrontational methods often succeed, but the guilt they induce tends to be short-lived. They force the offender to make an earnest or perfunctory apology to settle the matter ("OK, I'm sorry!"). Or the accused may become defensive and deny the accusation ("I said nothing of the sort") or lash back in anger ("I'm sick and tired of your making a mountain out of a molehill").

An alternative tactic is to prod the offending partner indirectly. One can do this by nonverbal cues (such as by looking upset), or by complaining to a third person within the hearing of the offender ("I can't believe he would embarrass me like that"). This gives the culprit an opportunity to either explain or apologize without getting defensive. However, the offender can also avoid the issue by pretending not to hear what is being said.

A third approach is to adopt the perpetrator's perspective. The injured party may minimize the seriousness of the offence ("No harm was done"); take the blame for it ("I deserved what you said"); or make excuses for the offender ("You must have felt exasperated with me"). These strategies are quite effective in establishing the offender's guilt while pretending to deny it. Turning the other cheek or reinterpreting the act in a positive light gives the victim the moral high ground. Even ostensibly forgiving the offender binds the person in the grip of a deeper sense of guilt; but this tactic may also let the offender get off the hook if he or she actually believes, or pretends to believe, that he or she has been truly forgiven.[10]

Finally, one should insist on closure. After you have said and done all that can be reasonably expected, you are entitled to be released from your burden of guilt. This usually requires a measure of forgiveness and hopefully reconciliation (although the two do not always go together, as we shall discuss later on).

The more we are attached to someone, the more we are vulnerable to being manipulated by induced guilt. The standard reproach among lovers starts with "If you loved me" you would do such and such. The accusation may be just or it can also be a manipulative tactic:

> In my last serious romantic relationship, my evil and manipulative boyfriend would always make me feel guilty whenever I tried to break up with him. He would tell me how I let him down, how I was the only one in the world that he could trust, and now I was hurting him and not even trying to save our relationship, and how I obviously didn't care about him and was just using him. He would use my past mistakes against me, even when I had already admitted that I had been wrong and was trying my best to be more considerate. Even though I would always take him back, I believe in my heart that it would have been best for both us if I had not done so. But he knew how to make me feel guilty and used it to control me.

Dealing with the unrequited love of another person toward us is one of the most difficult situations we could face. Sometimes it is almost easier to have one's own love rejected than to reject someone else's love. Even when we have neither encouraged nor made any commitments, we still feel guilty for rejecting the love offered us. To break someone's heart is hard even for the hard-hearted. Moreover, the guilt we feel makes us vulnerable to being manipulated by the would-be lover.[11]

In *Don Quixote*, the young man whose unrequited love leads to his death, heaps invective on the beautiful Marcela in a three-page poem for rejecting his love. Marcela defends herself at his funeral with the following words:

> According to what I have heard, true love is not divided and must be volun- tary, not forced. If this is true . . . why do you want me to surrender my will, obliged to do so simply because you say you love me? . . .
>
> If I had kept him by me, I would have been false; if I had gratified him, I would have gone against my best intentions and purposes. He persisted though I discouraged him, he despaired though I did not despise him: tell me now if it is reasonable to blame me for his grief![12]

Leila A., a 22-year-old intelligent, gifted, compassionate, lovely young wom- an became the object of the obsessive love of a young man who had lost the use of his legs due to polio. She liked him but could not return his ardent love, nor could she bring herself to sever her relationship with him. She finally consented to her parents' pleas to stop meeting him out of guilt—meetings he imposed on her insistently. She wrote to him, as gently as she could, that she could no longer see him. Soon after, the young man showed up at her house and asked to see Leila for one last time. She did not have the heart to refuse. As the young man wheeled himself into the room, he took out a pistol and shot her, then killed himself. This was a double tragedy that might have been averted if matters had not been allowed to go as far as they did. Or perhaps there was no other way out; not every problem has a good solution.

Inducing guilt provides certain advantages, but it is not cost-free. It causes resentment that leads to withdrawal and alienation. Ultimately, it is self- defeating. Another consequence is *metaguilt*—feeling guilty for inducing guilt. This traps the guilt-inducer and the victim in a vicious cycle. For example, John and Jim are a gay couple in a committed relationship. John is a successful bank manager. Jim, who is quite a bit younger, is a writer who has not yet found his "voice." John says,

> I work long hours and do most of the work around the house as well. Jim con- tributes very little yet he complains bitterly that I do not take his career aspi- rations seriously and instead treat him like a "wife." When I lose my patience

once in a while and tell him to get off his ass and make himself useful, he says I hurt his feelings and make him feel like shit, [and then] I feel bad and apologize profusely.

Inducing guilt is more effective if the criticism is pointed at a deed rather than the doer of the deed: "You didn't do the dinner dishes as you promised," rather than "You don't hold to your promises." If guilt is induced in a diffuse and indiscriminate manner, all it does is make the other person feel bad with no tangible benefit. If one does not allow the offending partner a way out, then guilt has nowhere to go. It places the person in a "double bind" where you are damned if you do and damned if you don't—a no-win, catch-22 situation.

Consider a couple in their late thirties. Eric is a physician and Emily is a nurse. They were married while he was in residency training and she worked at the same hospital. It is not clear if they would have done so had she not gotten pregnant. This made Emily fret over whether Eric married her out of a sense of obligation rather than love. When Eric had a brief affair with a fellow resident it intensified Emily's anxieties and made her resort to making him feel guilty by construing evidence that he did not love her (which became increasingly true). Eric says,

I don't know why Emily keeps trying to make me feel guilty by accusing me of not loving her. She says she loves me, but I see no sign of real affection. All she does is complain about how little I care about her. As proof, she points to my repeated failure to remember what she calls "special occasions." These are not standard birthdays or wedding anniversaries—nothing like that. It's more like when I kissed her for the first time or when we had an anniversary picnic at the beach. I don't know how in hell I am to remember all this. But since she does and I don't, it means that she loves me and I don't love her. It's like keeping track of saints' days—one for each day of the year. The whole thing is crazy, but I still can't stop myself from feeling guilty.

Eric has no reasonable way of satisfying Emily. If he rejects what she says, it confirms her accusation that he does not love her. If he agrees to remember all their "special occasions," he is bound to fail since Emily comes up with new ones. Eric cannot get out of this predicament except by getting out of the relationship, which is ultimately what he did. (We do not have Emily's side of the story.)

The roles are reversed in the next example. Alexandra is a lawyer who stayed home when her three children were young. She then went back to work with the ostensible encouragement of her husband, Arthur:

> I gave up my job to stay home with my children even though I was on my way to be made a partner. Arthur appreciated my willingness to be a full-time mom but deep down he pretty much took it for granted that this was the "natural" thing to do. When our youngest daughter finally started school, I decided to go back to work. Arthur went along with my decision, but was not terribly enthusiastic. He welcomed the second income, particularly since I made more money than he did. But he was expecting that I would continue to take care of the house, just as I had been doing.
>
> What really upsets me is that Arthur never complains openly about household matters because he knows that he could not get far with it. Instead, he constantly refers to children being better off if mothers looked after them full time. He knows that is what will make me feel guilty—and it does—crazy as it may sound.

SITUATIONAL AND PERSONALITY
FACTORS IN FEELING GUILTY

Guilt in interpersonal relationships does not occur independent of situational and personality factors. Situational factors are related to the context or setting under which an interaction takes place. Personality factors have to do with the sort of person you are. The matter of relational context is reflected by the fact that an action can make us feel guilty under some relational contexts but not others. For instance, you may feel guilty lying to your child or spouse but not your employer or client. Moreover, a general precondition for feeling guilty is that both relationship partners share a common view about the acceptability of a given behavior. It is when a common understanding is violated that guilt ensues. Ultimately we only feel guilty when we, not someone else, thinks that we have done something wrong.

Some reasons for feeling guilty are independent of relational considerations. For instance, my spouse may not care if I lie to my clients but I would still feel guilty if I believe lying is morally wrong. Conversely, even if a behavior I consider morally justified has a negative impact on my partner, then I may feel guilty on that count alone. This requires, of course, that I care about the person. We do not need to be well regarded by everyone, but only by those who matter. To be thought well of by the wrong people is not a good thing.[13]

Whether or not a certain action is deemed wrong or makes us feel guilty depends on several considerations. The first is *intentionality*. This is important in both relational as well as broader ethical or legal contexts. If we did not mean to hurt someone, we are less likely to be considered having done wrong, or feel guilty. A corollary is *controllability*: Could we have prevented what happened or was it out of our power to do so? If I had an accident because the brakes of my rented car failed, that would be different than if I were driving recklessly. Finally, the level of guilt may depend on the *consequences* of our actions. If our action did not seriously impact another person's well-being, we are less likely to feel bad about it. (In criminal conduct, all three considerations have important legal ramifications, which we will discuss in the last chapter.)

The focus on the interpersonal aspects of guilt should not make us lose sight of personality factors, which are also highly relevant. Whether or not the branches of a tree move in the wind depends both on the strength of the wind as well as how stout the branches are. Some people are more guilt-prone than others, just as some relationships are more conducive to guilt than others. Some will feel guilty even if their partner is the devil himself; others cannot be made to feel guilty by hurting the sweetest and most tolerant angel. Typically, personality and relationship characteristics interact and reinforce each other. In the worst case, when a guilt-prone person is matched with a guilt-inducer, the relationship becomes drenched with guilt.

The key personality requirement for feeling guilty is the capacity for *empathy*.[14] Empathy ("feel in") means projecting oneself into another person—putting oneself in another's shoes. It entails both understanding and sharing the feelings of another person. *Sympathy* ("feel with") is a sense of affinity with another person (or idea). It has more of an element of sharing another's joy and sorrow without the element of necessarily understanding it.

The propensity to feel guilty has been linked with shyness, loneliness, and resentment, an issue we touched upon in earlier chapters. This implies that guilt-prone individuals are likely to have less satisfactory personal relationships. Similarly, those with a low self-esteem tend to blame themselves. They feel socially more vulnerable and hence are more prone to be concerned with the judgments of others. They see themselves as less valuable partners, and thus take particular care not to give offence. Conversely, proneness to guilt itself may cause low self-esteem with all its attendant problems. As a group, those brought up with strict religious and ethical standards may be more prone to guilt. But within that group, some will be less and others more liable to feeling guilty based on personality and relational considerations.

What about the personality factors that predispose a person to *induce* guilt in others? Guilt-inducers are also typically shy and not self-assertive. They come across as being irritable, suspicious, and resentful. In many respects, guilt-inducers turn out to be quite similar to those who are vulnerable to feeling guilty.[15]

CONSEQUENCES OF FEELING GUILTY

Since guilt is a distressing feeling, people have a generally negative view of it. Nobody *wants* to feel guilty. That is different, however, from whether or not we *should* feel guilty. Most religions foster the need for feeling guilty as a moral safeguard. Freud recognized the necessity for the feeling when it was warranted, but he also emphasized the damaging effects of neurotic guilt arising from repressed conflict. Psychologists now view guilt as an emotion that promotes *prosocial* effects. It motivates people to admit responsibility for their wrong actions, to make amends and repair damaged relationships. However useful it might be, guilt still carries a serious pathological potential.

The expression of guilt is but a first step, or a down payment, for the more concrete steps that must follow. Guilt motivates the wrongdoer to confess and mollifies the injured party. Sometimes, simply acknowledging that one was wrong and apologizing for it is enough to settle the matter. On the other hand, confession may make transgressors feel that having admitted their guilt there is nothing left for them to do ("I already admitted I did wrong, what more am I supposed to do?"). It also runs the risk of leaving the guilty party vulnerable to retaliation in contentious situations. (That is why defendants in court are not expected to testify against themselves.)

Guilt induces people to be more helpful and compliant toward their victims and others as well.[16] A child who breaks a sibling's toy becomes overly solicitous. One gives an expensive present to a spouse one has offended. Such altruism may extend beyond the victim. For instance, after firing an employee, a manager may give money to the first beggar who comes along. Not all forms of altruism are of course due to guilt. One may be motivated by pity, by identifying with the victim, or by a sense of religious, ethical, or social responsibility.

Guilt also has negative and antisocial consequences. We would rather avoid the person we have offended, as well as avoid the person who has offended us. It feels awkward. This is less of a problem in exchange relationships (you do not have to go back to the same store if you had a problem). However, in a communal relationship, the resulting alienation places a strain on the relationship. It is awkward to have breakfast with the person you upset at dinner.

Excessive guilt is a drain on our psychological reserves and a burden on our relationship partners. It is just as hard to live with a person burdened with guilt as with someone who is chronically depressed. Guilt takes its toll, which is why there are psychological defenses to dampen it. Just as the body has regulatory mechanisms to maintain homeostatic balance, similarly, when a person's emotional balance is disturbed by guilt it needs to be brought back into equilibrium to keep life on an even keel.

The *punishment* of the guilty is a cornerstone of our moral and legal systems. There is a common belief among clinicians that the guilty want to be punished in order to alleviate their guilt. For instance, criminals may act in ways that will lead to being apprehended (such as returning to the scene of the crime). Police interrogators use various tactics to induce guilt to make the accused confess. However, empirical studies have failed to confirm this association between guilt and the wish for punishment. The dominant feeling in these situations may be the fear of punishment that gets confused with the wish to expiate for it; when the fear is absent, the person no longer feels guilty. In other cases, people who know they are going to be punished may want to be done with it sooner rather than later.

VIRTUAL GUILT

The internet has opened unprecedented opportunities for people to share their innermost thoughts and feelings with each other, including anonymously. In chat rooms one may share confidences with strangers that one would not dream of doing in person. Such *virtual relationships* have an interesting bearing on guilt.

In an internet-based virtual world called *Second Life*, participants (called "Residents") assume fictitious identities ("avatars"). For instance, a puny person may have an avatar who is a muscular giant with wings. Residents interact with each other in individual and group activities. They can also conduct business such as buying and selling properties and services with "Linden dollars" (named after Linden Labs, the creator of *Second Life*). Since these can be converted into real currency, *Second Life* is linked to the real world. Several million people have registered in *Second Life* and many thousands log in every day.[17]

Avatars engage in a wide range of activities including sexual interactions. Although there are limits to what one can do (for instance, pedophilia is excluded), the programs still make possible a good deal of activity that is likely to induce guilt in real life. Beyond the erotic, the opportunity for intimacy and open communication is a powerful magnet, as one woman testifies: "You talk about your day, your dreams, that kind of thing. I couldn't get that from my real-life boyfriend."[18]

One woman was spending up to eight hours a day online with an avatar (presumably a man, but one cannot be certain) to whom she became so emotionally attached that it led to the breakup of her real-world marriage. In another instance, a woman who was married to a man both in their real and virtual lives, divorced him because he had been unfaithful to her with a "prostitute" in cyberspace, even though he remained faithful to her in their real marriage, thus blurring the distinction between the real and imaginary worlds.

The technology of *Second Life* is new; its psychology is not. Fantasy, after all, has always been a staple of our inner lives. And "unreal" as they may be, they can induce guilt just as if one had acted out these fantasies. The fantasy world of the cyber world is therefore not entirely guilt-free. Some people feel guilty over the amount of time they spend with their avatars at the cost of real-life relationships, while others feel guilty over neglecting their avatars. If what one does within the fantasy cyber world involves aberrant sexual practices, which lead to virtual betrayals and breakups, do they generate guilt the way they do in the real world? Moreover, the virtual and the real world are not totally disconnected from each other; there is a real person behind every avatar.

If however, what we have here is the opportunity for guilt-free emotional release and enjoyment, that might explain the popularity of this virtual world. It is too early to predict the long-term prospects and consequences of participating in this novel environment. Are these activities nothing more than elaborate video games or do they open up new opportunities for emotional expression, enjoyment, and growth? Are they a search for new forms of human relationships, or are they nothing more than pathetic attempts to substitute what is contrived and fake for the real world—with its joys and sorrows?

DEALING WITH GUILT IN
INTERPERSONAL RELATIONSHIPS

In the preceding chapter we discussed the differences between the authentic and inauthentic ways of dealing with guilt. How do these two modes apply to guilt in interpersonal relationships?

The *inauthentic resolution* of guilt typically starts with denial of guilt but it is not quite the same. Denial short-circuits the feeling of guilt altogether. In inauthentic resolution, the person does feel guilty but tries to resolve it by wiggling out of it instead of coming to terms with it.

In a broader sense, denial is part of our everyday life, almost by necessity. This may involve an occasional trivial issue or we may be "in denial" with respect to a more serious problem such as being an alcoholic ("OK, so I drink quite a bit, but I can stop it anytime I want"). Denial may be a protective defense against unbearable reality, such as having a terminal cancer. We use denial in interpersonal relationships because the pain of admitting a transgression may be worse than the burden of denying it.

Denial comes in several varieties that escalate its seriousness. Its relatively benign form is *inattention* that allows us to get away from a minor lapse by forgetting it ("I meant to pay you back for the book but it just slipped my mind"). The next stage is *passive acknowledgment* where we recognize a problem but make light of it and take no action to correct it ("I gossip, but I don't mean any harm"). When there are serious transgressions, they are *reframed* by being cast as mistakes ("Yes, I lied to you but I was flustered and used the wrong words"). The most serious form of denial is through *willful blindness* when one refuses to even acknowledge or talk about the misdeed.[19]

Denial may also operate at several levels of consciousness. In what psychoanalysts call *unconscious denial* of guilt, we are not even aware of feeling guilty. Denial feeds on itself—we deny that we are denying it. Consequently, we cannot deal with it on our own. We need help from a therapist who understands what unconscious guilt is and knows how to help us deal with it.

If guilt is unconscious, how would we even know when to ask for help? One way is to be aware of its associated states: If we feel anxious, depressed, or distressed for no apparent cause, it may be due to repressed feelings of guilt (but also for other possible causes). These may arise from unacceptable sexual or aggressive feelings we harbor toward others, which may hark back to long-forgotten childhood experiences. If you find yourself gratuitously revealing to others intimate details of your life, you may be engaging in a substitute form of confession. The same is true for behaviors where the person seems to be courting punishment. Other cues may come from conflicts in our personal relationships that have no reasonable justification.

Conscious guilt is more within our reach. In this case, we know we have done wrong and feel guilty about it, but we refuse to admit it. We can lie ("I did nothing wrong") and get away with it. Deceit may work but it is costly to live with, especially when we lie to ourselves.

The denial of guilt is not always absolute. We may admit to being at fault and express some remorse over it, but we then blunt its impact through "deconstructing" our actions by turning them into something other than what they are. We may say, "I struck my child but not that hard; it happened only once (maybe twice)"; "I was provoked; I was upset and didn't know what I was doing; it'll teach the child a lesson." In other words, we modify what happened, how it happened, why it happened, and how often it happened. We admit being "technically" at fault but "not really" guilty; we accept the facts but reject moral responsibility for them.

A more sinister tactic is to demean the victim. We consider the person we offended to be unworthy of better consideration. The man got cheated because he is stupid. The woman was raped because she is a slut. The person was unfaithful because the spouse is a miserable lover. In even more extreme examples, before we torture and kill we dehumanize our victims first—we turn them into vermin to be exterminated.

Since guilt is based on intentionality and the consequences of one's actions, the inauthentic resolution of guilt aims at negating both: We admit to doing wrong but it was not our *intention* to cause harm; we admit there was damage done, but contend it was not that extensive, or permanent, or serious. Sometimes we start dealing with guilt in an authentic mode but then fail to follow through to completion (for instance, we confess but stop short of making amends). Or, when the discomfort of the authentic mode gets too much to tolerate, we switch to inauthentic means of handling it.

The consequence of inauthentic tactics is that the damaged relationship is not repaired; rather, it gets further undermined. The guilt we suppress does not go away but festers and erodes other aspects of our relationship. If guilt becomes a prisoner that must be kept under lock and key, that drains our psychological resources and turns us into a prisoner within our own prison.

Authentic resolution has the opposite effect. It heals the rupture of the damaged relationship and removes the sense of isolation that guilt produces. The first step in the authentic mode is *confession*. It starts by admitting to myself that I did wrong and taking responsibility for it. A full acknowledgment of guilt requires that you know it in your head and feel it in your heart; it cannot be an abstract notion or a vague feeling. It must truly emanate from our own self. We feel guilty not because someone else wants us to, but according to our own lights.

After we first acknowledge guilt privately, within ourselves, the next step is to admit it to the person we have wronged. We need to do this in a forthright manner without obfuscation, qualification, or self-justification; with sincerity and without making light of it by dismissive gestures. It is not enough to say, "I did it," but also to say "I am sorry for it"—and mean it. To be effective, confession has to be done freely, honestly, and with a level of contrition commensurate with the offence. Making light of it trivializes it; groveling cheapens the experience.

Confession fulfills two functions. It takes the burden off the guilty person's chest and it engages the offended person. This "down payment" on the debt is a necessary first step toward full restitution. The practice of confession in the Christian church is primarily for spiritual purposes, but it also fulfills important psychological functions. Sharing an inner secret with a trusted and compassionate person—such as a priest—has an enormous effect by relieving the pressure of guilt that weighs heavily on the conscience. The secular counterpart of confession is talking to a trusted friend or therapist. Confessing to a family member or colleague is problematic if it makes it harder to face them. In Christian spirituality, it is essential to have one person who knows everything about you.[20] Pent-up emotions need to be released. The ancient Greeks called it *catharsis* ("cleansing" or making pure). Bottled-up guilt feelings—like pus—fester unless the abscess is lanced.

Confession is not risk free. It may short-circuit the process of resolution. Having confessed, I may decide that I have paid my debt and need go no further. There are also risks to ourselves. Confession puts us at a disadvantage by making us vulnerable to censure and retaliation. We need to use discretion before baring our chest. It is safer to be candid in relationships that are based on trust and affection than in more impersonal and contentious circumstances. In such cases, civility requires a formulaic expression of regret ("I'm sorry this happened") rather than a fuller admission of guilt ("It's all my fault").

Professionals who deal with confession advise caution. For instance, confessing hurtful behavior from the past is a step in the Alcoholics Anonymous recovery process. However, when its negative consequences outweigh the need

GUILT AND RELATIONSHIPS 81

for candor, then counselors advise against disclosure.[21] Nor does the law require that we incriminate ourselves. If we are guilty of a crime, we are under no legal obligation to confess even though it would greatly help resolve the case.

A full confession may not always be in the best interest of all parties, even in intimate relationships. The truth hurts and may make reconciliation more difficult. Therefore, what we reveal should be on a need-to-know basis. For example, if I have been unfaithful to a relationship partner, I need to provide sufficient detail to count as an honest confession; but there is no need for going into graphic descriptions of what went on. (Even if the partner insists on knowing.) During the 1960s, the notion of "letting it all hang out" gained popularity, but many of its proponents came to regret it.

We also need to protect the privacy of other parties involved in our misdeeds. Dragging others into the picture to get ourselves off the hook is uncalled for. Much depends, of course, on the role other people have played. If others are co-conspirators who aided and abetted your actions, then they must share in the responsibility for the consequences. But if other persons were merely witnesses to what went on, why drag them into the mud?

In revealing the truth, we can be discreet without being secretive; transparent without standing naked. The need to take full responsibility does not mean unconditional capitulation. When defending ourselves, we can get this across firmly but without sounding defiant. How you say things is as important as what you say.

The step that follows confession is *making amends*—be they material or emotional. Here again, we must be careful that the level of restitution be commensurate with the degree of damage. We should not let the sting of guilt push us overboard. Compensation is essential, but full restitution may not be possible. If you have destroyed someone's cherished possession, you may not be able to make it whole again; some debts can never be paid in full. Do not let that turn you into a hostage, or derail the orderly process of resolving your feelings of guilt.

Having come this far, we may feel that after going through these steps we should no longer be liable to punishment. That is, however, not the case and we must be willing to accept punishment as part of our responsibility, unless we are forgiven. Excessive as it may sound, punishment is a necessary part of paying our debt to an individual or society. Pope John Paul formally forgave Mehmet Ali Agca, who tried to assassinate him, but the man is still in jail.

The last step is the commitment not to repeat the offence. This requires a change of heart as well of mind and is not easy to do. We cannot change ourselves overnight. Repairing the damaged relationship may require more than patching it up. It may be necessary to restructure or terminate it. Not all marital conflicts are resolved by kissing and making up. Once the "plate is broken" (as they say in Turkish) it may not be possible to mend it.

Ideally, the outcome of this process of resolution is *forgiveness* and *reconciliation*. This means you are forgiven by the person you have injured, you have accepted that person's forgiveness, and you have forgiven yourself. Forgiveness normally leads to reconciliation, but the two are not the same, as we shall shortly discuss.

It is not possible to draw a sharp line between the authentic and inauthentic ways of dealing with guilt. As with all human affairs, this too is not a matter of absolutes. We may try to deal with our feelings of guilt in authentic ways but fall short. When we realize an inauthentic tactic is not working out, we may move on to a more authentic mode. What ultimately defines our moral character is not how we act in an isolated instance, but the way we behave more generally. It is the pattern and consistency in our behavior that define us as moral beings, not what we do on a particular afternoon.

The process of resolution need not follow a rigid formula. One does not need to go through the entire script each and every time. Sometimes the mere recognition that one has done wrong is enough. If someone makes a critical remark and then says, "I'm sorry if I hurt your feelings," the gracious response should be, "I understand, don't worry about it" (unless this is happening for the tenth time). But in more serious situations we should neither try to bring the process to a premature closure nor drag it out.

It is tempting to rush for premature closure of a conflict by absolving the offender at an early stage, for instance, right after an apology is offered. You may do this because you feel uncomfortable by being owed something by another. If you have low self-esteem, you may feel you do not deserve any better. In a precarious relationship (especially if you are the more dependent party), you may be afraid of alienating the offender on whom your life depends. Or, you may think forgiving reflects generosity of spirit. That may be true, but easy forgiveness may also lead to "cheap grace." Premature closure shortchanges both parties. Victims do not get their due and offenders do not have the benefit of a sense of closure. Justice is not served.

How should we deal with the prospect of inducing guilt? As we noted earlier, inducing guilt is an effective influence tactic, but it is costly. Whether you should resort to it or not depends on a number of factors. If the offender accepts responsibility and embarks on an authentic manner of resolving the ensuing guilt, then you let the process play itself out; there is no need to fan the flames.

However, if the offender shows no sign of remorse, then you have several options. The first is to do nothing. Life is too short to go to war over every provocation. Some people will not let any misdeed escape to uphold a principle. ("I don't care about the money—it's the idea of being ripped off that I can't stand"). But what exactly is the principle? Overly touchy and litigious people are insufferable, so one needs to assess the cost-benefit ratio of getting embroiled with an unrepentant offender.

If you must press your grievance, the first step is to bring the matter to the offender's attention in a clear and calm manner. Give the person the benefit of the doubt since you may have been hurt inadvertently. If you are not satisfied, restate the facts and express your feelings more emphatically ("I'm upset that you broke your promise not to divulge what I told you"). Then wait for the response. If the person persists in denying responsibility, or becomes defensive and belligerent, then you must decide whether to dig in your heels and escalate the issue, or withdraw by distancing yourself from that person temporarily or for good.

If the offender is receptive, then state how you want the problem to be resolved. So much of what you say and how you say it depends on the circumstances and the nature of your relationship with that person. No single example will cover all contingencies. Two considerations need to be stressed. First, pitch your grievance at the person's actions and words, not at his or her character. "You lied to me" is more likely to elicit an appropriate response than "You are a liar," which will induce a defensive reaction (especially if the person is a liar). Second, present your demands in such a way that they will lead to a reasonable resolution: Allow the offender a way out; facilitate a constructive resolution.

You may be tempted to induce guilt for reasons that go beyond legitimate expectations. If you give in to this temptation, ask yourself why. Are your actions motivated by vengeance and the wish to inflict suffering? If so, remember that "Vengeance is mine . . . says the Lord" (Deut. 32:35). Vengeance is also self-destructive. The saying, "If you devote your life to seeking revenge, first dig two graves" is attributed to Confucius but he may not have said it. Nonetheless, it is a compelling metaphor.[22]

The next question to ask yourself is whether you are taking advantage of a person who is in a vulnerable position by being in your debt. Instead of recovering only what is due to you, you may be trying to extort all you can. You do this by exaggerating the damage and imputing bad faith: "You hurt me more than you realize / are willing to admit"; "You did it on purpose to hurt me"; "It's not the first time you've done this"; "No one else has ever treated me like this." Such claims escalate the offence by making it unique and more deliberate, repetitive, and unforgivable.

To drag this process out and milk it for all its worth by refusing to be satisfied by the offender's attempts to achieve a resolution condemns the offender to a state of perpetual penance. Some people will accept this and remain hostage. Others will walk out, ending the ballgame.

The impulse for self-preservation will blunt the relentless bite of the offender's conscience. Guilt will give way to feelings of resentment and alienation, which will eventually lead to withdrawal. You end up pushing away the very person you are so desperately trying to keep in your life. Moreover, the unwillingness to achieve closure will get you trapped in the role of a perpetual victim (which only a masochist would enjoy). Besides, repeated accusations of guilt loose their efficacy. Like an addictive drug, you need to induce more and more guilt to obtain the same effect. Therefore, guilt as a tactic of eliciting compliance is riskier and more costly than other influence tactics.[23]

How can we protect ourselves against being "guilted"? If you are not at fault, stand firm and, like Job, refuse to admit or feel guilty, and you too may be vindicated in the end. The fact that a relationship partner is distressed does not necessarily make you responsible for it. There may be occasions when one admits to some responsibility to mollify the person and keep the peace, but one does this deliberately and not by being dragged into it.

The principles for dealing with a recalcitrant offender also apply to protecting yourself against being seduced or bullied into feeling guilty. Once again, start laying out the facts: "Yes, I said / did that and this is how and why it happened." Be honest with yourself and fair to the other person. Listen with an open mind to the accusations being leveled against you and hear the person out in good faith. However, it is for you, not someone else, to define the limits of your responsibility ("I admit I was rather quiet during dinner at your parents' house, but it was because I was tired, not because I wanted to be rude"). If the boundaries are not clear, redefine them, and if the stakes are big enough, renegotiate the terms of your relationship, or if all else fails, end it.

Focus on the objective reality of your actions, not their symbolic significance. Symbols are important for understanding our motives, but in a conflict-laden situation their interpretations are too subjective to allow a common understanding. For instance, if you said something upsetting to your spouse, focus on your actions and not on his or her inferences about your affections. Whether or not you love your spouse is important, but that issue must be resolved separately and outside the context of feelings of guilt. (Leave interpreting unconscious motives to therapists.)

It is best to stick to matters that exist in the present, in the here and now. This may be difficult. Actions should not be judged in isolation. There is a valid difference between how you deal with a first offence and a larger pattern. On the other hand, you cannot let each and every offence be the occasion for an exhaustive review of all your faults. There are two potential traps here: one is using temporal bracketing ("I only did it once") to minimize the guilt, the other is over-generalizing ("You do this all the time") to maximize it. Focusing on the present makes clear that what is at issue is your *behavior*—not your *person*. You are not on trial—your misdeed is. Do not allow it to engulf your whole self.

Avoid excessive sensitivity to those you may have hurt. This is not a call for callous disregard of suffering, especially if you have caused it. Take responsibility for the hurt you have caused and do something about it—but do not feel responsible for the pain your victims suffer for reasons of their own. Compassion—yes; servitude to the feelings of others—no. Moral responsibility—yes; moral perfectionism—no.

FORGIVENESS AND RECONCILIATION

Forgiveness is the overcoming of feelings of resentment directed toward a person who has hurt you. It means canceling a debt. *Reconciliation* entails reestablishing an amicable relationship with someone one has become estranged from. We may think of forgiveness as a precondition for reconciliation, or reconciliation as a natural outcome of forgiveness. Yet, achieving both may not be possible or even desirable. You may forgive a spouse but not become reconciled and stay married to the person. Or, you may decide to remain married without having forgiven a person. This may be because of the impact on others (such as children) or due to your life circumstances (you may have nowhere else to go). There is, thus, a difference between *decisional* forgiveness as a calculated rational decision and *emotional* forgiveness, which reflects a deeper level of acceptance.[24]

Forgiveness need not be immediate. You may need time before forgiving someone or being forgiven. It is natural to want closure, but the process cannot be rushed. If, however, after a reasonable time the injured person continues to refuse to forgive you, there may be nothing further for you to do but to put the matter behind you and move on with your life. Should you become obsessed with the need to be forgiven, you may end up a hostage to that wish. The same is true for reconciliation. To have the offence also *forgotten* would also be nice, but it may be too much to ask. Nor is it necessary as long as the offended party does not keep throwing your offence in your face.

The failure to achieve closure may also be the result of the decision to live with one's guilt rather than try to resolve it. There may be many reasons for this, not all of which have to do with other people. The psychological cost may be higher than the burden of guilt in stopping a harmful behavior. For instance, those who feel guilty because they smoke, drink excessively, or abuse drugs may put up with their guilt rather than give up their addiction ("After all, I can live with guilt, but I'd hate to live without cigarettes").

Others resign themselves to living with guilt because they cannot come to terms with it. As an older man put it, "Guilt is a fact of life. There's no way you can undo what you've done. I still shudder when I think of things I did forty years ago. It's likely I'll carry my guilt with me to the grave."[25]

In some cases one becomes dependent, almost addicted to guilt. The memory of the events that led to the feeling of guilt becomes part of one's identity. A young man I treated some years ago was so imbued with guilt that I thought, should I manage to free him of the guilt, there would be nothing left of him.

An offer of forgiveness may actually be a form of accusation:

Patricia and I were divorced over forty years ago and have hardly been in touch since. As we were both getting on in years, I received a letter from her in which she said that now that we were entering the sunset of our lives, she wanted to meet with me to make sure that she had forgiven me. I first thought, how nice to hear this, after all these years. Then, I realized it implied that I was the one that needed to be forgiven for ruining our marriage.

It may have been too much to expect her to say that she hoped that I had forgiven her. But at least she could have said that we *both* needed to make sure that we had forgiven each other. But forgiveness was not what she was after; she just wanted to take another shot at me. After all these years, she had not changed.

Since a moral or legal offence involves a deliberate wrongdoing, it must be distinguished from *justification*, which removes the fact of wrongdoing, and *excuse*, which absolves the wrongdoer of responsibility for it. Forgiveness is also different from *mercy*, which involves the forgoing or curtailment of punishment without exonerating the offender. For instance, a woman convicted of an offence may be set free so as not to take her away from her children. Forgiveness is the personal prerogative of the aggrieved individual. Strictly speaking, we cannot forgive a person on somebody else's behalf, even though those close to the victim may feel that they have that prerogative.

Forgiveness is fundamental to all religious traditions. It has also attracted much attention in psychology and self-help books that focus on its health benefits.[26] Their basic message is that holding a grudge does more harm than good and festering resentment is a destructive and self-defeating emotion hazardous to one's health.

Forgiveness reduces the stress of anger, bitterness, resentment, and hatred that accompany nurturing a grudge. These feelings have physiological effects (such as hypertension) that increase the risk of cardiovascular disease and suppress the immune system, making the person vulnerable to various disorders. A spirit of forbearance helps sustain close ties to family, friends, and neighbors. Those with such strong social networks tend to be healthier. In these contexts, forgiveness is not only a matter of letting go of particular wounds, but incorporating forgiveness into one's way of life.[27]

Though most books on forgiveness endorse its merits, there are some that point to its limitations. Books like *Getting Even* argue that hasty and uncritical forgiveness is potentially damaging to self-respect, inimical to self-interest, and detrimental to respect for the moral order. However, despite their combative titles, these books do not endorse a spirit of vengeance but mainly caution against "cheap grace" that trivializes the virtue of forgiveness itself.[28]

In these first three chapters we have focused on experiences of guilt that result from moral transgressions and conflicts in interpersonal relationships. In the next chapter we shift to a different dimension of guilt, one where it occurs in the absence of personal transgression—in other words, when one has done no wrong. This involves guilt among survivors of disasters and tragedies—those who have lived while others have died; remorse for the actions of others with whom one identifies; and feelings of guilt that arise from being in a privileged position.

4 GUILT WITHOUT TRANSGRESSION

When I came to Auschwitz, my sister was with me. She was only 14. . . .

Needless to say, I know in my head I'm not the cause of her death . . . but in my gut I've believed that I caused her death . . . [because] we were separated.

I felt guilty for many years that maybe I should have run back and tried to get her with me or stay with her. Maybe I didn't do enough to stay together. Maybe I was too selfish about saving myself. You can excuse yourself and say if I had run back my fate would have been the same as hers. There is no logic to my feelings.

·   ·   ·

I could never forgive myself. . . . I had good connections in Auschwitz . . . but I didn't do enough to save my brother. He was with me from the beginning, but [even] with all the connections I had, I couldn't save him. I had many sleepless nights about him. That was depressing me for years. . . . Of all my brothers and sisters, he was the most idealistic, the best of us.

·   ·   ·

I'm guilty all my life. I'm guilty I didn't save my father, my mother, my sister. I feel guilty, I could have made Aryan papers for them. I'm guilty, I tried to talk them into going to Russia, but they wouldn't listen. I'm guilty, I don't want to be richer than my father. I had opportunities to make millions. I always feel guilty. Why should I have more than my parents? Maybe I'm wrong. I'm guilty. I feel guilty all my life.

·   ·   ·

I am grateful to Esther Hewlett, David Hamburg, and Ulla Morris for their comments and help with various aspects of this chapter.

You start taking stock and you know you came from a big family. I don't know how to explain it to you. You think, "Why me? Why did I survive?" I was often miserable about it. You can also explain it in mathematical terms. The Germans had to kill a certain number of Jews. If you survived, you did on account of others. We were lucky, but some would consider it not so lucky.[1]

THESE ACCOUNTS from former inmates of concentration camps during the Holocaust represent *survivor guilt*, a term used to describe feelings of guilt among those who survive conditions that engulf others. Typically, we feel guilty when we have done wrong. Yet there are instances when one feels guilty without having done anything wrong. Survivor guilt is one such example. It is the first of three forms of guilt without transgression that we will discuss in this chapter.

A second form of such guilt results from the feeling of personal responsibility for the wrong that the members of one's group have done—*collective guilt*. Finally, there is *existential guilt*—the feeling of guilt for more puzzling reasons ranging from being better off to merely being human.

These forms of guilt entail no moral or legal culpability. Otherwise, the circumstances that give rise to them are very different. Our awareness of such guilt experiences is quite recent, going back to the aftermath of World War II. Consequently, there is no historical religious, philosophical, or literary record to draw from. Yet, they are very much part of our modern consciousness.

SURVIVOR GUILT

The concept of survivor guilt emerged largely from the experiences of Holocaust survivors. Its use then expanded to include other tragic circumstances with similar consequences. For instance, suppose a leaky gas oven explodes into a fireball in the family kitchen, trapping the mother and her two children. The father tries to save them but by the time the fire is put out, his wife and children are burned to death. He is devastated by grief and an overwhelming sense of guilt. The grief is understandable, but why the guilt? The man is not responsible for the fire or the death of his family. There is nothing he could have done, and he knows it. Yet, he is tormented by the thought that his loved ones died, while he lived.

Tragic experiences like this take many forms. The disaster may result from natural causes, such as floods or earthquakes. It may be due to human error, such as an airplane crash. People are victimized in war or through persecution, as in massacres and genocides. The circumstances under which these disasters occur—what caused them, how they were handled—may influence survivor reactions, but the basic response of survivor guilt is the same.

Guilt among Survivors of Concentration Camps

The experiences of Holocaust survivors of the Nazi concentration camps during World War II have been studied extensively.[2] The atrocities in concentration camps resulted from willful criminal acts, not human negligence.[3] Unlike natural disasters, they took place over long periods. Consequently, although camp inmates had no more control over their fates than did victims of a flood or tornado, they had a wider range of experiences. The conditions under which they lived were so brutal that the need to survive overwhelmed other considerations. Inmates were reduced to the point where the only thing that counted was survival itself.[4]

In order to survive, some victims became collaborators by functioning as guards (*kapo*), who brutalized their fellow inmates (hence they had ample reason to feel guilty). Others merely took advantage of their fellow victims in order to survive. The memory of their actions tormented the survivors despite the moral ambiguity of how one should or can act under the circumstances. Still others would not compromise themselves and preferred to die. Yet others survived to be witnesses to their ordeal.

Another common source of guilt was tied to the regret of not having fled from the impending disaster while it was still possible to escape. Others felt guilt over their failure to fight back, even though the chance of prevailing was virtually nil. As Primo Levi, an Italian chemist, writer, and eloquent witness to the Holocaust recalls, "When all was over, the awareness emerged that we had not done anything, or not enough, against the system into which we had been absorbed. . . . Consciously or not he [the survivor] feels accused and judged, compelled to justify and defend himself."[5]

The purest expressions of survival guilt came from the burden of having survived while others died.

> It is no more than a supposition, indeed the shadow of a suspicion: that each man is his brother's Cain, that each of us . . . has usurped his neighbor's place and lived in his stead. It is supposition, but it gnaws at us; it has nestled deeply like a woodworm; although unseen from the outside, it gnaws and rasps.[6]

The most agonized were parents who were powerless to save their children. In a heartrending example in William Styron's novel *Sophie's Choice*, a mother is forced to choose between saving her young daughter or son.[7] Children felt less responsible for their parents since they were even more helpless than them. Guilt was particularly acute if the survivor was the only family member left; when there were other survivors, the grief was more readily shared. The idea that a "quota" had to die each day reinforced the feeling that if one survived, it was at the expense of someone else who died instead.

Not all Holocaust survivors felt guilty. Those who fought with the resistance felt exonerated. Others ascribed their deliverance to luck over which they had no control. Some credited their own tenacity for being alive, but the general feeling was that those who survived were no more resourceful or better persons than those who died.

The factors that induce survivor guilt also generate profound shame. The concentration camp stripped inmates of their dignity and the most basic elements of self-respect. When we are exposed to events over which we have absolutely no control, it makes a mockery of our sense of agency and personal adequacy. It is this combination of guilt and shame that made these experiences so overwhelming.

Most survivors had an excruciatingly hard time coming to terms with the massive psychic trauma. Some committed suicide. Even though inmates of the camps were exposed to the same inhumane conditions, each individual lived in his or her own personal hell. Primo Levi writes: "In my opinion, the feeling of shame and guilt that coincided with reacquired freedom was extremely composite: it contained diverse elements, and in diverse proportions for each individual. It must be remembered that each of us, both objectively and subjectively, lived the Lager [concentration camp] in his own way."[8]

Although it was hard to find rational explanations for the calamity that befell them, survivors sought to find meaning and purpose in their suffering. Some accepted it as God's will; others saw it as a punishment from God for their sins; yet others blamed God or lost their faith. Then there were those who refused to seek explanations for what happened so as not to diminish its horror. Ultimately, most survivors reconstructed their lives the best they could.

Guilt among Survivors of Natural Disasters

In February 1972 a massive flood devastated mining hamlets along the Buffalo Creek in West Virginia. The flood, caused by heavy rains, led to the collapse of an artificial dam formed by the coal waste that the mining company had piled up-stream. There were many casualties, but hundreds survived the disaster.[9]

Although the basic elements of survivor guilt associated with natural disaster are similar to the those experienced by concentration camp inmates, there were particular features that were different. The scenes of devastation left an indelible imprint of images of death on the survivors at Buffalo Creek. This *death imprint* was accompanied by severe anxiety triggered by events like the heavy rain. Terrifying dreams of death and destruction continued to trouble them for years.

Like concentration camp victims, survivors of the Buffalo Creek disaster experienced *death guilt*—the survivor's painful sense of remorse and regret over having lived, while others, particularly family members, died. They were tormented by thoughts that they should have saved those who perished, even when they could have done nothing more. One man, whose desperate efforts had failed to save his wife from drowning, accused himself of killing her. In vivid recurrent dreams the dead continued to haunt the living. One man said, "In my dreams, I never get caught in the water. What hurts is the people calling for me to come and help them but I can't do it."[10]

Another common reaction is *psychic numbing*. The initial reaction of being stunned is followed by feelings of apathy. This is a defensive reaction against being overwhelmed by the flood of grief and bewilderment ("I feel dead"; "I have no energy"; "I sit down and I feel numb"). This loss of feeling, including loss of sexual interest, affected mainly survivors who had lost people close to them. However, it had a contagious quality that extended to those who were there to help them. The apathy concealed a smoldering rage that could erupt unexpectedly. Since the mining company was ultimately responsible for what happened, it was an obvious target. However, the anger spilled over in the form of unfocused resentment. The sense of alienation was compounded by conflicting feelings over being helped and nurtured. Survivors craved help, yet they were suspicious of their well-intentioned helpers and considered their expressions of sympathy as fake and counterfeit.

Deep down, survivor guilt cries out for meaning and significance: Why did this happen? Why did people die? Why did I survive? As with concentration camp victims, some survivors of the Buffalo Creek disaster found solace in accepting the disaster as God's will, or as punishment for their sins. Others saw it as an act of nature with no moral significance. The ability to ascribe some sort of meaning to the disaster made it easier for survivors to come to grips with it and get on with their lives. The feeling of guilt eventually abated, but its memory lingered on.[11]

Guilt in Combat Experiences

Soldiers need to overcome feelings of guilt that could otherwise get in the way of their killing the enemy. Guilt is a serious problem especially in the death of noncombatants and the committing of atrocities. However, what concerns us here is not the guilt soldiers experience when they have done wrong, but when their own companions get killed or wounded while they escape unscathed. When one's incompetence, cowardice, or negligence have led to the death of others, the guilt is compounded.

Psychological problems resulting from combat experiences established the concept of *post-traumatic stress disorder* (PTSD; called *shell shock* in World War I and *combat neurosis* in World War II). The same reactions are now being reported from the war in Iraq. Captain Lisa Blackman, a 32-year-old clinical psychologist serving in Iraq, sent the following e-mail to her family and friends:

> A quick word about guilt. No one ever felt they are doing enough. If you are in a safe location, you feel guilty that your friends are getting shot at and you aren't. If you are getting shot at, you feel guilty if your friend gets hit and you don't. If you get shot at but don't die, you feel guilty that you lived, and more guilty if you get to go home and your friends stay behind. I have not seen one person out here who didn't check off "increased guilt" on our intake form. . . . I can't stop thinking about the fact that these folks have lost something that they will never get back—innocence (and a life free of guilt). My heart hurts for them.[12]

Veterans who have survived combat have the feeling of living on borrowed time. For instance, the member of a bomber crew that had suffered a crash appeared to have readjusted to civilian life, with a successful career and a happy marriage. Yet, he continued to be troubled by feelings that he should have died with the rest of the crew, and he went to bed with the hope that he would not wake up in the morning.[13] The psychological after-effects of war with their attendant guilt can be as seriously debilitating as physical injuries.[14]

Guilt among Survivors of Individual Traumas

Survivor guilt among victims of natural disasters is submerged in the plight of many others. The guilt that results from surviving individual tragedies is more private. We have already cited the example of the man who loses his family in a fire. More commonly, survivors of car accidents feel guilty, especially if they were driving the car. Among couples, when a partner develops AIDS, the person who is not infected feels guilty. It feels unjust to them that exposure to the same risk should not have the same outcome. In such cases, there is no satisfactory answer to the question, "Why not me?"

Survivor guilt may also be part of the larger experience of feeling guilty when someone close to us dies of natural causes, such as illness or old age. Freud referred to this (in connection with his father's death) as the "tendency toward self-reproach which death invariably leaves among the survivors."[15]

Although it is natural to grieve the loss of someone we love, why should we feel guilty over it? The answer may reside in the ambivalence we feel toward those we love. It is impossible not to nurture some measure of anger or disappointment, no matter how much we love the person. These feelings may be repressed, but the finality of death brings them to the surface. There is nothing we can do anymore to resolve these issues and to set things right. The person is dead, and we feel responsible for all that went wrong in our relationship. In cases of a lingering terminal illness, we have a greater opportunity to settle these matters but when death comes suddenly, one is unable to achieve a similar resolution.

Finally, guilt may result from an apparent inequity as, for instance, when some employees are laid off but others are not. In such cases, friends can become alienated from each other if they do not share the same fate. The guilt that may follow assault and rape does not quite fit the model of survivor guilt (since there are no others who are affected simultaneously). However, if victims of crimes feel that what happened was their fault, then the fact that they survived the experience compounds the guilt.

If survivor guilt has no rational justification, why do we feel it? What possible function can it serve? On the face of it survival guilt appears to be an unnecessary burden. Would it not be more useful to limit our taking responsibility for things over which we have control?

Actually, survival guilt may have an adaptive value if it helps sustain emotional engagement with those one has lost. It gives a semblance of control over events that feel overwhelming and arbitrary—if we can do nothing else, we can at least feel bad about them. Survivor guilt may also help preserve a sense of connectedness with those with whom one has suffered. Painful as it may be, some people do not want to be rid of such guilt. Jacobo Timerman, a journalist who wrote about civil rights violations in Argentina, was imprisoned and tortured, but, unlike many of his companions who died in prison, Timerman survived. In an interview with Bill Moyers, he describes his reasons for clinging to his survivor's guilt:

> I know that going to a psychiatrist, I will lose all the world of pain to which I am so loyal, after seeing the people who were killed in prison. And I don't want to lose this relation with the world I was in. . . . I feel a kind of loyalty to the people, to the people who were killed. . . . I feel [abandoning my guilt and putting it behind me] is disloyal. I belong to that world, and I want to belong to that world, and I don't want to belong to any other world.[16]

Dealing with Survivor Guilt

The victims of inhumane treatment, like Timerman, may resent having their suffering cast into a pathological mold. They do not want to be "cured" of the guilt that they hold as a hallowed trust to honor the memory of those who have been lost. Nonetheless, most sufferers of survivor guilt welcome all the help they can get in resuming a life of normalcy, even though they can never erase the memory of the horror they lived through.

Currently, survivor guilt is treated as a form of PTSD according to the following format. The sufferer of PTSD is encouraged to talk freely and at length about the traumatic experience and its aftermath (often repeating the same account over and over). This helps the person to relive and unburden the bottled-up painful emotions. Talking also helps to overcome feelings of isolation, alienation, and helplessness. Feelings of guilt have to be accepted as natural and necessary, but also as something that becomes irrational and unnecessary beyond a point. The sufferer must come to accept the fact he or she is not at fault, has done nothing wrong, and is not responsible for the death or suffering of others. One can grieve for them without taking on the responsibility for what happened to them. The healing takes place over time, with the person reengaging in the normal routine of work and reestablishing family connections.

Various therapeutic approaches are used to achieve these aims. For instance, in *cognitive-behavior therapy*, the focus is in helping the person understand how certain thoughts are causing the painful feelings and to replace them with more reality-based and less distressing thoughts. The exposure to the painful memories helps to control and neutralize them through a process of "desensitization."

Psychotherapy aims at a deeper emotional insight into past experiences and how they may be contributing to the anxiety and distress of the traumatic experience. It may be supplemented with *group therapy* that brings together those who suffer from similar symptoms by sharing their emotional experiences and providing support to each other. *Family therapy* accomplishes a similar purpose in connection with members of one's family who are often experiencing a good deal of stress themselves. Finally, antidepressants and other drugs can be used to alleviate and treat the symptoms of depression and anxiety associated with PTSD.[17]

COLLECTIVE GUILT

Collective guilt results from feelings of culpability for unjust or criminal actions perpetrated by a group one identifies with. The common bond may be based on nationality, ethnicity, or some other social bond. Collective guilt embodies the idea that a group, or a government, can be held responsible—above and beyond the guilt of particular individuals—for perpetrating a criminal action, such as genocide. While in survivor guilt you are a member of a group to which something bad happens, in collective guilt, you are a member of a group that has done something wrong.

Just as the modern concept of survivor guilt largely arose from the experiences of Jewish victims of the Holocaust, the subsequent German response to it is the key example of admitting collective responsibility. It was the Nazi state that was clearly responsible for the conception and operation of concentration camps—from its high-level planners down to the guards who ran them—but what about those who helped the Nazis come to power and tolerated their actions? Were they innocent bystanders, or "Hitler's willing executioners"?[18] Would it matter whether or not they knew of the existence of the concentration camps? What about Germans born after these tragic events—should they also feel guilty simply by virtue of being German?

Sociologist Amitai Etzioni addresses this thorny issue by distinguishing between several types of collective guilt. *Criminal guilt* pertains to the perpetrators of the Holocaust as judged by the courts; *political guilt* to the leaders of the Nazi state and the citizenry who shared in the responsibility for the actions of those they put in power; and *moral guilt* to individuals who must take responsibility for own their actions (claiming that they were following orders does not absolve them).

For Etzioni, none of these considerations apply to the generations of Germans who were not yet born (or were too young) during these events. He differentiates *collective* guilt from *hereditary* guilt. The former applies to the generation that was involved in these events at one or another level. However, one cannot impute hereditary guilt to those in subsequent generations simply for being German. Nevertheless, these newer generations still have a *communal responsibility* based on the shared heritage of the community they were born into.[19]

The president of Germany, Richard von Weizsäcker, expressed the German view in a speech to the Bundestag on May 8, 1985 (the fortieth anniversary of the end of World War II):

> There is no such thing as the guilt and innocence of an entire nation. Like innocence, guilt is not collective but personal. There is acknowledged or concealed individual guilt which people proclaim or deny. Everyone who directly or consciously experienced that era should today ask himself about his involvement in these awful events.
>
> The vast majority of today's population were either children then or had not been born. They cannot confess guilt of their own crimes that they did not commit. No discerning person can expect them to wear a hair shirt simply because they are Germans. But their forefathers left them a grave legacy. All of us, whether guilty or not, whether old or young, must accept the past. We are all affected by consequences and liable for it. . . .
>
> As human beings we seek reconciliation. Precisely for that reason, we must understand that there can be no reconciliation without remembrance. . . . Remembrance is experience of God in history. Remembrance is the source of faith in redemption.[20]

The justification for collective guilt goes back to the biblical injunction that children will pay for the sins of their fathers for many generations. There is, nonetheless, a fundamental problem with the concept of collective guilt in that it breaks the crucial link between an action and personal responsibility, thus undermining a basic tenant of justice.[21]

A particularly flagrant example of how collective guilt can victimize the innocent is the practice of *trocosi*. In some traditional communities in Ghana, when a person commits a serious crime, the family must provide the priest with a young girl as a "slave of the gods." The girl has to act as the priest's servant and concubine for as long as he wishes. She can be freed only in exchange for another girl. The family of the offender feels compelled to follow the custom of *trocosi* to avert calamities that would otherwise befall them as a punishment for the crime.[22]

Some of the problems associated with collective guilt have to do with the difficulty in establishing responsibility for crimes like genocide. Since these crimes usually take place during wartime or periods of political turmoil, it may become difficult to establish who did what to whom. Those responsible, of course, use these problems to try to exonerate themselves. It is particularly disheartening when yesterday's victims become today's victimizers. People will argue that what was done to them and what they are doing to others is not the same. Their treatment was unfair, while their own actions are due to dire necessity. Consideration of "moral equivalency" is a valid distinction when, for instance, we are comparing a criminal shooting at a policeman with a policeman shooting at a criminal in self-defense. Yet, more often than not, moral equivalency all too often becomes a self-serving tool.

Collective Responsibility

It is important to differentiate between collective *guilt* and collective *responsibility*. There is collective responsibility at the bottom of all cases of collective guilt, but the opposite need not be true—there can be collective responsibility without collective guilt when harm is done without deliberate wrongdoing.

Collective responsibility often takes the form of *corporate responsibility*, where a company is held liable for damages, without its directors being held personally responsible. For example, shortly after midnight on March 24, 1989, the oil tanker *Exxon Valdez* struck a reef in Prince William Sound, in Alaska, spilling more than 11 million gallons of crude oil, damaging the delicate food chain that supports the area's commercial fishing industry, and endangering many species of animals.[23] The captain of the tanker was drunk and asleep in his cabin when the accident occurred. The officer on the bridge may have averted the collision had the tanker's radar been functioning. The captain was clearly guilty of dereliction of duty, but punishing him would have hardly settled the matter. It was the seven companies that owned the tanker that had to take collective responsibility for the gigantic task of the cleanup.

In other cases, assigning collective responsibility is harder to justify without punishing the innocent. In 1914, Austria held Serbia collectively liable for the assassination of Archduke Ferdinand by a Serbian citizen who had no connection with the Serbian government—an event that triggered World War I.

Corporations can be held liable, but can we ascribe guilt to them? As a British lord chancellor put it, how can you expect a corporation to have a conscience when it has no soul to be damned and no body to be kicked? More-over, corporations are interconnected with so many other entities and involve so many people that it is hard to delineate the ethical boundaries. Suppose that a tobacco company is held responsible for the harm caused by cigarettes. What about its thousands of suppliers and distributors? Or those who drive the trucks that transport the boxes of cigarettes? After all, without their de-liveries cigarettes would not make it into the stores. Where does one draw the line? Nonetheless, to deal with such concerns, there are "socially responsible" mutual funds that screen out the purveyors of undesirable products, thereby sparing its stockholders from feelings of collective guilt. Are such measures ef-fective beyond making us feel better? Boycotting companies doing business in South Africa helped bring about the end of apartheid. However, such tangible effects are harder to see in most other cases, even though one should, perhaps, do what one can to at least uphold the principle.

The collective responsibility of public officials is another complex issue. The doctrine of sovereign immunity shields governments and civil servants from personal liability where there is no dereliction of duty. With the growing power of government and the immense impact that corporations have on our lives, questions of collective moral responsibility become increasingly more important.[24]

In the account of his involvement in the tragedy of Vietnam, former sec-retary of defense Robert McNamara states: "We were wrong, terribly wrong. We owe it to future generations to explain why."[25] This is an unprecedented admission of responsibility by a high government official and stands in sharp contrast to the more usual self-serving memoirs of public servants that justify their actions.

If Robert McNamara was burdened personally by guilt over actions that took place during his watch he does not say so. His account is not intended to serve as a personal catharsis but to set the record straight, and to let the coun-try and its leaders learn from the experience. The failures that McNamara atones for are not in his personal life but in the conduct of his duties. His mo-tives are not in question; his actions in office could have been carried out with the best of intentions. Nonetheless, the war resulted in 58,000 American casu-alties and many more enemy dead, including many civilians. It left Vietnam devastated and America deeply divided. If McNamara felt guilty for having blood on his hands, it is not for blood he spilled himself. The United States is now in another disastrous war in Iraq, but so far there have hardly been any admissions of individual or collective responsibility (some may find even the idea to be offensive).

Collective responsibility also motivates some special groups into action. An example is animal rights activists who become vegetarian, refuse to use animal products, and try to induce guilt in others to do the same. At a broader level, collective responsibility and guilt are now associated with global issues like poverty, overpopulation, and environmental degradation. Increasing awareness of our interdependence has fostered the idea of the world as a global village, which makes it everyone's responsibility.

Problems like widespread poverty mostly affect developing countries and so feel quite remote for many people. The guilt we might feel about their plight is more likely to be due to compassion rather than collective responsibility. That is not the case with environmental degradation. The awareness that its consequences are going to affect everyone is generating a greater sense of collective responsibility and guilt over our overuse and abuse of the earth's limited resources. The fact that Americans account for 15 percent of the world's population but use 85 percent of its natural resources may not sound as dramatic as a gigantic oil spill, but its effects are more far reaching. Nonetheless, unless a greater sense of collective responsibility induces governments and businesses into more vigorous and drastic measures, environmental problems are going to get worse.

The field of professional ethics now prompts medical, legal, and other organizations to take greater collective responsibility for the actions of their members. The idea of a professional code of conduct goes back to the Hippocratic Oath from ancient Greece, which specifies the ethical responsibilities of physicians to patients, including prohibitions against sexual abuse and divulging of confidences. Given their life-and-death decisions, physicians have ample occasion to feel guilty. Misdiagnoses, bungled operations, and failure to respond to pleas for help generate both guilt and shame over incompetence, negligence, and misjudgment. Physicians realize that to err is human, yet their conscience and professional pride still nag at them when things go wrong. Similar considerations apply to other professions like law, business, and an increasing number of other service professions.[26]

Dealing with Collective Guilt

Dealing (or not dealing) with collective guilt follows the same basic process that individuals use with regard to personal guilt: It starts with acknowledgment and ends with compensation, possibly with reconciliation. If anything, it is even more difficult for nations than it is for individuals to swallow their pride and own up to their misdeeds. The charge of genocide is a particularly bitter pill to swallow. It is also harder to substantiate than other atrocities since it requires the deliberate intention of exterminating the victim population (as in "ethnic cleansing"). The prospect of compensation is a further obstacle to admitting collective responsibility.

This is why the case of Germany is so remarkable. Following the defeat of the Nazis, subsequent German governments accepted responsibility for the actions of their predecessors. In particular, they acknowledged collective responsibility for the Holocaust and made amends, including financial compensation on an unprecedented scale to the state of Israel and world Jewry. Coming early in Israel's history, such massive assistance played an important role in building the infrastructure of the country.[27] The feeling of German contrition was symbolized by Chancellor Willy Brandt when he went down on his knees at the memorial of the Warsaw ghetto in 1970. Many Germans, including those born after these events, continue to struggle with a lingering sense of collective guilt.

The more usual response on the part of governments is to deny collective responsibility. Perpetrators negate or minimize the consequences of their actions by claiming that the alleged crimes did not happen; or that they were perpetrated by only a few powerholders; or that they were isolated events; or that they inflicted suffering on only a few, and that those who suffered did not suffer much; or that they were not premeditated or centrally planned; or that they were due to necessity and there was no choice. On their part, victims may magnify the blame by inflating the number of victims, expanding the range of responsibility ("everyone took part in it"), and turning isolated events into patterns of persecution in order to hold the perpetrators hostage and extract all the compensation they can get out of them.

An example of denial of collective guilt is the continuing refusal by the Turkish government to acknowledge the Armenian genocide of 1915 that virtually exterminated the Armenian population in the Ottoman empire, through death and exile.[28] Turkey admits that large numbers of Armenians died tragically during World War I, but claims this was due to chaos and the ravages of war and to fighting instigated by rebellious Armenians.

In 1985 Dr. Sukru Elekdag, the Turkish ambassador to the United States, upheld this position in a letter to members of the House of Representatives, who were considering the passage of a resolution to mark the Armenian genocide:

> The Armenian allegations regarding the events of 1915 have been challenged and found by unbiased scholars to be unsustainable. Those events stemmed from an armed uprising by large numbers of Armenians who were Ottoman citizens seeking to impose the establishment of an exclusively Armenian state in an area of Eastern Anatolia that was predominantly non-Armenian.[29]

International opinion now widely supports the Armenian claims, and voices are being raised in Turkey to allow discussion of these issues. Since the beginning of December 2008, 27,000 Turks have signed a manifesto that declares, "My conscience cannot accept that we remain indifferent to the Great Catastrophe that Ottoman Armenians were subjected to in 1915, which we are made to deny. I reject this injustice and, for my part, I share the sentiments and sorrows of my Armenian sisters and brothers and ask for their forgiveness."[30] Nevertheless, Turkish law still prohibits even using the term *genocide* in this connection (prompting an editorial in the *New York Times* to state, "Turkey's self-destructive obsession with denying the Armenian genocide seems to have no limits").[31]

It is hard enough to deal with the guilt of individual criminals, but that difficulty pales in comparison with dealing with the "guilt of nations."[32] The list of the crimes of nations all over the world against hapless populations seems endless. In the recent past, the killing, torture, and uprooting of hundreds of thousands of people in places like Rwanda, Bosnia, Sierra Leone—and currently in Darfur—have yet to elicit any significant evidence of collective guilt or responsibility on the part of the perpetrators. It is even hard to know whom to hold responsible when so many of those guilty of atrocities are "ordinary" people, including child soldiers.

In the United States itself, the legacy of slavery and the mistreatment of Native Americans, and the internment of Japanese Americans during World War II, among other historical events, weigh heavily on the national conscience. In righting such wrongs, how far back should nations go? Should there be a statute of limitations? How does one set limits on monetary and other settlements?

Given the sovereign power of countries and their alliances, it is even harder to bring international pressure to bear on another country. Besides, since so many countries have blood on their hands, not many have the moral authority to act. Consequently, justice seems to be done only when an offending country has been crushed militarily. It was not hard to bring Hitler's henchmen to justice, but who could have touched Stalin's murderous state apparatus, which instigated the deaths of millions? The problem is even more complicated since the attempt to prosecute an entrenched leader accused of war crimes creates its own problems. For instance, the president of Sudan has been indicted for war crimes in Darfur and a warrant issued for his arrest by the International Criminal Court. Even if he can be brought to justice, which is quite improbable, it is feared that it would lead to more chaos and suffering. Idealism and pragmatism thus get pitted against each other.[33]

At an individual level, how do we decide to accept or reject collective responsibility for the actions carried out by those who represent us, or with whom we share a social bond? One may wonder, what difference can an individual make, and what would be the cost of engagement? Yet to remain passive while a crime is, or has been, committed in our name means shirking our moral responsibility. Particularly since democratic governments are supposed to be subject to the will of the people, what excuse do their citizens have to remain silent?

Another issue of importance is the complex prospect of forgiveness in order to bring about national reconciliation. South Africa achieved a remarkable task in this respect after decades of struggle against apartheid, through the work of the Truth and Reconciliation Commission. President Nelson Mandela signed into law its recommendations on July 19, 1995. This successful conclusion of a painful era in that country's history can serve as a model of overcoming, without forgetting, the hatred and strife that may appear beyond resolution. It reaffirms the premise that we should never forget, but we can forgive.[34]

In survivor guilt there are victims to be mourned. In collective guilt, there are victims to be compensated. In the next several categories of guilt there are no victims of any kind. This kind of guilt is based on who one *is* rather than what one *does*; it is a matter of being, not doing (although the two are hard to separate).

POSITIVE INEQUITY AND THE BURDEN OF WEALTH

Inequity is inequality that is neither justified nor fair. It is "positive" since it arises from the sense of having the good things in abundance that we want in life—health, wealth, and other material and social advantages—in short, leading a privileged life. Since this is what everyone wants, why feel guilty over it? Is it because others do not have what we have, or because we do not deserve it as much as others do? Here is a typical example:

> I have begun to feel a strange sense of guilt for the privileges in my life that I feel have not been deserved. I have been fortunate to have a close family, with my parents still happily married. My parents have been fortunate to afford a large house, many vacations around the world, and plenty of material possessions for all of us. I have never had to worry about basic survival or the support of my family, and I have always been fairly confident about the future.

Since the value of what we have is relative to what others have, the guilt of positive inequity is expressed not in absolute but relative terms. It is not an issue of having too much or too little, but having more or less relative to others we compare ourselves with. Nevertheless, there is also a sense of the excessive that bothers some people. Those who live in two-room houses are not likely to feel positive inequity because others live in only one room; it is those who live in mansions that are typically bothered by it (or should, some might say).

To put this matter in perspective, suffering from positive inequity is not exactly a moral issue of epidemic proportions. Most people who are better off are hardly bothered by it; on the contrary, they would like to have more and envy those who do. The more you have, the higher your social and self-esteem. Nonetheless, fair-minded people want their lot in life to be equitably matched with those they compare themselves with. We want outputs (what we have) to be proportional to inputs (what we contribute)—in short, giving and getting a fair shake in life. If we get less than we deserve, we feel resentful; if we get more than we deserve, we feel guilty.[35] On the other hand, winning the lottery raises no qualms because we do not feel responsible for the quirks of luck.

A number of additional considerations also matter. One is a sense of deservedness. Those who have earned their wealth through their talent and hard work, and who are generous in sharing it, are widely admired and would have the least reason to feel guilty (though some do so anyway). Misers, and those who have not earned their wealth fairly, are despised; ironically, they may also be the least likely to feel guilty.

Inherited wealth has its own burdens and contradictions. Children of the rich may consider themselves undeserving of their wealth and be viewed by others with a mixture of disdain and envy. Hence they may be more likely to suffer from the guilt of positive inequity. On the other hand, inherited wealth carries with it more prestige ("old money") and those with long pedigrees have a greater sense of entitlement and are less predisposed to feel guilty since their status has now become part of the order of society.

What troubles most people is the inequality between family members and close friends; others, one cares less about. Nor is the issue always money; being my parent's favorite child may be a more potent inducer of positive inequity than having done well in the stock market. Our earliest experiences of envy, after all, are sibling rivalries:

> One of the toughest and most emotional challenges that I have faced has cen-tered on my older sister. Two years ago she was diagnosed with depression, severe enough that she could no longer function at school and had to come back home. Her life seemed to be stagnating while my life seemed to be falling in place. I had a summer job I loved, hung out with my friends frequently, and was preparing to move to college. I didn't have time to deal with her problems and, honestly, it became easier to avoid them. The contrast was heartbreaking. I tried to suppress my excitement. The situation was unfair—my sister was losing a lot while I was gaining so much. While the feelings of guilt have faded in the past two years, the cycle continues to this day.

I was astonished to learn in student surveys that the most commonly cited reason for feeling guilty was "being at Stanford" (or any select institu-tion for that matter). I assumed young people felt guilty for failing to get into a good college; but now it looked like a case of being damned if you do, and damned if you don't. Students from middle class families feel guilty over the financial burden on their families (the rich can afford it and the poor get financial aid). Many wonder if they are making the best use of their educational opportunities. Some are bothered by the fact that they got a coveted spot while others, such as their friends in high school, did not, even though they were just as deserving. Some feel like an imposter ("imposter syndrome") because they think they do not belong where they are because they imagine they lack the intelligence, diligence, and talents expected of someone in their position.

> I met a girl who had gotten into a good college but had not received enough financial aid to come here. I felt guilty, though I had no control over the situ-ation, because I had the financial capability of attending an expensive univer-sity. I felt guilty for the opportunities I had, and someone else didn't simply because of socioeconomic reasons.

During the political turmoil of the 1960s, activist youth agitating for social justice were typically not the children of the poor or the disadvantaged but college students who came from better-off families. On the one hand, it has been argued that guilt over their privileged status (and guilt over their exemption from the draft) fueled their opposition to the Vietnam War. Consequently, they turned on their affluent parents—to their bafflement and consternation—and trashed the campuses of colleges that were grooming them for lives of affluence.[36] What started as guilt over acts of omission (not helping the poor and socially disadvantaged) evolved into guilt over acts of commission (responsibility for causing the plight of the poor and those in third world countries).[37] On the other hand, it seems wrong and unfair to explain away the actions of these idealistic youth on psychological grounds instead of crediting them with the political insight and moral sensitivity for seeing the Vietnam War for what it was much earlier than their parents and elders.

Positive inequity is not the same as guilt caused by ill-gotten gains. Those who have swindled or exploited others or have been ruthlessly competitive and self-serving have good reasons for feeling guilty. That, however, is not the issue here. Rather, the question is whether or not wealth in itself is a moral liability, an issue we considered earlier in connection with greed and envy.

Western attitudes toward wealth have been ambivalent. The rich are both envied and resented, especially if they have accumulated their wealth by exploiting others or through greed.[38] Jesus said it is easier for a camel to go through the eye of a needle than for a rich man to enter the kingdom of heaven (Matt. 19:24). Taken literally, this means the rich are doomed. Taken metaphorically, it means it is difficult, but still possible, for the rich to inherit eternal life. When a rich young man, who already observed the Law, asked Jesus what he should do to enter the kingdom of heaven, Jesus told him to give away his possessions and follow him. The young man walked away dejected because he owned so much. Nonetheless, Jesus did not shun the company of the rich. When a woman anointed his hair with a costly perfumed oil, some of the disciples were indignant and grumbled that the oil could have been sold and the money given to the poor; but Jesus said to them, "For she has done a beautiful thing to me. For you always have the poor with you, and whenever you will, you can do good to them; but you will not always have me" (Mark 14:3–10).

Christian monastic orders imposed a vow of poverty, but the princes of the church lived in luxury during the Renaissance. As noted earlier, the Protestant Ethic introduced the idea that wealth was a sign of God's favor. This idea has found particularly fertile ground in the United States, feeding into the American gospel of success. In the late nineteenth century the Baptist minister Russell Conwell delivered his "Acres of Diamonds" sermon six thousand times:

> I say the opportunity to get rich, to attain unto great wealth, is here now within the reach of almost every man and woman who hears me speak tonight! . . . I say that you might get rich, and it is your duty to get rich. Money is power . . . and you can do more good with it than you could without it.[39]

Some Protestant churches today continue to preach the "Prosperity Gospel," which unabashedly celebrates wealth as a blessing bestowed by God on the faithful.[40] It has been suggested that Americans retreat from this ideology during times of economic downturn, but always get back to it as the quintessentially American spirit of commercial optimism ultimately prevails.

Prosperity is also associated with what sociologist Thorstein Veblen called the *conspicuous consumption of the leisure class*. Perhaps it is conspicuous consumption that is the pitfall of the affluent rather than wealth itself. Nonetheless, inequality remains entrenched in the world even in relatively egalitarian countries. For example, the top 1 percent of Americans own 33 percent of the nation's wealth while the bottom half own only 3 percent. Some have billions of dollars, while over a billion people in the world subsist on less than a dollar a day.[41]

One of the ways the wealthy deal with positive inequity is through philanthropy. At the turn of the twentieth century Andrew Carnegie and John Rockefeller established the model of private American philanthropic foundations (of which there are now over thirty thousand). Most recently, Bill Gates and Warren Buffett raised the bar by jointly contributing over $70 billion to the Gates Foundation. There is no country in the world with a more extensive tradition of philanthropy than the United States (helped by its tax laws). In 2006, American gave $295 billion to charity (of which nearly $100 billion went to religious organizations alone). It is estimated that over the next fifty years, Americans will contribute a staggering $21 trillion to charities.[42]

There is a perception that the rich give away their money to soothe their conscience. Actually, despite the spectacular generosity of some, most wealthy Americans (the richest sixty of whom are worth $630 billion) do not give away their fortunes. This is hard to understand: If they do not give their money away, can spend but a fraction of it, or will pass only a small part to their children, what is the point of having it? Does the making or possession of money become an end in itself?[43]

When we discuss the evolution of guilt, we will consider the roots of altruism based on kinship or the prospect of reciprocity that prompts people to share their wealth. Other explanations include enhancing one's reputation (or rehabilitating it, as the case may be) and the desire for prestige (such as by having one's name on a public building). Such actions are some of the surest ways for people to join the social elite.

People may also be generous for psychological rather than material rewards. They are generous because it makes them feel good (the "warm glow" theory) or enhances their self-esteem. In this view, people are not giving money merely, for example, to save the whales; they are doing it to be the kind of person that gives money that saves the whales.[44]

Is it also not possible for people to be genuinely altruistic without seeking to benefit themselves in some fashion? As a former foundation executive, I have been impressed by how some wealthy individuals make philanthropy the center of their lives with no apparent ulterior motives. Guilt may be an entry point into philanthropy, but it is not enough to sustain it without genuine altruism. Nor is it only a matter of money. As one philanthropist expressed it, "One can contribute one's talent, time and treasure."[45] Moreover, public service is not wholly dependent on money. Millions of people dedicate their lives to the service of others, or make that an important part of what they do in their life and work. To say that they are simply motivated by guilt, or some other self-serving motive, would seem simplistic and overly cynical.

EXISTENTIAL GUILT

The last category of guilt without transgression is the most enigmatic. *Existential guilt* is a nebulous entity and entails a way of looking at guilt in the context of human existence. It is also referred to as *ontological guilt* (ontology being the branch of philosophy that deals with the nature of being).

The idea of ontological guilt is tied to existentialism, the philosophical and literary movement that gained prominence in Europe following World War II. Existentialism is popularly associated with French intellectuals like Jean Paul Sartre, Simone de Beauvoir, and Albert Camus. Its language is complex and its ideas hard to state in simple terms. Briefly, existentialism focuses on the uniqueness of the individual for whom death is the central fact of human existence. Consequently, one should act from *authenticity*—being true to oneself and free from conventional expectations about human nature—and one should accept personal responsibility. Authenticity rejects bad faith (insincerity and duplicity), lying to oneself, refusing to face reality, and making choices based on what is merely conventional. Ultimately, the choice we face is to either descend into "nothingness" or have the "courage to be."

Literary works with existentialist themes make these ideas somewhat easier to understand it. An important example is Franz Kafka's novel *The Trial*, an account of extraordinary events in the life of an ordinary person that are incomprehensible in everyday, rational terms.[46]

Joseph K., the protagonist of the novel, is a hard-working, junior official in a bank located in a central European city (presumably Prague); he is a single young man leading an ordinary, rather lonely life. On the morning of his thirtieth birthday, Joseph K. is arrested by two mysterious agents for unspecified reasons. He has not committed a crime, nor is he charged. Yet, he gets trapped in a bewildering web of accusations issued by a shadowy court that exists outside the legal system.

The case never comes to trial. What K. goes through is more like an investigation than a formal trial. Yet his presumed guilt relentlessly engulfs him. He professes his innocence, but his very denial evolves into proof of his guilt. Joseph K.'s life becomes unraveled. Events that start by being odd turn bizarre. The final encounter takes place in a cathedral where K. goes to meet a client who never shows up. The priest turns out to be the prison chaplain who knows all about his case. He tells K., "it is not necessary to accept everything as true, one must only accept it as necessary." Joseph K. finds that "a melancholy conclusion" that "turns lying into a universal principle." Shortly thereafter, he is taken out to a quarry and killed, "like a dog."[47]

The Kafkaesque world that K. inhabits is oppressive, alienating, undecipherable, and nightmarish. Expressed in Kafka's lucid language, each sentence in the novel is perfectly intelligible, yet taken together their cumulative effect is enigmatic and sinister. Taken at face value, *The Trial* represents the arbitrary and cruel way individuals are treated in an oppressive and corrupt dictatorial society. The deeper meaning of the novel goes beyond the conventional experiences of being guilty.

There have been many interpretations of *The Trial* and of Kafka's work more generally. *The Trial* is not autobiographical, but there are some hints that link Kafka's personal life to his work. Joseph K. and Kafka's other literary characters all suffer from an ineluctable sense of guilt, and Kafka himself was burdened with guilt. The origin of his guilt has been attributed to his relationship with his father; unconscious conflicts; culturally induced self-hatred; being Jewish in an alien society; the values of Western society; or even simply being human. Ultimately, the enigma of Joseph K.'s guilt, and perhaps Kafka's guilt as well, epitomizes the idea of existential guilt—the elemental guilt of human beings who have lost their moorings in a senseless world.[48]

Existential guilt is rooted in an *existential anxiety* associated with a feeling of *dread*, or deep apprehension (German, *Angst*), that comes from the realization that we are ultimately alone in the world and responsible for our own actions. Such anxiety is not to be confused with ordinary anxiety, such as that associated with the fear of death, or even neurotic anxiety generated by repressed unconscious conflicts. Existential anxiety is vaguer, but no less painful. It is the feeling of being ill at ease in one's skin and not at home in the world. The guilt associated with it may be useful in helping us become more responsive and responsible beings in facing the challenges of life with courage, but it is also a source of anguish.[49]

Our inability to change the past leads to *existential regret* for having failed to make conscious, wholehearted choices. It is this sense of self-betrayal and inauthenticity that fills us with existential guilt. We feel guilty not because we have transgressed moral boundaries (which are arbitrary), offended God (who does not exist), or failed to meet social standards (that should not matter), but because we have fallen short as human beings—we have failed to live authentic lives. Since we can do nothing to avoid this feeling, we are bound to feel existential anxiety and guilt because we are condemned to be free: "Consequently, man's ontological guilt resides within his irresolvable tension resulting from between what he is and what he would like to be, between what he would like to be and what he will never be able to be."[50]

In its more popularized versions, existential guilt can also said to arise from the failure to develop our full potential as human beings. It arises from our sense of separateness that sets us apart from other human beings, and from our alienation from nature. But given the countless potentialities we are born with, how could we possibly fulfill all of them, especially since fulfilling some would preclude fulfilling others? We aspire to be close with others, but also to be apart. To be part of nature is wonderful, but separation from nature is the price we pay for urban life. Most pertinently, how can we be or feel guilty unless there is some deviation from a norm that sets us apart? If everyone is guilty by virtue of being human, then can anyone be guilty in a meaningful sense of the word?[51]

Nonetheless, conceptions of existential guilt are interesting because they go deeper than our everyday guilt in psychological terms. In Martin Buber's words,

> Existential guilt—that is, guilt that a person has taken on himself as a person and in a personal situation—cannot be comprehended through such categories as "repression." . . . Existential guilt occurs when someone injures the order of the human world whose foundations he knows and recognizes as those of his existence and of all common human existence. . . .
>
> The psychotherapist into whose field of vision such manifestations of guilt enter in all their forcefulness can no longer imagine that he is able to do justice to his task of guilt-ridden men merely through the removal of his guilt feelings. . . . The psychotherapist is no pastor of souls and no substitute for one. It is never his task to mediate salvation; his task is always only to further healing.[52]

Buber tells us how *not* to deal with existential guilt by turning it into a psychological problem. How to deal with it in a broader philosophical sense is an issue when we take up we will turn to our discussion of guilt in the light of reason.

Where does all this leave us? The material discussed in this chapter has taken us away from the standard psychological conceptualizations of guilt as subjective experiences played out in interpersonal contexts. The forms of guilt discussed here are more baffling, but they add a more nuanced and a subtler appreciation of what guilt is all about. We will have more to say about these humanistic approaches to guilt when we consider religious and philosophical perspectives in subsequent chapters. But we are not there yet. In the next chapter we will consider, mostly in a clinical context, what constitute healthy and unhealthy forms of guilt. What is it that makes guilt pathological; how does it make us sick?

5 THE PATHOLOGY OF GUILT

HOW DOES A WELL-FUNCTIONING CONSCIENCE differ from one that is dysfunctional? Why and how does guilt become excessive? When does it make us sick? Is guilt a problem only when it is excessive, or does the lack of guilt constitute an equally serious problem? What are the consequences when one has too little guilt or a deficient conscience? These are the questions that we will address in this chapter.

Emma L. is a 19-year-old bright, thoughtful, attractive, and self-confident college student. The account of her struggles with guilt illustrates how guilt caused by her recurrent episodes of depression find expression through her religious beliefs. Emma's religious beliefs are not the cause of the depression that generates her guilt. Hence, her story is not intended to represent a typical experience of guilt by a Christian, nor is it an indictment of Christianity as a guilt-inducing religion. Rather, it shows the complex tangle of psychological, pathological, and religious factors that shape an individual's moral sensibilities, including the experience and expression of guilt.

> I was a fundamentalist Christian by my own choice; it was in no way forced upon me by my parents. My mom is very eclectic in her beliefs and my dad says he sees more of God while he is watering the lawn than he does in church. It never occurred to me at the time I was involved with the church, but in retrospect I think that a major reason I decided to become a Christian had to do with my history of clinical depression. I am now nineteen years old, and

I am grateful to Sanford Gifford and John Racy for their most helpful critique of this chapter.

I'm taking medication to prevent me from falling into what would be my fifth bout of major depression. The first time I was depressed, I was nine years old.

My first couple of years of high school were a good period in my life: I was making new friends, had started a new school, and was doing well in band and drama. The possibilities of my future seemed endless, and my faith in God helped me feel like someone was listening to my prayers and watching over me. There was, however, another side to my faith: Even in my happiest days as a Christian, I was plagued by guilt. The guilt stemmed primarily from the sense of indebtedness I had toward God, from my belief that I was inherently sinful and wicked, and finally, because I believed my guilt was a good thing—it served as a buffer that kept me from going too far astray from the path of God. I did not know why God had chosen to save me, or even why he had decided to create me in the first place, but I was determined to spend the rest of my life repaying the debt. It was this sense of indebtedness that laid the foundations for the guilt I began to experience each time I felt I'd disappointed God, by breaking His rules or lacking in faith.

While attributing any purity of spirit within myself to God, I came to view the essence of my being as evil. I learned to feel guilty not only about my moral transgressions, but I was ashamed of my inherent nature. Thank goodness, I would remind myself, that Jesus had come into my life to save me from my sinful self. It didn't occur to me to be bitter that I was beginning to feel almost unceasingly guilty; on the contrary, I was grateful for my guilt. Although I do not consider the "normal" guilt I experienced as a Christian a healthy thing, it was tame in comparison to the guilt I experienced in my junior year in high school when my third round of depression hit at age sixteen.

I am not attempting to generalize about the "Christian experience," but I know that in my life it was Christianity that led to a rift within myself. I think I have always had a tendency to view my world in black-and-white, all-or-nothing terms, but my religious beliefs helped this tendency to blossom. It was especially powerful in helping me to disown the parts of myself that I labeled as evil: from lust to selfishness to pride. I tried to bury the parts of myself that didn't fit into my scheme of righteousness; when I saw "evil" in myself, I became terribly afraid that Satan was gaining control of my soul.

"Please don't leave me, God; I am nothing without you," I wrote in purple ink in my diary. I decided that night I was ready to try loving God again. I have always looked back upon that night as the beginning of my recovery from depression, and symbolically at least it was. But there was more to it than that one-night conversion experience. I began to see a therapist and to learn to take care of myself. I distanced myself from several unhealthy friendships, and perhaps most importantly, my depression had run its six-week course.

There was one sentence that came to be the cornerstone of my new image of God: "Love me first and above all, and all other loves will follow." But the God I perceived in my mind was a jealous lover who competed with my boyfriends for my allegiance and my body. The fact that I was sixteen years old and beginning to be confronted with sexual decisions made my sexuality a logical target for guilt. I was torn apart by guilt every time I felt that I had chosen my sexual desires, or my boyfriends', over my relationship with God. I will carry with me forever the memory of one Sunday afternoon I spent sobbing in the graveyard, consumed by guilt I felt for "going too far" with my first really serious boyfriend.

Overall, Christianity was healthier for me the second time around. As I continued to grow stronger emotionally, it became easier to trust in the goodness of God. As I learned to accept myself, I could begin to believe that my God loved me too. Nonetheless, rare is the person who wouldn't hate the Christianity I created for myself.[1]

How are we to understand Emma's struggle with guilt? One way is to look at it from a clinical perspective. Emma suffered from a depressive illness with guilt as one of its key symptoms, a condition over which she had no control. In this view, her religious views, no matter how prominent, become secondary: It was not Christianity as such but a Christianity that she created for herself in the throes of her depression that fueled her guilt. It would have hardly mattered if she had belonged to some other faith, or no faith at all; her guilt would have found some other vehicle to express itself. In this view, guilt was a product of illness; religion was its vehicle of expression, not its cause.

An alternative view would ascribe a greater role to Emma's religious beliefs as an integral part of her guilt. Her guilt would be part of a true spiritual response to sin, as defined by a particular form of Christianity. In other words, had Emma been, for instance, a Buddhist, her experience of guilt caused by her depression would have been different, possibly less intense (even though Buddhists get depressed too). So, in this view, Christian conceptions of a particular cast directly contributed to Emma's struggle with guilt, aiding and abetting it.

However one chooses between these two conflicting explanations, or tries to reconcile them, it is clear that Emma's experience of guilt was excessive. It caused her intense pain and suffering and was disruptive of her young life.

There was no realistic moral reason why she should have felt so guilty since she was a child. She had done no wrong. (Emma is now a happily married woman with two children and works as a psychotherapist. Her youthful struggle with guilt feels like a distant nightmare.)

CULTURAL THRESHOLDS OF GUILT

Pathological guilt is the domain of psychiatrists and other clinicians. It is not possible, however, to understand the psychology of guilt in a cultural void. The proper measure of guilt—how, when, and to what extent people should feel guilty—is part of our social conventions that have changed over the centuries. For example, until modern times people thought of guilt mainly in moral terms. In the medieval period, popular sentiment, usually but not always backed by church doctrine, fostered the idea that feeling guilty was a good thing—it reflected a healthy conscience—hence, the guiltier one felt, the better could one resist sin. This ideology that led to the excesses of guilt has come to be associated with medieval Christianity. It developed mostly among monks and nuns who wished to save their souls by mortifying the flesh; it is hard to know the extent to which ordinary people adhered to such views. Those held in the grip of these beliefs resorted to ascetic practices like the wearing of hair shirts and refusing to bathe; and some went further in their mortification of the flesh: "St. Margaret Marie Alacoque sought out rotten fruit and dusty bread to eat . . . and drank water in which laundry had been washed. . . . She cut the name of Jesus on her chest with a knife, and because the scars did not last long enough, burnt them with a candle."[2] The thought of drinking pus and washings from the sores of the sick is disgusting but such practices were meant to overcome the disgust one feels in serving the sick.[3] During epidemics, penitents flagellated themselves to expiate for the guilt that presumably caused the calamity. Tertullian—a renowned father of the early church—castrated himself to overcome lust.

The church formally disapproved of these excesses, recognizing their disordered nature, but it also canonized some of their practitioners. Many who took religious vows were seeking lives of devotion and service, but medieval convents in particular also served to house social outcasts, including the mentally ill, who had nowhere else to go. (St. Bernardine called them "the scum and vomit of the world.")[4] Consequently, such beliefs and practices were often the result of mental illness, rather than genuine piety. They were pathological in terms of their excess as well as their cause.

The increasing secularization during the Renaissance, which marked the end of the medieval period, contributed to new ideas that viewed individuals as autonomous and masters of their own destiny (famously expressed by the Victorian poet William Earnest Henley, "It matters not . . . / How charged with punishments the scroll, / I am the master of my fate: / I am the captain of my soul"). This secular frame of mind generated a new ethic, a new conscience, and a new threshold for guilt. It was an ethic that made earthly happiness, not eternal life, the highest good. Guilt over the pursuit of pleasure and happiness gradually replaced the striving for happiness.

The greater emphasis on individual autonomy led to new attitudes toward guilt in the twentieth century. As conceived by J. A. Amato, the first form it took was a lack of guilt. The *guiltless man/woman* has a deficient sense of guilt and is devoid of empathy, charity, and pity.[5] People such as this absolve themselves by claiming to be doing their duty in following orders—even if this leads to the death of thousands. These ordinary, insignificant individuals, who may cause monumental damage, embody the "banality of evil" (as in the case of Adolf Eichmann).[6] We see the same attitudes in mobs and gangs, with their callous indifference to human suffering. These people may be written off as the "toxic waste" of modern society. Yet it is much harder to deal with the devastation caused in "good conscience" by the bombing of cities of no strategic importance, especially when this is done by one's own country. It has been documented that the worst and most extensive carpet bombing of German cities, such as Dresden, by the Allies during World War II was carried out when the end of the war was already imminent and served no strategic purpose.[7] The wholesale destruction of Hiroshima and Nagasaki raises similar concerns, although it is argued that it shortened the war and saved lives.

The opposite of the guiltless character is the *man/woman of guilt*, one who is burdened with excessive guilt. People such as this anguish over everything and, by making everything a matter of conscience, they become morally defenseless and paralyzed: "The world of the guilty man is a 'moral' minefield," says Amato. "He is forever turning back on himself. It is as if his whole existence is tethered to his anxious conscience. . . . His mind is a tribunal before which he always stands as defendant. . . . What he pleads makes no difference. His trial continues but sentencing never occurs."[8]

This pervasive sense of guilt constitutes a "cultural neurosis" that became endemic in the twentieth century as a result of wars, revolutions, genocides, purges, and economic crises that afflicted entire populations and became the landmarks of our modern existence.

These circumstances have led to a process of "social conscience loading" with a heightened sensitivity to the suffering in the world exemplified by the *man/woman of guilt*. People of this type are ethical beings who feel morally burdened, not only by the wrong that they may do but also all the good that they fail to do. The religious guilt of the past was dependent of God. Secular guilt must be shouldered by autonomous beings who bear the entire burden of responsibility for their own actions. This idealized conscience is the ethical reaction to the increasing interdependence of the world. It is the realization of Father Zossima's vision, in Dostoevsky's *Brothers Karamazov*, that "everyone is responsible to all men for all men and for everything."[9]

Consequently, we need to understand individual experiences of excessive guilt within the historical and cultural contexts in which we live. It is important to distinguish excessive guilt imposed by cultural factors from that generated by our own psychology. The need to restrain socially disruptive behaviors must be pitted against the extent to which society may limit our personal freedom to do as we please. When social constraints are too lax, we risk chaos; when they are too stringent, they suck the joy out of life.

By the end of the nineteenth century, the strictures of Victorian morality led men like Nietzsche and Freud to protest against prevailing social mores that induced needless guilt. Freud's basic thesis in his *Civilization and Its Discontents* is that there exists an irreconcilable conflict between human natural desires ("instincts") and the restrictions of civilization. As societies evolve, more constraints are imposed on human drives—particularly sex and aggression—in order to maintain the social order. However, the greater the need for curtailing human freedom, the greater is the cost in neurotic suffering.[10] Freud illustrated this with the story of a farmer who fed his horse less and less hay each day until it starved to death. Likewise, human beings can be denied their instinctual satisfactions until the game of life is no longer worth the candle. Freud's somber conclusion is that human beings cannot live without civilization but neither can they be happy within it.[11] That is the human predicament. All we can do is to find some way of living with it.

PSYCHOLOGICAL ASSESSMENTS OF GUILT

When is guilt normal and when does it become abnormal? Normality is first of all a statistical concept that represents what would apply to the majority of ordinary people. Since it represents the "average," whatever is normative is not pathological. If the majority of the population have crooked noses then a crooked nose would be part of a normal human face. In a cannibalistic society, eating human flesh is no different from our consuming beef.

The statistical norm, however, is not the only determinant of normality. Moral judgments may be independent of numbers; thus, lying may be considered wrong even if everyone lies. However, as a practical matter, moral and legal standards usually represent the common ethical assumptions of the majority. We cannot send everybody to jail, or to hell, no matter what they do.

Despite the great diversity of human behavior, we categorize some people as ill, immoral, or criminal. Where to draw the boundaries that separate them from those who are healthy, moral, and law-abiding follows certain rules, but it is ultimately arbitrary. Experiences of guilt are no different. Normally, the appropriate response to everyday transgressions is to feel guilty. Then, at the extremes, are some who feel guilty for everything they do, or fail to feel guilty for anything they do. Most of us fall somewhere in between. Consider the following examples and decide whether the person should or should not feel guilty, under the circumstances:

> Whenever someone asks me for a personal favor, I feel compelled to say yes. No matter how distant our relationship is and how time-consuming or inconvenient the request is, I will usually acquiesce. Whenever I endeavor to refuse, I am overwhelmed by a sense of guilt, as though I had let the person down. This feeling is so oppressive that I find it easier and less stressful just to go ahead and do the favor. There is no logical basis for this guilt. Yet my sense of social responsibility is overdeveloped to the extent that refusing such appeals makes me feel uncomfortable and unhappy for the remainder of the day. I feel trapped, yet I seem to be unable to extricate myself.

Does this person's willingness to help make him a valued friend or a sucker? Without more information about the impact of the problem on himself and others, it is hard to tell. Next is the opposite problem:

> Maybe I'm just too prideful to feel guilty, but the feeling of guilt has rarely come across my life. The events of my life that probably should have violated some moral code all seem to have failed to instigate any feelings of guilt in me. For instance, when in middle school I was caught shoplifting, I was furious that I didn't do a better job of sneaking out. So far as romantic and interpersonal issues are concerned, I would prefer to use the word "sorry" rather than "guilt." Since I am usually the one who terminates a relationship, the internal

pain and contrition is absent. I also seem to always be able to justify my actions to myself so that self-blame becomes unreasonable. Maybe I'm just too prideful to allow myself to experience guilt.

It may be harsh to call this person a psychopath, but there is a chilling note in his attitude that borders on callousness. On the other hand, he does not seem to have inflicted any serious harm on anyone. He is willing to say he is sorry. Finally, there are those who cannot decide whether they should or should not feel guilty:

> It is hard to pinpoint if and when I feel guilty. I am neither religious (in a traditional sense) nor judgmental of myself or others. I don't believe in principles of right and wrong. Instead, one should live life according to one's own principles and not be made to feel bad about it—unless it adversely affects others. Sometimes, however, I feel a bit guilty for holding such ideas; whether they are truly my ideals or my unconscious way of justifying my behavior, is hard to tell. I suppose one might say that I feel guilty—for not feeling guilty.

What counts in these assessments are not isolated incidents but general patterns of behavior—their consistency, magnitude, and the circumstances under which they occur. What is it that makes us *habitually* feel guilty? What are the conditions under which feelings of guilt arise? Most important, does guilt interfere with our life or the lives of others? If my crooked nose does not interfere with my breathing (or make me feel ugly) then it is a healthy nose for all practical purposes. The element of *dysfunction* is a basic requirement for calling someone sick.

CONSCIOUS AND UNCONSCIOUS GUILT

We generally think of guilt as a conscious emotion—a feeling we are all too painfully aware of. This is also the sense of guilt that most psychologists are concerned with. However, psychoanalysts distinguish between conscious and unconscious guilt.

The idea of unconscious guilt was central to Freud's theory of the mind. Freud made a critical distinction between conscious feelings of guilt, which we are fully aware of, and unconscious guilt, which is not accessible to our consciousness (though it may leak into our dreams or reveal itself through slips of the tongue). Conscious feelings of guilt are a response to life events that involve committing a misdeed; in that sense, they constitute "real guilt."

(For instance, we lie and feel guilty.) Unconscious guilt arises from repressed feelings and thoughts that we are unaware of but nonetheless influence our thoughts, feelings, and actions. For instance, if I yell at an older person and feel guilty I may be actually expressing unconscious feelings of anger at my father.

Freud called conscious guilt "remorse." He was not particularly interested in it even though, in his later years, he wrote extensively on how guilt in Western culture encumbered people's lives. The guilt that Freud was concerned with was unconscious guilt—the irrational, dreadful feeling of moral condemnation that induces a need for punishment. This is the guilt that lay at the bottom of neurotic conflicts ("neurotic" referred to all forms of emotional and mental problems).[12]

Freud developed these ideas in his work with his patients, but he extended them to ordinary people whose unconscious guilt was manifested by pervasive discontent in trying to live moral lives in civilized society. Guilt could also be manifested in religious piety, asceticism, or irrational fear of death—it could even act as a motivation for various crimes. Freud ascribed this guilt to the conflict between the ego (the executive component of our psychological self) and the superego (which corresponds roughly to our conscience).

We deal with conscious guilt just as we deal with other emotions, like fear and anger. However, we cannot deal with unconscious guilt the same way because we are not aware of it. That is what makes it especially problematic. Repressed feelings and thoughts form "complexes" that, like tangled knots, are not easy to unravel. Keeping them out of our consciousness uses up psychological energy. Like keeping prisoners in jail, it is costly. Moreover, such guilt warps our relationships with others without our realizing it. For instance, instead of recognizing our repressed hostile feelings, we project them on others who have not caused them and accuse them of persecuting us. This make our behavior look odd and erratic.

Most behaviorist psychologists currently do not accept the idea of unconscious guilt. Like much else in psychoanalytic theory, unconscious guilt cannot be verified by empirical or experimental studies. However, more recently, neuroscientists have confirmed the presence of unconscious thoughts and feelings in the brain, but they call them "subcortical" rather than unconscious.

GUILT AND DEPRESSION

We all feel sad from time to time in response to the vicissitudes of life. At such times, we describe our mood as low, blue, dejected, gloomy, downhearted, unhappy, sorrowful. Sadness may even have a wistful quality ("sweet sorrow").

Depression is a more severe form of sadness (conveying the sense of being downcast). The older term, *melancholia*, was derived from the ancient notion that severe sadness was caused by an excess of black bile (*melanina chole*).

Given its prevalence, depression is the so-called common cold of psychiatry.[13] It forms part of many psychiatric conditions, especially those subsumed under "mood disorders."[14] Ordinarily, we feel sad when we have lost a valued object or person, most poignantly when we grieve the death of someone we love. In the clinical literature, the element of loss—real or imagined—is central to all experiences of depression, sometimes by triggering earlier, childhood memories of experiences of loss. In childhood depression, there may be feelings of abandonment and a sense of the loss of part of oneself. However, while manifested in psychological symptoms, severe depressions have important biological determinants (including disturbances in hormones and neurotransmitters) and can be treated effectively with antidepressant drugs.

The psychological symptoms of depression include feelings of pessimism, worthlessness, and guilt.[15] Such feelings are usually not due to significant, real-life transgressions. No matter how guilty they feel, severely depressed persons have not committed serious wrongs. They ruminate instead over minor past failings, such as trivial acts of dishonesty. Long-forgotten events flood back into the mind. The depressed misinterpret events as evidence of personal defects, or feel responsible for misfortunes over which they have no control. They may even develop delusions of being responsible for catastrophes like natural disasters or feel condemned to hell as agents of the devil.

Freud, in his comparison of grief (a normal reaction to loss) to melancholia (the pathological reaction to loss), gives a compelling description of the devaluation of the self or the sense of moral inferiority that is suffused with guilt:

> The melancholic displays something else . . . which is lacking in mourning—an extraordinary diminution in his self regard. . . . In mourning it is the world which has become poor and empty; in melancholia it is the ego itself. The patient represents his ego as worthless, incapable of any achievement and morally despicable; he reproaches himself, vilifies himself and expects to be cast out and punished. He abases himself before everyone and commiserates with his own relatives for being associated with anyone so unworthy.[16]

Psychoanalysts also ascribe the intense feeling of guilt to repressed aggression. The accusations the depressed direct at themselves may be unconsciously intended for others. Moreover, their hostility is turned inward and directed at themselves, most dramatically manifested when it results in suicide.

Depression may also appear as a personality trait. Those suffering from it have a gloomy, cheerless outlook on life. They are overly serious, incapable of enjoying themselves, and lack a sense of humor. They brood, worry, expect the worst, and are particularly harsh in their judgments of themselves. Their low sense of self-esteem exaggerates their shortcomings and makes them prone to guilt. The dispositional tendency to guilt is not uniform; some are prone to feel guilty under a wide variety of circumstances; others feel guilty under certain specific conditions only (such as sexual interactions).

Another personality type that gets entangled with guilt is the *masochistic character*. Masochism is typically associated with obtaining erotic pleasure through pain and humiliation. However, it can also exist without a sexual element (*moral masochism*). The harsh conscience of masochists leads to feelings of guilt that they try to assuage by inviting hostility and punishment (which is why it looks like they are "asking for it").[17] For example, a masochistic character married to an abusive spouse will suffer for years until freed by divorce or death only to marry another abusive person of the same sort and start over again. The element of hostility may be hidden in masochism, but it is ever present. When a masochistic character says "Look how miserable I am," the hidden accusation it conveys is "Look how miserable you make me feel."[18]

GUILT AND OBSESSIVE-COMPULSIVE DISORDERS

The association between guilt and obsessive-compulsive conditions is less obvious than in depression but no less significant. These conditions may take several forms. They may be isolated traits in an otherwise normal person; they may be manifested as a more global personality disorder; or they may constitute a neurotic disorder. The boundaries between these conditions are not always sharp but generally are discrete enough.

Some people enjoy a measure of perfectionism while others are irritated by it. Orderliness and attention to detail help us to be well organized, but when exaggerated they interfere with flexibility and efficiency. Relentless perfectionism and nitpicking get in the way of getting the job done; unrealistically high standards lead to frustration. For such individuals, nothing is ever good enough and the best becomes the enemy of the good. Difficulty in delegating responsibility compounds the excessive devotion to work beyond economic necessity; leisure and pleasure are a waste of time. They are stingy with money as well as with praise. They have difficulty expressing affection, or do it in a stilted fashion. Reason trumps emotion in their lives.[19]

For example, Anthony M., a 48-year-old professor of mathematics, as a teenager developed a streak of perfectionism that dominated his life. Though he was at the top of his class, he fretted endlessly over every little mistake he made on exams. The failure to do everything just right made him feel guilty. His perfectionism and guilt fed into each other. Issues that did not concern him caused needless distress. He could not look at a newspaper without reading every obituary and "grieving" over it. Like Atlas, he carried the burden of the world on his shoulders. By the time Anthony graduated from college, his symptoms had become less problematic. As he got older, his perfectionism actually helped him to be more meticulous and successful in his work, although it continued to be a handicap in his personal life.

It is easy to see why such individuals would be prone to guilt feelings. They are excessively conscientious and inflexible about matters of ethical conduct, hence they are in constant fear of doing wrong. Sticklers for rules, they are mercilessly critical of themselves and others. Their literal compliance with rules and deference to authority turns morality into a rigid and joyless ordeal, trapping them in a mindless maze of rituals that enforces their need for control. The satisfaction that comes from doing the right thing is marred by doubts of having failed to do enough of it, not doing it the right way, or at the right time; something is always missing.

Such personality traits and symptoms are particularly prominent in *obsessive-compulsive disorders* (OCD).[20] Obsessions are persistent and unwanted ideas that typically revolve around fears of contamination (hence a preoccupation with germs); persistent doubts ("Did I close the door properly?"); or imagery involving forbidden impulses (often sexual or deviant). Compulsions are repetitive behaviors (such as hand washing) or mental acts (repeating certain words). The person feels compelled to perform these rituals in order to reduce the distress that accompanies the obsession or to magically prevent some dreaded prospect from coming true. The following excerpt from an autobiography illustrates this:

> My mother became unwell. . . . I neither rested day or night. . . . Suddenly, I found myself doing that which even at the time struck me as being highly singular; I found myself touching particular objects that were near me, and to which my fingers seemed to be attracted by an irresistible impulse. It was now

the table, or the chair I was compelled to touch . . . now the handle of the door; now I would touch the wall. . . . So I continued to do day after day . . . ; frequently I would struggle to resist the impulse, but invariably in vain. . . . What impelled me to these actions was the desire to prevent my mother's death.[21]

The association of guilt with OCD is twofold. An excessive sense of responsibility, even for matters beyond one's control, makes the person prone to feel guilty. And once the guilt sets in, it becomes difficult to get rid of; like a rat on a treadmill, the person cannot get out of the loop. The reason is that obsessions are very difficult to get rid of and guilt becomes one more obsession.[22]

Long before clinicians identified obsessive-compulsive disorders, the Catholic church characterized such behaviors as *scrupulosity*.[23] A person with a scrupulous conscience sees sin where there is none and feels guilt over matters that do not warrant it—despite all argument to the contrary. During confession, the person may relate a real, or presumed, sinful act in excruciating detail and then repeat it to make sure that it was properly conveyed to the priest. The priest's attempts to give absolution will get nowhere; and when he gives up, the person is likely to go to another confessor and start over. The Catholic church recognized this as the sign of a disturbed mind rather than a sensitive conscience and instructed confessors to deal with the scrupulous with a combination of kindness and firmness, forbidding repetitive confessions.

Rabbis have also confronted this issue in the form of devotion to a religious text or ritual so excessive that it comes to dominate one's life. Judaism considers this to be a form of idolatry where the text becomes a substitute for God and a substitute for carrying out good acts.

Some key Christian figures struggled with scrupulosity. As a Benedictine monk, Martin Luther was beset with scruples over whether he was truly forgiven by God, a forgiveness he sought with repeated confessions, but to no avail. Finally, his great doctrinal breakthrough of salvation by faith set him free. His salvation no longer depended on what he did but on the grace of God. Luther excluded the confessional from Protestant practice because Christians could relate to God without intermediaries.

Another example is St. Ignatius Loyola, the founder of the Jesuit order (Society of Jesus). Loyola was a Spanish nobleman who experienced a profound conversion while recovering from severe wounds sustained in battle. His newly found faith was marred by recurrent doubts about whether his past sins had been forgiven. He knew his doubts were irrational, yet they still plunged him into despair: "Show me, Lord, where I can obtain help: and if I have to follow a little dog to obtain the cure I need, I am ready to do just that."[24]

John Bunyan, one of the great religious and literary figures of the seventeenth century (and the author of *Pilgrim's Progress*), has provided a poignant account of his struggles with scrupulosity in *Grace Abounding to the Chief of Sinners*:

> . . . the tempter came upon me again, and that with a more grievous and dreadful temptation than before.
>
> And that was, 'To sell and part with this most blessed Christ, to exchange him for the things of this life, for any thing.' The temptation lay upon me for the space of a year, and did follow me so continually, that I was not rid of it one day in a month; no, not sometimes one hour in many days together, unless I was asleep. . . .
>
> . . . I could neither eat my food, stoop for a pin, chop a stick or cast mine eye to look on this or that, but the temptation would come, 'Sell Christ for this, or sell Christ for that; sell him, sell him.'[25]

INADEQUATE GUILT

Excessive guilt is a problem at the personal level; inadequate guilt is more serious in social terms. In the former, the suffering is mostly personal; in the latter, one makes others suffer through antisocial behavior. We react with bafflement, even sympathy, to those with excessive guilt, whereas those with an inadequate guilt make us dismayed and resentful.

We associate antisocial behavior with criminals, and rightly so. However, who has not engaged, now and then, in some antisocial act in good conscience? We justify it by invoking extenuating circumstances; because of our wish to serve a higher cause; or because we victimize strangers but not family and friends. It is all part of human frailty and Erik Erikson considers allowing oneself to get away with something once in a while to be the sign of a healthy ego.

Antisocial acts by otherwise socially responsible individuals are more apt to occur under special circumstances: Soldiers in uniform will do things they will not in civilian life; we behave differently when away from home, on vacation, or acting as part of a group. Alcohol is a potent catalyst in weakening self-restraint. (The conscience is said to be the part of the brain that is soluble in alcohol.) We will often do "this" but not "that." Such selective lapses are like holes in our conscience, and hence are called *superego lacunae*. The result is a "Swiss cheese conscience." Such antisocial behavior is ascribed to inconsistent moral expectations and contradictory behaviors by parents ("Do as I say, not as I do") that are internalized in childhood.[26]

A peculiar aspect of antisocial behavior is the harm ordinary persons are willing to inflict in the name of obedience. In a classic series of experiments, Stanley Milgram was able to induce volunteers to deliver what they thought were increasingly painful electric shocks to a protesting subject (actually a collaborator of the investigator). Women participants felt guiltier than men doing it, but obeyed just the same.

In another study, by Philip Zimbardo, college students were assigned as guards in a simulated prison experiment. Within a week, these "guards" had grown punitive, at times to the point of being sadistic, in their treatment of their fellow students (the "prisoners") because they had been made to think by the experimenter that it was necessary to do so to maintain order.[27]

It is also possible to induce people to do strange things outside a psychological laboratory. A prankster, posing as a police officer, instructed an assistant manager at McDonald's, over the telephone, to strip search a teenage employee who had supposedly committed a theft. By the end of the day, the employee was induced to perform oral sex on the fiancé of the assistant manager. Some seventy others were duped into committing similar offences.[28] In *Lord of the Flies*, William Golding shows how a group of schoolboys stranded in the wilderness regress to acting like savages.[29]

From such contrived situations it is but a short step to the criminal behavior of ordinary people who commit atrocities in war. The ring leaders at Abu Ghraib or Mai Lai may have been psychopaths, and it is comforting to soothe our conscience by ascribing criminal acts to a few "bad apples." Yet, the number of average, "normal guys" who act in similar ways seems much larger. Are these soldiers victims of circumstances that make them do things abroad that they would not dream of doing back home? Does war brutalize them? One veteran declares, "I felt like there was this enormous reduction in my compassion for people. . . . The only thing that wound up mattering is myself and the guys that I was with. And everybody else be damned."[30]

The more charitable view is that these soldiers suffer a temporary lapse of moral judgment and on their return home they will revert to their more moral selves. The darker view is that they are covert psychopaths with a dysfunctional conscience that releases their brutal impulses when given an opportunity. The likelihood is that none of these explanations will apply to everyone. Perhaps it takes a confluence of factors to bring about a moral collapse.

ANTISOCIAL PERSONALITIES AND PSYCHOPATHS

At some point, antisocial behavior goes beyond relatively benign and sporadic actions and turns to criminal behavior which is habitual and part of a lifestyle. Antisocial individuals have been a source of dismay and bafflement: We can neither understand them nor figure out what to do with them.

Traditionally, antisocial individuals have been considered *evil* (and still are by some people), and thereby the problem has been attributed to a nefarious external influence, such as the devil. This primarily religious perspective shifted, at the turn of the nineteenth century, to a more secular view that regarded antisocial behaviors as a form of mental illness (*moral insanity*). The term *psychopath* ("suffering soul") was coined in Germany in the 1880s. This internal focus on the individual came into conflict with more liberal ideologies that put the blame for social deviance on external causes, like poverty, and the term *sociopath* came into vogue in the 1930s.[31]

The formal diagnostic term that is used in current psychiatric classifications refers to these conditions as *antisocial personality disorders.*[32] It includes what was called psychopathy, but some investigators object that including psychopathy with antisocial disorders would be akin to confusing pneumonia with the common cold. While the two conditions share some common features, psychopathy is far more severe and may have its own distinctive causes. Nonetheless, for our purposes here, we will treat psychopathy as the more severe form of antisocial disorders, rather than as a separate entity.

Psychopathy was the first personality disorder recognized in psychiatry and has been the subject of a great deal of investigation and speculation by clinicians and social scientists.[33] While its ultimate causes remain largely uncertain, we have a good idea of its behavioral manifestations:

> On the interpersonal level, psychopaths are grandiose, arrogant, callous, dominant, superficial, and manipulative. Affectively, they are short-tempered, unable to form strong emotional bonds with others, and lack empathy, guilt, or remorse. These interpersonal and affective features are associated with a socially deviant (not necessarily criminal) lifestyle that includes irresponsible and impulsive behavior and a tendency to ignore or violate social conventions and mores.[34]

A key characteristic of all these conditions is the woefully inadequate capacity to experience guilt, a feature long noted by clinicians and law enforcement officials. This results from a severe form of *emotional detachment* that leads to a lack of empathy and remorse; these individuals simply do not seem to care about the consequences of what they do to others. Clinical experience and empirical studies show that guilt proneness actually makes one less likely to engage in aggressive or criminal behavior. Conversely, lack of the capacity for guilt has the opposite effect. In that sense, guilt works.

The sexual abuse of children and sexual violence are among the most prevalent and serious crimes carried out by antisocial characters. Though women are the victims in most cases of sexual assault, men also do get raped (usually in prison) and react to it quite similarly to the way women do. While it cannot be claimed that no rapist or child-abuser ever feels guilty, ironically it is often the victims who end up feeling guilty by holding themselves responsible for provoking the assault by being careless, being drunk, or not resisting enough.[35]

Psychopaths are particularly dangerous when they end up in professions, like medicine, where their clients are highly dependent on them and vulnerable. One of the most egregious examples of such professional misconduct, which could have only been carried out by a psychopath, was related to me by a young woman in a conservative foreign country. Leila M. was working as a secretary in a law firm where one of the young lawyers became interested in her. She was flattered then shocked when he propositioned her. However, when he persisted in telling her that he loved her and wanted to marry her, she yielded to him. After he got what he wanted, he lost interest. She was heartbroken, then horrified to realize that she was pregnant. She could not tell her parents without disgracing herself, nor go to a physician since abortion was illegal in that country. She did not know where to turn, until a former classmate she confided in told her about a gynecologist who performed surreptitious abortions outside of his regular practice.

Leila called and made an appointment for a Sunday afternoon when the building would be closed and no one would see her come and go. She showed up at the appointed time full of fear and embarrassment. The man who let her into the clinic was an ordinary looking person in his forties whose smile made her uneasy. After she paid him, he asked a few questions and asked her to get undressed. As she lay down for the procedure, the gynecologist strapped her arms to the table and lifted her legs into the stirrups. He began to examine her but in a manner that made her tense up and then she became horrified when she realized that he was trying to arouse her. She began to fight and scream, but there was no one to hear her. He raped her, then calmly performed the abortion and let her go.

As she sat in her car, Leila felt numb. She could not believe what had just happened to her. Then a wave of anger washed over her. She wanted to go back and stab the man. Go to the police. Run home and beg her parents' forgiveness. Most of all she felt horribly guilty. If she had not had sex, she would not have gotten pregnant, thus she would not have needed an abortion, and gotten raped. The fact that she also felt relieved for no longer being pregnant made her feel worse. She decided the only course open to her was to say and do nothing. The cost of doing anything looked prohibitive; it would have led to her disgrace and ostracism. Even having the man who had raped her unmasked and punished would not have been worth it. Over the years, she learned to live with all this, although she has hardly gotten over it.

Among antisocial characters, a pervasive pattern of disregard and violation of the rights of others appears early in life. They start by acting cruelly toward animals and grow up into adults who wreak havoc. They are reckless, disregard the safety of others, and destroy property by malicious mischief and arson. Such persons are deceitful and lie, steal habitually, default on debts, fail to provide child support or to take care of dependents. At worst, they become rapists and murderers. Such conduct lands them in jail, which does little in changing them into socially responsible individuals.

What causes the moral deficit? Jesus prayed on the cross, "Father, forgive them; for they know not what they do" (Luke 23:34). Socrates also ascribed wrongful behavior to ignorance. Does that mean that it is all a matter of not knowing any better? Perhaps there is some truth to that when ordinary people do wrong. However, the problem with psychopaths does not seem due to lack of moral knowledge. They know the rules and understand the harmful consequences of their actions, but they do not care because their *emotions* are not engaged. There is a disconnect between their moral thoughts and feelings. Their conscience malfunctions through lack of empathy.

Psychopaths refuse to take responsibility for their actions and express neither remorse nor regret (except for getting caught). In effect, the lack of guilt is so fundamental that to say that a psychopath has no guilt would be an oxymoron (whereas some other types of antisocial characters may be capable of feeling guilty). Psychopaths blame everyone but themselves: They blame society (as "corrupt"); hold their victims responsible ("they had it coming"); hide behind rationalizations ("life is unfair"); or simply do not give a damn. In short, they have a special talent of absolving themselves of moral responsibility. Some years ago, I asked a prison inmate if he would sell a nuclear weapon to a hostile country knowing that it would then be dropped on an American city. He promptly said he would. How would, then, he feel about causing the death of millions of innocent people? He said it would not bother him because he would not be dropping the bomb himself, hence he would not be "personally" responsible for anyone's death.[36]

The fact that men vastly outnumber women among psychopaths raises the possibility of differences in moral judgment due to biological (but not excluding social) factors. The sexual engagements of psychopaths, in particular, tend to be superficial, promiscuous, and exploitative (some women fall for their glibness and superficial charm). Their irresponsibility and need for instant gratification, along with their frequent abuse of drugs and alcohol, make it difficult for them to hold on to a job. However, what stands out most of all is their lack of empathy and remorse.

Psychopaths are estimated to represent only 1 percent of the American population but account for a quarter of those in jail. Psychopathy and criminality, however, do not always go together. Some criminals (for instance those who kill in a fit of jealousy) are not psychopaths. Violent antisocial behavior may also result from an inability to control anger rather than inadequate guilt. By the same token, some psychopaths engage in antisocial behavior that is not considered criminal (such as being habitually unfaithful).

Psychopathic criminals show a strong streak of sadism and are more likely than other criminals to be responsible for cold-blooded murders, brutal sexual assaults, and gratuitous and sadistic violence. When psychopaths commit crimes, they are less likely to be motivated primarily by the prospect of gain (as in burglary) but rather act in response to psychological impulses that are unrestrained by guilt.

How violent such behavior can be is illustrated in the following account by Kent Kiehl, a prominent investigator in this field. It concerns a man who, following his release from prison, had an altercation with his mother. When she tried to call the police, he was enraged ("Man, can you believe the balls on that chick"). So he wrapped the telephone cord around his mother's neck and strangled her. "Then," he said, "I threw her down the basement stairs, but I wasn't sure she was dead, so I got a kitchen knife and stabbed her, and her body made these weird noises, I guess gas escaping, but I wasn't sure, so I grabbed a big propane canister and bashed her brains in." He then went out and partied for three days before disposing of his mother's body.[37]

Although we usually equate psychopaths with violent criminals, there are others who inflict immense harm on their victims without spilling a drop of blood. Corporate scandals, such as at Enron, revealed how executive greed and malfeasance wreak havoc with people's lives. Even more spectacular is the more recent case of Bernard L. Madoff, who eventually confessed to having swindled individuals and institutions—including charitable foundations—out of sixty-five billion dollars, through a Ponzi scheme. (The Elie Wiesel foundation lost $15.2 million, while Wiesel and his wife lost their life savings.)[38]

Bernard L. Madoff appeared to be the very antithesis of the image of a criminal. He was an urbane, charming, and highly successful financier; a compassionate man who treated his employees like family; a philanthropist and pillar of his community; a man who was widely admired and courted by prominent and sophisticated people. Then, when the truth was known, he looked like a textbook case of a psychopath. What made his actions so galling was that many of the people he victimized, and the institutions he damaged, belonged to his own community. And he showed little remorse. In his widely circulated photograph, he has a faint, enigmatic, and chilling smile. His only early expression of regret was to the other tenants in his building for being inconvenienced by the media.[39] Later on, he made an unemotional admission of guilt in court.

Calling someone like Bernard L. Madoff a psychopath is comforting; labels provide explanations and make us feel better by providing us with a measure of control over baffling situations. However, they also blur the subtleties and complexities that drive men like Madoff. Financial gain is a key motivation in these cases, but insufficient as an explanation; a man of Madoff's competence could have made money some other way, or he could have avoided pushing his scheme to a point of no return. What motivated him may have also been the sense of mastery in manipulating financially sophisticated people, including regulators; reveling is in some sense a sign of invulnerability, of being above the law. His civic and philanthropic activities may not have been merely a strategic cover but a way of assuaging his guilt by making amends. Or, there was perhaps a Jekyll and Hyde duality to his character where virtue and vice coexisted side by side. Actually, what brought Madoff such notoriety was not only the nature of his wrongdoing but its scale and magnitude. There have been many others who have perpetrated Ponzi schemes (starting with Ponzi himself) and not doubt there will be others. Moreover, the reason such swindlers succeed is because of the misplaced trust, gullibility, and greed of their victims, who in some ways make their actions possible.[40]

Some antisocial personalities are not altogether free of guilt, nor of anxiety or depression (which they may fight with alcohol and drugs). Ultimately, it is the presence of guilt that differentiates antisocial personalities from psychopaths, rather than the nature of their offence. I encountered a dramatic example of this when I was a consultant to the California Youth Authority. "Jim," an 18-year-old, was in prison for killing a 3-year-old girl. She was the daughter of a teenage prostitute who worked for him. One night, when the mother was out, the child kept crying until Jim lost his temper and punched her in the stomach. By the time he got her to the hospital, the girl had died of a ruptured spleen.

This had happened several years earlier, but Jim remained greatly troubled by it, so much so that I felt moved to help alleviate his burden of guilt. I told Jim such feelings were like the flames of a fire that burned hot until the ashes gradually dampened it down; in other words, time healed. As Jim caught the drift of my comments, he began to shake his head and said, "That won't work for me." I asked why not. "Because," he replied with tears in his eyes, "my fire is like Kennedy's fire"—the eternal flame on the tomb of the president that generates no ashes. If I had read a newspaper account of what Jim had done (particularly since my own daughter at the time was about 3 years old), I would have concluded that the man had no conscience—but not after I heard his story.

A variety of biological, psychological, and social causes have been proposed to explain the dysfunctional conscience of antisocial and psychopathic personalities. Biological causes range from our evolutionary heritage (animals also cheat "shamelessly") to genetic and hormonal factors. Other explanations rely on socioeconomic conditions, such as poverty and injustice, that are thought to breed crime (even though, while many criminals are poor, most of the poor are not criminals).

None of these explanations is conclusive. In some instances biological factors are associated with psychopathy, but these are special cases. Many psychopaths come from dysfunctional homes and have been abused as children. Their lives have been characterized by early deprivation, parental separation, rejection, and deviance. However, there are countless others who come from similar backgrounds who do not become antisocial characters.

Severe antisocial behaviors are particularly disturbing when they occur in children. We may be inured to crimes committed by teenage gangs, but it is startling to learn that some twenty homicides are committed each year in the United States by children younger than ten. Some of these are particularly gruesome. In Chicago, a 5-year-old was tossed out of a window by a 10-year-old and his 11-year-old pal. In Liverpool, England, two 10-year-old boys threw more than twenty bricks at the head of a 2-year-old, then, "kicked him, tore off his lower lip, stripped him, and possibly molested him . . . and left the raggedy corpse on the train tracks" to make the murder appear accidental.[41] Do children such as this suffer from a congenital inability to feel guilty? Do they learn such behavior from television and video games that are rife with violence? We will return to these issues in the next chapter when we discuss the development of moral judgment and the capacity for guilt.

Finally, there are some people who share certain antisocial elements with criminals but are not themselves criminals. For instance, those with a *narcissistic personality* are self-centered, lack empathy, and use and abuse others for their own purposes. Similarly, *histrionic characters* are manipulative and constantly seek to be the center of attention. Some of the popular figures in the entertainment industry—who are idolized as romantic and exciting—are good examples of both personality types.

Some exciting current research focuses on the association of brain dysfunction and psychopathic behavior. An early and dramatic demonstration of this was the famous case of Phineas Gage. In 1848, this 25-year-old construction worker, a man much valued for his competence and good character, sustained a horrific brain injury. When blasting rocks, an iron rod accidentally shot through Gage's head, destroying a substantial part of his brain. He survived the injury but began to manifest personality changes. He became irreverent, indulged in gross profanity, showed little deference to others, acted capriciously, and lost his sense of responsibility and ability to plan for the future. These new traits contrasted so sharply with his previous character that he seemed to have become a new person ("Gage was no longer Gage"). He had lost his sense of social responsibility even though the rest of his intellectual functions remained intact. His case established the principle that ethical and socially responsible behavior requires an intact brain.[42] Since then, numerous other cases involving brain damage due to trauma, tumors, and surgery have reaffirmed the linkage between brain damage and failures in social functioning. Such malfunctioning is associated with lesions in the frontal lobes of the brain, particularly the orbitofrontal regions, which are involved in the regulation of social behavior, including the complex appraisal of self-conscious emotions such as embarrassment, shame, and guilt.[43] Other investigators place the problem elsewhere in the brain (such as in the amygdala) and associate psychopathy with a marked attention deficit (which impairs the exercise of moral judgment) or a lack of fear of the social consequences of antisocial behavior.

Neurologist Antonio Damasio calls these conditions *acquired sociopathy*. They are characterized by aberrant behavior, including high levels of aggression and a low tolerance for frustration, among formerly normal individuals. These individuals show a callous disregard for and an insensitivity to the feelings of others. Their disregard of social rules and lack of empathy for others lead to the sort of antisocial behavior usually associated with psychopaths.[44]

Studies such as these based on a limited number of special cases are highly instructive but they cannot be generalized. Moreover, they raise difficult questions. If their findings mean that the human conscience has a specific location in the brain, is ethical behavior simply a function of how well that "ethical center" works? Such a reductionist view is rejected by Damasio:

> I am not attempting to reduce social phenomena to biological phenomena, but rather to discuss the powerful connection between them. . . . In human societies there are social conventions and ethical rules over and above what biology already provides. . . . Does this mean that love, generosity, kindness, compassion, honesty and other commendable human characteristics are nothing but selfish, survival-oriented neurobiological regulation? . . . That is definitely *not* the case.[45]

Nagging questions remain about how to integrate moral principles and practice with neural functions. Most antisocial individuals have no demonstrable brain dysfunction, therefore we do not have a consistent causal relationship between the two. Does the brain merely provide the neural circuitry for moral feelings like a soulless computer? Whatever the answers to such questions, one thing is clear: Whatever else we may or may not need for sound moral judgment, we do need an intact brain—but an intact brain is not enough for a healthy capacity for guilt.

WHICH IS MORE DAMAGING: GUILT OR SHAME?

Guilt, rather than shame, has been the dominant moral issue in the Western world. This is true for much of its religious, philosophical, as well as literary heritage. Moreover, over the past century psychiatrists have considered guilt rather than shame as the more problematic emotion with a greater pathological potential, particularly when it occurs as part of larger clinical entities like depression. Shame in this regard has attracted much less attention.[46]

As we discussed in Chapter 1, this view has been challenged recently by psychologists who claim that it is shame rather than guilt that is the more damaging emotion. Their central argument is that shame engulfs the global self whereas guilt arises from reactions to particular transgressions. Shame leads one to deny, hide, and escape from a shame-inducing situation; guilt motivates one to take reparative action to undo the damage. Guilt enhances empathy toward others; shame disrupts it. Shame is likely to lead to anger, hostility, and blaming others; guilt leads to constructive responses to anger. A proneness to shame is associated with a wide variety of psychological symptoms (including low self-esteem, depression, anxiety) and conditions such as eating disorders and post-traumatic stress disorders. On the other hand, guilt is more effective than shame in restraining people from engaging in risky, illegal, and immoral behavior. Thus guilt is more "moral" an emotion than shame.[47] As summed up by June Tangney and Rhonda Dearing:

> In brief, shame is an extremely painful and ugly feeling that has a negative impact on interpersonal behavior. Shame-prone individuals appear relatively more likely to blame others (as well as themselves) for negative events, more prone to a seething, bitter, resentful kind of anger and hostility, and less able to empathize with others in general. Guilt, on the other hand, may not be that bad after all. Guilt-prone individuals appear better able to empathize with others and to accept responsibility for negative interpersonal events. They are relatively less prone to anger than their shame-prone peers—but when angry, these individuals appear more likely to express their anger in a fairly direct (and one might speculate, more constructive) manner.[48]

This highlighting of the damaging potential of shame is an important contribution. Clinicians have tended to understate shame's potential for harm. This is partly due to the influence of Freud's views that gave a much more prominent place to neurotic guilt than shame. The recognition of shame's potential for harm is thus long overdue and provides a necessary corrective. The same is also true for tempering the overly negative way clinicians have viewed guilt. Hence, looking at guilt in more psychologically positive terms is also a welcome corrective.

This new psychological paradigm for the pathological potential of the self-conscious emotions clearly contradicts some of the long-established views in psychiatry. And it runs counter to the assumptions of religious and philosophical traditions. There would be little point in discussing here whether empirical and experimental methods of studying guilt and shame in psychology are more or less useful than clinical or other approaches since they rely on different conceptual schemes and rules of evidence. In addition, their usefulness varies with the purposes to which their findings are put. In that sense, they are complementary.

However, there are also dissenting voices within psychology itself that are based on both methodological and conceptual grounds.[49] For instance, it has been pointed out that there is a tendency "to consider almost all negative self-evaluations as shame, and to restrict guilt to specific actions unconnected with self-judgments," in the wording of TOSCA.[50] Moreover, TOSCA's descriptions of the thoughts and actions associated with experiences of guilt and shame involve relatively minor or isolated mishaps.[51] In studies using such instruments, guilt emerges as the more adaptive and positive emotion because these studies use measures that rely on the sort of clear moral violations for which subjects would normally feel guilty. Furthermore, the damage such guilt causes can be readily repaired. In other words, more "healthy" forms of guilt seem to be compared with "unhealthy" forms of shame.

The proponents of the new view agree that some forms of guilt do carry a significant pathological potential. However, they attribute this mainly to the "contamination" of guilt with shame. Otherwise, they consider "shame-free guilt" to be largely unrelated to psychological dysfunction. However, shame-free guilt may sound like nicotine-free cigarettes or nonalcoholic wine. Without nicotine, a cigarette is not a cigarette and alcohol-free wine is grape juice. Given the inevitable overlap between shame and guilt, the search for their "pure" forms may itself be futile. And even if there were such a thing as shame-free guilt, it would be too "anemic" an emotion to serve any meaningful social or moral function.[52]

An even more central concern arises in making the issue of global involvement of the self the primary, if not the sole, criterion in differentiation between guilt and shame. The question is not if global involvement of the self is significant in determining how damaging an emotion is; that seems self-evident. Rather, the question is if this happens only with shame but not guilt. If we start by defining shame on the basis that in involves the global self, then the conclusion that it is the more damaging emotion becomes a self-fulfilling prophecy. If, however, we make the engaging of the self the criterion of how damaging either shame or guilt can be, then we may reach more even-handed conclusions.

Consequently, there is no warrant for calling shame an "ugly feeling" any more than there is for considering guilt in its pure form an unalloyed blessing. It would make better sense to view guilt and shame as we do other emotions, such as fear and anger. They are neither good nor bad in themselves, but just part of our nature. They become a blessing or a curse depending on how they are used. In light of this, the new perspective on shame and guilt does well by pointing to the beneficial effects of guilt, but errs in downplaying its potential for damage; conversely, it does well by pointing to the damage that shame does, but errs by downplaying its beneficial uses. This will become even clearer after we discuss the relatively greater reliance of Asian religions and cultures on shame rather than guilt as the primary moral sentiment of social control.[53]

DEALING WITH PATHOLOGICAL GUILT

If the nature and intensity of guilt raise it to the level of being pathological, then, by necessity, dealing with it requires professional help. A key consideration here is whether the experience of guilt is part of a larger psychiatric illness, such as depression, or exists independently. If guilt is part of a larger entity, then treatment is aimed at dealing with the illness, rather than the guilt itself that is one of its symptoms.

As we discussed in connection with post-traumatic stress disorders, an array of psychiatric and psychological methods is available to treat such conditions, ranging from the use of drugs to psychotherapy and cognitive-behavior therapy; most effective is a combination of methods. The treatment of depression by drugs typically relies on antidepressants, which fall into several groups. Of these, selective serotonin reuptake inhibitors (SSRIs) are most commonly used. They include drugs like Prozac and Zoloft, which are some of the most heavily prescribed drugs in the United States. Antidepressants work by controlling the chemical imbalances in the brain that influence mood. These medicines may take some time to be effective, but they work well and are generally safe. The treatment of OCD by drugs is also mostly through SSRIs, which increase the level of the neurotransmitter serotonin.

In cases where severe guilt is the primary symptom, psychotherapy and cognitive-behavior therapy may be used to help the person deal with it. Each of these approaches in turn includes a variety of techniques. For instance, insight-oriented psychotherapy aims at helping the patient understand the psychological roots of the problem. It often entails delving into the past as well as understanding the patient's current interpersonal relationships. Cognitive-behavior therapy also has variants and may, for instance, help the person understand how one's thoughts, rather than people, situations, or events, determine how one feels. Thus changing the way we think will in turn change the way we feel. Ironically, the very fact that one has psychological problems, or is in psychotherapy, may itself cause shame and guilt. Moreover, since facing problems, let alone repressed conflicts, is painful, those in therapy often resist the therapist's efforts to help them understand the roots of their problems.

Difficult as dealing with excessive guilt may be, it pales by comparison with dealing with inadequate guilt. Currently, we have no effective ways of treating or managing the lives of psychopaths. Everything from drugs, psychotherapy, group therapy, and behavior therapy to castration of sex offenders has been tried. (Currently the same effects as castration can be obtained by treatment with testosterone-antagonist drugs.) This does not make a child molester change his (most are in fact men) sexual orientation, but it does diminish the drive to act out his sexual impulses. Each of these methods may well have helped some psychopaths, but their results generally have been inconsistent and disappointing. A better understanding of the brain mechanisms involved in psychopathy may lead to more effective chemical treatments.

So far we have been dealing with guilt as it exists in our present experience. However, a true understanding of any issue requires that we learn about its origins and development. We need to know how moral judgment and the capacity for guilt develop within an individual, particularly during childhood. It is this subject that we turn to in the next chapter. Then, in Chapter 7, we will consider how the capacity for guilt developed within the human species through evolution. These two chapters will bring to a close our examination of guilt from primarily the perspective of individual psychology.

6 THE DEVELOPMENT OF MORAL JUDGMENT

WE HAVE SO FAR concerned ourselves with various experiences of guilt and delineating when guilt is healthy and when it is not. Now we need to go behind the scenes, as it were, and examine how the capacity for moral judgment that underlies the experience of guilt develops within an individual's lifetime. I must forewarn you that some of this chapter is quite theoretical, in the sense that it deals with concepts and ideas rather descriptions of human behaviors. That does not mean, however, that it should only be of academic interest. Theory is essential for providing an intellectual framework for understanding guilt.

There is a widely shared belief, almost an intuitive understanding, that human beings are endowed with the capacity to make moral judgments. This is an essential part of our humanity which sets us apart from animals. This capacity may be taken as given by God, part of our evolutionary heritage, a product of socialization in childhood, or a combination of such factors. Moral responsibility is closely tied to the idea of *free will*—another quintessential human quality—which enables us to make moral choices and constitutes the justification for holding people responsible for their actions.

The agency that allows us to make moral judgments is our *conscience*—a moral compass that points to what is right and wrong. How does the conscience develop? While there are various theories, it is clear that its primary development takes place during childhood. Freud introduced the concept of

I am grateful to Anne Fernald, James Gross, and Cendri Hutcherson for their critique of and help with this chapter.

the *superego*, which dominated clinical practice for almost a century. While no longer as widely accepted, it retains its historical importance and has become part of our mainstream understanding of how moral capacity operates. Consequently, we will start with one of Freud's famous case histories that has a direct bearing on how the conscience develops.

"Little Hans" was the 5-year-old son of a Viennese couple who belonged to Freud's circle of adherents (his mother had been Freud's patient). Hans was a precocious child raised in a permissive manner. He showed a frank interest in sexual matters and talked about them freely. Hans developed a fear that a white horse would bite him. He became afraid to leave the house and the phobia of the horse developed into a serious problem. Hans's father consulted Freud and they agreed that the father would embark on a "psychoanalysis" of his son under Freud's direction. The case history that Freud later published was mainly based on the father's reports. Freud spoke with the boy only once.[1]

Hans's father attributed the boy's anxieties to the excessive tenderness of the mother. He was concerned that Hans was preoccupied with his penis (which he called the "widdler") and was stimulating himself sexually. Initially, Hans had to be prodded into recognizing the sources of his symptoms, but he gradually became adept at interpreting them in his childlike way (which greatly endeared him to Freud).

The story that gradually emerged is as follows. While growing up, Hans had become aware of the pleasurable effects of stimulating his penis and had developed sexual feelings toward his playmates. However, the primary object of his affections and erotic longings was his mother, who doted on him. Hans was particularly fond of cuddling with her in bed, which his father disapproved of. Although Hans was very fond of his father as well and had a close relationship with him, he began to see him as a rival for his mother's affection, and he resented his father's intrusion into their relationship. He began to wish that his father would go away on trips more frequently and eventually hoped that the father would be gone altogether. Freud described Hans's feelings for his mother:

> Some kind of vague notion was struggling in the child's mind of something he might do with his mother by means of which his taking possession of her would be consummated. . . . "I should like," he seems to have been saying, "to be doing with my mother, something forbidden; I do not know what it is, but I know that [my father] is doing it too."[2]

When Hans's mother became pregnant and gave birth to his younger sister, he became more aware of sexual matters. He suspected that his father had something to do with his mother's pregnancy (having figured out that the story of the stork was nonsense). He then developed the wish to have children with his mother himself. As Hans watched his little sister being bathed, he wondered if she too had a penis. He was preoccupied with the fact that his father had a bigger penis than he did. This then became linked in his mind with horses having large penises.

Freud instructed the father to tell Hans that only boys and men had penises. This raised the frightening prospect for Hans that he could lose his penis and become like his sister. The idea had already been implanted in his mind when his mother had told him earlier that if he did not stop touching his "widdler" the doctor would cut it off.

Hans was in a dilemma. He was torn between his love for his mother and his love for his father. He wanted his mother all for himself but realized that she belonged to his father as well. If Hans tried to displace his father, he was afraid his father would retaliate. Even if he could get rid of his father, he did not want to lose him:

> This father, whom he could not help hating as a rival, was the same father whom he had always loved and was bound to go on loving, who had been his model, had been his first playmate, and looked after him from his earliest infancy: and this. . . . gave rise to his first conflict.[3]

> Hans's anxiety had two constituents: There was fear *of* father and fear *for* his father. The former was derived from his hostility towards his father, and the latter from the conflict between his affection, which was exaggerated at this point by way of compensation, and his hostility.[4]

Little Hans had developed an "Oedipus Complex." Since there was no way of satisfying his forbidden wishes, he dealt with them by *repressing* them. Burying them in his mind was the next best thing to not having them. Nonetheless, these thoughts and feelings would not disappear and Hans's fear of his father was transformed into a phobia of horses.

The symbolic choice of the horse was the result of a number of chance events: Hans had seen the father of a little girl across the street go away in a horse-drawn cart (just as Hans wished his own father would do). On another occasion, Hans saw a horse pulling a cart fall down (which is what

Hans wanted his father to do—fall down and die). It is through these and related associations that Hans equated his threatening father with a horse that would come and bite him for his evil thoughts; or more precisely, bite off his penis as a way of punishing and "neutralizing" him (Freud called it "castration anxiety").

Hans was not aware of any of these thoughts smoldering in his unconscious, hence he could not deal with them. When he became conscious of them, the phobia of the horse disappeared and the analysis ended. What does the case of Little Hans have to do with the development of conscience and feelings of guilt? Freud considered the Oedipal conflict, as played out in Hans's story, to be the crucible in which the superego was forged, as we shall discuss shortly.

CONSCIENCE AND GUILT

The words *conscience* and *consciousness* both come from the Latin verb "to know" (*conscire*). To be conscious is to be aware, and it is the conscience that makes us aware of the difference between right and wrong. It determines the moral quality of our feelings, thoughts, words, and acts. It is the sting and bite of conscience that induces the gnawing feeling of guilt.

> Almost by definition [conscience] must be understood to be as vast as consciousness and as complex as the mind itself. No faculty of the mind—intellect, imagination, judgment, and will—nor any passion of the spirit, however subtle, can be understood to be without a relation to conscience. Conscience in turn, is joined so intimately to a person that it is considered to be inseparable from his personality, temperament, character, and habits. Likewise, conscience is not discussed without reference to the person's society and its traditions, laws, customs, and values.[5]

Religious Views of Conscience

Concepts of moral judgment are integral to religious beliefs and practices.[6] All religions encourage moral reflection and self-evaluation. However, the concept of a discrete moral agency based on free will has been particularly prominent in Christianity, although its antecedents can be traced to older traditions in Judaism.[7]

In the Old Testament, God is privy to every thought and feeling we harbor. The Psalmist prays, "Search me, O God, and know my heart. Try me and know my thoughts! And see if there be any wicked way in me" (Ps. 139:23–24). In the Judaic tradition, a person becomes morally responsible for observing the Law after attaining maturity at age thirteen.

These themes reach their full force in the New Testament, particularly in the letters of St. Paul. In Romans 2:15, Paul sees conscience as a witness within everyone, including pagans. It is a gift of God that represents the Law as written in their hearts. Paul's conception reflects the earlier views of Philo, the Hellenistic Jewish philosopher of Alexandria, who saw conscience as the true self within every individual, which acts as a judge and umpire, witness and accuser—a source of "reproof." Philo had the serene notion that God welcomes a contrite heart; for Paul, God requires a broken heart and conscience takes on a more accusatory and judgmental tone.[8]

The church fathers whose teachings shaped the early medieval church retained the notion of conscience as the inner moral voice of divine origin. Present in all human beings, its voice is obeyed to please God. The most influential of these patristic figures in the Western church was St. Augustine, who blended into the Latin term *conscientia* ("conscience") divine judgment, moral self-evaluation, and introspection.[9] In his *Confessions*, the voice of his conscience resonates with his sense of guilt: "Indeed, Lord . . . what could be hidden within me, even if I were unwilling to confess it to you? . . . My groaning is witness that I am displeased with myself. . . . I am ashamed of myself and reject myself. You are my choice, and only by your gift can I please either you or myself."[10]

In the late Middle Ages the notion of conscience was developed more fully into a theory of moral judgment. The Scholastics, who taught in the early universities of Europe, ascribed two functions to moral judgment: *Synderesis* is the God-given innate capacity to know the moral law that enables us to grasp moral principles, and *conscientia* is the faculty that applies the moral law to concrete cases. It connected knowledge to moral action, not unlike our idea of conscience as a moral agency. *Synderesis* is divine and never errs; *conscientia* is a witness to our actions, and like any other witness, it can err.[11]

In 1215 the Catholic church instituted the obligation to confess one's sins and receive communion at least once a year. Known as the *tribunal of conscience*, this was to help bring the lives of Christians into closer conformity with moral principles. The church took a keen interest in moral instruction and developed catechisms, which conveyed the principles of Christianity in the form of questions and answers.

The idea of *stages* of moral development emerged as early as the thirteenth century when St. Thomas Aquinas drew on the analogy between the development of charity (*caritas*) and physical and intellectual maturation. In its first stage, one withdraws from sin and resists the appetites that lead to vice. Next, one becomes proficient in the good, thus moving from a reactive to a proactive stance.

The Protestant Reformation in the sixteenth century recast the Catholic conception of conscience in a new light. Luther considered the Christian conscience oppressed and weighed down by human laws and practices that passed as church doctrine. As the heir to the spiritual legacy of Paul and Augustine, Luther saw himself as the militant defender of the *freedom of conscience* that made one directly accountable to God. Luther viewed the church as having failed as a guide to the conscience of believers. Human efforts to please God with good deeds could not produce a clear conscience no matter how hard one tried. This plunged Luther into despair until he realized that he could be justified through faith but not good works.

Luther's Reformation rejected the idea of a tribunal of conscience and abandoned the practice of confession to priests. Freed by grace, Christians received a clear conscience as a gift from God directly and without intermediaries. Only God could judge the human heart. Thus Luther felt his conscience to be safe in God's hands, free of the need to please others and immune to their opinions. Conscience was not an agency of the church, nor its moral police; it was only answerable to God. The Counter-Reformation in the seventeenth century eventually narrowed the breach between the Protestant and Catholic doctrines, thus establishing a more consistent Christian view of the conscience.

In the eighteenth century the English theologian Bishop Joseph Butler provided conscience with its modern philosophical underpinnings, while retaining some of its religious roots. Butler argued that one's moral sense was based on a *rational* consciousness of right and wrong rather than on faith alone. Nonetheless, he claimed for it divine authority: God instills within us "a principle of reflection" through which we disapprove of actions like fraud and injustice. Conscience stands on its own authority—it is not just a method of social control.[12]

This self-confident Christian conscience had serious political consequences. Armed with their sense of moral certainty, Europeans came to see their destiny as the saviors of "inferior" people whose consciences were compromised by false beliefs and superstitions. This provided the moral justification for colonial subjugation, which was thus undertaken with a clear conscience.

Secular Views of Conscience

The secular idea of a moral agency goes back to Plato and Aristotle. In the *Republic*, Plato devised a curriculum for teaching virtue to the future leaders of the ideal Greek city-state. It was not until men reached the age of thirty that they attained moral maturity through a philosophical understanding of the concept of the Good. Conscience for Plato was a rational faculty for recognizing the Good.[13]

Aristotle thought of conscience as linked to self-indulgence and self-control. The self-indulgent person feels no regrets over wrong actions, whereas the person lacking self-control does feel guilty. (The first would be a case of inadequate guilt; the second of moral weakness.) The self-indulgent person has no incentive to change and is not curable; the person who lacks self-control is.[14]

In the Hellenistic period, the Greek Stoics became particularly concerned with moral issues that led to a good and happy life. Stoic ethics was founded on the principle that virtue is good and vice is bad, while things like health, wealth, and honor are morally indifferent. As we develop our rationality, our choices require sacrificing some natural preferences for the sake of others. For example, one may forego the accumulation of excessive wealth for the common good. Stoics also saw morality as being rooted in the impulse for self-preservation. This made what is virtuous accord with what is natural.

The idea of conscience became more explicit with Roman thinkers like Cicero. For Cicero conscience represents an internal moral authority that evokes pleasurable feelings in response to good deeds and unpleasant feelings for bad deeds: "Great is the power of conscience," Cicero writes, "great for bliss or for bane."[15] Good conscience is independent of public opinion and has more authority than the applause of any audience.

For René Descartes—the leading philosopher of the seventeenth century—conscience is more autonomous, skeptical, socially oriented, and secular. Descartes drew a sharper distinction between the idea of conscience and consciousness. Conscience is a firm and stable moral entity, while consciousness is ephemeral and vague. In the eighteenth century, models of moral development became more explicit. Jean Jacques Rousseau put forth the idea that individuals pass through age-related stages of maturation, a model of moral development that persists to this day. Rousseau had an idyllic view of human nature in its original form. Early humans were "noble savages," but the development of society required that individual freedom give way to a "social contract" binding people in mutually agreed rules of governance. Moral behavior is part of this contract between people, not a covenant with God. Especially significant is Rousseau's idea that a child's thinking matures over time. During the earlier stages leading to adolescence, children are incapable of moral judgment; it is only after adolescence that a person can be held morally accountable.[16]

In the nineteenth century there followed an even stronger emphasis on the importance of conscious moral choices over merely obeying social conventions. Goethe has Faust reject his conscience to expand his consciousness instead. In Dostoevsky's *Notes from the Underground*, conscience turns obsessive; it is a stern judge in an oppressive inner court where the self is the accuser as well as the accused. When detached from social life, conscience leads to retrospective, solitary, and relentless self-condemnation.

In the late nineteenth and early twentieth centuries, Emile Durkheim, one the founders of sociology, addressed issues related to conscience from a societal perspective.[17] To act morally is to further the collective interest. It requires that one obey moral authority, as determined by a particular society, and exercise sympathy in dealing with others. John Dewey, the influential American philosopher and theorist of education, described three levels of moral development in his *Ethics*.[18] At the first level, one is driven by biological and social needs and desires that have no moral motivation. Next, one accepts the moral standards and customs of society more or less uncritically. In the last stage, action is based on one's own values and moral judgments whereby one becomes more rational, social, and ethical. The result is a person with a deeper set of social connections as well as interests in artistic and religious pursuits.

Despite its vicissitudes, conscience has retained a positive character. As Aristotle pointed out, no matter how perversely human beings behave, there will always remain the realization that one must do good and avoid evil. As Freud put it with respect to reason, the voice of conscience is soft, but persistent. We may give up on it, but it never gives up on us.[19]

The Superego and Unconscious Guilt

Freud attached great importance to the case of Little Hans but not because he learned anything new from it. He already had formulated his theory about the Oedipal conflict from his adult patients. However, whereas he had reconstructed this psychological process among adults, with Little Hans he could see it developing in real time, thus confirming for him the validity of his theory.

First, the experience of Little Hans demonstrated the existence of infantile sexuality. The sexual impulse, or *libido*, did not arise at puberty but was already present in childhood, albeit suppressed by society and repressed by the individual. Moreover, that sexual element was a key component in the psychological and social development of the individual and a critical determinant of the person's subsequent mental health and emotional well-being.

Second, the culminating event in the child's psychosexual development was the resolution of the Oedipus complex. Earlier, the sexual impulse was invested in bodily orifices and represented immature ("pre-genital") forms of sexuality. Most important, the resolution of the Oedipus complex resulted in the development of the *superego*. Conversely, the development of the superego made possible the resolution of the Oedipal conflict.

These ideas might sound quite improbable if we attribute to them an adult quality. However, infantile conflicts must be understood in the elementary terms accessible to a child's mind. At this age, children have a hazy idea of sexuality. Obviously, children could never fulfill their Oedipal wishes. Little Hans could never replace his father, or *be* his father; he could only be *like* his father by identifying with him. He could not have *his* mother, but one day could have a woman *like* his mother and establish his own claims as a husband. (This model applies to girls also, but is more convoluted.) Consequently, Oedipal impulses must not only be *suppressed*, by being consciously set aside, but also *repressed*—buried in the unconscious—so that the child cannot even be aware of their presence. These impulses may leak out, but only in disguised form in neurotic symptoms (such as Hans's horse phobia), in dreams (Freud called them the royal road to the unconscious), and in other forms (like slips of the tongue).

The Greek tragedy *King Oedipus*, by Sophocles, explored this human drama twenty-five centuries before Freud tapped into it to develop the first comprehensive model for the development of a psychological moral agency—the *superego*. In Freud's model, *conscience* is the *conscious* moral entity that embodies socially defined moral precepts whose violation results in what he called remorse. The superego, by contrast, is primarily an *unconscious* entity and the violation of its precepts leads to *unconscious* guilt, as we discussed earlier. The conscience is subject to change as individuals rationally rework their moral principles; the superego remains fixed in the unconscious, hence is not subject to reason. The superego is thus harsher, more uncompromising, and more punitive than the conscience. When the superego is particularly harsh, it leads to pathological guilt.[20]

The *id* represents "instinctual energy" that is experienced as a psychological drive—a motivational impulse or state of arousal that pushes for gratification. The libido fuels the sexual impulse experienced as erotic pleasure and serves reproductive functions. The second key instinct—aggression—enables mastery of the environment, the acquisition of vital goods, and overcoming of forces injurious to the self.[21]

The instinctual needs of the id should not be indulged freely yet must be allowed some gratification, albeit in sublimated or camouflaged forms that are socially acceptable. For instance, aggressive impulses are sublimated through competitive sports where one fights within rules. The task of reconciling these competing demands of the id and social constraints falls to the *ego*—the rational component of the self. The id heedlessly follows the *pleasure principle*; the ego abides by the *reality principle*, which takes into account the limitations and constraints of the social environment.[22]

The young child is not born with a superego and hence cannot experience guilt. This leaves the ego to deal with the unruly impulses of the id. It is a thankless job. The ego relies on reason, which is not the id's strong suit. Help comes when the superego develops and acts as judge and jury of moral behavior. Ego and superego now combine forces in dealing with the id—the ego uses sweet reason; the superego cracks the moral whip.[23]

The superego is a mixed blessing. It is an ally of the ego in restraining the id. Yet it can be just as irrational as the id. If its harsh and uncompromising demands are not reined in, it ruins one's life. Thus the id must be controlled but not crushed; the superego must be attended to, but not blindly obeyed. It is a balancing act where the instinctual demands of the id, the strictures of the superego, and the dictates of society must be reconciled. Guilt is a key player in bringing this about, but it too may be a blessing or a bane.

C. G. Jung disagreed with Freud's single-minded emphasis on the psychosexual origins of conscience and focused more on a lifelong process of *individuation* that led toward integration and wholeness. Jung proposed a twofold conscience: a *moral conscience*, which is more or less similar to the superego; and an *ethical conscience*, which arises from critical reflection when faced with conflicts between duties. Hence, the latter constitutes a more mature form of moral reasoning with philosophical and religious overtones. Rather than being a battleground between the superego and id, the ethical conscience entails an internal dialogue with one's own wiser inward self (the *Thou*).[24]

Psychoanalyst Erik Erikson revised Freud's theory of psychological development into a model that encompasses the entire human life cycle from infancy to old age, not just the early years of childhood.[25] His model, which became popular in the 1960s, divided the life span into eight stages of *psychosocial* (rather than *psychosexual*) development, thus emphasizing the importance of the social components.[26] Guilt and shame play key roles in Erikson's model.

Erikson believed that by about age two children have a mind of their own and know the difference between "me" and "you." Sweet and gentle one minute, contrary and willful the next, they erupt in anger if their will is frustrated ("the terrible twos"). This stage of development normally ends with the formation of a sense of *autonomy*; failure to achieve autonomy results in *shame* and *doubt*. Erikson linked the origin of shame with the self-consciousness that results from being exposed and looked at. In this unruly period, children need both parental love and restraint. Shaming may be effective in restraining the child, but too much shame may push the child into taking refuge in shamelessness.[27]

The sense of autonomy establishes the child as a person; but what kind of person is the child going to be? Children look up to their parents as the most important people in their lives. They identify with them and want to be like them. Children's increasing motor ability to move about and their developing ability to communicate expand their imagination and make their behavior more intrusive and aggressive. Children come to engage in more overt sexual play and exploration. Gender identity develops beyond being a boy or girl and acquires the characteristics of *masculinity* and *femininity*. Greater initiative becomes synonymous with action; hence the need to know how to behave and not to behave. The positive outcome of this third stage is *initiative*; failure at this stage results in *guilt*. Out of this conflict develops the capacity for moral judgment. Erikson says:

> The child . . . now hears, as it were, God's voice without seeing God. Moreover, he begins automatically to feel guilty even for mere thoughts and for deeds which nobody has watched. This is the cornerstone of morality in the individual sense. But from the point of view of mental health, we must point out that if this great achievement is overburdened by all too eager adults, it can be bad for the spirit and for morality itself. For the conscience of the child *can* be primitive, cruel, and uncompromising, as may be observed in instances where children learn to constrict themselves to the point of over-all inhibition;

where they develop an obedience more literal than the one the parent wishes to exact.[28]

The Freudian model of the superego is widely invoked by clinicians and humanists. In effect, it has become part of our folk psychology of moral judgment. However, the concept of the superego has no purchase on the thinking of behavioral scientists and clinicians outside the Freudian fold. Psychologists in particular are skeptical that the Oedipal conflict represents a universal stage in human development or is the basis of the development of human moral agency. They cannot empirically confirm these claims, and thus they remain neither proven nor disproven.

Currently, there is no single overarching theory of moral development in psychology corresponding in its scope to the Freudian model. Instead, what we have are a number of theories of moral development based on empirical studies that highlight one or another aspect of moral maturation. It is to these that we turn next.

Social Learning Models of Guilt

When psychology emerged as a scientific discipline in the nineteenth century, its pioneers relied on introspection and self-observation to study thoughts and feelings. At the turn of the twentieth century, John B. Watson took psychology in a radically different direction. His theories, known as *behaviorism*, were to dominate psychology for the next fifty years and remain quite influential, as is seen in, for example, the work of B. F. Skinner.

Behaviorism is the study of observable behaviors. These include not only actions but thoughts and feelings as well. Moreover, all behavior is learned. As Watson claimed, "Give me a dozen healthy infants, well-formed, and my own specified world to bring them up in, and I'll guarantee to take any one at random and train him to be any type of specialist . . . doctor, lawyer, artist, merchant-chief and, yes, even beggarman and thief!"[29]

Behaviorists explain moral behavior in terms of "conditioning history": events to which individuals are exposed and their response to them. Moral judgment develops in response to contingencies—unpredictable events—in the social environment. We behave a certain way and are rewarded; we behave some other way and are punished. Thereby we learn how to behave so as to be rewarded and not be punished. Since at some level life experiences are unique to the individual, the behaviorist approach does not envisage general stages of moral development.[30]

In a strictly behaviorist approach, guilt is just another product of social conditioning. Watson could presumably create guilt-ridden or guilt-free individuals on demand.

Social learning theorists now deviate from this strictly behaviorist line. In addition to reward and punishment experienced at the personal level, they ascribe a role to observational learning whereby we learn from the experience of others. Seeing your older sibling being punished for lying teaches you not to lie; you do not have to be punished yourself in order to learn a lesson.

By making morality a purely social construct, behaviorism leaves little room for the exercise of free will. There is no intrinsic or abstract moral principle regulating behavior, no abstract entity called conscience except as the pooled residue of past learning.

The ways that child-rearing practices reinforce these tendencies vary in different cultures. American parents discipline their children primarily for breaking rules. They induce them to reflect on the consequences of their misdeeds by suspending privileges, by grounding and time outs. They consider an appropriate level of remorse as a way to strengthen the child's sense of moral responsibility.

Japanese mothers (who are the primary disciplinarians) use ridicule and embarrassment to induce the child to behave properly. Instead of trying to induce guilt, they resort to ostracism by ignoring the child. The child may cry and scream to get the mother's attention only to be ignored; the child may even be locked out of the house. (Americans find this cruel, while Japanese mothers are appalled at how children are handled in the United States.) In each case, the punishment reflects the fundamental values of each culture. Taking privileges away strikes at the child's sense of autonomy; ridicule and ostracism convey to the child the risk of rejection, social exclusion, and abandonment.

Learning theorists include cognition in the process of socialization; hence their developmental models are referred to as *social cognitive theories*.[31] Cognition provides the capacity to interpret social symbols, to foresee the probable consequences of one's actions, and to act accordingly. In the next set of theories, cognition takes center stage.

COGNITIVE-DEVELOPMENTAL MODELS OF MORAL JUDGMENT

Children need to develop a certain level of cognitive ability to think and reason. Since young children lack such an ability, we cannot hold them accountable for moral choices. Innate moral capacity is not enough; we need to teach children how to behave morally. Morality is like language. We are born with the capacity to use language, but whether we speak Spanish or English depends on what language we learn to speak. The same is true for moral judgment.

The first systematic studies of this issue were carried out by Swiss psychologist Jean Piaget in the 1930s. Based on his observations of childhood behavior, Piaget set out a theory of moral development that entailed two main modes of moral reasoning: pre-moral and moral. During the first few years, the child has no conception of morality based on a real consciousness or comprehension of rules. This pre-moral state is followed by two moral stages of development: the morality of constraint and the morality of cooperation.[32]

The *morality of constraint* (characteristic of ages four to eight) is based on the unquestioning obedience to adult rules, which the child accepts as absolute, unchangeable, and applicable under all circumstances. "Right and wrong" is understood by the child as conformity to rules, with no clear understanding of their derivation or justification. You do what you are told, and never mind why.

The *morality of cooperation* (ages eight to ten) develops in children based on their interactions with their peers. Rules are no longer imposed from above and immutable; they are created and modified by mutual agreement among children and aimed at common interests. Responsibility shifts from the *consequences* of actions to the *intention* behind the actions. At earlier ages, a child judges events in terms of the magnitude of the damage. For instance, breaking ten cups would be worse than breaking one cup. However, as the child's moral reasoning becomes more sophisticated, breaking one cup intentionally becomes worse than breaking ten cups accidentally.

This maturation of thinking makes possible the move from *concrete* to *abstract* reasoning. Concrete thinking differentiates between specific instances of good actions and bad actions. For instance, Barbara observes that her friend Amy shares her toys with her friends and helps her younger sister get dressed. She identifies these as two separate good actions but does not connect them. Abstract thinking allows Barbara to make that connection and to think of Amy as a *kind* person. Being kind is an abstract idea that applies to any number of good actions.

Psychologist Lawrence Kohlberg expanded Piaget's ideas into a more comprehensive theory of moral development based on stages of cognitive maturation.[33] In this scheme, socialization still counts but it is contingent on the child's intellectual readiness for it. We generally credit or blame parents for their children's moral qualities. Yet parents may not be solely, or even primarily, responsible for them (which may free some from the nagging question, "What did we do wrong?").

Kohlberg was interested in how his subjects reached their moral judgments, not the moral value of the judgments themselves. He studied a group of American boys by presenting them a story involving a moral dilemma to see how they reasoned their way through it. They were then retested periodically over the next twenty years to determine changes in their moral reasoning. The scenario involved a woman who was dying of a form of cancer for which a local pharmacist had discovered a drug that would save her life. However, he was charging an exorbitant price for it and the woman's husband could not afford it. He asked the pharmacist to reduce the price, but the pharmacist refused. So he stole the drug to save his wife's life. Was the husband right or wrong in what he did and why?

There are no right or wrong answers to these questions. The point is to determine how subjects reach moral conclusions—that is, the moral reasoning behind their answers. Based on their responses, Kohlberg proposed six stages of moral development reflecting progressively more sophisticated forms of moral judgment.

The first two stages constitute *pre-conventional* morality, where one accepts and applies culturally defined moral standards of right and wrong. Stage 1 has a punishment-and-obedience orientation: You obey the rules and avoid punishment. Stage 2 shifts to a reward-and-reciprocity orientation: Do the right thing and others will return the favor. Stage 3 ushers in *conventional morality*, where one conforms to social expectations by doing what is considered to be right and avoiding wrong. It begins with the good-boy / good-girl orientation of children and moves on in Stage 4 to the law-and-order orientation of adults, where rules and regulations define what is moral. We readily recognize these levels of moral judgment since they apply to most people.

The last two stages consist of *post-conventional morality*. The basis of morality now rests on one's autonomous conscience. Social expectations matter but are not paramount. It is the moral principle that counts. Stage 5 is predicated on the idea of social contracts, where moral action is based on what people freely agree on as the common good. Finally, we come to Stage 6, where universal ethical principles guide one's conduct based on justice, equality, and human dignity.[34]

Along the same lines, James Fowler has a theory of *faith development*, which closely follows Kohlberg's developmental stages. For instance, in Stage 3 one's faith reflects the conventional beliefs of one's society. In the next stage, faith becomes more individualistic. Stage 6 culminates in a universalizing faith defined by a feeling of being at one with God. Those who reach this stage invest their lives in larger causes irrespective of personal cost. These stages also bear on moral development and the experience of guilt.[35]

Kohlberg's theory was dominant for several decades, but it has now come under criticism based on his methodology and the applicability of his findings across genders and cultures. His primarily cognitive approach to moral development does not pay sufficient attention to the role of emotions and to the way children are socialized at home, in school, and through peer interactions.[36] There is good empirical evidence that some forms of moral reasoning are already present in very young children. Children as young as two may already show a "moral sense," although the content of that sense may vary from individual to individual. Preschool children learn the need to adhere to standards of correct behavior and get distressed when they fail to do so. Therefore, at least the antecedents of moral judgment are present much earlier than postulated in cognitive developmental models.[37]

INTEGRATIVE MODELS OF MORAL JUDGMENT

Historically, psychology focused on developing theoretical models that were universal and applicable to all cultures (like theories in the natural sciences). Currently, there is a move away from such overarching formulations and instead toward models that are more culturally specific. Applied to guilt, this means looking for different ways in which the capacity for guilt develops in social settings instead of searching for a single basic model of guilt that works everywhere.[38]

This new perspective is coupled with a more integrative approach that does not dwell on a single aspect of mental functioning, like cognition, but brings together the affective, cognitive, and other developmental aspects of moral judgment. The work of psychologist Martin Hoffman has been influential in ushering in this more integrative approach. Hoffman's theory of moral development is based on *empathy*—a key concept we referred to earlier.

Empathy is understanding and sharing the feelings of another person, as we noted earlier in connection with interpersonal relationships.[39] Empathy is essential for the experience of guilt. However, simply knowing that we have hurt someone is not enough to induce guilt. We need both a cognitive awareness of having done something wrong and the affective capacity to share the other person's emotional distress in order to feel guilty. Thus, *empathic distress* is the response to another's pain and discomfort ("sharing one's pain"); in that sense, it overlaps with sympathy. *Empathy-based guilt* is the negative feeling about oneself in response to having hurt someone.[40] The capacity of empathic distress appears to be innate. It is already present in infants, who cry when they hear other infants cry.[41] This is a very specific response that does not occur in response to the crying of adults or chimpanzee babies; therefore, the infant's crying is not due to being startled by the noise or some other extraneous factor.

Hoffman assumes a common core of empathy for both negative ("You shall not") and positive ("You shall") forms of moral injunctions. His developmental sequence starts very early and goes through several stages. During the first year of life, infants cannot differentiate between their self and others. They respond to the distress of others as if it were their own. Thus there is no basis for feeling guilty. During their second year, children become more aware of their difference from others. This allows them to empathize with the distress of others without confusing it with their own. (One child who saw her mother crying put her pacifier in her mother's mouth.)

The sense of guilt appears in the context of an emerging sense of relatedness. In the third year, children become more aware that the feelings of others may differ from their own. As they acquire language, they can express a broader and more complex set of feelings, which allows them to articulate their distress for having done wrong. By late childhood and early adolescence, there is a clearer sense of having one's own distinct personality and sense of identity. This allows experiencing negative and positive feelings that go beyond reactions to immediate circumstances, such as feeling sorry for someone who gets hurt; one can also empathize with others for being poor or persecuted.[42] As with other psychological characteristics, adult versions of guilt become consolidated during adolescence.

Current studies identify two components in the development of conscience in children: biologically based *temperament* and *socialization* in the family. Out of their interaction emerges an inner guidance system for self-regulation. It is these inner guidance mechanisms that constitute conscience as a psychological entity.[43] The early conscience encompasses three interrelated mechanisms of control: emotional, behavioral (or executive), and cognitive. Guilt is the moral emotion that infuses misdeeds—actual or contemplated—with negative feelings. Moral conduct reflects the child's executive capacity to abide by the rules, and moral cognition reflects the child's growing understanding of rules and standards of conduct and the negative consequences of violating them. These strands come together rather than vie with each other as competing explanations of moral behavior.

The earliest precursor of conscience appears in the attitude of young children by their showing an eager and willing acceptance of parental directives and demands. This trait-like quality is consistent across situations and over time, and as well is subject to individual variations. How do we account for these differences? The child's biologically based temperament interacts with socialization in the family to determine these outcomes. A child's mind is not a blank slate on which socialization writes the moral script. Rather, socialization molds the raw clay of biological temperament, which is not blandly neutral, and hence also helps determine the outcome. This biological element is part of our evolutionary heritage we will discuss in the next chapter.

Styles of parenting have been the subject of an enormous amount of study. What is particularly significant is that gentle parental discipline, in affectionate and reciprocal parent-and-child relationships, fosters greater compliance on the part of the child. This leads to development of a more robust conscience with a healthy sense of guilt. By contrast, the assertion of parental power and the use of punitive measures lead to resentment and anger toward parents and to a lower capacity for guilt. A child who is harshly punished for a misdeed has already paid the penalty, therefore has less need to feel guilty. Fear and fearfulness also appear to be closely associated with the emergence of the feeling of guilt. Fear is an important antecedent and consequence following wrongdoing. Fearful children also tend to be more guilt-prone.

It appears that guilt and shame are not yet differentiated in early childhood. Following wrongdoing, children show a blend of negative emotions—they just feel "bad." As embarrassment begins to be associated with experiences like nudity, children begin to differentiate between moral and amoral transgressions and then go on to knowing the differences between guilt and shame.

Virtually all psychological models of moral development have an underlying assumption that moral judgment and behavior are the result of moral reasoning. (The same view has prevailed in moral philosophy.) In other words, when faced with a moral dilemma, we consider the evidence, match the facts with our conception of what is moral, and reach a moral decision through a conscious and rational process. Psychologist Jonathan Haidt challenges this view by proposing an alternative model where moral judgments are made *intuitively* and only then followed by a process of rationally justifying the moral judgment after the fact.[44]

To illustrate this, Haidt uses the following example. Suppose a brother and sister have consensual sex. When research subjects are asked if incest under these circumstances is wrong, their immediate reaction is that it is. If asked why, they will offer a variety of reasons (such as it results in pregnancy or the child may have genetic defects). If subjects are presented with cogent arguments that no such negative outcomes will result in this particular case, they will run out of rational objections, yet will continue to argue that incest is immoral. They just *know* that incest is wrong.

Intuitive judgments occur quickly, effortlessly, and automatically, without conscious awareness of why they are being made, whereas their rational justifications come more laboriously, through intellectual effort. Moreover, we think of morality as something that has to be put *into* the child through a process of *internalization*. In Haidt's model, morality is already in the child, it just needs to be brought out through of process of *externalization*. What makes this approach of particular interest is its broadly integrative nature. It brings together not only the various strands of psychological functioning but combines them with social, cultural, evolutionary, and biological elements.

GUILT, GENDER, AND FEMINIST ETHICS

Are women and men different in the ways they experience guilt? This is a question we have raised before. But we now need to consider, if there are differences, how they come about. It is relatively easy to identify gender differences with respect to embarrassment and shame. Women are more prone to these feelings because of the sexual *objectification* of the female body. This valuation takes place both in interpersonal encounters as well as through representation in the media from advertising to pornography. It leads women to develop a greater sensitivity and self-consciousness, which in turn leads to a higher sense of shame.[45] Women also have special physiological functions (such as menstruation) that may be potential sources for embarrassment. Women generally are more self-conscious than men with respect to issues like obesity and other physical features. Traditionally, expectations of modesty, purity, and chastity have weighed more heavily on women than men.

What about guilt? If women are more likely to feel guilty than men, is that because of a greater capacity for feelings as such, or a greater willingness to express feelings? Or, do women and men have different moral dispositions? Freud claimed that men had harsher superegos. Yet, the more common view is that it is women who are more prone to feel guilty, just as they are more likely to induce guilt in others.

Psychological studies support this more common view.[46] Sex differences can be explained on biological, social, and political grounds. However, nothing we say about male and female behavior would apply to every single woman or man. There is so much overlap in how women and men feel, think, and behave that we cannot speak in absolutes, only in relative terms as to how each sex is likely to behave under a set of circumstances. Moreover, gender identity and gender roles have undergone great changes during the past several decades and continue to change. Therefore, much of what we ascribe to gender differences may apply to traditional relationships rather than the newer patterns still evolving around us.[47]

Probably the most important factor that leads women to be more prone to feel guilty is their greater sense of empathy. Women are more sensitive to the feelings of others. A woman or a man will recognize equally well when a friend is sad; but the woman is more likely to express concern for the friend's sadness. When someone's feelings are hurt, it is women who are more likely to be distressed. That in turn leads to a greater propensity for feeling guilty. This is one reason why women often believe that men are not sufficiently sensitive to their feelings.[48] ("My boyfriend does not notice if I'm sad or worried unless I'm really upset. So to get his attention, I have to get really upset; and that really upsets me.")

Greater female empathy may also serve a self-protective function. Given that women have been more dependent on others than have men, they must be more sensitive to the feelings of others, such as knowing if someone is displeased or angry with them. Consequently, when women are responsible for hurting another, their greater sense of vulnerability makes them more likely to feel guilty.

Traditionally, women have adopted the *expressive* role in being responsive to the needs and feelings of others, particularly their children. Therefore, they more easily acquire expressive traits like empathy and compassion. Men take on the *instrumental* role, especially in the occupational sphere. Women are more likely to cast their relationships in communal terms ("I wish my husband would not treat me like a business partner"), while men are more likely to follow the exchange model even in their personal relationships ("If my wife could deal with me in a more businesslike way, we would get along much better").

Women take on the responsibility of caring for others as an extension of their traditional role in caring for children. This means a greater readiness to involve themselves in the problems of other people, be they relatives, friends, or neighbors. The women's movement encouraged women to pay more attention to their own needs, which generated a tension for some women between their traditional sense of responsibility to others and their newly found awareness of what they owed to themselves. Favoring one over the other leads to guilt, and trying to have it both ways makes life difficult.[49]

> When I was studying for an exam, my roommate came in looking like hell because she had an argument with her mom on the phone. What was I supposed to do? Pretend not to notice it and go on studying, or drop everything and comfort her? I felt bad going either way.

When parents discipline their children, they are more likely to use the threat of withdrawal of love with girls than boys, who are more likely to be punished. This early association of wrongdoing with the withdrawal of love results in female self-blame, which in turn leads directly to guilt.

When something goes wrong, it leads to a mixture of regret and guilt ("I could have prevented this but didn't"). In these cases, women are more likely than men to take responsibility for the outcome, even when it is not their fault. By contrast, men are likely to blame others even when it is their fault. And instead of feeling guilty, they get angry. Anger becomes the substitute emotion. When children have problems with drugs, sex, and delinquency, both parents feel responsible, but typically, mothers feel (or are made to feel) more responsible than fathers.

These vulnerabilities place women more at risk for *false guilt*—guilt that arises not from wrongdoing but from the fear of disapproval and the threat of damaging relationships. The threat of withdrawal of love turns feelings of loneliness, fear, and anger into guilt and self-blame ("It's all my fault"). Self-blame leads to the expectation of a greater measure of self-control at whatever cost ("I'll try harder next time").[50]

The clash between responsibility to oneself and the ethic of responsibility to others comes to a head as women try to balance the requirements of career and family. The problem is often not marriage, or cohabitation, where there are various ways of sharing the burdens. The real problem is parenthood, where the prospect of full-time motherhood fills many well-educated women with guilt for not achieving their intellectual and social potential, while pursuing a full-time career means feeling guilty for failing to devote their full attention to their children. A 55-year-old woman says, "I still feel guilty for neglecting my sons while burning the midnight oil trying to excel at my job. They're now dysfunctional in many ways and I blame myself, even though I'm not sure I was actually the cause."

Women have found many solutions to this dilemma, but none of them is easy, even though some women are hardly fazed by it. (A medical school colleague, who is married, the mother of five children, manages the house, runs a large lab, and takes care of numerous patients, commented, "What's the problem?") Men who are interested in doing their share in the upbringing of their children also face this problem, but not to the same extent. Moreover, no matter how much men get involved with their children, it is usually the mother who feels the ultimate responsibility for them.

> My husband and I are both attorneys and do more or less the same type of work. We can afford to have excellent child care for our kids. So my husband rarely thinks about the kids while at work, unless there's an emergency. Yet, there is always some worry at the back of my mind if everything is alright at home. And if something comes up, I'm the one who gets called, and I'm the one who wants to be called.[51]

Jean Piaget observed that boys and girls resolved conflicts differently. Boys relied on rules, while girls were more concerned with relationships. When a dispute arose, boys would invoke rules and looked for ways to apply them fairly. Girls were inclined to manage the conflict by bending the rules, or ignoring them altogether, in order to safeguard their relationships. Boys placed rules ahead of playmates; girls put playmates ahead of rules. Boys' games lasted longer because when problems arose they argued over them. Girls' games were shorter since if a dispute arose, they stopped the game. When push came to shove, boys fought; girls resorted to social ostracism.[52]

Psychologist Carol Gilligan has argued that theories of moral development tend to be based on male models, which are then misapplied to women; this would be true of the work of Freud as well as more recent examples like Erikson and Kohlberg. Gilligan points out that females and males interpret moral problems from two different orientations, based on different conceptions of the self and its relationship to others. Women follow an *ethic of care* and responsibility; men follow an *ethic of rights and justice.* The ethic of rights and justice is morality-driven by the abstract principles of fairness and equality. The moral self is characterized by autonomy, separation, and disinterestedness in the impact of one's moral judgment of others. The ethic of care, by contrast, emerges from a sense of responsibility for others. Consequently, boys are more likely to feel guilty for violating rules, while girls feel guilty for damaging their friendships.

Is there is an innate aspect to being male or female that accounts for these differences, or is it a matter of culturally defined gender roles? Western societies (and America in particular) have *individually oriented* moral codes that stress the independence and autonomy of individuals. Asian societies emphasize the integration of the individual into the group, hence they have *duty-based* interpersonal moral codes (an issue we will return to in the next chapter).

Joan Miller argues that even if Gilligan's morality-of-caring framework differs from Kohlberg's justice-based model, it too reflects a Western cultural orientation, which stresses personal freedom of choice and individual responsibility. If Gilligan's viewpoint were extended to different cultures, concepts of self and morality would be more similar among individuals of the same gender from different cultures than among individuals of different genders from the same culture. In other words, American women would be more like Indian women than American men. However, this is contradicted by evidence that shows a great deal of difference between cultures, irrespective of gender. This means that American women and men would have more in common with each other in their experiences of guilt than would American women and Indian women, or American men and Indian men. The critical factor is therefore not gender but culture. Even if Gilligan's claim is true that American men and women vary in their moral orientations (with men following an ethic of justice and women an ethic of caring), they still have more of a common core that reflects an individually oriented Western morality that would set them apart from Asians, who follow an ethic of duty. In this respect, culture trumps gender.[53]

Gilligan's work is part of the larger field of *feminist ethics.*[54] The main thrust of this approach is a critique of traditional Western ethics as lacking concern for women's interests, neglecting women's issues, depreciating feminine values, and devaluing women's moral experience. It points to traditional moral philosophy as having a male bias that neglects the domain of domestic activities and family and personal relationships. Feminist ethics focuses on moral issues that have a particular relevance to women's lives, such as abortion, gender orientation, and social equality. It aspires to give equal weight to women's moral concerns, broadening the domain of ethics and rethinking fundamental issues of morality.[55]

Feminist ethics is an expanding field. However, apart from the sort of issues addressed above, there are as yet no distinctive philosophical views on how guilt in women differs from that among men at the conceptual level, if it actually does.[56] Moreover, although gender differences between women and men with respect to guilt are important, *differences* should not be confused simplistically with *superiority*:

> To say that the two sexes differ is not the same as saying that morality defined as justice and fairness is superior to morality defined as benevolence and caring. Everyone applies various combinations of principles and feelings to the management of moral problems. . . .
>
> It is difficult to say exactly how these gender differences, to the extent that they exist, emerge. Nature and nurture interact in ways that are complex and hard to disentangle.[57]

DEALING WITH GUILT AMONG CHILDREN

It is comforting to think that children are free from the guilt that burdens adults. That, however, is not the case. Virtually every form of adult guilt has a counterpart among children, even though the occasions and manifestations of such guilt may differ. As parents, we actually expect children to show remorse when they misbehave and feel upset when they do not. Nonetheless, when children and adolescents suffer guilt of a problematic nature, it becomes necessary for adults to deal with it.

In the accounts of guilt we have cited all along, childhood experiences of guilt and shame continue to trouble men and women, even in their more mature years. In addition to the usual reasons for feeling guilty associated with misbehaving, children also manifest guilt in more unusual circumstances. For instance, siblings of cancer patients (particularly those who die) experience survivor guilt. They may feel guilty for being angry at parents who neglected them because they were preoccupied with taking care of a chronically sick sibling.

Children often blame themselves and feel guilty for family conflicts and breakups, for which they feel personally responsible. The pain of seeing their parents get divorced is compounded by the feeling that they were somehow the cause of it. This is made worse when parents recruit the child as an ally in their domestic battle. If these situations do not resolve themselves, they will require counseling or therapy. Children who feel guilty will not simply outgrow the feeling. The important element in dealing with such guilt is to allow and encourage children to express their feelings of guilt, to let them talk in whatever form or however long they wish. The very fact of being listened to validates their feelings; they are no longer alone in facing them. Their free expression releases the psychological tension caused by guilt. These experiences of childhood are fresh and not yet hardened through years of repression. They require much less in the way of elaborate interpretations. They are close enough to the surface to address directly.

Also important is to help the child recognize that negative feelings like anger toward parents and siblings that engender guilt are normal and acceptable ways of feeling. The fact that one feels angry does not mean that one hates the person. And even if one hates the person, it does not mean that one does not also love them.

In many such instances, children can be helped by parents or other caring and sensitive adults to deal with their guilt. However, in more complex situations, such as when anger and guilt (as well as guilt over anger) results from sexual abuse, especially by a family member, professional help would be necessary. It would be very difficult for a child to confront an abusive parent. Not infrequently, if the father (or more often the stepfather) is the offender, the mother may side with him—refuse to believe the child, get angry at the revelations, or accuse the child of instigating the sexual interaction.

During adolescence, mood swings with elements of guilt are part of the turmoil of growing up. However, more serious behavioral problems deserve special consideration since behaviors that often induce guilt (for example, the use of alcohol or drugs, and sexual misconduct and delinquency) may have particularly serious consequences. Guilt works both ways in these situations. Risky behaviors may induce guilt, or they may be induced by guilt (from whatever cause) as a way of getting relief. Eating disorders and self-inflicted wounds (such as cutting, in particular) may also be manifestations of trying to obtain relief from pain.

Young people are more likely to see a psychiatrist or psychologist if their feelings of guilt are part of a larger problem like depression. The rates of clinical depression among children may be as high as 2 percent and among adolescents over 8 percent. There may be both genetic as well as psychological factors that account for these rates. Consequently, a combination of antidepressant drugs (usually serotonin reuptake inhibitors) and cognitive behavioral therapy or psychotherapy is used. Such a combination is generally quite effective. However, since depression is a chronic and recurring illness, the ongoing use of drugs raises special problems with children and adolescents, some of whom have to be on them for decades.[58] On the other hand, given that untreated depression entails serious risks, physicians have usually little choice but to keep these youngsters on drugs.[59]

The most serious risk of depression is suicide. In most developed countries other than the United States, suicide is the second most common cause of death among adolescents (after accidents). In the United States, homicide is second and suicide comes third. Suicidal thoughts, attempts, and threats account for a high proportion of all psychiatric referrals in this age group. One in five U.S. high school students has thought of suicide during a given year. Only a small proportion of those who attempt suicide actually will kill themselves (but among those who do, boys vastly outnumber girls).[60] Not only does guilt often play a central role in such cases, but the tragedy of having a child die of suicide leads to intense feelings of guilt among the parents and siblings.

It is important to deal with feelings of guilt in childhood, but it is equally critical to raise children with a healthy sense of guilt without unduly burdening and warping their lives. Who should be responsible for this critical task— parents or teachers? The responsibility usually falls on parents, and they seem like the natural choice. They have the earliest and greatest impact on the lives of their children, and since the issue of guilt is tied with morality, it is the parents' moral values that should prevail. On the other hand, instruction is the primary task of teachers and they have the pedagogic skill and training to be most effective in imparting moral values to children. Many parents may actually be delighted to have teachers relieve them of this task, but some are not.

Public schools on their part find it difficult to take on the formal task of moral instruction. It is hard to give moral instruction with no reference to religious beliefs, but public schools cannot indoctrinate students in religious values. Besides, the moral views of which religion should they endorse? The scope of instruction raises other problems. John Dewey was critical of the common tendency to treat morality as a thing apart from the rest of life; he wanted moral teachings to be incorporated in all aspects of education.

But teachers can only do so much. More than anyone else, it is parents who must play the dual role of providing love and support for their children and also acting as the disciplinarians who must set limits and deal with their misbehavior. They are both the primary source of love and support for children and also the disciplinarians who must set limits and deal with their misbehavior. These two functions may seem in conflict but in fact they are complementary.

Much has been written about successful parenting with respect to exercising effective and healthy discipline and providing children with clear standards and expectations. There are many ways of approaching this issue. Those with religious convictions make the instilling of moral values part of their broader aim of bringing up their children within their particular tradition. Others rely on a more secular basis to achieve the same end. The degree to which guilt is used as a moral vehicle will vary accordingly. There are also popular books that offer guidance to parents for building "moral intelligence" in children: to instill empathy, self-control, and a healthy conscience to foster respect, kindness, tolerance, and fairness. Despite the diversity in their assumptions and values, these various approaches are remarkably similar in the outcomes they try to achieve.[61]

Consistency is particularly important for effective discipline and instilling a healthy moral sense. Permissive and restrictive styles of parenting each have their positive and negative sides. However, in either case, it is important for children to know the consequences of their actions. Parental inconsistency wreaks havoc with the child's ability to predict these outcomes and to act accordingly, as well as to know when to feel guilty and when not to. Such inconsistency can take a number of forms. One is inconsistent parental standards for judging the morality of actions: for instance, permitting lying under some circumstances but not others, or with respect to some people but not others. This makes moral judgment a matter of playing it by ear rather than following a reliable moral principle. This does not mean laying down absolute rules never to be breached. Some leeway in making moral decisions is healthy and necessary. However, before children can learn how to make responsible exceptions for exceptional circumstances, they need to have a solid grounding in the rules. Another pitfall is the "Do as I say, and not as I do" attitude toward parental privilege. This too undermines moral foundations and punches loopholes in the child's conscience. It allows an out for not doing the right thing whenever it is unpalatable and bypassing the healthy remorse that should follow doing wrong.

Knowing how to instill a healthy ethical sense in children is not easy. As parents, we are often unsure of drawing moral boundaries in our own lives and living by them. As a parent, reprimanding or punishing a child you love may hurt you more than it hurts the child. However, even that is easier than knowing how to get across moral principles that a young mind and heart can make their own. Abstract principles often do not make sense to children. One day, when my son, then a little boy, had misbehaved, I tried to use the occasion to go beyond the minor misdeed and draw larger moral lessons from it. My son interrupted me and said, "Dad, if I did something wrong, tell me what it is, but cut the side talk."

Ultimately, how effective parents are as moral guides depends on the deeper quality of their relationship with their children. Parents are the models that children identify with and emulate, or reject and react against. If there is no mutual love and respect binding parent and child together, then what the parent says or does hardly matters, or is an incentive to do the opposite.[62]

Understanding how moral judgment develops in individuals is only half the story. The other half is to learn how human beings, as a species, have developed moral judgment through evolution. How did the capacity for guilt evolve to become part of our innate nature? That is the subject of our next chapter.

7 THE EVOLUTION OF GUILT

DO ANIMALS FEEL GUILTY? Perhaps dogs but not cats? Konrad Lorenz, one of the founders of ethology, tells the following story of Bully, his old and faithful French bulldog. One day, Lorenz returned home from a ski trip with a handsome younger dog; Bully was devastated and tormented by jealousy:

> For days the atmosphere was heavy with tension which finally discharged itself in one of the most embittered dog fights that I have ever witnessed, and the only one which took place in the master's room where normally even sworn enemies observed a cease-fire. Whilst I was separating the combatants, Bully accidentally bit me deep in the ball of the right little finger. That was the end of the fight, but poor Bully had received the severest shock . . . : he broke down completely and although I did not admonish him and indeed stroked and coaxed him, he lay on the carpet as though paralysed, a little bundle of unhappiness, unable to get up. He shivered as in a fever and every few seconds a great tremor ran through his body . . . [and] from time to time a deep sigh escaped his tortured breast, and large tears overflowed his eyes. As he was literally unable to rise, I had to carry him down on to the road several times a day; he then walked back himself . . . but he could only crawl upstairs with an effort. Anyone who saw the dog . . . must have imagined him to be severely ill. It was several days before he could eat and even then he could only be cajoled into taking food from my hands. For many weeks he approached me in an

William Durham's lectures to my seminar introduced me to the field of evolutionary psychology. I am most grateful to Robert Sapolsky for his insightful critique of this chapter and his helpful comments.

attitude of humble supplication, in sad contrast to the normal behaviour of this self-willed and anything but servile dog. His bad conscience affected me the more in that my own was anything but clear towards him. My acquisition of the new dog now seemed an almost unforgivable act.[1]

Touching as this account may be, the question of whether or not animals feel guilty is still unsettled. Why should that matter to our understanding of human guilt? Since we associate what is natural with the animal world and what is cultural with humans, this question is relevant for determining to what extent our capacity for guilt is part of our evolutionary heritage—our so-called animal nature. Knowing our origins makes a lot of difference in understanding how we behave. This is not only true at the individual level but at the societal level as well. What is at issue is not only whether animals have a moral sense, but how guilt evolved during human evolution and became refined through culture.

In the last chapter, we discussed how the capacity for guilt develops within an individual's lifetime—its *ontogenesis*. In this chapter, we turn to the development of guilt at the level of the human species—its *phylogenesis*. As we turn our attention from the individual experience of guilt to our collective human experience, we shift from a micro to a macro perspective. We will be primarily concerned with two issues: Do we have an *innate* sense of guilt—one that we are born with; and are there *continuities* as one moves from the way animals exhibit a moral sense, albeit in less developed forms, to the way humans do?

The cultural evolution of guilt, which will occupy us in the second part of this chapter, is equally important. We are social animals that share a great many characteristics with our closest evolutionary relatives, like the chimpanzees, but we have an entire category of characteristics—those that make us human—which sets us apart from them. According to the theory of evolution, modern humans appeared about 100,000 years ago. Since then, what has shaped us is primarily our culture. The cultural evolution of the moral emotions like guilt has been an integral part of that process.

GUILT AND HUMAN NATURE

The quest for understanding human nature is motivated partly by our need to control unruly behavior.[2] The biblical account of the disobedience of Adam and Eve has been particularly important in shaping Western ideas of how human nature became corrupted. Stoicism introduced ideas of eternal laws directing the actions of rational beings. These became elaborated into the Christian concept of natural law whose most prominent early exponent was St. Thomas Aquinas: the law of nature emanated from God's eternal wisdom and was engraved in the human mind. This was supplemented by moral laws that had to remain consistent with natural law:[3]

> Every law framed by man bears the character of law exactly to that extent to which it is derived from the law of nature. But if on any point it is in conflict with the law of nature, it at once ceases to be a law; it is a mere perversion of law.[4]

This is a highly naturalistic view but it is not based on the actual study of nature. Rather, it is based on presuppositions of how nature functioned as God intended it. The medieval church's view of human nature was laden with guilt. The secular perspective that followed it in the Renaissance was equally bleak. Niccolò Machiavelli described his contemporaries as "ungrateful, fickle, dissembling, anxious to feel danger, and covetous of gain."[5] The English philosopher Thomas Hobbes characterized human beings in their natural state as living in constant fear and danger of violent death—a life that was "solitary, poor, nasty, brutish and short."[6] People survived by looking out for themselves, not by being altruistic. Societies maintained peace and order through imposing horrendous punishments, not by relying on good will. In the Enlightenment these gloomy views were challenged by some thinkers, like John Locke and Jean-Jacques Rousseau, who argued that human beings in a state of nature were "noble savages"; it was civilization that corrupted their good nature, but corrupted they were.[7]

It was against this background that, in the nineteenth century, Charles Darwin formulated his theory of evolution, which has shaped our modern consciousness of the natural world and our place in it. Darwin's views proved revolutionary. Just as Copernicus had taken the earth out of the center of our universe, Darwin took humans out of their central place in nature by turning them into just another species of animal, albeit superior to all others in their evolutionary endowments.

The basic validity of Darwin's theory of evolution is now accepted by the overwhelming majority of biologists, even though it continues to be modified in light of new findings. (The fact that it is called a "theory" does not detract from its validity; gravity is also referred to as a theory.) However, those who adhere to a literal interpretation of the account of creation in the Bible continue to reject it. Others qualify it by ascribing its basic design to a higher intelligence ("intelligent design"). The Catholic church accepts the theory of evolution, on condition that God's creative role in it is given its due.

Evolutionary theory maintains that organisms evolve as they interact with their environments in complex ways. *Natural selection* is the process by which individuals with heritable characteristics (which enhance their ability to survive and reproduce) are selected over others that are not similarly endowed. Fitness is the key factor in this process, not in the sense of physical fitness as we commonly understand it, but *reproductive fitness*—the capacity to produce offspring who will reproduce in turn. What counts here is not the absolute number of offspring (thus the point is not to have as many children as you can) but their number relative to those the individual competes with. Therefore, if guilt is an innate capacity, its development must be understood in terms of the selective advantage it provides to reproductive fitness.[8] It was initially thought that selection operated at the level of the species; in other words, individuals acted in ways that helped the survival and reproductive success of the group. This view shifted in favor of natural selection operating at the level of the individual, whereby each person aims at enhancing his or her reproductive fitness.[9]

Darwin did not confront the issue of human nature head on, but his early followers tended to side with the hawkish and materialist view espoused by Hobbes rather than the dovish and romantic vision of Rousseau. These ideas were popularized by the English philosopher Herbert Spencer into the image of a ruthless nature where the strong survived and the weak perished. Under the rubric of Social Darwinism, *survival of the fittest* became the watchword of self-serving capitalists and politicians who justified aggression and exploitation on the grounds of social progress.

In the 1970s biologists extended the theory of natural selection to the social behavior of animals and humans. This opened up the field of *sociobiology*, the title of a book by E. O. Wilson published in 1975.[10] Wilson described this field as the *new synthesis* and it became a new paradigm for understanding the evolution of human behavior. In books that followed, like *The Selfish Gene* by Richard Dawkins, these ideas kicked up a storm of controversy, especially with regard to politically hot topics like sex, gender, and aggression.[11] The notion that human beings are naturally self-serving has continued to dominate the thinking of most evolutionary biologists and psychologists.

The emergence of sociobiology in the midst of resurgent feminism and other ideologies fueled the controversy. Wilson was vilified and sociobiology

tarred with the brush of Social Darwinism. Nonetheless, evolutionary theorists generated new models for the evolution of morality and guilt, which is
what we will be concerned with here.[12]

THE EVOLUTION OF MORALITY

Natural selection is not an irresistible force that compels us to act in predetermined ways, like a biological robot. Genes are complex chemical molecules—
not our conscience. Calling genes "selfish" is a figure of speech. All genes can
do is to *predispose* us to behave in certain ways, under certain circumstances,
and within a particular environment. The effects of genes do not negate the
critical importance of culture in shaping behavior. Even biologically oriented
scientists estimate that genetic factors account for no more than 10 percent of
the variance in human behavior.

Similar considerations apply to the term "innate." When we say that our
capacity for feeling guilty is innate, what we mean is that moral behavior can
be adaptive in genetic terms by virtue of having provided our ancestors with a
reproductive advantage. It does not mean that an innate trait will assert itself
irrespective of the environment. Nor does it mean that it will lead to universal
patterns of moral behavior across all cultures at all times and in all places. To
avoid the use of nebulous labels, ethologists now use the term *fixed action pattern* to refer to behaviors that emerge without prior learning. For instance, a
captive young squirrel will crack a nut on its first encounter with it without having learned it from other squirrels. Yet this skill can be refined by learning.

That something is natural does not necessarily make it good or bad. Nothing in nature can be "unnatural" in the sense of having an ethical value. To
equate what *is* with what *ought to be* is called the "naturalistic fallacy."[13] The
same considerations apply to social realities. The fact that women have been
primarily responsible for childrearing in the past does not mean that they
should continue to be so. Circumstances change: A practice that may have
been adaptive in the past may no longer be adaptive.

Natural selection may appear to be inflexibly rigid, but it actually favors a
degree of flexibility. Since ecological and social circumstances are not always
predictable, a flexible code of morality will have a higher adaptive potential to
fit prevailing conditions than a rigid one. Evolutionists are accused of being
uncritical advocates of the values of nature. Yet they recognize the need for social constraints to "bridle the horse" of untamed nature, thereby moderating
nature's values with *social values* shaped by cultures.[14]

We do not know when during the long period of human evolution the capability for guilt was "hard-wired" into the human brain, but this critical change must have occurred in the harsh *ancestral environment* during which early humans subsisted as hunters and gatherers, living in small groups of related individuals.[15] That ancestral environment is long gone and far from the world we live in now. Innate patterns that worked then were not designed to work for all time in all places. The behavioral patterns of moral behavior selected in response to the prevailing physical and social conditions may have been adaptive then, but may be maladaptive in the modern world.

In reconstructing the evolution of morality, we rely on two sources of information. First is the behavior of animals that are closest to us genetically and in social organization, in particular the great apes (chimpanzees, gorillas, and orangutans). Second are studies of preliterate societies whose life circumstances are close to those of our evolutionary ancestors living in the ancestral environment (such as inhabitants of the Kalahari desert in Africa).

The (Almost) Moral Animal

Dog owners have many stories about how their pets act "guilty" when they have misbehaved, as in the earlier account of Konrad Lorenz. The following account is more skeptical:

> When I was a child, we used to keep the family dog fenced in the back yard much of the time. The dog was forever trying to escape into the exiting world of the neighborhood, though he knew it wasn't allowed. . . . If grabbed in the middle of the escape, he would be overcome with guilt and disappear submissively into his kennel. . . .
>
> . . . Speaking strictly, I don't believe that my dog "knew that it wasn't allowed" or that he genuinely had "guilt." He knew he would be punished, granted, and he didn't want that. He had internalized a rule of the household, but didn't know it *as* a rule. His mind, though impressively devious in many ways . . . did not have the capacity to form a thought about escape from the yard, or anything else, as being *prohibited*.[16]

Such skepticism is supported by experiments. In one case, a dog would chew up the papers and books of its master then act "guilty"—slinking around looking sheepish with gaze averted. On one occasion, the owner shredded the papers himself in the dog's absence. When the dog came in and noticed the shredded papers, it again acted "guilty"—this time for no good reason.

The dog was reacting to being in the same room with shredded paper, and that spelled trouble. It was the fear of disapproval that was troubling the dog, not guilt. The dog's behavior is normative (that is how dogs behave), but not moral. It is meant to signal *submissiveness* to avert punishment and regain the master's favor; pet owners may interpret this as guilt because that is how they would have felt in the same situation. (This explanation will not convince everyone.)

More instructive are systematic studies of primates, especially chimpanzees.[17] Based on such studies, primatologist Frans de Waal considers morality and the capacity for guilt to be part of our human nature—not a thin social "veneer" that conceals our innate selfishness. He traces the roots of human morality to a number of animal traits that form the basis of sociality, such as empathy, reciprocity, peacemaking, and social order.

Since chimpanzees are our closest evolutionary relatives (we share 95 percent of our genes with them), one would expect that they should also be closest to humans in their level of moral development. (While that is generally true, it is puzzling that helping behavior is also present in some animals, like dolphins and elephants, that are far from us on the evolutionary scale.)

Just as in human society *empathy* plays a central role in the experience of guilt, among chimpanzees also there is a remarkable capacity for empathy. For instance, some chimps have drowned in zoo moats trying to save other chimps. Chimps help the injured and disabled and assist stranded young chimps to get down trees. They will console the loser after a fight.

Chimps also have a keen sense of *reciprocity*. When one chimp grooms another, the other chimp will do the same. Chimps will also share food with those that have groomed them. They remember who did them a favor and who wronged them. In these and similar interactions, they exhibit the animal counterpart of the human sense of equity and fairness.

A sense of *social order* exists in many animal species based on a hierarchy where each individual knows its place (until that changes through ongoing competition). This social order is particularly well developed among chimps. Their young learn to adhere to it, and if they fail, they are punished. Social order is also maintained through peacemaking. To keep the peace, chimps accommodate each other and resolve conflicts through negotiation. Females, more often than males, take the initiative at containing aggression. For instance, they will take away a stone from the hands of males that are about to fight. After fights, chimps have ways of achieving reconciliation.

The Grammar of Morality

We noted earlier the parallel between the development of language and of moral judgment. In both cases, we are born with an innate capacity for language / guilt, but we need to learn a particular language or a moral code. This parallel between language and morality has been further elaborated in terms of deeper functional similarities.

In Noam Chomsky's conception of language, when I say that I speak English, what I mean is that I can communicate with others by expressing myself through that language. However, when I speak it, I am neither aware of, nor concerned with, its underlying grammatical rules. Chomsky's primary interest is not only the ordinary grammatical rules, but the deeper linguistic principles that constitute a *universal grammar* that applies to all languages, living or dead. This universal grammar is hard-wired through evolution and accounts for the innate human capacity to use language in ways that animals cannot.[18]

Similarly, an innate capability for moral action is hard-wired in our brains through evolution.[19] This makes possible the acquisition of particular moral rules and principles based on appropriate cultural instruction. However, there are also deeper moral principles, which we are unaware of, that guide our actions. These function at an intuitive level without our having to stop to think about them. Since moral decisions have serious consequences, the fact that we can make these determinations spontaneously and without prolonged reflection is of great adaptive significance. This is the same idea we touched upon in the last chapter.[20] For instance, when faced with a situation where I must either kill or be killed, there may not be time for moral reflection—I need to act fast in a way that is consistent with my ethical principles.

It is also possible that the development of language and morality have been interdependent. The capacity for language would make sophisticated moral reasoning possible. Language greatly facilitates moral instruction and the formulation of moral laws. Conversely, the need to communicate sophisticated moral rules may have been instrumental in the evolution of language.

The grammar of morality and its components—empathy, reciprocity, peacemaking, and social order—are tied with the idea of *altruism*. As we discussed earlier, altruism consists of acting out of selfless concern for the well-being of others, with no expectation of personal gain or even at a cost to oneself. It is the very opposite of selfishness. Like morality, altruism has been traditionally considered an exclusively human trait, in contrast to the blind "selfishness" of animals. Evolutionary theorists now challenge that view and see the roots, or counterparts, of human altruism among animals.

THE EVOLUTION OF ALTRUISM

Darwin was puzzled by the altruistic behavior of certain species. He took it for granted that human beings should behave compassionately, but could animals be induced to do likewise? Why would bees die for other bees or sterile ants spent their lives in the service of other ants? Why would a bird walk out into the open, or a ground squirrel utter an alarm call, to distract a predator at the risk of endangering its own life? If natural selection operated in the service of the group, this would be easy to understand, but it does not; it is individual reproductive fitness that is in play.

Consider the interaction between two individuals: One is the *performer* of the act, the other is the *recipient* of the act. The outcome of the act entails a *benefit* or a *cost* to each participant. In this case, benefit or cost have to be understood strictly with respect to the individual's reproductive fitness—it would either enhance it or reduce it. There is no conscious *moral* intent involved in this act. We are simply dealing with the way genetic scripts are acted out.

To illustrate this, suppose that you and I are desperately trying to get off a sinking ship where there is only one seat left in the last lifeboat. If I shove you aside and take the seat, my action is *selfish* and benefits me at a cost to you. If I cannot get into the boat but also stop you from getting in as well, then I am being *spiteful*, and both of us lose. If we act together and shove somebody else out of a seat, our action is *cooperative* and will at least benefit one of us (heartless as it may be). Finally, if I voluntarily let you take the last seat and I die, my action is *altruistic*, which is the very opposite of being selfish. The selfish and cooperative choices are in my interest, hence natural selection would enhance both. To be spiteful is self-defeating and makes no evolutionary sense. That leaves us with the question of why anyone should behave altruistically since it entails a benefit for another at a cost to ourselves.

The first answer was provided by the idea of *kin selection*.[21] The reason social insects like bees, ants, and wasps act altruistically is because they share the same genes with their kin. As long as these genes are transmitted to the next generation, that is all that matters. Consequently, reproductive fitness had to be redefined as *inclusive fitness*, which means that I would do for my kin what I would do for myself. This idea may look deceptively simple but it had momentous implications. It essentially took altruism out of altruism by turning it into just another facet of the self-serving evolutionary game. Moreover, it left unresolved the issue of why individuals act altruistically toward others who are *not* their kin, that is genetically unrelated to them. The answer to that question came with the theory of *reciprocal altruism* proposed by Robert Trivers.[22] Reciprocal altruism is behavior that benefits others not closely related at a cost to oneself. How would it work?

Consider the following scenario. Suppose you see someone floundering in a lake. If you do nothing, the person will drown. If you jump in, you reduce the chances of the person drowning by 50 percent, but at a 5 percent risk of drowning yourself. What should you do? It depends on the drowning person's relationship to you. Here are the options: If you jump in irrespective of who the drowning person is, whether related to you or not, your action represents *random dispensation*—the willingness to die for anyone. If you consistently risk your life for anyone randomly, then indeed you will not live long. If you jump in only when you recognize the drowning person as a relative, then we have *non-random dispensation to kin*. You are altruistic, but only to your kin, not just anybody—your altruism is not randomly extended to everyone. The choice can be refined further. If the person drowning is your identical twin, then it is as good as saving yourself since you share exactly the same genes. If the person is an ordinary brother or sister, then you are saving 50 percent of your genes. With cousins and distant relatives, the genetic gain gets progressively less until the game is no longer worth the candle. However, suppose I love my cousin more than I do my brother. Or, the person drowning is Mozart, whose music I adore. Would such considerations make no difference?

The answer depends on the last alternative, which is *non-random dispensation to non-kin*. Following this alternative, you can be altruistic to non-kin but not randomly—it does not include everybody. There should be something in it for you—some prospect of payback. It is this that makes it *reciprocal altruism*. Think of it as a long-term investment in your reproductive fitness.[23]

Smart investments are based on a cost / benefit balance. Reciprocal altruism is no exception. The cost / benefit ratio should be in one's favor to make it worthwhile; simply getting equivalent value does not get you ahead. The best deal provides maximum benefit for the minimum cost. There is also the consideration of the time frame. When you invest in the stock market, you do not expect to make a fortune right away; on the other hand, you do not want to wait to cash in until you are on your deathbed. The same considerations apply to investments in altruism. Getting an early payback is good, since the person who owes you might die or go away (the memory of favors does tend to fade). On the other hand, insisting on early returns may preclude maximizing your gains or getting back anything at all.

Reciprocal altruism is characterized in game theory as *tit-for-tat*. It is based on the assumption that altruistic reciprocity is not a zero-sum game: One person's gain need not be at the cost of another's loss. In cooperative relationships (where favors are done simultaneously), or in reciprocal altruism (where there is a time lag between giving and getting back), both parties win. However, in reciprocal altruism there is still no point in being moral merely for the sake of being moral.

Animal studies have shown that the likelihood of reciprocal altruism depends on a number of factors. The same is true of reciprocal altruism among humans. One factor is group size. Since reciprocal altruism is based on individual interactions, it is necessary that interacting parties know each other. This generally means that the group be small, so that the individuals within it interact repeatedly—in other words, reciprocal altruism would be more likely to work in a rural area or a small town rather than, say, New York City (unless one is talking about an enclave that functions as a cohesive community). Other factors are living under circumstances where there is a likelihood of needing mutual assistance (such as several farm families living in an isolated area). Pairs of individuals that normally interact should be exposed to needs or dangers of a comparable kind. And they must have equivalent levels of ability to help each other. Since the reciprocal benefits may take a long time before bearing fruit, the interacting groups should be stable and have a low dispersal rate (thus migrant workers are not good candidates). This is why we are more likely to invite a longtime neighbor to dinner than someone renting the house next door for a month (unless the people are delightful or might be useful to you). Having young children leads to a higher degree of mutual dependence and encourages collaboration and reciprocity, thus adding an additional incentive.[24]

The type of social organization is also significant. The more egalitarian it is, the higher the likelihood of reciprocal altruism working effectively. For instance, in a hierarchical baboon troop, the dominant alpha male is not dependent on its inferiors. Yet chimpanzees, which have a less rigid social hierarchy, are more interdependent (for instance, they will share food); therefore, they are more likely to engage in reciprocal altruism. Similarly, where money is concerned, the rich and the very poor are not good candidates to engage in reciprocal altruism; the rich do not need the poor, and the poor have no money to offer in return. Altruism in those cases takes the form of charity (or it may have its own non-monetary rewards).

No matter how altruistic the act, the calculation of self-interest is close to the surface. For instance, we are less likely to enter into reciprocal alliances with the very young and the very old than with those in the prime of their lives. On the other hand, one can invest in a younger person with the hope of reaping the benefits in the future. Moreover, the currency of exchange need not be the same. When you are a mentor to students or younger colleagues, what you want in return is not career advancement for yourself but respect and the satisfaction of having helped a worthy individual or paying your debt to society. Gratitude and sympathy also enter into the altruistic calculus. Ingratitude and being taken for granted are upsetting. By contrast, a heartfelt appreciation ("I will never forget what you did for me") is gratifying to the donor and increases the likelihood that the recipient of the favor may reciprocate one way or another.[25]

Reciprocal altruism is also a way of extending the benefits of communal relationships to exchange relationships. Kinship does not guarantee automatic altruism. There are parents and children who do not help, and may even hurt each other (some of the worst feuds occur within families). Consequently, one can argue that underneath the most selfless parental love runs an expectation of reciprocal gain, even if it is wholly emotional. Traditionally, parents have expected to be cared for by their children as they get old. Even though that may no longer be the case in industrialized societies, parents still hope for some measure of affection and care from their offspring.

Self-sacrificing individuals are called "saints," but they do not appear to be shining examples of reproductive fitness. Does that make them evolutionary misfits? Does their benevolence result from some hidden sense of guilt that needs to be expiated by public service? Is their payoff the admiration and esteem they receive, or the hope of entering paradise?

Mother Teresa, perhaps more than any other person in the modern world, has come to symbolize selfless love for the world's poorest of the poor. For almost half a century, she ministered to the destitute, sick, orphaned, and dying (including washing the bodies of the dead). Her followers operate 610 missions in 123 countries. Mother Theresa received the Nobel Peace Prize in 1979 and was beatified by Pope John Paul II. Yet in recently published letters to her spiritual advisors, she expresses terrible sorrow about her life, describing it in terms like, "dryness," "darkness," and "sadness."[26] Does this mean there is no such thing as "pure" altruism? If so, what was the payoff of Mother Teresa's altruism? It is hard to answer that question without being naïve or cynical.

Guilt, the Cheater Detector

Like all other transactions based on trust, reciprocal altruism has a basic pitfall. The persons you are dealing with may fail to live up to their obligations—they may cheat. If so, what was intended as a reciprocal exchange ends up as a selfish deal. We call cheaters derogatory names (swindlers, impostors, frauds) and treat them with disdain and may even consider them immoral. However, in evolutionary terms, the term "cheating" is used solely to denote the failure to reciprocate and has no implications of moral censure.[27]

The roots of cheating run deep and are even traced to animals.[28] Some similarities are close enough to be comical. For example, among long-tailed macaques, sexual access to females is limited to the dominant alpha male. When the alpha male moves indoors in a zoo compound, the subservient males hustle eagerly to copulate with the females (who are happy to oblige). Should the dominant male catch them, they will be in deep trouble. But even when the alpha male rejoins the group unaware of what has transpired, the culprits act in an ingratiating and submissive manner, with wide grins on their faces to appease the cuckold.

Cheating provides short-term benefits. Like stealing, you get something for nothing. If cheaters regularly got away with it, then cheating would be selected as enhancing reproductive fitness. Yet there are risks associated with cheating. The defrauded party may retaliate by either punishing the offender or refraining from future altruistic gestures.

The cheater may chalk this up to the cost of doing business, but the matter does not end there. Cheaters who develop a reputation of being untrustworthy are shunned and punished not only by the victim but by the group itself. Blatant offenders are put out of business in short order, but more subtle cheaters represent a more insidious threat to the workings of reciprocal altruism.

The most effective way of being a free rider is to conceal one's intentions under a cloak of honesty. This is done by mimicking the characteristics of true altruism through acts of generosity, friendship, sympathy, even sham indignation at cheating, and by relating to an exchange relationship partner as if one were in a communal relationship ("You are like family"). (Bernard Madoff could act as the poster boy for such characters.) Cheaters may not even be conscious of their own deception. The most effective liars are those who actually believe in their own lies. (In which case, can we call them liars?)

Typically, guilt-free cheaters will not claim outright that it is fine to cheat; rather, they will rationalize and find mitigating reasons for why they cheat ("Everybody does it"; "I need to survive"; "I can't help it"). How can we protect ourselves from cheaters? We can apply tests of consistency, judge trustworthiness by actions rather than words, and apply a healthy dose of skepticism. We also need to guard ourselves against misguided compassion ("He can't help it; he had a hard life") and being charmed by cheaters. In short, we should rely on some of the same strategies we use against psychopaths. However, while we need to protect ourselves against cheaters' tactics, our defenses are not cost-free. For instance, being overly suspicious may stop us from taking calculated chances in being altruistic to a relative stranger who could have ended up as a good friend or even a benefactor. Moreover, since altruistic relationships span a long time, with many "goods" changing hands, calculating net gains and losses is often difficult—and cheaters take advantage of that. Crime sometimes does pay.

In dealing with cheaters, societies may engage in *moralistic aggression* by punishing the culprits severely so as to make an example of them. Moralizing leads to a sense of righteous indignation, which in turn can lead to exacting revenge (as in lynching by a mob). More pragmatic considerations also enter the picture. In eighteenth-century England, debtors who failed to pay their debts were put in prison like criminals. The point was that the failure to honor contracts would undermine the economic basis of society. Capital punishment is another form of moralistic aggression that is perpetrated by the state against offenders, who are often prejudicially selected by ethnicity or social class (in 2007, half of those executed in the United States were African Americans).

When cheaters face the prospect of discovery, they may engage in *reparative altruism* by admitting wrongdoing, compensating the victim, and giving assurances there will be no further cheating in the future. This may represent an honest coming to terms with one's misdeeds or an attempt to get off the hook. The *feeling of guilt* has evolved in order to motivate the cheater to come clean. Since no external policing alone can stop cheaters effectively, the emotion of guilt acts like an internal moral enforcer. This is why guilt is called a *cheater detector*: it motivates offenders to reveal their misdeeds to the world.[29] Guilt has thus evolved as an *algorithm* in its function as an internal moral agency.

An algorithm is a simple mathematical procedure that does not require an understanding of its logical structure. It is the way a computer follows a series of established steps in solving a problem. It requires no "thinking." Similarly, the guilty response is supposed to function "automatically."[30]

The Expanding Circle and the Floating Pyramid

To illustrate the web of human relationships within which altruism operates, philosopher Peter Singer has envisaged a set of expanding concentric circles. At the very center would be our own self (at least in individualistic Western societies). In the next circle would be members of our nuclear family (our parents and siblings, or our spouse and children). This is followed by members of our extended families, including relatives by marriage (in-laws and their circles of relationships). We can expand these connections as far as our kinship ties remain recognizable, such as in clans and tribes.[31]

In the next set of circles would be those unrelated to us by blood or marriage: for instance, our friends, co-workers, neighbors, and acquaintances, and more broadly, religious communities, associations, nations, and civilizations. Despite their distance from the center, those encompassed by this circle may call upon us to serve or even give our lives, such as by dying for our country or as martyrs to our faith. It may be argued that dying for one's country ultimately means dying to protect those near and dear to us; thus, patriotism and religious faiths put forth their own intrinsic reasons worth dying for. The final circle ultimately takes in all of humanity, and beyond that (at least for some people) all forms of life. The ideal is the universal unity of all human beings, as has been expressed by many visionaries. Here is Darwin's version:

> As man advances in civilisation, and small tribes are united into larger communities, the simplest reason would tell each individual that he ought to extend his social instincts and sympathies to all the members of the same nation, though personally unknown to him. This point being once reached, there is only an artificial barrier to prevent his sympathies extending to the men of all nations and races.[32]

The expanding circle of concern is a useful metaphor but it is not a rigid system. For instance, we may feel closer to some of our friends than to our relatives. Even a pet may elicit more altruism than a family member. (One woman reportedly left 12 million dollars in her will to her dog, while two of her grandchildren got nothing.) Virtual relationships on the internet may come to mean more to some people than living and breathing creatures. However, when we are thinking in evolutionary terms, we are concerned mainly with universals that apply to large groups of people over an extended time, not individual aberrations.

The basic rule here is that the degree of empathy, and hence the level of altruism, is directly proportional to the closeness of the object of concern to the person at the center of the circles. However, another critical factor has to do with the availability of *resources*. To be altruistic, we need something to be altruistic with; we cannot give away what we do not have. Frans de Waal illustrates this with his model of a *floating pyramid*.

Instead of concentric circles, consider a pyramid consisting of a series of rectangular compartments of decreasing size stacked on top of each other. The largest compartment at the bottom represents our obligations to all life forms. Successively higher levels correspond to progressively smaller groups of people who are closer to us. The self occupies the top compartment of the pyramid (corresponding to the center of the circles). The pyramid floats in a sea of resources. The density of the water (like a saturated salt solution) represents the level of resources available and determines how high the pyramid will float. The higher it floats, the larger the area of altruistic concern above the water. When resources are scarce, the pyramid sinks down and fewer groups are within the range of moral concern. In a hypothetical worst case, only the top is above water—only one's own self counts. This puts altruism on a more secure, pragmatic basis, and makes it less of an abstract principle.

Not everyone is convinced that human altruism has animal antecedents. For the more skeptical, animals lack the capacity for true moral reasoning. Just as animals can communicate quite effectively but cannot use language, the same is true of morality. The grammatical universals for language and morality have not been hard-wired or encoded in animal brains. What animals have are the *precursors* of these human capabilities. But that does not amount to having a moral conscience that makes feeling guilty possible. Animals may know what to do and what not to do, but they cannot differentiate between right and wrong—between what *is* and what *ought to be*. It is the ability to make that differentiation that defines the moral dimension. In other words, animals know what the rules *are* but not why there *should* be rules in the first place. They know what to do, but not why. It is the uniquely human knowledge of moral responsibility that leads to true feelings of guilt.[33]

THE CULTURAL EVOLUTION OF GUILT

The evolutionary roots of guilt would explain its universal features. However, guilt, shame, and moral emotions generally have undergone a great deal of further change that would account for their variations within different cultures. That is part of the heritage of the cultural evolution of guilt, which has determined how it is experienced, under what circumstances, and to what ends.[34]

After the capacity for guilt evolved in the ancestral environment, it is not clear what happened next. During much of prehistory, humans continued to live as hunters and gatherers. They went around looking for food, interacting with each other within small kinship groups, and reproducing. But that is not all they did. They began to bury their dead, which implies some sort of belief in life after death. They increasingly evolved sophisticated rules of behavior that reflected a growing awareness of right and wrong.

About 30,000 years ago human populations began to grow larger more rapidly and people lived longer. With more grandparents around there was more opportunity to pass on cultural traditions, including rules of behavior. A dramatic upsurge in creative activity led to the production of sophisticated cave paintings and female figurines (called "mother goddesses") with exaggerated hips and breasts, suggestive of religious symbols of fecundity. The capacity to produce such symbolic objects implies the existence of abstract thought and the beginning of belief systems. It is perhaps by this time that a more distinct and self-conscious sense of guilt / shame made its appearance.

The development of agriculture about 10,000 years ago, during the Neolithic period, led to the growth of more complex sedentary societies. This had enormous social implications. Archeological evidence suggests the growth of more formal religious systems, and a further refinement of moral reasoning, during this time. From then on, it is only a matter of a few thousand years until the invention of writing in Mesopotamia and Egypt some 5,000 years ago, which ushered in the historical period and with it the establishment of organized religions. By this time, the experiences of guilt and shame may well have attained their more or less modern forms.[35]

The Origins of Guilt in Primal Religions

Theories of the origins of religion are speculative—the archeology of material cultures cannot tell us directly about what ancient peoples thought or believed. Anthropologists have tried to re-create this past by studying the religious beliefs and practices of preliterate traditional cultures (such as that of Australian aborigines) whose religious beliefs and practices approximate those of older, extinct human societies.

We call these earlier beliefs *primal religions* (not "primitive" religions).[36] The general premise is that early religious beliefs emerged out of attempts to deal with natural forces. Faced with threatening natural phenomena, like thunder and lightning, early humans must have wondered *who* rather than *what* was causing these events. This attribution of forces to external agents led to the belief in supernatural beings—ghosts, spirits, and ultimately gods. (For instance, the ancient Canaanites associated lightning with the god Hadad; the Greeks, with Zeus.)

Early people lived in an *animistic* world where every natural object or phenomenon possessed a life of its own and its spirit exerted a beneficial or malevolent influence on human lives. Shamans communicated with this world of spirits through magical rituals and trances. They warded off evil, provided healing, and foretold the future. The world was full of hazards, but it also sustained and nurtured people. People in turn lived in harmony with nature rather than trying to defy, challenge, or reshape it (actually, nomadic pastoralists did a lot of damage by overgrazing). Anthropological pioneers like James Frazer saw religion as the result of human attempts to deal with the powers that direct and control the course of nature and human life.[37]

Preliterate people had a profound sense of the *sacred*. They saw the world divinely ordered, with everything in its proper place. This made certain objects sacred; taking them out of their place interfered with the order of the universe. They developed rituals to influence nature, such as inducing rainfall, but they had no institutionalized religious beliefs or practices dedicated to abstract ideas like sin and salvation. Life after death was a shadowy existence out there somewhere.

How would one experience guilt in such a world? What would be the transgressions that would induce the sense of having done wrong and feeling bad about it? While we have no certain answers for these questions, it is likely that the earliest transgressions which induced a sense of guilt were of a ritual, rather than of a moral, nature; they were more concerned with pollution than ethics. And the prohibitions that arose were associated with magical practices through which people tried to relate to and propitiate the powerful forces ruling their world.

When we make someone angry, we try to appease that person by humbling ourselves and making amends by offering gifts. We expiate our guilt by paying a debt. Ancient people treated supernatural powers the same way by ascribing human feelings and motives to them. And the most common way of propitiation and expiation was through animal sacrifice. Closely related to this practice were concerns over purity and pollution that arose from the violation of taboos.

Totem and Taboo

The ethical lives of preliterate people were guided by oral traditions derived from archetypal ancestors. The individual's identity was shaped by the tribe, represented by an *animal totem* symbolizing the ancestor. Totems linked the tribe to an animal species (such as the wolf or the crow) in a ceremonial union that gave them a common life. The totem animal bonded the members of the tribe together and offered them help and protection. In return, it was treated with respect and not hunted or harmed.

Taboo is a Polynesian word that refers to the prohibition of behaviors involving a person, animal, object, or word. A taboo object is forbidden because it is sacred or unclean. In either case, it is endowed with a special power that is dangerous. The fundamental taboo object in preliterate societies was the totem. Other typical taboo objects could be persons endowed with power (such as chiefs or priests) as well as the dead, whose spirits lived on. The basic taboo in preliterate societies pertained to harming or violating the totem. Other taboo behaviors were related to food, sex, and the relationships between people and nature. Breaking a taboo brought supernatural retribution as well as social ostracism and punishment, including death. In fact, people who accidentally touched taboo objects, even inadvertently, could be so terrified that they would get sick and die.[38]

Darwin assumed that prehistoric societies consisted of small bands of people under the domination of a sexually possessive male. Freud extended this idea into that of a primitive horde ruled over by a tyrannical father who kept the women to himself and drove away his sons when they came of age. The sons then banded together and killed their father. However, since they also loved their father, they were stricken with remorse. This led to the emergence of a "consciousness of guilt." The dead father became the model of the ancestral totem and harming the totem / father became taboo. Remorse induced the rebellious sons to deny to themselves their father's women (their mothers and sisters), thus instituting the universal incest taboo.

In elaborating his ideas on totem and taboo, Freud relied heavily on the work of contemporary social anthropologists like James Frazer. His own contribution was to apply psychoanalytic principles to these issues by drawing parallels between the thinking of "primitive" people and those of children and neurotics (in particular, obsessive-compulsives).[39] These early anthropological interpretations and their elaborations by Freud have been largely discredited. Nonetheless, it is interesting to note how in *Totem and Taboo* Freud makes explicit the association between taboo, guilt, and conscience:

> If I am not mistaken, the explanation of the taboo also throws light on the nature and origin of *conscience*. It is possible, without any stretching the sense of the terms, to speak of a taboo conscience or, after a taboo has been violated, of a taboo sense of guilt. Taboo conscience is probably the earliest form in which the phenomenon of conscience is met with.[40]

GUILT AND SHAME CULTURES

Guilt, shame, and embarrassment are forms of *social control*. Whether these are cast in evolutionary, psychological, or cultural terms, we should not lose sight of that basic function. These emotions may not always be portrayed in these terms, but that is how they have evolved and become embedded in our cultural beliefs and practices. It is in this context that we should raise the question: Are there *shame cultures* as opposed to *guilt cultures*, with corresponding differences in how people within them experience guilt and shame?

The issue of such a cultural contrast was introduced in 1946 by anthropologist Ruth Benedict in her book *The Chrysanthemum and the Sword*.[41] Its purpose was to provide a better understanding of Japanese culture in connection with the reconstruction of Japan in the postwar period. Benedict designated Japan as a shame culture in contrast to the American guilt culture. This led to a furious controversy because shame was seen as a more "primitive" moral emotion that is elicited by external judgments, whereas guilt was seen as a more highly developed moral feeling arising from an internalized moral conscience.[42] Benedict's critique pointed out that the Japanese are also highly sensitive to feelings of guilt for the plight of others, even when they are not personally responsible for it. Guilt was integral to Japanese culture; the reason shame appeared to be prominent was because of its collectivistic, group-oriented values and the desire for unity, belongingness, and interdependence.[43]

As a cultural relativist, Benedict had no intention to denigrate Japanese culture or to suggest a sharp dichotomy between guilt and shame cultures. She pointed to Japanese guilt ("Japanese sometimes react as strongly as any

Puritan to a private accumulation of guilt"), as well as to the role of shame in American culture. The difference was a matter of relative emphasis, with the Japanese attaching a greater importance to shame than guilt:

> The early Puritans who settled in the United States tried to base their whole morality on guilt. . . . But shame is an increasingly heavy burden in the United States and guilt is less extremely felt than in earlier generations . . . [even though] we do not expect shame to do the heavy work of morality. We do not harness the acute personal chagrin which accompanies shame to our fundamental system of morality.
>
> The Japanese do. A failure to follow their explicit signposts of good behavior, a failure to balance obligations or to foresee contingencies is a shame (*haji*). Shame, they say, is the root of virtue. A man who is sensitive to it will carry out all the rules of behavior. 'A man who knows shame' is sometimes translated 'virtuous man,' sometimes 'man of honor.' Shame has the same place of authority in Japanese ethics that a 'clear conscience,' 'being right with God,' and the avoidance of sin have in Western ethics.[44]

INDIVIDUALISTIC VERSUS COMMUNITY-BASED MORALITY

Discussions of cultural differences between shame and guilt have shifted away from the more value-laden earlier conceptions. Moreover, there has been a greater appreciation of the cultural influences in the way moral codes are shaped. As we pointed in the preceding chapter, both Kohlberg's cognitive model as well as Gilligan's morality-of-caring alternative of moral judgment are based on Western ideals of individual autonomy. In contrast, in Asian cultures, moral responsibility is based on duties determined by one's obligations to others.[45]

In American culture (and Western cultures generally), personal identity is conceived of as being independent and autonomous. Society is seen as a collection of self-contained individuals who are held responsible for their own behavior. One's interests are best served by allowing maximum freedom and responsibility in choosing one's objectives. Moral precepts are based on conceptions of justice. Even when these are tempered by interpersonal obligations, the focus remains on individuals who must balance their responsibilities between the self and significant others.

The primary moral obligation is to avoid harming significant others. It is when you cause harm, or are unjust, that you feel guilty. Being responsive to the needs of others is desirable, but is not a moral duty. Individuals are free to follow their inclinations within the limits of the law and in consideration of the rights of others. Their obligations to others are defined in negative terms—what they should not do—rather than as positive duties of what they should do. Whereas the failure to uphold justice is a vice, the failure to be beneficent to others is only a lack of moral virtue.[46]

By contrast, in Asian contexts, one's identity is defined in relation to the group one belongs to, typically the family. Whereas in the West, a person would be known as Jane or John Doe, in the East, they would be identified as members of the Doe family. In her study of Indian Hindus, psychologist Joan Miller found that the primary basis of determining moral conduct was not justice but a person's duties to significant others. Among Americans, moral duty is imposed on the individual to constrain that individual's actions. For Hindus, doing one's duty meant both meeting one's obligations as well as realizing one's own nature. Therefore acting benevolently toward others was not an aim secondary to considerations of justice, nor was it a matter of acting above and beyond the call of duty—fulfilling one's social duty was the primary purpose of moral conduct.[47]

These differences lead to contrasting ways of determining what is moral. For instance, if there is no other way to help a friend in need, it would be ethical for an Indian to steal but unethical for an American to do so even if it means failing to help the friend. These differences are not absolute; nonetheless, twice as many Indians as Americans would give priority to interpersonal considerations over abstract ethical principles. Moreover, Indians were more prone than Americans to make contextual exceptions (where the morality of an action depends on the nature of the relationship and the circumstances of the case), whereas Americans took a more absolute view about an action being right or wrong, irrespective of other considerations. The moral objective in the West, as noted above, is to avoid doing wrong and is more objective; in the East, it is to do what is right and is more subjective.

Similar considerations apply in other Asian cultures. In China, the family is the "great self." One starts by literally owing one's life to one's parents. One's primary obligation in life is to serve and protect social ties, not pursue personal goals. Similarly, while Americans place a high premium on self-reliance, the Japanese favor interdependence and harmonious integration within the group. Individuals in both groups are highly competitive but in different ways. Americans want to *get ahead* of others; the Japanese are concerned with not falling behind; instead of pushing ahead, they *line up sideways*. The personal boundaries of Americans have been compared to the hard shell of an egg; those of the Japanese, to an egg's soft internal membrane.[48]

This individualistic-versus-interdependent basis of moral judgment helps clarify the problematic distinctions between shame and guilt cultures. Instead of these designations explaining differences in such a way that makes one culture seem morally superior to another, they explain cultural differences as the outcome of serving different needs. In the Western context of individualism, guilt, with its emphasis on autonomy, provides a better moral foundation for guiding individuals who are responsible for themselves. With a lesser sense of responsibility for others, there is less need for shame as a form of social control. By contrast, in the Asian cultural context, where maintaining harmony in relationships is most valued, shame is a more effective means of moral control. Since personal boundaries extend beyond the individual, it becomes more difficult to generate guilt. When someone does wrong, it is not only the person but everyone related to that person who shares in the guilt. Therefore, shame in Asian cultures fulfills some of the same functions of social control that guilt does in the West and vice versa.

These considerations are important to our understanding of differences in the ways guilt and shame are perceived in Western and Eastern religion, which we will discuss in the next two chapters. For instance, the centrality of shame in Confucianism has led to the general impression that Confucian China is a shame society, and hence is ethically less developed. Mark Berkson has raised cogent arguments that this characterization is not valid. Confucian ethics, being far from being ethically less well developed, offers much to others to learn from.[49] While generally framed in East / West terms, these differences between guilt and shame can also be seen within Western culture itself in historical perspective. As noted earlier, Homeric heroes in ancient Greece were driven by the twin virtues of honor and fame. In their warlike society such virtues were best manifested on the battlefield. The self-esteem of heroes like Achilles, Odysseus, and Oedipus depended on their standing in the eyes of their peers, with whom they were in fierce competition and often conflict. Failure led to loss of face and shame. Consequently, shame has been generally assumed to be the predominant moral sentiment that motivated and restrained the ancient Greeks. Their shame culture was based on public esteem. What mattered was where one stood with respect to one's peers, who constituted an honor-group. This view has been challenged by moral philosopher Bernard

Williams, who argues that that Greek conceptions of shame also included elements of guilt as well.[50]

These cultural differences are embedded in various languages as well. This makes translating terms like guilt and shame a common source of confusion. For example, when we look for synonyms for shame and guilt in Chinese, we do not find single terms that correspond to them. Rather, we find a number of terms that correspond to various types of shame, making distinctions that do not exist in English. In some contexts, even guilt may appear as a subsidiary form of shame.

Even if the terms to designate them vary, are these emotions universal or culture specific? Do an American and an Indian experience guilt and shame the same way, whatever they call them? There are no simple answers to this question. Some emotions appear to be more universal than others; for instance, it is hard to imagine a culture that does not recognize expressions of fear or anger. However, when it comes to complex emotions like guilt and shame, which are more subject to cultural variation, the picture becomes less clear. Even the fact that a culture has no word for an emotion does not mean that the emotion it represents is absent.

Linguists point out that even if certain emotions are universal, their terminology is not. For instance, there is no word for "disgust" in Polish. And in one Australian aboriginal language, "fear" and "shame" are expressed by the same word (associated with the impulse to retreat). The common error is to start with one's own language and look for exact translations in other languages. Ultimately, it is not through specific terms like "guilt" or "shame" but through *metalanguage*—descriptions of the essential elements in emotional states—that we can test the universality of the emotions. For instance, the answer to "How do you feel when you have lost someone dear to you?" would convey the idea of sadness better than would the answer to the question "Do you feel sad?"

How does the evolutionary view help us in *dealing with guilt*? This is not a matter explicitly addressed by evolutionary psychologists, therefore we will have less to say about it than in previous chapters. Nonetheless, the evolutionary basis of the capacity for altruism and the capacity to feel guilty provides us with a natural foundation for guilt, and hence the need for its acceptance and usefulness. If guilt is indeed part of our nature, and there are good reasons for it, it makes no sense to fight it or deny it. Accepting guilt as a fact of life therefore makes it easier to approach it in a positive manner, and perhaps helps us to resolve it in more authentic and adaptive ways.

In the next two chapters, we will return to some of the issues discussed in this chapter, particularly with regard to the cultural evolution of guilt. However, the religious perspectives on guilt that we will turn to in the next two chapters differ sharply in their approach to moral judgment, and hence to the experience of guilt. Most fundamentally, whereas above we described conceptions of divinity as human creations, in monotheistic religions God exists as an independent entity who creates human beings, and not the other way around. It is God who imparts to humans moral laws through revelations to select individuals. These divine messages constitute the sacred texts that contain the ethical principles and moral prescriptions for leading one's life. We will therefore let the voices of six world religions speak for themselves in conveying how guilt functions in human lives.

8 GUILT IN JUDAISM, CHRISTIANITY, AND ISLAM

GUILT AND RELIGION have a long-standing association in Western culture. Even in an increasingly secular world, religious beliefs continue to shape our moral values, including those of nonbelievers.[1] As the Colombian novelist Gabriel García Márquez put it, "I don't believe in God, but I am afraid of Him."

With this chapter we shift our focus from the secular to the religious perspective. We will first deal with Judaism, Christianity, and Islam, then in the next chapter we turn to Hinduism, Buddhism, and Confucianism. Religious conceptions of guilt in these great religious traditions are embedded in their particular social and psychological contexts. In the monotheistic traditions, God reveals his moral precepts to select individuals by speaking to them in their own language and at a particular time and place in history. The expressions of the divine are less personal in Asian religions. Nonetheless, all sacred teachings must be understood within their cultural contexts. These contexts change over time, and religions change with them while maintaining a core of beliefs and practices.

The life of St. Augustine is not a model for the experience of guilt in Christianity, let alone Judaism or Islam. However, given the enormous impact that

The lectures of the following colleagues to my seminar introduced me to their respective areas: Arnold Eisen, Charlotte Fonrobert, Mark Mancall, and Steven Goldsmith (Judaism); Robert Gregg, George Brown, Barbara Pitkin, and Lewis Spitz (Christianity); Ebrahim Moosa and Carol Delaney (Islam).

I am grateful to Shahzad Bashir, Arnold Eisen, Robert Gregg, Mark Mancall, William McLennan, Ebrahim Moosa, and Ernlé Young for their critiques and invaluable help in the preparation of this chapter.

Augustine has had on conceptions of guilt in Western culture, and his own personal struggles with guilt, he is a good choice for an introductory account of guilt.

Augustine was born in 354 into a family of modest means, in the small town of Thagaste in North Africa, during the declining years of the Roman empire. Augustine's mother was a devout Christian and the dominant influence in his life; his father was a pagan who converted to Christianity toward the end of his life and was a less significant figure for Augustine.

Augustine wrote the *Confessions* in his middle years; it is not an autobiography, even though it contains a good deal of biographical material. Rather, it was intended as an account of his spiritual journey following his conversion, a testament addressed to God in which Augustine disowns his worldly aspirations in favor of a Christian life.[2]

As a bright boy who was not fond of school, Augustine excelled in Latin but hated Greek. He grew into a boisterous adolescent. The *Confessions* is brimming with remorse over his youthful indiscretions. For instance, he is overwhelmed with guilt over having stolen some pears from a neighbor's tree:

> I wanted to carry out an act of theft and did so, driven by no kind of need other than my inner lack of any sense of, or feeling for, justice. . . . I stole something which I had in plenty and of much better quality. My desire was to enjoy not what I sought by stealing but merely the excitement of thieving and the doing of what was wrong.[3]

The memory of his sexual awakenings filled Augustine with moral dismay:

> The single desire that dominated my search for delight was simply to love and be loved. . . . Clouds of muddy carnal concupiscence filled the air. The bubbling impulses of puberty befogged and obscured my heart so that it could not see the difference between love's serenity and lust's darkness. Confusion of the two things boiled within me. It seized hold of my youthful weakness sweeping me through the precipitous rocks of desire to submerge me in a whirlpool of vice.[4]

Peer pressure led Augustine to "pretend I had done things I had not done at all, so that my innocence should not lead my companions to scorn my lack of courage, and lest my chastity be taken a mark of inferiority."[5] At age sixteen, Augustine was sent to study in Carthage, where he seems to have jumped from the frying pan into the fire: "I came to Carthage and all around me hissed a cauldron of illicit loves. As yet I had never been in love and I longed to love. . . . I sought an object for my love; I was in love with love."[6]

These are the recollections of a 47-year-old revered bishop looking back on his life. His experiences illustrate his tortuous spiritual journey that led to his salvation. There is no evidence that Augustine experienced much guilt while he was actually going through these experiences. The guilt was after the fact, in hindsight.

At the age of seventeen, Augustine met a young woman in Carthage who became his concubine, a common practice at the time that even the Catholic church was willing to recognize provided the couple remained faithful, as Augustine did for fifteen years. Given her lowly origins, he could not marry her, but they had a son early in their relationship (who died in adolescence) and Augustine appears to have been very fond of his concubine, but he does not provide any more details about her, not even her name.

As a young man, Augustine went through a lengthy and anguished religious quest. He became a Manichee then a Neoplatonist. He earnestly struggled with the desire to embrace Christianity, but he did not want to relinquish his way of life. He prayed for chastity, "but not yet." Augustine became a brilliant scholar and a renowned teacher of rhetoric in Rome and Milan. Eventually, the woman he lived with became an obstacle to his social aspirations because of her humble origins, and he was persuaded by his mother to break off his relationship in favor of a socially more advantageous marriage. Augustine then became engaged to a very young girl, but he had to wait for her to reach marriageable age (twelve under Roman law) in order to marry her. However, in the meantime he converted to Christianity and took monastic vows. Five years later, he went back to North Africa and spent the remaining thirty-four years of his life as the bishop of Hippo, teaching, preaching, and writing voluminously.

Much can been made of Augustine's views on guilt based on his personal life, especially his relationship with his mother. The struggles with guilt that he dwells on are sometimes inconsistent. He frets over adolescent escapades, but reports no remorse for concealing from his mother the fact that he was going to go away and leave her behind. Nor does he express any guilt for abandoning the woman he had loved and lived with for years, and who was the mother of his child. His keen sense of guilt is linked with the residues of the various ideologies he was exposed to (such as aversion to the physical body in Manichaeism), his vision darkened by the gloomy outlook of life in the tottering Roman empire. What is important for us is not so much who he was but his enormous impact in shaping the conscience of the Western world, an issue we will address shortly.

That we will no longer dwell on the psychology of guilt here on does not mean that psychological factors cease to be significant. Nonetheless, the religious approach to guilt does differ significantly from that of the behavioral sciences. Whereas psychological approaches are primarily concerned with the subjective experience of guilt, religions focus on guilt as moral culpability based on objective behaviors. Psychology is interested primarily in *how* people behave, while religions are more concerned with how they *ought* to behave and why they do not behave as they should. The first is primarily *descriptive*, the second *prescriptive*.

Do religions relieve or intensify guilt? The question makes guilt sound like an ailment to be made better or worse—a negative emotion with no redeeming features. Moreover, we cannot assess the impact on guilt by "religion" as a whole. There are important differences between how various religions perceive and use guilt as a spiritual vehicle and a form of social control, and encourage or discourage it. There is a world of difference, for instance, between Christianity and Buddhism in this regard.

The key concept underlying guilt in the monotheistic religions is that of *sin*. The word is derived from the Latin for guilt (*sont*), but the two are not the same. Sin results from violating a religious ordinance. Guilt is not a moral violation but the result of one, both as culpability as well as feeling remorseful. Although sin typically arises through human interactions, in monotheistic traditions all feelings of sin and guilt are experienced in relation to God. Guilt is a sign of alienation from God through sin. God is Lord (to be worshipped), Judge (to be feared), and Creator (to be loved like a parent). Therefore, one can offend God by being disrespectful, disobedient, and ungrateful. Only God can absolve one from sin and guilt. Redemption and forgiveness are therefore essential in dealing with guilt.[7]

In the Hebrew scriptures sin is understood as the breaking of the covenantal relationship between God and his Chosen People through their willful disobedience of the Law. In the New Testament, sin and guilt originate in the fall of Adam and Eve, and are perpetuated by human wrongdoing. Modern Christian theologians see sin in broader relational contexts. For instance, for Paul Tillich, sin represents estrangement from our true selves and others, and alienation from God; for Reinhold Niebuhr, sin results from pride and insatiable desire; for Karl Barth, it is caused by ingratitude.[8] In Islam also sin is opposition to God rooted in human pride and ingratitude.

The conception of guilt in these great religious traditions is a monumental topic. We have already discussed religious views on conscience in Chapter 2, which is directly relevant to the issue of guilt. Our discussion will be limited to a few key aspects. With respect to Judaism, we will focus on its ethics imbedded in the Law and the teachings of the prophets. In Christianity, we will consider briefly five key figures: Jesus, Paul, Augustine, Thomas Aquinas, and Martin Luther. And in Islam, we will discuss guilt in the context of Islamic law and mysticism.

GUILT IN JUDAISM

Many Jews seem to have a fascination with guilt. They both complain about it as well as take pride in their guilt-proneness ("I am Jewish. I know all about guilt").[9] The sensitivity to guilt is seen as an essential part of Judaism. Rabbi Harlan Wechsler writes:

> Deep in the Jewish tradition, deep in the psyche of the Bible, is a human being who can experience guilt. And it is true, whether one seeks to praise the fact or bury it very deep, that the culture of the Jews is a culture rooted in that conception of a human being. More than guilt's being a problem, it is second nature to Jews.[10]

The Jewish experience of guilt has a strong communal aspect. During the period of penitence culminating in the Day of Atonement (Yom Kippur) Jews plead for forgiveness collectively: "We are guilt ridden, we have been faithless, we have robbed. . . . We have committed iniquity, caused unrighteousness, have been presumptuous. . . . We have counseled evil, scoffed, revolted, blasphemed. May it be therefore Your will to forgive our sins, pardon us our inequities, to grant remission from our transgressions."[11]

There is also an important individual component of personal reflection and repentance. The individual stands alone before God, possessing no merits but trusting in God's mercy and love: "I am dust in my life, more so after death. Behold I am before You like a vessel filled with shame and confusion. May it be your will . . . that I may no more sin, and forgive the sins that I have already committed in Your abundant mercy."[12]

Jewish ethics is largely derived from the Law as well as prophetic conceptions of justice, fairness, and compassion. Jewish laws are not only negative injunctions, nor ethics merely a matter of refraining from immoral actions; they entail a positive commitment to moral action.

Judaism started as a priestly religion organized around the temple in Jerusalem. Like other ancient religions, its central ritual was sacrifice. Following the destruction of the temple by the Romans in the year 70, sacrifice could no longer be practiced; it was replaced by Rabbinical Judaism. Rabbis are not priests but legal scholars and teachers within the Jewish tradition. In some respects, religious scholars in Judaism are more like constitutional lawyers (as are Muslim scholars), while Christian theologians are more like philosophers.

There is no centralized religious hierarchy in Judaism. In the nineteenth century, Reform Judaism arose in Germany, representing the first significant religious alternative to Orthodoxy in the West. Reform Judaism retains the ethical component of Judaic law but dispenses with its cultic practices (such as its dietary requirements). Conservative Judaism then developed to bridge the gap.[13] All three forms of Judaism are developments of the modern period, although Orthodoxy more closely approximates premodern forms of Judaism.

The Hebrew scriptures (the Old Testament of the Christian Bible) consist of three parts. First comes the Law (Torah), consisting of the first five books (traditionally attributed to Moses); next come the Prophets (Nevi'im); and the rest constitute the Writings (Kethuvim). The first letters of these three terms make up the word *Tanakh*, which is the Hebrew name of the Jewish scriptures.[14] Another very important source in Judaism is the Talmud, which consists of the writings of rabbis from the fifth century, but also incorporates older legal traditions and legal precepts (the Mishna). The Talmud uses parables and sayings that address concerns associated with all of Jewish life, hence it has been singularly important in traditional Jewish education.

Judaism is a coherent religious tradition but it is not a monolithic entity. Over its long history it has undergone profound transformations. The biblical, Talmudic, medieval, and modern periods have their own particular ethical concerns. While it is convenient to refer to Judaism as a single entity, it encompasses a vast and diverse religious tradition spanning 3,000 years. Therefore, whatever we say about guilt in Judaism is not going to apply to all Jews at all times and in all places.

Law and Culpability
Judaic law is embodied in the Halakha, primarily based on the Torah and the Talmud. It represents the "way" by which life should be lived to be holy.

Its commandments regulate virtually all aspects of Jewish life. A devout Jew "observes" the Law—not "believes" in it; its validity does not require faith or rational proof; it is taken as a given.

Guilt in Judaism derives primarily from culpability for violating the Law. Being guilty is essentially the same as having sinned. The word for both guilt and sin is *awon*, translated as "iniquity." (To "bear one's iniquity" means to be guilty.)[15] Implied in *awon* is the idea of lawlessness and rebellion that point to the centrality of the Law in Jewish ethics. The Law encompasses many rules but at heart it is a covenant—a solemn contract—between God and his Chosen People that imposes reciprocal obligations on both. Laws typically refer to conduct, but Judaism is also concerned with moral intentions and motives, and rabbis inveigh against hardening of the heart and wrongful desire.[16]

Judaic law applies to everyone—rich and poor, ruler and subject—even to God.[17] As God was planning the destruction of Sodom, Abraham dared to argue, "Will the judge of all land not act justly?" (Gen. 18:25). Jewish ethics is especially concerned with the protection of those who are vulnerable, like the poor, the widow, and the orphan.[18] It can be quite harsh, but it also invokes love and compassion to moderate justice. The supreme commandment is, "you shall love the Lord your God with all your heart, and with all your soul and with all your might" and "you shall love your neighbor as yourself" (Deut. 6:4). (Christians associate these commandments with Jesus but he was actually quoting the Jewish scriptures; Mark 12:29–31.)

Transgressions in Judaism are of two kinds. They may result from the violation of *moral laws* as exemplified by the Ten Commandments. Then there are ritual transgressions that violate *cultic laws*. A ritual transgression is like a victimless crime. It does not involve doing anything morally wrong; it may even result from praiseworthy acts such as burying one's father (touching a dead body makes one "unclean"). Such cultic practices may have arisen from the awe ancient people felt toward processes of life and death or health considerations (which may, for example, be associated with eating pork). Other ritual prohibitions are more puzzling (like mixing cotton and wool in garments).

It may come as a surprise that there is no word for "conscience" in biblical Hebrew. In modern Hebrew, the word *matspun* (derived from "what is hidden") was created to represent a moral compass. The fact that there is no word for conscience does not mean that Jews do not have a conscience (just as the absence of a word for spleen in ancient Hebrew does not mean that Jews have no spleens).[19]

Biblical Hebrew uses body parts as metaphors for emotions.[20] "Heart" comes closest to the idea of conscience as in "David's heart smote him" (1 Sam. 24:5). The kidneys (reins) have a similar meaning, as in "Thus my heart was grieved and I was pricked in my reins" (Ps. 73:21).[21] There is no term that directly conveys the subjective feeling of remorse, but David's "heart smote him" conveys the same idea. Another term that comes close to guilt is the expression of deep regret (*tsa-ar*).[22]

Some other ancient terms also bear on the concept of guilt. *Asham* is associated with a guilt offering as an act of reparation mandated for an individual for a specific offence, such as desecrating a sacred object or making a false oath.[23] *Asham* implies legal culpability and requires that the offender make a sacrifice to God and compensate the victim. It also implies paying a fine (hence guilt as debt).[24] In modern Hebrew, *asham* has evolved into two meanings: *Ashem* stands for being guilty, and *ashma* for feeling guilty, thus replicating the dual meaning of guilt as in English.

The second term—*khatta't*—is linked with sacrifice as a purification offering in response to the violation of a ritual law. It has the same root as *khet'*, or sin, so it is also referred to as "sin offering." Its central function is purification. What purifies the sinner is remorse and repentance, but the ritual itself is also important. For instance, if the impurity is caused by contact with blood (such as in menstruation or childbirth) a ritual bath (*mikvah*) accomplishes the purification. There is no need for remorse or repentance in such a case since no moral wrong has been committed.[25]

The idea of sin in Judaism is closer to the ancient Greek idea for it than the Christian concept. Both *khet'* in Hebrew and *hamartia* in Greek mean "missing the mark"—in this case, making a mistake by failing to observe the law. The major sins in Judaism are idolatry, murder, and adultery. The Hebrew word for shame is *busha* and is related to nudity, the exposure of the body to those who should not see it. Seeing the nudity of the father by the sons is particularly objectionable in the Old Testament.

The Prophets and Repentance

Prophets played a key role in shaping the ethical consciousness of Judaism. We tend to associate prophecy with foretelling the future, but the primary function of Jewish prophets was to speak for the Lord in denouncing heathenism and demanding justice. Prophets represent the voice of ethical monotheism. Their call is for repentance—returning to God—addressed both to individuals and to the community at large.

Some early prophets were part of the religious hierarchy; others, like Isaiah, Amos, and Hosea, were not. Prophets attacked social injustice, which reflected Israel's failings in its relationship with God. Amos equates social ills with sins against God. Isaiah exhorts the people to have their public and private lives manifest God's justice and righteousness in order to receive the Lord's blessings or else suffer his wrath.

The confrontation between the prophet Nathan and David illustrates the boldness with which prophets spoke truth to power. Bathsheba was the wife of Uriah, a Hittite soldier in the king's service. David saw Bathsheba bathing and he was smitten by her. He sent for her and got her pregnant. To get her husband out of the way, David ordered Uriah into battle where he was certain to die. David then married Bathsheba, who bore him a son. The Lord was displeased and sent Nathan to confront David with what he had done. Nathan began by giving David an account of a man who had committed a grievous injustice. David flew into a rage and told Nathan, "as the Lord lives, the man who did this deserves to die." Nathan responded, "That man is you" (2 Sam. 12:5–6). Chastened, David acknowledged his guilt ("I have sinned against the Lord"). By the law of retaliation, he should have died to atone for Uriah's wrongful death, but the Lord took pity on him and instead it was the child—the fruit of his iniquity—that got sick and died to pay David's debt. (His next son was Solomon.)

Ethical responsibilities in Judaism are at two levels. At the first, the moral obligations of Jews are to other Jews. The Lord gave Moses the Law for the use of the Israelites, not the world at large. Moral obligations are to one's neighbor, consisting of one's kin, or fellow Jews, not everybody. The prophetic messages were addressed to God's Chosen People, not to their neighbors (except for warnings for their hostility to Jews). However, there is also a wider dimension whereby the words of the Lord are meant for all of humanity—a universal ethic transmitted to the world through Judaism, as "a light unto all nations."

Guilt and the Evil Impulse

"God created man in his own image . . . male and female he created them. . . . And God saw everything that he had made, and behold, it was very good" (Gen. 1:27, 31). It was an excellent start, but things went wrong soon after.

Adam and Eve, deceived by the serpent, disobeyed God's command not to eat from the tree of knowledge of good and evil. When they ate the forbidden fruit (the Bible does not say what it was) "the eyes of both were opened," so they covered their nudity and hid themselves from God. The serpent personifies an evil spirit later on characterized as Satan—God's antagonist who induces human beings to commit sin. Adam and Eve were culpable for disobeying God, and were expelled from the Garden of Eden. Life on earth was to be one of toil and suffering culminating in death. Cain killed his brother Abel out of envy. Evil was now loose in the world.

The actions of Adam and Eve are more suggestive of shame and fear than guilt. Does the reference to nudity imply that the transgression was somehow sexual? The Lord had decreed that man and woman would become "one flesh" and beget children. There is only one way human beings can reproduce, but Adam and Eve had no children until after they were cast out of the Garden of Eden. Did the forbidden fruit awaken lust? Was sex the cause of the fall? The Bible does not say.

There have been various interpretations of the Genesis account but Judaism puts the blame on disobedience. Adam and Eve are punished but they are not tainted with sin, and they do not transmit sin to their progeny—there is no doctrine of Original Sin in Judaism. Instead, Judaism assumes that human beings are naturally endowed with an ethical intuition—conscience as a gift of God—that lets them know right from wrong. However, moral intuition is not wholly reliable, which is why revelation and the Law are necessary to guide human conduct.

Human beings are essentially good, but like unruly children, they misbehave (". . . for there is no man who does not sin"—1 Kings 8:46). Hence they need moral instruction. To that end, God gave Moses the Law so that ethical intuition could grow into moral maturity. Adult responsibility for observance of the Law is attained when a boy reaches age thirteen and goes through a rite of passage called the *bar mitsvah* ("son of commandment"); this has been extended in modern times to girls as the *bat mitsvah*.

Jewish ethics took a more philosophical turn during the Middle Ages when scholars like Moses Maimonides adopted Aristotelian principles of moral virtues. The idea of a dual human nature—one good, one evil—became more prominent, even though the idea goes back to earlier traditions.[26] The good impulse (*yetzer tov*) is the inner voice that prompts Jews to study the Torah and reminds them of God's law when they are tempted to do something forbidden.

The evil impulse (*yetzer ha-ra*) is more difficult to define. It is not the sort of evil that leads to senseless harm. Rather, it reflects selfish human nature that presses for the satisfaction of desires (such as for food and sex) without regard for the moral consequences (resulting in gluttony and adultery).

Judaism sees sex in positive terms. It is the relational context of sex, not sex as such, that determines its morality. It is good within marriage; bad outside it. There is no monastic tradition in Judaism requiring celibacy or abstinence. Sexual offences are dealt with like other offences, even though their penalties can be harsh (like death by stoning for adultery). Essentially all sexual behaviors outside of marriage, including premarital sex and homosexuality, are unlawful in traditional Judaism.[27]

There is one book in the Old Testament that presents a courageous challenge to the common idea that suffering is the punishment for guilt. The book of Job starts with a conversation between God and Satan (who is not yet the personification of evil). God praises Job (who is a Moabite, not a Jew) as a blameless and upright man who shuns evil. Satan ascribes this to Job's having received so many blessings from God and claims that should God take all this away from him, Job will turn from God and curse him.[28]

To prove Satan wrong, God places Job in Satan's power and Satan turns Job's life into rack and ruin. His friends tell him to seek God's forgiveness and end his suffering, for he must have surely sinned to deserve these calamities. Job refuses to do so for he has done no wrong. Nor does Job blame or curse God for his seeming injustice. He just suffers and demands justice. Ultimately, he is vindicated by God and restored to his former life. The story conveys a powerful message that suffering is not a punishment for sin; bad things also happen to good people, the good also suffer. It is part of life and the inscrutable ways of the Lord. There is no need to add the insult of guilt to the pain of injury.[29]

Secular Jewish Guilt

There are two main aspects to being Jewish. One is religious—practicing the precepts of Judaism. The second is secular and means having a Jewish ethnic identity (however that may be defined).[30] Many secular Jews, nonetheless, selectively participate in religious rituals, often after they have children, in order to provide them with a moral anchor and a sense of kinship with Jewish traditions.

Secular Jews reject the religious elements of Judaism while considering themselves to be no less Jewish. This strong association between culture and religious belief is not limited to Judaism. It also holds true for Confucianism and being Chinese, as well as Hinduism and being Indian. It is difficult in such cases to reliably separate the religious from the cultural elements in the experience of guilt. For example, are the feelings of guilt of Orthodox Jews in Israel and in the Diaspora more similar than the experiences of guilt for their secular counterparts who may be more subject to external cultural influences?

Some aspects of guilt seem to be quite distinctive of American Jews, judging from the writings of authors like Philip Roth and Woody Allen (who have elevated Jewish guilt almost to a genre of literature). In these accounts, and in popular humor, Jewish sex comes across as being particularly guilt ridden ("All the guilt without the fun"). Another caricature is the "Jewish mother"—the master guilt inducer ("A Jewish mother gives her son two neckties—one red, one blue. When the son shows up wearing the blue, the mother says, 'What's the matter, didn't you like the red one?'"). In the following passage from *Portnoy's Complaint*, Roth brings Jewish guilt over sex and the Jewish mother together: "Mother . . . what my conscience, so called, has done to my sexuality, my spontaneity, my courage! You can travel the length and the breadth of my body over superhighways of shame and inhibition and fear."[31]

Beyond such literary characterizations and hyperbole, it is difficult to make meaningful distinctions between secular and religious Jewish guilt. With a Jewish philosopher like Martin Buber, it is hard to even discern a distinctively "Jewish perspective" on guilt (whatever that may mean).[32] This may be disappointing to some but if creeds and doctrines divide religions, should not shared moral principles unite them?

GUILT IN CHRISTIANITY

What do a Catholic doctor, an Anglican accountant, an Evangelical mechanic, and a Greek Orthodox housekeeper have in common in their experiences of guilt by virtue of being Christians? Given the bewildering diversity among Christians (with a billion Catholics and over five hundred Protestant denominations), is there any point in even discussing guilt in Christianity as if it were a single entity? Emphasizing the diversity within a religious tradition would seem to dispel any hope of understanding its essential moral elements. Yet to assume a monolithic moral stance is equally misleading given the importance of historical and cultural differences. For instance, the vaunted "Catholic guilt" seems to apply more to Irish than Italian or French Catholics, who are nonetheless just as Catholic.

Christian views on guilt are particularly important because Western nations, even if only nominally Christian, dominate the world politically, economically, and culturally. Consequently, Christian conceptions of guilt influence people all over the world. So much so that we have come to take it for granted that guilt—as understood in the West—should be part of all religious traditions. That, however, is not the case, as we shall see in the next chapter.

A number of major historical influences have shaped Christian ethics and its conceptions of guilt. There is the Judaic heritage embodied in the Old Testament, the Hellenistic culture within which the early church developed, and the Roman (later Byzantine) state through which it became the dominant religion in the Western world. In 1054, the Christian church (after centuries of gradually moving apart) effectively split between Western Catholicism and Eastern Orthodoxy. The Reformation, in the sixteenth century, further separated Protestants from the Roman Catholic church. These schisms have resulted in significant differences in attitudes toward guilt. Protestants have since splintered into hundreds of denominations and sects, each with its own particular take on guilt. Moreover, though basic moral principles that determine when and why we feel guilty are quite similar between Jews, Christians, and Muslims, there are also important differences. For instance, Christianity has no cultic requirements and Judaism and Islam have no doctrine of Original Sin. Most important, freedom from sin and guilt for Christians comes through the saving grace of Jesus Christ but, obviously, not for Jews and Muslims.

We will look at the more distinctive features of Christian guilt through the lives and teachings of five key individuals: Jesus, whose life and ministry form the basis of Christianity; St. Paul, who laid the foundations of Christian doctrine in the early church; St. Augustine, who heavily influenced Western Christian conceptions of sin and guilt; St. Thomas Aquinas, who is the dominant figure in Catholic theology; and Martin Luther, who led the Reformation, which established Protestantism.[33]

Guilt in the Teachings of Jesus

Jesus referred often to sin but not to guilt or shame. We cannot therefore discuss his ideas that specifically pertain to guilt; we can only infer what we can from his teachings and the example of his life and ministry. There is no suggestion in the gospels that he ever felt guilty himself, for he was without sin (even though he did experience regret, sadness, and anger). That is not true for his apostles. Following the arrest of Jesus, Peter denied being one of his followers and then, "he broke down and wept" (Mark 15:66–72). After he betrayed Jesus, Judas told the high priest, "I have sinned in betraying innocent blood," and went out and hanged himself (Matt. 27: 3–5).

Jesus frequently cites the Jewish Law, but then qualifies it:[34]

> You have heard . . . "You shall not kill; and whoever kills shall be liable to judgment." But I say to you that everyone who is angry with his brother [without cause] shall be liable to judgment. (Matt. 5:21–22)

> You have heard . . . "An eye for an eye and a tooth for a tooth." But I say to you . . . if any one strikes you on the right cheek, turn to him the other also. (Matt. 5:38–40)

> You have heard . . . "You shall love your neighbor and hate your enemy." But I say to you, Love your enemies and pray for those who persecute you. (Matt. 5:44)

> You have heard . . . "You shall not commit adultery." But I say to you that everyone who looks at a woman lustfully has already committed adultery with her in his heart. (Matt. 5:27–28)

These commandments seem to raise the moral bar impossibly high as Jesus goes beyond the morality of conduct and looks into the motives behind actions. We can expect people to control their actions, but how can they control their thoughts and feelings? On the other hand, since thoughts and feelings precede actions, how better to control actions than by nipping in the bud the motivations that induce them?

At the same time, Jesus softens the Law by taking a more forgiving attitude, as for instance, in the story of the woman caught in adultery, where he asked the one without sin to throw the first stone, and told the woman to go home and sin no more. This spirit of forgiveness that infuses the teachings of Jesus is a powerful antidote to the guilt that otherwise would arise from his demanding teachings.

The terms for sin and guilt are used interchangeably in the New Testament. The forgiveness of sins is the same as the remission of guilt. However, the various renditions of the Lord's Prayer convey significant differences in how guilt is perceived. The version in Luke 11:14 says, "Forgive us our *sins* as we forgive those who sin against us," while Matthew 6:12 reads, "And forgive us our *debts*, as we also have forgiven our debtors." The idea of debt is central to guilt. (The Greek word in the original text is *opheilemata*, "that which is owed.") Mark 11:25 introduces the idea of trespass (*paraptoma*): "And whenever you stand praying, forgive, if you have anything against anyone, so that our Father also who is in heaven may forgive you your trespasses." To trespass means to cross over a forbidden line, to intrude into another person's property (or rights and prerogatives). Sin is heavy with overtones of hell and damnation. Debt and trespass sound less ominous; debts can be cleared, mistakes rectified, trespasses retreated from.[35]

We must also be mindful that Jesus spoke Aramaic while the gospel accounts are in Greek. So, strictly speaking, we do not know what his actual words were. Moreover, Jesus spoke in parables and metaphors not meant to be taken literally. Therefore, we may understand better the moral perspective of Jesus, and his views on guilt, by relying on the overall context and spirit of his teachings rather then dissecting his words.

The temptations of Jesus provide a glimpse into what Satan thought were his moral vulnerabilities. Satan did not offer Jesus women, wine, and song since he knew they would have no purchase on him. Instead he challenged Jesus to turn stone into bread (to feed the poor), promised him power to rule the world (to bring justice), and dared him to throw himself from the pinnacle of the temple to test his faith in God's ability to protect him. Jesus refused to yield to any of it. Whether we think Jesus literally stood face to face with Satan, or was engaged in an internal dialogue with his conscience, does not significantly change the ethical and spiritual dilemmas he was facing.

When people called Jesus "Good Teacher," he said, "Why do you call me good? No one is good but God" (Luke 18:19). The poor and social outcasts were the objects of his special concern and sympathy. To the shock of his pious contemporaries, he associated with pariahs, like tax gatherers. He reached out to them as human beings to rescue rather than condemn them. Unlike most men of his time, Jesus never married and was celibate. (Allegations that he was married to Mary Magdalen are fiction.) This was not a rejection of marriage and sexuality. His first miracle was turning water to wine at the wedding at Cana, and several of his apostles were married. Nor did Jesus shun the company of women; Mary and Martha were his friends. Consequently, there is little in the words and actions of Jesus that would support the burden of guilt that has characterized traditional Christianity. The responsibility for that can be placed mainly at the doorstep of St. Paul.

St. Paul and Guilt

Next to Jesus, Paul is the most significant figure in Christianity. Raised as a devout Jew, and a Roman citizen, Paul lived in the Hellenistic culture of Rome's Eastern provinces. His letters to the early churches (which are the earliest texts in the New Testament) laid the formal foundations of Christian theology and ethics. Paul never met the historical Jesus yet he could rightfully claim to be the apostle to the Gentiles; it was he who led the early church from its modest Jewish origins to become the most all-encompassing institution in the Western world.

Paul drew on the Hebrew scriptures and in the process changed some of their basic precepts. Singularly important for the Christian conception of guilt is his interpretation of the fall of Adam (who carries the brunt of moral responsibility, rather than Eve). Although Jesus makes no specific reference to Adam, Paul made it a pivotal point in explaining the origin of sin and guilt. The book of Genesis ascribes sin and death entering the world through the disobedience of Adam and Eve; but it does not state that human beings *inherited* Adam's guilt. That idea came from Paul, who interpreted the Genesis account in the light of Christ's mission. For Paul, Christ is the second Adam and through him the effect of Adam's fall is reversed: "For as by one man's disobedience many were made sinners, so by one man's obedience many will be made righteous" (Rom. 5:19). On this foundation, St. Augustine was to develop fuller the doctrine of Original Sin three centuries later.

Unlike the serenity of Jesus, Paul is at war with himself. He does not understand his own actions: "I can will what is right but I cannot do it. For I do not do what I want, but I do the very thing that I hate" (Rom. 7:15). Compressed in these few words is the enigma of why we do wrong when we earnestly try to do right. Paul feels burdened with guilt for a "sin" that dwells in him. He does not specify what that sin is but its origin is the legacy of Adam's fall that predisposes him to moral failure. However, when confronted by the chief priest, Paul would declare, "Brethren, I have lived before God in all good conscience up to this day" (Acts 23:1).

Paul's views on sex and marriage have attracted special attention and have a direct bearing on guilt. It has been suggested (without good evidence) that the sin Paul was constantly struggling with may have been sexual in nature (whatever it entailed). Paul never married and he allowed marriage, rather grudgingly, as a safeguard against fornication (it is better to marry than to "burn") and as a concession to the need to reproduce. As for himself, he did not want to be distracted from his consuming mission for the Lord. Paul sounds quite judgmental when he lumps adulterers with the "immoral, idolaters, and sexual perverts." He has harsh words for homosexuals and sees their passions as the penalty God had imposed for idolatry: "For this reason God gave them up to dishonorable passions. Their women exchanged natural relations for unnatural, and the men likewise gave up natural relations with women and were consumed with passion for one another, men committing shameful acts with men" (Rom. 1:26–27).

Paul refers to such acts as *shameful* rather than sinful; should that matter with respect to invoking guilt?[36] His views have strongly influenced Christian moral perceptions of homosexuality (and still do) even though liberal churches no longer view homosexuality as immoral and ordain gays and lesbians (an issue that has come close to splitting the Anglican church).

There is a significant distinction between committing a *sin* and being a *sinner.* The first refers to an action; the second, a state of being that reflects on one's character. One could say, "I have sinned" in reference to a particular act. However, sin dwells in Paul, imbedded in his body, as a permanent disability, making him a sinner (although he never refers to himself as such). There is no resolution to Paul's sin in the Law. Only God can free ("justify") him through faith in Jesus Christ.

There is a common perception that heavy-duty guilt made its way into Christianity with St. Paul. It is Paul who is held responsible for the guilt-burdened introspective conscience of Christianity, distorting the more tolerant original message of Jesus. This somber view is rejected by those who see Paul as having put flesh on the bare bones of the moral teachings of Jesus while remaining faithful to his message. Moreover, some of the most damning passages in Epistles ascribed to him may not have been written by him. Paul is used as a whipping boy, it is argued, by those who are hostile to Christianity itself.[37] His defenders claim that Paul had a robust conscience but was not a guilt-ridden soul. He was proud of being an observant Jew and did not wallow in sin as a Christian. We should also remember that Paul lived at a time when the word, or idea, of "Christianity" did not yet exist as we understand it. He spoke of *weakness* rather than sin, *justification* rather than forgiveness, and *call* rather than conversion.[38]

St. Augustine and Guilt

We began this chapter with biographical vignettes from the life of St. Augustine. We now turn to his more specific contributions to the conception of guilt in Christianity. Augustine belonged to a group of men, called the Fathers of the Church, who exerted a great influence on early Christianity as it developed within the Roman empire, both in the West and the East. Augustine's influence was particularly strong on the Western (Latin-speaking) Christian conceptions of guilt; the Greek-speaking Eastern Orthodox church never fully adopted his ideas on sin; Orthodox doctrine remains more mystical than legalistic to this day.

Augustine took the doctrine of the fall from Paul, where sin and death enter the world by Adam's disobedience, and expanded it into the doctrine of Original Sin.[39]

We referred earlier about the possible associations of Adam and Eve's shame and guilt with sexuality. Some early Christian writers hinted at such a connection and condemned it. John Milton, in *Paradise Lost*, refers openly to "connubial love" between Adam and Eve and rebukes those who condemn it ("Whatever hypocrites austerely talk / Of purity . . . and innocence / Defaming as impure what God declares . . . pure").[40]

Augustine introduced a new conception of human nature into Christianity whereby human beings are born into a condition of sin by being the progeny of Adam (inheriting his guilt by genetic transmission as it were). Baptism erases this original sin but the propensity to sin remains throughout life because the fall weakens (but does not destroy) the freedom of the will. Sins after baptism are dealt with by confession and penance.

Augustine further implicated sexuality by the concept of *concupiscence*— an overweening desire as exemplified by the "heat and confusion of lust." This expanded the condemnation of immoral sexual behavior by striking at the very core of sexual desire. A Jew sins by committing adultery. Jesus extended this to committing adultery by merely lusting after a woman. Augustine makes the very desire for sex—even for one's spouse—sinful in and of itself, if contaminated by lust. This means a huge shift from immoral behavior, to immoral desire, and on to desire that is immoral in itself, thereby escalating the prospect of guilt.

Augustine did not condemn sexual intercourse for procreation in marriage and for emotional intimacy between husband and wife, as long as it was free of concupiscence. How would sex then feel? Controlled by reason and free of passion, it would be like a cordial and hearty handshake. (Presumably that is how Adam and Eve would have eventually reproduced, had they stayed in the Garden and Eden.) This reasoning widened the split between sexual desire and love that was to bedevil the lives of so many people over the centuries.[41]

Even though he gets blamed for it, sex was not Augustine's most urgent moral concern. The core problem was the human unwillingness to let God take over one's will. All sins ultimately resulted from human willfulness, which comes from the will to dominate. This push to mastery challenges and offends God, disrupts human relationships, and sows social injustice and conflict.

Beyond guilt as moral culpability, Augustine is quite explicit in his references to the subjective sense of guilt: "the human conscience feels guilty"; "I stood naked to myself and my conscience complained against me."[42] He speaks in our language of guilt (or perhaps it is we who speak in his). His insights into human motivation are sharp and hint at human actions driven by unconscious forces that resist the control of reason (anticipating Freud).

The Christian doctrine of sin offends rationalists who reject the idea that sin may be "inherited" and who will not hold people accountable for sins they themselves have not committed. Augustine gets the blame for much of this. "A great deal of what is most ferocious in the medieval Church," writes Bertrand Russell, "is traceable to his gloomy sense of universal guilt."[43] Nonetheless, St. Augustine remains one of the towering figures in Christianity—guilt and all.

For seven centuries after Augustine, Western culture went through a period of stagnation followed by rebirth. During the Middle Ages, the consciousness of sin became increasingly important in the teachings of the church as exemplified by the Cardinal Sins, discussed earlier. The excesses in the mortification of the flesh that we discussed were part of this picture.

The penitential system that was to deal with sin had three components. First was contrition of the heart, where one recognized one's sins and regretted them. Remorse—feeling guilty—was an essential first step. Contrition was followed by confession, the private admission of sins to a priest. Finally, there had to be restitution to those harmed by one's actions. That cleared the debt and allowed one's reintegration into the community.[44] It was this theology of sin that mostly led to the perception of Christianity as a guilt-ridden religion.[45]

St. Thomas Aquinas and Catholic Guilt

Catholic moral philosophy reached its apex in the thirteenth century with St. Thomas Aquinas. Born into an aristocratic family, Aquinas started his education in a monastery at the age of five and eventually studied theology in Paris. He joined the Dominican Order and devoted his life to study and teaching, resisting attempts to elevate him in the hierarchy of the church.[46]

In his monumental *Summa Theologiae*, Thomas Aquinas aimed for the synthesis of Christian doctrine with the philosophy of Aristotle.[47] For Aquinas, guilt results from disobeying the voice of God and remorse leads to repentance. Although Aquinas laid the formal foundations of Roman Catholic ethics, the church did not agree with everything he taught. For instance, his belief that the soul enters the embryo—"ensoulment"—on the fortieth day of pregnancy, which presumably would make abortion morally acceptable until that time. Aquinas discusses sexual behaviors in almost clinical detail, addressing such topics as touching, kissing, fondling, seduction, virginity, marital sex, fornication, adultery, rape, incest, prostitution, homosexuality, and bestiality. He offers detailed arguments for and against involuntary nocturnal emissions being sinful.[48] Aquinas remains to this day the quintessential Catholic theologian.

Catholics (especially those who attend parochial schools) seem to vie with Jews as being more guilt-driven than everybody else. Some Catholics may fit this stereotype more than others, probably because it reflects cultural rather than religious differences. Nonetheless, guilt remains central to Catholic teaching as reflected in its catechisms that provide instruction in a question-and-answer format. However, Catholic moral teaching is currently also informed by secular insights, which led to a differentiation between "real moral guilt" that has a religious basis and guilty feelings due to psychological problems. The following passage is from a website aimed at Catholic youth:

> Guilt is positive and necessary: Despite jokes about guilt being the ultimate Catholic emotion, the Church wants us to deal with it, not wallow in it. Just like a warning signal on a car's dashboard, guilt feelings tell us there is something wrong "under the hood." . . . You need to see the difference between actual guilt and guilty feelings. . . . If you have real moral guilt, you need to repent. Don't rationalize it away—and forgive yourself prematurely. If your feelings are false guilt, however . . . you may need to talk to someone to get your feelings out. You may need to learn new skills that prevent you from taking on guilt that other people enjoy laying on you.[49]

The Catholic practice of confession plays a distinctive, cathartic role in dealing with guilt. It unburdens penitents and leads them to make peace with God and their conscience. Catholics are free to confess any time but they are required to do so at least once a year. Other Christian denominations use confession differently. Orthodox churches rely on group confession where the priest recites a list of sins and communicants respond by asking forgiveness without specifying which particular sin they are confessing to. Protestants confess directly to God without the mediation of clergy.

Martin Luther and Protestant Guilt

Luther is one of the great transformative figures in Christianity. There are more books written about Luther (over 9,000) than any other Christian figure except Jesus. Luther's own collected works fill 120 volumes.[50] Although Luther set out to reform rather than break away from the Roman Catholic church, the Reformation in fact had that effect.

Luther made the Bible the sole moral authority; his conscience was "captive" to the word of God. One of Luther's most important legacies was enabling Christians to approach God directly through his Word and their personal religious experience. Luther considered one religious experience worth a thousand miracles and one miracle worth a thousand theological arguments. By translating the Bible from Latin into German, Luther made it accessible to everyone who could read, not just the clergy. Since then the Bible has been translated into more languages than any other book (estimated at 2,400 languages for at least one of its books).

Luther's life, like that of Augustine, whom Luther revered, has interesting links with his views on guilt. Luther was brought up by severe parents and at the age of twenty-one he set out to become a lawyer at his father's urging, but he changed his mind after he survived a severe thunderstorm and decided to become an Augustinian monk.[51] His years at the monastery were troubled by a tormented conscience (*Anfechtung*), as we discussed earlier in connection with scrupulosity. He suffered from bouts of depression and fits of anger. He was obsessed by doubts and lived in fear of Christ's judgment:

> I went to confession frequently, and I performed the assigned penances faithfully. Nevertheless, my conscience could never achieve certainty but was always in doubt and said, "You have not done this correctly. You were not contrite enough. You omitted this in your confession." . . . I did not know Christ other than as a severe judge from whom I desperately wished to flee but whom I was never able to escape.[52]

In his psychobiography, Erik Erikson refers to Luther's "lifelong burden of excessive guilt." In Luther's own words:

> And this is the worst of all these ills, that the conscience cannot run away from itself, but it is always present to itself and knows all the terrors of the creature

which such things bring even in this present life, because the ungodly man is like a raging sea. . . . The worst of all ills is to have a judge. . . . For this is the nature of a guilty conscience, to fly and to be terrified, even when all is safe and prosperous, to convert all into peril and death.[53]

Though he had devoted his life to the church, Luther could not be certain of his salvation. He finally realized that salvation came through the grace of God, not through his own efforts, no matter how hard he tried. This religious insight, which shaped Protestant doctrine, emerged from the midst of his personal anguish. Despite his internal conflicts, Luther had a robust character that made it possible for him to challenge the awesome authority of the church and to deal with the momentous religious and political consequences of his revolt (which he did not always handle well).

After Luther left the church, he was happily married to a former nun. He thought there was no lovelier, more friendly, and charming relationship or company than a good marriage. Luther had an earthy sense of sex and expressed himself with candor. He rejected the Catholic doctrine of marriage as a sacrament because he could find no biblical basis for it. He saw marriage as a divinely ordained duty and privilege. The sexual urge was part of God's creation to be harnessed within marriage (which he compared to a hospital that cured unbridled lust and saved one from fornication). Marital sex was not only for reproduction but also for the expression of affection between spouses.[54] Impotence and rejection of conjugal sex were grounds for divorce. Having blessed sex in marriage, Luther disapproved of all other forms of sexual expression; since a legitimate sexual outlet was available, there was no need or excuse for anything else.

Although Protestantism has also been portrayed as suffused with guilt, it is not Luther but John Calvin who introduced the deep sense of self-denial that disapproved of all that was sensuous or frivolous. (At one time, even whistling on Sundays was frowned upon.) English Puritans elaborated these attitudes into a distinctively dour form of sexual morality. Transplanted to the New World, these attitudes proved highly influential in shaping the moral sensibilities of the American colonies. A classic literary account of how these attitudes ruled people's lives is Nathaniel Hawthorne's novel *The Scarlet Letter*. The climactic confession of the Reverend Dimmesdale, quoted in Chapter 2, is a classic expression of Puritan guilt.

Residues of the Puritan legacy endure to this day in those Protestant

churches that adhere to a conservative morality that is absolutist and stringent in its requirements, particularly with regard to sexuality. However, where
Evangelical preachers used to thunder with threats of hell and damnation,
some of their modern heirs preach a much more optimistic and positive message. The focus is now on Christians leading good and prosperous lives and
the punitive aspects of guilt are played down or rejected. Joel Osteen, billed as
"America's best-known pastor," writes:

> Too many people live under condemnation, listening to the wrong voices. The
> Bible refers to the enemy as "accuser of the brethren" who would love for us to
> live our lives guilty and condemned. He constantly brings accusations against
> us, telling us what we didn't do or what we should have done. . . .
>
> Many people swallow these lines with little or no defense. Consequently,
> they walk around feeling guilty, condemned, and extremely discontented with
> themselves.[55]

Osteen advises to develop a "tender conscience" and listen to its voice, but
refuse to live guilty or condemned because of past mistakes: Know that you are
forgiven by God, so when you do something wrong, make a fresh beginning.

Liberal Protestants now tend to feel less guilty for traditional transgressions and focus instead on more modern issues like social injustice. Liberal
morality is more subject to individual discretion than to traditional Christian
doctrine. A good example is the relativistic and contextual *situation ethics* of
the 1960s.[56] In this view, the morality of conduct depends on not *what* one
does but *why* one does it. The guiding principle that makes an act moral is
agape—selfless love. This liberal perspective became popular, especially
among college youth, who substituted romantic love for agape ("It's OK if
you're in love").[57]

The do-it-yourself morality of the sexual revolution faded away by the
1980s, but the older conventional morality has not come back in full force. As
noted before, premarital sex and cohabitation have now become essentially
guilt-free (if done in a more or less responsible manner), but extramarital sex
still engenders guilt. Same-sex relationships are no longer censured and birth
control is actively encouraged. Americans are about evenly split on the moral
permissibility of abortion between pro-choice and pro-life groups.

Mainstream Christian conceptions of morality and guilt are currently
struggling to find ways to preserve religious moral traditions while adjusting
to the changing circumstances of the times. Many Christians are looking for

new ways of enhancing the spirituality in their lives without the constraints of organized religion.

Guilt and Spirituality

There are currently important changes in the views of many Christians with respect to traditional attitudes toward morality and guilt, which can be loosely subsumed under the rubric of *spirituality*.[58] For those outside mainstream churches, spirituality does not yet constitute a coherent doctrine of new beliefs or a systematic code of ethics; the disavowal of doctrine is actually one of its hallmarks. Nonetheless, it appeals to a significant number of individuals of diverse backgrounds.[59]

Actually, traditional, or classic, spirituality has been part of established religious traditions for a long time, not only in Christianity but also in Judaism and Islam. Spirituality aspires to a more intimate and personally satisfying relationship with God based on love as opposed to doctrinal obligations. In its more contemporary versions, Christian spirituality combines religious traditions with broader secular concerns, such as overpopulation and environmental degradation. It is a pluralistic view that stresses diversity in its search for a global ethic including the cultivation of healthy personal relationships and the pursuit of peace. Its appeal to compassion is not only idealistic but is also based on pragmatic grounds as necessary for the survival of life on earth. When one fails to be compassionate in this context, the ensuing feeling is more like regret over failing to make the right choices rather than guilt over moral failure.

Spirituality can also speak in a more dissident voice. This is clearly seen among some practicing Catholics, in particular in the United States, who are highly skeptical of or reject the traditional moral teachings of the church hierarchy, particularly with respect to issues like contraception, abortion, premarital sex, homosexuality, the ordination of women, and marriage for the clergy.[60]

Pushed further, spirituality becomes an alternative to religion—a sort of a religion without religion ("the religion of no religion").[61] Its adherents say, "I am spiritual but not religious." Some were religious once, but the church let them down or they outgrew it. They came to reject the inflexibility and authoritarianism of the church's traditional religious beliefs bolstered by its myths. (St. Paul and St. Augustine are key targets for blame for their views on sexuality and women.)

Spirituality encourages people to choose more individualistic moral paths that are autonomous and inclusive, to pick and choose what is appealing from various traditions—such as Hinduism, Buddhism, and Daoism—without being saddled with the rest of their baggage. The idea of integrating what is best in Eastern and Western spirituality has attracted both serious intellectuals as well as pseudo-intellectuals, dilettantes, and seekers of fig leaves for free-wheeling sex.[62]

Among the adherents of spirituality, guilt is not a popular idea; actually they see it as part of the religious legacy they are trying to undo. They believe the "negativistic" aspects of guilt make people feel bad to no good purpose. At best, they try to tame guilt and turn it into a vehicle for the exploration of the self or for the enhancement of one's "human potential." Instead of guilt, spirituality emphasizes the need to feel good about oneself by behaving in ways consistent with the exigencies of life in the modern world. Some bristle at the mere mention of the word "conscience" because of its overtones of moral censure. Instead, they speak of "an inner voice" or a "spiritual compass" that guides ethical choices toward more fulfilling and authentic lives. It is this nonjudgmental tone of popular books like *Care of the Soul*, by Thomas Moore, that appeals to so many. On the other hand, critics see the more popularized forms of spirituality as pandering to the self-indulgence and faddism that do-it-yourself morality makes possible.

GUILT IN ISLAM

O my Lord,
if I worship you
from the fear of hell, burn me in hell.
If I worship you
from the hope of Paradise, bar me from its gates.
But if I worship you
for yourself alone, grant me then the beauty of your Face.[63]

This prayer by the eighth-century Sufi Rabi'a al-Adawiyya expresses eloquently the centrality of God in Islam—God as the ultimate end, never the means, of all things. Rabi'a was orphaned as a young girl and sold into slavery but eventually was freed and became an eminent figure in Islamic mysticism—a "friend" and "beloved" of God—who initiated a new phase of Sufism based on love.[64]

In the seventh century, the prophet Muhammad converted the polytheistic people of Arabia to monotheism by elevating the worship of Allah to that of the only God, to the exclusion of all other gods. After a decade of dissent and persecution by the rulers of Mecca, in 632 Muhammad and his followers fled to the oasis town of Medina, where he became the secular and religious leader of the community. This journey (*al-hijra*) is a transformative event in Islam and marks the beginning of the Islamic calendar. Ten years later, following the Prophet's death, his successors (*caliphs*) began to expand Islam into a vast empire stretching from Spain to China.[65]

The Prophet characterized pre-Islamic society as ruled by ignorance (*al-jahiliyya*) and rife with corruption and exploitation. This did not reflect an evil human nature, but immaturity and ingratitude. As a law-based religion, Islam has as the core of its ethics the injunction to "command the good and forbid the evil."[66] Islam also has ritual requirements such as dietary restrictions (no pork, no alcohol).

The word *Islam* (derived from the Arabic *taslim*) means submission. Muslims (or Moslems) have totally and irrevocably submitted themselves to God. One becomes a Muslim by professing the declaration of faith: "There is no god but God and Muhammad is the prophet of God." This declaration of faith (*Shahadah*) is the first of the Five Pillars, or basic foundations, of Islam. The others are: prayer, almsgiving, fasting during the month of Ramadan, and pilgrimage to Mecca.

The primary scriptural basis of Islam is the Al Qur'an ("The Recitation"). It represents for Muslims the literal words of God, transmitted to the Prophet Muhammad by the Archangel Gabriel, in Arabic.[67] It is supplemented by the Hadith, which consists of the account of the life and teachings of the Prophet Muhammad by his early followers. The Prophet was a beloved figure whose humane and sensible nature inspired deep affection, in addition to unwavering loyalty, among his followers.

The Qur'an (which is about the length of the New Testament), is divided into 114 chapters (*surah*) that are organized by length rather than chronologically in sequence of revelation. Islam shares many of the moral precepts of Judaism and Christianity (both Moses and Jesus are revered as prophets in Islam) and as well has its own distinctive aspects.

Sin in Islam is the result of pride that leads to opposition to God's will (like Satan's refusal to obey God's command to prostrate himself before Adam). However, sin is more like a weakness rather than evil: there is no Original

Sin in Islam. Adam and Eve disobeyed God's command by eating the fruit of the forbidden tree (Eve did not tempt Adam—they were equally responsible). Hence they became tainted with *forgetfulness* (*al-ghaflah*), which character- izes human beings and distorts their moral nature.[68] Moreover, human beings still carry deep within their souls their primordial nature that attests to the unity of God. Human beings are free to make moral choices. When people err, forgiveness is within their reach.

Religious and legal responsibilities are defined by Islamic law (*shariah*), which is both a legal code and a moral guide as well. It is a way that leads to happiness and success in this and the next life. The interpretations of Is- lamic law amplify and apply these responsibilities to everyday circumstances. Experts of Islamic law (*mufti*) issue legal opinions (*fatwa*) that determine if actions and rulings are consistent with the shariah.[69] There is no central re- ligious hierarchy in Islam that speaks for the entire community of Muslims. Fatwas are only binding for those who choose to obey them. Moreover, Islamic law may follow one of four major schools of jurisdiction and has evolved over time to meet changing requirements of Islamic communities. Muslim jurists use various means of extrapolating from the shariah through analogy. For instance, the Qur'an prohibits the drinking of wine. What about whisky? If the problem with wine is due to its being made from grape juice, then whisky should be allowed since it has nothing to do with grape juice. However, if the problem is the alcohol in wine that leads to inebriation, then the prohibition would apply to whisky and all other alcoholic beverages.

The major subdivision of Islam between *Sunnis* and *Shiites* began in con- flicts over the succession to the Prophet but over time it involved doctrinal differences as well. Like Judaism and Christianity, Islam is a mosaic, not a monolith. As a world religion, it has wide regional and cultural differences.[70] Thus, attitudes toward morality, shame, and guilt, such as between Arab, Pakistani, or Indonesian Muslims, are apt to reflect their indigenous cultures in addition to the overarching principles of Islam. This makes attempts at generalizations difficult and potentially misleading.

Guilt as Culpability
Guilt in Islam primarily involves legal culpability. The terminology of guilt in Arabic reflects this aspect of wrongdoing rather than the subjective experi- ence of guilt. *Jurum* means "crime," and a person who has committed a legal offence is *mujrim*, or guilty of a crime. The word *dhamb* also implies culpabil-

ity, but may convey a sense of feeling guilty. The word that comes closest to capturing the emotional component of guilt is *nadama*, which means "contrition." Muslims experience it especially when they offend God. A term that is closer to "sin" is *esm*. Major sins include idolatry, murder, theft, and adultery; minor sins are the occasional failure to perform the requisite prayers or giving offence inadvertently.

The Arabic word that comes closest to "conscience" is *damir*. The idea is captured in the image of an "inner torch" that lights the way to preserve *taqwa*—reverence for God. The Qur'an guides those with *taqwa* to develop the ethical consciousness to tell right from wrong and deal with the ethical implications of actions under ambiguous moral circumstances.

Another key term—*jahada*—forms the root of several relevant words with different, but related, meanings. First is *mujahadeh*, an effort of the will or the application of self-discipline not to yield to temptation. It requires that one be aware of personal proclivities and moral weaknesses and avoid temptation. Second is *ijtihad* or intellectual effort. Through it, one acquires the capacity to make the right ethical interpretations and exercise moral judgment.

Finally there is the much misunderstood term *jihad*. It means striving for one's faith or struggling for justice ("in the path of God"). It is the moral obligation to defend Islam against its enemies, as exemplified by the war Muhammad waged against the Meccan expeditionary force sent to kill him. This, however, is the *lesser jihad*. The *greater jihad* is waged against one's own immoral inclinations. In any case, jihad is not intended to be an indiscriminate call for aggression. The Qur'an says, "Fight those in the way of God who fight you, but be not aggressive: God does not like aggressors."[71]

However, the idea can be, and has been, exploited to justify aggression for self-serving political purposes (as has been the case with the Western concept of "just war"). Consequently, *jihadist* (or *jihadi*) has now become in the West a term of opprobrium. Suicide bombers invoke it but they actually violate fundamental Islamic prohibitions against suicide and the taking of innocent lives. By linking terrorism with Islam, the term *jihadist* puts a religious cast on what are political conflicts, thus implicating Muslims as a whole, although most Muslims oppose the use of violence by extremists in the name of Islam.[72]

The subjective experience of guilt emanates from the "heart." The heart not only encompasses moral sentiments but has a rational aspect. Its sentiments are like a fatwa—a legal ruling—with regard to personal moral judgments ("Solicit a fatwa from your heart").[73] Ultimately, morality entails a deeply personal choice. The fatwa of one's heart trumps the ruling of the mufti. One who has done wrong must both acknowledge it as well as feel it. While Islam clearly acknowledges the experience of guilt, it does not dwell on it. Rather, it puts the emphasis on how to get rid of it through repentance and return to God.

Guilt and Shame in Islamic Cultures

Guilt in its Western sense has not been a prominent feature in Islam; historically, shame has played a more important role. In that sense, Islam is closer to Asian religions. However, the importance of shame may be primarily an outgrowth of Islam's Arab heritage. The Arabian desert is a harsh environment; in order to survive, its inhabitants had to evolve a combative culture. The nomadic tribes of Arabia (the Bedu or Bedouins) lived in a state of chronic warfare fueled by raids. The dominant social ethic was loyalty to the clan and the larger tribe; no individual or family could survive alone. The virtue necessary to sustain the group is "manliness" (*murruwwa*), which incorporates courage in battle, endurance in hardship, and avenging wrongs done to members of the tribe. The sentiment to conform to this ideal was that of honor (*'ird*). A man upheld his honor through his valor in battle, a woman by her sexual modesty (*hasham*) and deference to social superiors, in particular older men of her clan.[74]

A life taken had to be avenged by the clan, which would otherwise be indelibly tainted with shame and invite more aggression. There are striking parallels between the values of Arab warriors that shaped Islam and those of Homeric heroes. Honor and fame achieved in battle were what drove these men—the very qualities that allowed the strong to survive. Their failure led to shame. The expectation to preserve honor also drives the gruesome practice in some traditional Arab societies of the "honor killings" of sexually errant women (or even victims of rape) by members of their family, usually a brother. These are, however, culturally endorsed practices rather than precepts prescribed by Islam.

Manliness has not been the only Bedouin virtue. Hospitality and generosity have also been highly valued. Care for one's kin and for widows and orphans, and fairness and justice were traditional values Muhammad endorsed. These virtues were the closest thing to an ethical system that the Bedouins had before they embraced Islam.

The idea of shame is best conveyed by the Arabic word *hayah*, which corresponds to "modesty," "bashfulness," or "reserve." It is viewed as a virtue, especially for women. A more cultural rather than religious term is *aib*, which has sexual connotations for women but reflects boorish, uncivilized behavior for men. Consequently, Islam views the capacity for shame as a positive quality—a protective armor that helps maintain one's reputation and guards against shamelessness, which is demeaning.

Closely linked with the idea of modesty is the segregation and veiling of Muslim women. These practices have attracted much attention in the West, where their critics see them as symbols of the subjugation of and social discrimination against women. These were established practices in pre-Islamic Arabia that were adopted by the Prophet's wives to protect their privacy. Since the wives of the Prophet were the most honored of women in the Islamic community, veiling came to be seen as a symbol of prestige (like foot binding in China).

The traditional justification for veiling and covering the body in public (generally referred to as *hijab*) is that it shields women from the prying eyes of men and helps guard their modesty and honor. This practice is now mandatory only in a few Muslim countries (notably Iran and Saudi Arabia) and forbidden in Turkey. In much of the rest of the Muslim world the practice is voluntary and relatively more common among older and traditional women, thus reflecting social convention rather than religious practice. However, there is now a revival of the custom among younger women in European countries, like France, with large Muslim communities, which becomes problematic under certain circumstances.

Guilt and Moral Behavior

Human beings are born in a "state of nature" (*fitra*) that allows free choice. One may make a wrong moral choice but then return to God in repentance. This prospect of return and reconciliation (*tawbah*) is deemed better than not falling into sin at all. This is because it avoids self-righteousness and religious pride, which diminish one's utter dependence on God.

Disobedience to God (*isyan*) and ingratitude (*kufr*) are key sources of immoral behavior. Given the many blessings of God, ingratitude is a grave offence. God forgives those who err, but ingrates do not deserve his mercy. Islam classifies human behavior into five categories: permitted (*halal*); prohibited (*haram*); discouraged (*makruh*); ethically neutral (*mubah*); and encouraged (*mustahabb*). Islamic ethics is liberal in the sense that whatever God has not expressly forbidden is permitted (a sign of his generosity). Intentions behind actions are as important as the actions themselves in determining their moral valence.[75]

Islamic law views sexuality as a gift of God as long as it is limited to a lawful relationship like marriage. All other sexual practices that threaten the integrity of marriage are prohibited, including adultery and homosexuality. The punishments in countries that follow the shariah are quite severe, such as death by stoning. However, the standard of proof is so high that it is hard to establish guilt (the act must be witnessed "as if a pen is being dipped in the inkwell"). Therefore, as a practical matter a judgment of guilt is usually based on compelling circumstantial evidence such as pregnancy in an unmarried woman or acts supposedly committed during the absence of the woman's husband.[76]

Islamic marriages are predominantly monogamous but it is the prospect of occasional polygamy that has attracted the attention (and fantasies) of Westerners. The Prophet was monogamous in his first marriage, to Khadija (who was the first convert to Islam and fifteen years older than him). Following her death, the Prophet married a number of women, some of them for political reasons. The Qur'an decrees that a man can have up to four wives, provided that he treats them with scrupulous fairness. The practice was pre-Islamic, but it gained momentum as a response to the need to take care of widowed women and orphaned girls (it also obviously appealed to the male desire for sexual variety). Polygamy is rarely practiced in most Muslim countries and forbidden in secular states like Turkey. In the few places where it is allowed (such as Saudi Arabia), only a small fraction of men have more than one wife.[77]

So far, we have largely dwelled on mainstream Islam. The Sufis have a somewhat different perspective on guilt and shame. Given the focus of the shariah on culpability, Islam does not dwell on subjective elements of guilt. By contrast, the Sufis, who seek a closer personal and mystical experience with God (as exemplified by Rabi'a's prayer at the opening of this section), dwell more on the subjective self (*nafs*). Sufis follow the "dictates of the soul" and seek the love of God. Sufi spiritualism is often contrasted with Islamic law. However, the Sufis do not reject the law; what they object to is the carrying out of ritual practices for egoistic reasons or without devotion.[78]

There are two conditions necessary for moral virtue in Sufism: a heart free from bondage to others and an appetite free from worldly desires. The first step on one's spiritual path is recognizing one's own ignorance. Moral error is in most cases due to ignorance. When one discovers having committed an error, the reaction is one of shame, not guilt. Shame is useful for leading one to repentance, provided it results from the person's own recognition, not the condemnation of others.

Guilt at best also points to one's errors and serves no useful purpose if it merely represents institutional condemnation used to manipulate individuals. Responsibility comes with knowledge; acting in ignorance leads to shame; acting irresponsibly in the face of knowledge induces guilt. If one seeks guidance and follows it, diligently, then one should not be judged and no guilt should follow. Guilt is a form of derivative suffering, like an interest payment on a bigger debt that will come due when God catches up with us. However, God is most merciful and ever forgiving if one is repentant.[79]

DEALING WITH GUILT

How do the monotheistic faiths deal with guilt? What do their adherents do when they feel guilty? We know by now that there is no single answer to such questions. What Jews, Christians, and Muslims do when burdened with guilt depends not only on their particular religion but also on the cultural and folk traditions of their societies, and, no less importantly, on their psychological predisposition to guilt as individuals. People are first and foremost who they are apart from the religious tradition they belong to.

The basic sequence of dealing with guilt in the monotheistic religions is fundamentally the same as in dealing with guilt in other contexts discussed earlier. For example, the steps for dealing with guilt indicated by Rabbi Harlan Wechsler are: remorse (feeling bad); recantation (confessing); renunciation (turning away from doing wrong); resolution (resolving not to repeat wrongdoing); and reconciliation (receiving the forgiveness of the person you have wronged).[80]

The key *religious* elements for dealing with guilt in monotheism consist of repentance and redemption. *Repentance* in Judaism means to return (*teshuvah*) to God. The Psalmist prays for forgiveness with the conviction that God will not spurn a contrite and humble heart. The call for repentance continues in the New Testament, where it is a central theme in the teachings of Jesus and Paul.

The same is also true for Islam, where return to God in repentance and reconciliation (*tawba*) is open to all.[81] In the Qur'an, the theme of divine forgiveness is pervasive: all but one of its chapters open with the phrase "In the name of God, the merciful, the compassionate."[82] Forgiveness is one of the attributes of God and a characteristic of the Prophet to be emulated by the faithful. It is a change of heart through which mercy replaces resentment, even where resentment is morally justified.[83] Forgiveness does not imply servility or lack of self-respect, nor should it be a matter of gain or loss. Nonetheless, given the legal basis of Islam, dealing with guilt is largely a matter of determining culpability and ensuring adequate compensation of the victim. The resolution of feelings of remorse that may follow a guilt-inducing action does not attract much attention in the law. As a practical matter, however, Muslims probably do not behave any differently than others in trying to repair the damage to relationships that results from guilty acts.

Redemption (from the Latin *redimere*, "to buy back") is modeled on paying ransom to redeem people from captivity. In the Hebrew Bible, God is the redeemer (*go'el*) of the people of Israel from captivity—first in Egypt and then again in Babylon. Redemption is also tied to God's promise to the people of Israel for a messiah who will free them from oppression.

In Christianity, this promise finds its fulfillment in the redemption through the death and resurrection of Jesus Christ. Through Christ, the estrangement from God through human disobedience is healed. Christ pays the ransom to redeem humanity from sin through the sacrifice of his own life followed by his victory over death through his resurrection.[84] In Islam, God will settle the accounts of believers and unbelievers on the Day of Judgment. Islam and Christianity, more so than Judaism, count on this settling of accounts by the eventual punishment of the guilty and the vindication of the faithful in the life to come.

There is an additional method of dealing with guilt based on the spiritual exercises of St. Ignatius of Loyola. Called the General Examination of Conscience (or *Consciousness Examen*), it is part of the Catholic tradition, but it can be adapted by people who follow other religious traditions or are secular. It is essentially a form of self-appraisal that has also been the basis of other religious, philosophical, and psychological practices.[85]

The Examen is aimed at moral ordering and discernment. It is a form of prayer—but different from the daily prayers offered by Jews, Christians, and Muslims. It is a form of contemplation—but not the sort of contemplation undertaken by Hindus and Buddhists; a form of rational analysis—but not the sort of analysis undertaken by philosophers. It allows our thoughts and feelings free reign—but it is not a form of psychological free-association. Nor is it a form of stocktaking or planning schedules. The use I propose here for it is as a form of "conscience maintenance" for the monitoring and resolution of guilt.[86]

Like any other exercise, Examen works only if done regularly and as part of everyday life, rather than imposed on it. In order to be sustained, it should not be burdensome, tedious, or unpleasant. The ten to fifteen minutes it requires should be easily fitted into our daily schedule and not be yet one more thing to do.

In preparation for the Examen, it is necessary to clear the decks by calming your heart and opening your mind. For a religious person, it means standing in the presence of God being fully aware of your utter dependence on him, like a child standing in front of a loving parent. You need to resist the intrusion of thoughts and feelings that are extraneous to your immediate concern, which is the examination of your thoughts, feelings, and actions since the last Examen the day before—not your whole life.

The first step is to acknowledge and be thankful for all that is good in your life; not only for spectacular successes (few and far between), but also for the everyday blessings we take for granted. The second step is more directly linked to guilt. What have you done during the past day that troubles your conscience? Having identified what (if anything) makes you feel guilty should determine how you have, or have not, dealt with it. (Recall the authentic and inauthentic ways of dealing with guilt.) You need to be firm with yourself without being either picky or punitive. This is not an exercise in self-flagellation. Do not obsess over issues in order to find something to feel guilty about, nor be dismissive of your actions. The point is to examine yourself with honesty and compassion, but with neither self-condemnation nor complacency.

The third step focuses not on guilt as such but on the ways our thoughts and feelings feed into guilt and fan its flame. This is as much a psychological exercise as it is a form of moral discernment. For instance, do you find yourself needlessly fretting over issues that you have already come to terms with, or over which you have no control? If you have fallen short of your own expectations, have they been realistic and significant? Look for patterns and do not get stuck on isolated incidents nor pile up a catalogue of failings.

The fourth and final step consists of looking ahead to the future, in particular, the next day. What are the things in life that you can reasonably and legitimately hope for? How can you apply the lessons learned from the past and not repeat your mistakes? How can you face the future with optimism and the determination to do better?

If nothing noteworthy has happened in connection with any of these steps, you can move lightly through them. If something of significance has happened, you have the opportunity to assess it while the experience is fresh in your mind; and if it is anything problematic and guilt-inducing, you can nip it in the bud and come to terms with it.

It is important to keep this process within bounds. The task is more like balancing your checkbook than an IRS audit. It is dusting and vacuuming, not spring cleaning. A particular issue may not be resolved within the time available to you. In that case, you can deal with it in installments, by taking it up again the next day. If, however, the problem is serious enough, it needs to be dealt with in a broader context that will allow more time for it and perhaps help from others. The Examen is only a form of moral *maintenance*. If what is needed is more than a simple oil change and lubrication, the car has to go to the garage for more extensive investigation and repair.

The Islamic practice of praying five times a day accomplishes some of the same functions. Though it is a more formal prayer that involves the recitation of particular verses from the Qur'an, it makes Muslims stop and reflect on their ongoing lives. To take such breaks, in whatever form, is an excellent antidote to being driven heedlessly by the pressures and distractions that make us forget who we are, what we are doing, and to what end.

Against this background, we turn next to the quite different perspectives on guilt and shame in Hinduism, Buddhism, and Confucianism, and Asian cultures more generally. Whereas in the monotheistic religions the moral impulse emanates from God and the moral consequences of human conduct are ultimately judged by God, there is no comparable personal divinity regulating the moral lives of Hindus, Buddhists, and Confucianists. Nonetheless, the basic human needs, proclivities, and conditions that lead to conflicts that generate shame and guilt are very similar among the followers of these traditions. How to reconcile these conflicts is the subject of the next chapter.

9 GUILT IN HINDUISM, BUDDHISM, AND CONFUCIANISM

MAHATMA GANDHI embodied the ethical ideal of modern India and Hinduism. Hence his personal experiences of guilt are a good way to introduce Hindu guilt. The following transformative episode took place when Gandhi was a 16-year-old, newly married, dutiful son caring for his dying father:

> Every night I massaged his legs and retired only when he had asked me or after he had fallen asleep. I loved to do this service . . . and never neglected it. . . . This was also the time when my wife was expecting a baby,—a circumstance which, as I can see today, meant a double shame for me. For one thing, I did not restrain myself, as I should have done, whilst I was a student. And secondly, this carnal lust got the better of what I regarded as my duty to study, my devotion to my parents. . . . Every night whilst my hands were massaging my father's legs, my mind was hovering about the bedroom. . . .
>
> My uncle would sit near my father's bed the whole day, and would insist on sleeping by his bedside after sending us all to sleep . . . It was 10:30 or 11 p.m. I was giving the massage. My uncle offered to relieve me. I was glad and went straight to my bed-room. My wife, poor thing, was asleep. But how could she sleep when I was there? I woke her up. In five or six minutes, however, the servant knocked at door. I started with alarm. "Get up" he said, "Father is

The lectures of the following colleagues to my seminar introduced me to their respective areas of expertise: Linda Hess and Mark Mancall (Hinduism); Carl Bielefeldt, Mark Mancall, and Mark Berkson (Buddhism); Lee Yearley and Mark Berkson (Confucianism); Huston Smith (Asian religions). I am also grateful to Raka Ray, Shireen Pasha, Smita Singh, Zulfiger Ahmad, Lee Yearley, Sheila Melvin, Jindong Cai, and Rachel Zhu, and in particular to Mark Mancall and Mark Berkson, for their critiques and invaluable help in the preparation of this chapter.

very ill." I knew of course that he was very ill, and so I guessed what "very ill" meant at that moment. I sprang out of bed.

"What is the matter? Do tell me!"

"Father is no more." So all was over! I had but to wring my hands. I felt deeply ashamed and miserable. I ran to my father's room. I saw that, if animal passion had not blinded me, I should have been spared the torture of separation from my father during his last moments. I should have been massaging him and he would have died in my arms. . . .

. . . This shame of my carnal desire even at the critical hour of my father's death, which demanded wakeful service . . . is a blot I have never been able to efface or forget, and I have always thought that, although my devotion to my parents knew no bounds and I would have given anything for it, yet it was unpardonably wanting because my mind was at the same moment in the grip of lust. . . . It took me long to get free from the shackles of lust, and I had to pass through many ordeals before I could overcome it. . . .

Before I close this chapter of my double shame, I may mention that the poor mite that was born to my wife scarcely breathed for more than three of four days. Nothing else could be expected.[1]

Gandhi related this event in the autobiography he wrote (in the Gujarati dialect) when he was sixty. The memory of his youthful transgression still rankled. Would Gandhi have felt differently if instead of making love to his wife, Kasturbai, he had been merely asleep when his father had died? Gandhi finally achieved his wish to "be free from the shackles of lust" when he told his wife years later that they would no longer have sexual relations (she was unhappy about it). However, by that time Gandhi's rejection of sex may have been due to his not wanting to be distracted from his all-consuming passion for justice and the liberation of India from British rule.[2]

Gandhi's experience had the standard ingredients of guilt: It followed a moral transgression (he failed in his filial duty) and involved a common cause of guilt (sexual passion), for which he was punished (by the loss of his child). Yet, Gandhi characterizes his feelings as those of *shame*, not guilt. As an English-trained lawyer, he knew perfectly well what guilt meant, but that is not the word he used. Yet, in his psychobiography of Gandhi, Erik Erikson refers to Gandhi as "a youth totally obsessed with matters of guilt and purity." Erikson refers to the episode involving his father's death as a "curse" that stayed with him for the rest of his life. Erikson says it was a curse Gandhi shared with other spiritual innovators who had a "similarly precocious relent-less conscience."[3]

In another context, Gandhi does refer to guilt in a letter he wrote to his father when he was fifteen, to confess that he had taken a bit of gold from his brother's armlet and sold it:

> In this note not only did I confess my guilt, but I asked adequate punishment for it. . . . A clean confession, combined with a promise not to commit the sin again, when offered before one who has the right to receive it, is the purest type of repentance. I know that my confession . . . increased his affection for me beyond measure.[4]

Why is Gandhi referring to guilt now? Is it because guilt in this sense refers to being culpable of wrongful conduct rather than the failure of a filial duty? What about transgressions of a more ritual than moral nature? As a strict vegetarian (influenced by Jainism), Gandhi did not eat meat. However, on one occasion in his youth, he was persuaded by a friend to do so because that would make them "strong like the British." Gandhi recalls: "I had a very bad night afterwards. A horrible nightmare haunted me. . . . It was as though a live goat were bleating inside me, and I would jump up full of remorse."[5]

Gandhi characterizes his feeling here as "remorse," which we equate with guilt. In his letters, he also speaks liberally of his conscience as the "clear voice within": "For me the voice of God, of Conscience, of Truth, or the Inner Voice, or 'the still small Voice,' mean one and the same thing."[6]

Gandhi considers conscience to be "the ripe fruit of discipline" acquired by laborious training. Children and irresponsible youngsters (as well as "savages") do not have a conscience. To hear the inner voice, one must have "divine ears." With these references to conscience, Gandhi seems to be speaking the language of guilt.

Some years ago, when I asked one of my colleagues who teaches Hinduism to lecture to my class on guilt, she responded, "But there is no guilt in Hinduism." I did not believe her. I assumed guilt was a universal experience, albeit with different social manifestations. So I began to look for what guilt was like in Hinduism, but my search turned into looking for the proverbial needle in a haystack. Finally, I began to wonder if there was a needle after all. So how do we make sense out of all this? Were Gandhi's feelings those of guilt or shame? And whatever they are called, what makes them distinctive in Asian religions? These are the sort of questions that will concern us in this chapter.

The adherents of Asian and Western religions follow more or less the same norms of ethical conduct. And when they violate these rules, they presumably feel equally bad. In Western languages like English, that is called *feeling guilty*, but there is no exactly equivalent term in Asian languages like Sanskrit or Chinese. Such feelings are typically translated as *shame*, but that represents something broader and more inclusive than what shame means in English. Does that mean that shame fulfills the same functions that guilt does in Western cultures? We already struggled with this issue in connection with our earlier discussion of guilt and shame cultures and we will reconsider it here in its religious context.

The Asian cultures within which Hinduism, Buddhism, and Confucianism developed share a strong emphasis on maintaining *harmony* between individuals, within families, in the larger society, and in the cosmos. However, we cannot subsume these religions under a single category as easily as we can monotheistic religions. Hinduism has many gods, Buddhism has no God (in the biblical sense), and Confucianism is accepted as a religion by some and an ethical philosophy by others (depending on what one thinks constitutes a religion).[7]

Problems in studying concepts like guilt and shame across cultural divides also arise from the fact that there are few studies that focus on the actual experiences of individuals instead of being derived from ancient religious texts or extrapolated from Western psychological models. Despite these uncertainties, there is much to learn from other religious and cultural traditions in understanding and managing our own experiences of guilt. At least that is the hope that informs this chapter.

GUILT IN HINDUISM

Hinduism has no founder. And its religious expressions and experiences are so varied that they defy easy categorization.[8] Nevertheless, there is a core of commonality that allows us to lump them together as *Hinduism*. Hindus believe in a cosmic force that governs all existence and cannot be fully known. Individual gods and goddesses are personifications of this cosmic force. Worshippers call upon familiar gods to help with their everyday hopes and problems. Among their array of gods (*deva*) three are most prominent: Brahma, the Creator; Vishnu / Krishna, the Preserver; and Shiva, the Destroyer. There are also goddesses under Devi (Protective Mother). These gods are also the attributes of a single Brahman, which represents all reality and consciousness. It is the Ultimate Being, Existence itself, an awesome presence that defies human understanding, "before whom all words recoil."[9]

A vast literature in Sanskrit encompasses the sacred texts of Hinduism. The earliest foundational texts are the Vedas.[10] In post-Vedic Hinduism, sages and kings, who exemplify moral conduct, came to be seen as incarnations of the gods, and their histories were accepted as divine epics. The two best known are the *Ramayana* and *Mahabharata*, which includes the *Bhagavadgita*—the primary sacred scripture of modern Hinduism. The Gita explores three dimensions of religious experience—knowing, feeling, and will to action—through dialogues between the warrior Arjuna and the god Krishna.[11]

In the nineteenth-century struggle for independence from British rule, the idea of a single Hindu God became prevalent. As an equivalent to the Christian God of the British, a single Hindu deity would provide a common ethical ground for the resolution of the political conflict. For Gandhi,

> God is ethics and morality. . . . God is conscience. God is even the atheism of the atheist. . . . God is patient, but God is also terrible. With God ignorance is no excuse. And with all, God is forgiving for God always gives us a chance to repent. . . . God leaves us "unfettered" to make our own choices between good and evil.[12]

Where do notions of guilt and shame fit into all this wealth of beliefs and ideas? Let us first try to clarify the terminology in Sanskrit and Urdu. I noted earlier that there is no exact term for "feeling guilty" in Hinduism. There is actually no equivalent in Sanskrit for the English word *guilt* itself. The Urdu word *kharab* comes closest to the subjective feeling of guilt (as in, "When I do something wrong, I feel kharab"). The Sanskrit word *dosa* conveys both the sense of being at fault as well as having a negative character trait, such as untrustworthiness. Wrongdoing (*aparadha*) makes one *dosa*, or guilty in the sense of culpability. There is a general word for shame (*lajja*), which may convey several meanings. It includes shame as embarrassment as well as regret for causing discomfort to another ("I feel lajja for putting you in a bad situation"). *Sharan* is close in meaning to the English word *dishonor*.[13]

The idea of ethics as a set of moral rules also does not have an equivalent in Hinduism. However, there is a word for conscience (*vivek*), a moral guide that everyone can tap into. Unlike Judaism and Islam, Hinduism is not a law-based religion. It has many rules but most of them have to do with cultic purity, not morality. The ritual and ethical components of Hinduism are closely intertwined. There is a cosmic order in the universe, and human beings must act in conformity with it by performing proper rituals as well as cultivating proper moral attitudes and behaviors (such as truthfulness and generosity).[14] In this regard, two fundamental principles—karma and dharma—are singularly important.[15]

Karma and Dharma

Karma and dharma, for which there are no exactly equivalent words in English, together provide the basic structure of Hindu ethics and rituals. These concepts are shared with Buddhism, but there are some differences (as discussed in the section on Buddhism, below). Karma is concerned with the consequences of actions, dharma with moral duty and conduct. These twin principles work in close conjunction to support and regulate the cosmic order, the natural order, and the social order. Morality is not a personal matter alone. The fate of human beings and the universe are bound together. It is through proper adherence to rules of ritual and ethical conduct that individuals and societies maintain a viable world. If all goes well, people are happy and the world is in good order; if not, people are unhappy and chaos reigns.

Karma (Sanskrit, "deed" or "action") is a fundamental law of nature. It is neither fate nor destiny, even though the word may be misused in that sense ("What can I do about it? It's my karma"). Originally, karma was linked to ritual activity, but its meaning was expanded to refer to all "residues" of human actions that have moral consequence. Karma connects ritual and ethically relevant actions to the prospects of rebirth. All that I am at present is the result of my karma from a past life, and all that I do now (or the karma I accumulate) will determine who I will be in my next life.

While karma results from actions, not all actions generate karma. Normal physical activities like walking, or physiological functions like breathing, do not generate karma. There are good and bad actions that lead to good and bad consequences, but Sanskrit does not differentiate between good and bad karma—there is just karma.

Bad conduct leads to rebirth in an inferior form of life, such as being reborn in a lower caste, or even as an animal (for instance, a glutton may be reborn as a pig). Karma may sound like a form of punishment for sins, but in Hinduism there is no sin or divine judge, no punishment or repentance or remission of sins.[16] It is simply a natural process of cause and effect. Nor is karma the Hindu equivalent of guilt. In this regard, there is an important difference between the Western and the Hindu modes of evaluating the consequences of actions. In the West, the moral concern is with the impact of one's actions on *others*; in Hinduism, the concern is the impact of actions on *oneself.*

Intention is of key importance irrespective of consequences. Gandhi made this a cardinal principle. As long as your motives are pure and your means correct, the rest will take care of itself. In one of his renowned acts of nonviolent resistance, Gandhi sat on the railroad tracks with no thought of the possible consequences. For Gandhi this is also an important theme in the Gita.[17]

Another antidote to guilt in Hinduism is its lack of the doctrine of Original Sin or innate evil. Human beings are born with certain dispositions that make them prone to certain personal afflictions called *kleshas.* There are five such afflictions: ignorance, selfishness, attachments, aversion, and the fear of death. They lead to conduct that generates karma; thus one has to struggle to overcome these tendencies. Hindu gods do not determine human fate. There is no Hindu Oedipus to be punished by the gods. Hinduism is not fatalistic. New choices present new opportunities to reshape the moral landscape of one's life. One is not mired in karma forever.

Dharma (Sanskrit, "custom" or "decree"), the other key concept in Hinduism (and Buddhism), originated from concerns over purity, but was expanded to include conformity to custom and duty; thus it represents moral duty: the norms for right conduct and proper ritual.[18] Dharma is inherent in all living things and ensures the smooth functioning of the social and natural world as well as the realization of one's true nature. To conform to the requirements of dharma a Hindu must observe three things.

First is to maintain *ritual purity.* As a ritual matter, purity may have no moral content but pollution nonetheless sets one back in the path to liberation. Purity may apply to the mind and the body. Some polluting behaviors are simply violations of rules of cleanliness (for instance, dipping your spoon into the common pot) or rules of etiquette (such as hugging someone in public). Others involve religious rituals that are quite flexible. For instance, when Hindus do not have the means to offer a sacrifice, they can perform the ritual mentally. This may look like shortchanging the ritual, but it is the intent that counts.

The second requirement of dharma is to live within the confines of the *caste system* into which all Hindus were born. The caste system was so deeply embedded in Hindu consciousness that it governed virtually all human interactions from the most intimate to the trivial. For instance, Brahmins would not only avoid touching a *dalit* or "untouchable" but even stepping into their shadow, since it was considered polluting. Consequently, ethical behavior meant staying within the confines of one's caste. The morality of a given behavior often depended not on *what* you did but *who* you did it with.

Crossing the caste barrier would make someone of lower caste face the threat of retribution, while those of higher caste would face disgrace. The caste system was abolished in modern India but it continues to influence some social relationships. Marrying below one's caste is often opposed by families. The law forbids job discrimination based on caste, but that does not mean it no longer occurs.

The third requirement of dharma is fulfilling the obligations of various *stages in life*. The first stage is that of apprenticeship, when a young man lives with a mentor who educates him and teaches him a trade. Next comes the householder stage, when family and work dominate a man's life. Finally there is the retirement stage, when a man withdraws from worldly life, ultimately living as a *sanyasin* ("one who neither hates nor loves anything")—a homeless wanderer begging for his food, unconcerned about the future and indifferent to the present.[19] There are no comparable stages for women, for their lives were determined by their fathers and husbands, which in extreme form included *sati*, whereby a widow would immolate herself on her husband's funeral pyre (a practice no longer allowed by law).

The traditional requirement of dharmic duty may no longer exert the force it once did on Hindus. However, it still makes Hindu ethics far less absolute than ethics in the monotheistic religions. The morality of one's actions is ultimately dependent on the context of one's actions. Things are not either right or wrong in the abstract, but depend on the circumstances. This makes Hindu morality less judgmental.

Hindus obtain moral instruction from parents and other members of their families. Priests primarily serve ritual functions rather than provide moral guidance. In trying to influence the behavior of their children, parents recognize their own limitations: Children are going to do what they want to do and will eventually find their own way. One cannot stop them from following the paths they choose. One can reason and argue with them, but a parent would not disown a child under any circumstance.

Paths to Liberation

Hindus believe that human beings are trapped in a cycle of birth, death, and rebirth (*samsara*). At each turn, the body is discarded but the immortal or true Self—the *atman*—lives on in its next incarnation. The *atman* is not the same as the soul but more like a sense of "consciousness," the essential core of everything. The rest is *maya*, or illusion. The ultimate aim in life is liberation (*moksha*) from the repetitive cycle of death and rebirth. In some forms of Hinduism, the cycle culminates with the *atman* merging with the *Brahman*, the Universal Being, itself. The merger leads to the loss of personal identity (unlike the Christian soul, which retains its identity after death). Where Christians yearn for eternal life, Hindus want to be part of eternity itself. Christians want to extend existence on earth to life in the next world; for Hindus, existence on earth is the problem. This may be yet another reason why the Western sense of guilt has no place in Hinduism. What keeps Hindus in line is not guilt but the prospect of rebirth, especially sliding down the ladder to a lower station in life.

Hinduism is also distinctive in providing a variety of ways for making progress toward liberation. Whereas morality in monotheistic religions focuses on subduing unruly human nature, Hinduism does not engage in this arduous, and often losing, struggle; instead, it rolls with the punches by offering paths that best fit a person's natural inclinations. Therefore, to be a moral person, you do not have to disown your basic inclinations; rather, you follow whatever path fits with your basic character. Some people are driven by the desire for sensual, erotic, and esthetic enjoyment (*kama*); others long for worldly fame and fortune (*artha*); yet others want to follow the path of duty and service to others (*dharma*)—not to be confused with the more general meaning of dharma discussed earlier. It is not a matter of which path is better but which *fits* a person best. To that end, the important thing is to do one's best. Thus, a teacher must be the best teacher possible, independent of what others may think.[20] One should act without attachment to the fruits of the action. What we do is undertaken for the sake of dharma, not for its consequences. This, too, is in sharp contrast to the Western idea that the consequences of conduct define its moral nature.

These desires have their satisfactions but they still leave us subject to pain, distress, boredom, and ignorance; the sooner one gets out of it, the better off one will be.

To that end, and based on their defining desires, human beings are classified as inclined toward one of four paths: *intellectual, emotional, active,* and *experiential*. For each of these paths there is a *yoga* ("yoke"), the means toward liberation. Yoga is not just a set of contorted postures. Its serious practitioners use it to direct psychic energy inward to the true Self. The practice requires meditation, cleanliness, and abstention from bodily cravings, in addition to prescribed postures (*asanas*) and special forms of breathing.

For Hindus, yoga is a way of burning up karma. There are four yogas to fit each of the four human inclinations.[21] *Jnana yoga* is the way of knowledge for those who are intellectually inclined. This does not mean becoming a philosopher or relying on the cold light of reason, but involves intensive reflection under the guidance of a master. *Bhakti yoga*, for the emotionally inclined, uses adoration. It may entail ritual expressions of devotion, passionate love of poetry, and the recitation of divine names. The use of erotic imagery, metaphor and, in some cases, sexual practices makes traditional Hinduism unique in its attitudes toward sexuality. An unorthodox variation is *tantric yoga*, which uses sexual intercourse as the path to liberation.[22] Thus, whereas sex has been one of the key sources of guilt in Western morality, it can lead to liberation in Hinduism. Paradoxically, Hinduism contains some of the most sensuous expressions of all religions (as in the erotic statuary of medieval Indian temples like Khajuraho), as well as the most extreme forms of asceticism and self-mortification that can put to shame its severest Christian counterparts.

The third option, *karma yoga*, is for action-oriented persons and involves work in everyday life. (Not to be confused with the broader concept of karma; both terms refer to action.) Such work must be chosen wisely and performed selflessly. You need to put your heart and soul into it and avoid going after trivial pursuits. Finally, *raja yoga* (which was popularized by the Beatles as "transcendental meditation") uses psychological exercises and physical postures to control body and mind. To follow any of these paths effectively, one needs a *guru*, a teacher and role model.

Hinduism shares with other great religions basic ethical precepts for right living such as truthfulness, honesty, self-control, and discipline. Particularly distinctive is its focus on nonviolence. While all religions have pacifist ideals, some forms of Hinduism extend injunctions against killing to all of life's creatures, even to spiders and ants (a tradition influenced by Jainism).[23] The ideal of nonviolent political resistance was effectively put into practice by Gandhi, who called it *satyagraha* ("holding to the truth"). However, that has not stopped Hindus from killing each other (Gandhi himself was assassinated by a Hindu) any more than the command to love one's enemies has turned all Christians into pacifists.

Dealing with Guilt in Hinduism

Since guilt is not a central concern in the moral universe of Hindus, there is not much to be said about dealing with it. When Hindus commit a wrongful act, they recognize some version of feelings of regret and remorse, but they do not dwell on them. They move on to dealing with their consequences. Hence, "feeling guilty" is not an intermediary station on the path to the resolution of guilt the way it is in Western contexts. Since Hindus accomplish the task of moral control with less recourse to feelings of guilt, it is much less of an issue. (This is what is meant by saying there is no guilt in Hinduism.)

Nonetheless, a Hindu must still deal with the fact of having done wrong. And since doing wrong is contingent on one's caste (or social class), stage of life, and the circumstances under which the action takes place, the ways of dealing with its consequences vary accordingly. In any case, the steps taken are emotional as well as practical. Thus, the first step in confronting the wrong one has committed is to admit it to oneself; but there is no emphasis on confession and forgiveness and no issue of paying a debt. One must simply try to act better the next time. One also recognizes the suffering one has caused and suffers oneself through *penance* (*prayaschitva*). For instance, a man who had neglected to care for his mother during her terminal illness made a vow not to eat meat for the rest of his life. Others may fast or deprive themselves in some other way.

A more constructive remedy is to do good. One can feed the poor, do a favor to someone in need, or give money to a temple. The religious counterpart of this is to appease the gods by doing *puja*, a religious ritual to show respect for the gods or one's guru through prayers, chanting, and making offerings. Even though gods do not usually intrude into human lives, one must respect them to keep harmony in the universe. These practices may appear strange to outsiders. Some years ago, I visited a Hindu temple in New Delhi, thinking it was an ancient structure. Instead, it turned out to be a modern building full of garishly painted statues. As I stood looking at a tacky image of the elephant-headed god Ganesha, I noticed standing next to me a young woman whose face was luminous with piety, like a medieval Madonna, and I felt ashamed.

GUILT IN BUDDHISM

A colleague and friend of mine asked the Dalai Lama about guilt in Buddhism. "There is no guilt in Buddhism," replied His Holiness. "Suppose," my friend persisted, "a son disappoints his parents deeply by failing to live up to their expectations. How would he feel?" His Holiness smiled and said, "It happens."[24]

Does the Dalai Lama mean to say that there is no guilt in Buddhism even though people feel bad when they do wrong or fall short of expectations? Is his Holiness contradicting himself? If what they feel is not guilt, then what is it? Does it have a name? When a colleague was discussing guilt in Buddhism in my seminar, students felt frustrated. They wanted to know what the Buddha meant *exactly* when he said such and such; they wanted precise and clear-cut answers. My colleague told them not to try to "fine tune it."[25] That is exactly what I was doing above, myself.

Siddhartha Gautama, the historical founder of Buddhism, was born in 563 BCE into an aristocratic family in one of the feudal domains in India. At sixteen, he married a princess who bore him a son. He had everything a man could wish for until he became aware of human suffering by witnessing four distressing sights: an old man, a sick man, a beggar, and a corpse. At twenty-nine, he left his home and family and for six years he went searching for enlightenment in the solitude of the forest, next seeking instruction from two Hindu masters, and finally joining a band of ascetics.

All was to no avail until he found the answer through rigorous thought and mystical concentration. The Buddha sought the *Middle Way* between the extremes of asceticism and worldly indulgence. One evening, while sitting under the Bo tree, he was tempted by the Evil One in the form of *kama* (sexual desire) and *mara* (death). He yielded to neither and achieved his Great Awakening and was transformed into the *Buddha*—the Enlightened One. For the next forty-five years the Buddha traveled across India preaching, teaching, and comforting sufferers. He established a monastic order and divided his time between meditative solitude and attending to the instruction and needs of the people. (While Gautama is referred to as the Buddha, he was not the first, or the only, Buddha. A Buddha—Sanskrit, "awakened one"—is a person who is fully enlightened. Anyone with an awakened mind has the potential for becoming a Buddha.)

The Buddha left no writings. The earliest texts recording his words appeared 150 years after his death. There are no revealed scriptures in Buddhism—only teachings. The Buddha instructed his followers to shun speculation and to avoid treating words as substitutes for the reality of experience. His sayings were often enigmatic; he could respond to questions with silence or by a symbolic gesture. In one instance, he silently held up a lotus flower by way of an answer. In Zen Buddhism, masters use paradoxical statements, stories (*koan*), and questions that defy rational answers ("Two hands clap and there is a sound; what is the sound of one hand clapping?"). Nevertheless, the Buddha's followers tried to conceptualize his teachings in intellectual terms.[26]

The teachings of the Buddha make no direct reference to guilt. Since original Buddhist texts are in Sanskrit, our discussion of the terminology of guilt in Hinduism is also relevant here. There is no evidence that the Buddha ever felt guilty. We will therefore have to infer the existence of such feelings from the teachings of Buddhism, as we did with Hinduism.

Buddhist Ethics

The Buddha started life within the Vedic tradition of Hinduism and despite his disenchantment with it, he retained some of its fundamental tenets such as karma, dharma, and the cycle of rebirth through the law of cause and effect. Karma in Buddhism is similar to its Hindu counterpart. It operates within an impersonal system. Deeds are the only thing that one can truly call one's own. Everything else in life must ultimately be left behind. In Buddhism, as in Hinduism, karma does not correspond to the idea of sin or guilt. There is no creator god to love or to fear; no god to reward and punish. We are solely responsible for our own actions. It is moral cultivation—not faith, worship, or sacrifice—that dictates human destiny.[27]

Japanese Buddhism conceived the idea of hell, with many levels of ferocious torments (in colder regions hells were freezing; in hot regions, boiling).[28] Hell is not, however, a place where one is damned for eternity. Rather, it is a way station where people suffer to burn up karma. In some forms of Buddhism, hell is not an actual place but a form of self-torment.

Intention is particularly important in Buddhism, as it is in Hinduism. It is not what we do but why we do it that determines the moral character of our actions and their karmic burden. Causing harm inadvertently still generates karma, but far less so than intentional wrongdoing. When we step on an ant inadvertently, the ant dies just the same, but it would be far worse for us if we killed the ant intentionally. The Buddha did not blame the man who unknowingly served him the spoiled food that led to his death at age eighty. (The Buddha knew the food was bad, but did not refuse it so as not to offend his host.)

Buddhism starts with the premise that human beings are born with the potential to become a Buddha (or have a *Buddha nature*). Life confronts people with *Four Noble Truths*, which the Buddha taught in his first sermon. First is suffering (*dukkha*), which makes the world a frustrating, unfulfilling, insecure, and unsatisfying place. No matter who you are, life starts with the helplessness of childhood and culminates in the decrepitude of old age leading to death.

The second noble truth points to *attachment* (more like clinging) as a prime cause of suffering. We get tied down to what we love only to lose it. Our selfish desires seek fulfillment at the expense of others, whom we use as means to our ends. Desire, bolstered by ill will and ignorance, keeps us trapped in the suffering of life. The way to overcome desire and get relief from suffering is to stop "wandering about," buffeted by the world. The third noble truth is *liberation* from suffering and the fourth is the *path* to that liberation.

Buddhist morality is based not on rules derived from abstractions, like good and evil, but on whether conduct reflects "skillful" ways of doing things (*kushala*) or "unskillful" conduct (*akushala*) that is self-serving. The resultant karma is based not on moral distinctions between good or evil actions but the difference between conscious attempts to avoid doing harm and harmful behavior.[29]

Simply stated, the aims of Buddhist ethics are to avoid evil, do good, and purify the mind. You should acknowledge your ignorance, appreciate kindness, and express gratitude. Transgressions in Buddhism may pertain to speech (lying, slander, and idle talk); the body (murder, theft, adultery); and the mind (covetousness, hatred, and error). Covetousness is the ultimate root of evil and suffering since it leads to attachments that cause wrongdoing; hence, by eliminating desire and craving, detachment leads to goodness. To avoid these moral pitfalls, a good person must associate with right-minded people and follow the *Eight-fold Path*, which consists of right views, right intent, right speech, right conduct, right livelihood, right effort, mindfulness, and concentration.[30]

Buddhism places a high value on the sanctity of life. It forbids the taking of all human and animal life (including through religious sacrifice) and extends loving kindness to all sentient beings. However, not all Buddhists are vegetarian. For instance, Tibetan Buddhists eat meat (there is not much else to eat in Tibet). There are some other minimal requirements Buddhists must fulfill, but monks have to observe 227 additional precepts largely aimed at leading a simple life.[31]

Buddhists see tangible worldly benefits to being a moral person. One can accumulate wealth through diligence, enjoy a good reputation, be confident and self-possessed in society, and die without anxiety. However, the ultimate objective in Buddhism, as in Hinduism, is liberation from the cycle of death and rebirth. But unlike Hinduism, the individual soul does not merge with the universal soul but is liberated through attaining *nirvana* (Sanskrit, "to blow out"). Since nirvana is unconditional nonexistence, our language is unable to capture its reality except in negatives, which leads to its enigmatic quality.

Modern scholarship interprets nirvana not as annihilation but the extinction of the finite self, leading to boundless peace and bliss. Nevertheless, nirvana remains, in Buddha's words, "incomprehensible, indescribable, inconceivable, unutterable."[32] It is not something to be understood but experienced. The same considerations apply to the concept of emptiness. The Heart Sutra, which embodies the Perfection of Wisdom, states: "Form is emptiness; emptiness is form. . . . Feeling, discrimination and consciousness are empty. . . . In emptiness, there is no feeling, no discrimination . . . no consciousness . . . no body, no mind . . . no ignorance . . . no aging and death."[33]

Buddhists are perfectly aware that the world is far from empty in a literal sense. What they mean by "emptiness" is that nothing has inherent reality or independent existence—what we see around us is what we have been conditioned to see. This is also true for feelings and thoughts such as guilt. Moreover, nothing is permanent in the world and everything is in flux, interconnected and interdependent on everything else.

The Poison of Guilt

How do Buddhists achieve their moral aims without recourse to guilt? They do not rely on obedience to absolute moral rules. Rather, Buddhism is highly pragmatic. Its ultimate purpose is to avoid causing suffering to oneself or to others. So one does whatever it takes to reduce suffering. To that end, if you have to lie, then you lie (as the Buddha was accused of doing). Even though the moral prescriptions of Buddhism may be stated in negative terms, they embody their positive counterparts as well. Thus, *do not lie* can also be phrased as *tell the truth*.

Buddhism recognizes that there is guilt in the world, but guilt does not exist as a metaphysical entity, in the abstract. Nor is it permanent. The world is in a flux—how we feel changes. Another way of looking at this is that while we have to live in the world, we should not get mired in it. The world is not a jail in which we serve a life sentence. This resonates with St. Paul's exhortation to be *in* the world but not *of* the world. Similarly, we can feel remorse but not wallow in it. Guilt and shame should be our moral guardians, but we should not be their prisoner.

Buddhism does not relentlessly pursue moral excellence or seek moral perfection; it places its aims within the reach of everyone. When someone does the wrong thing or fails to do the right thing, the appropriate response is not guilt but mending one's ways. Therefore, rather than denying the existence of guilt, Buddhism actively rejects it as a negative response to wrongdoing that damages our self-esteem.

In Buddhism, there are several "poisons" that are at the root of human suffering: desire / greed, ignorance / delusion, and hatred / aversion. Negative attitudes, like guilt, are a form of hatred, albeit self-hatred, that leads to self-loathing. They reflect an aversion to the self, which is not the way one should treat oneself, any more than others. Buddhism also condemns pride and egotism. When guilt leads to obsessing over one's faults in a self-centered way, it makes one feel special, albeit especially bad.[34]

Buddhism has a more positive view of shame. There are two forms of shame: one positive and the other negative. The positive form alerts us when we have acted in ways that are beneath our Buddha nature. Such shame is more like regret that makes us aware of our shortcomings and induces us to do better. In this sense, shame both helps us to maintain our integrity and acts as the guardian of the world order.

The negative form of shame leads us to feel worthless and has a destructive effect (like pathological guilt). Consequently, while the capacity or *sense of shame* is essential, *shamelessness* is to be avoided. The Buddha said,

> Life is easy for a person who is shameless, as bold as a crow, obtrusive, pushy, reckless, and whose life is impure. But life is difficult for a person who has a sense of shame, who constantly seeks purity, who does not cling, who is not reckless, who understands the life of purity.[35]

The Buddha considered the sense of shame and the fear of blame to be the "two guardians of the world." The first acted as an inner, and the second as an outer, restraint on wrongdoing.[36] A Buddhist verse widely used in repentance says,

> For all the evil deeds I have done in the past,
> Created by my body, speech and mind,
> From . . . greed, hatred and delusion,
> I now know shame and repent them all.[37]

Community Responsibility

Although the primary objective for individuals is to attain their own liberation, Buddhism places great emphasis on service to the community and to relieving human suffering. The Buddha set the model of combining a life of solitude with preaching, teaching, and comforting (but he refused to perform miracles). His immense compassion for all living things endeared him to the multitudes.

When the Buddha attained enlightenment, he was eager to enter nirvana. Yet he delayed leaving the world so he could help others, which he did steadfastly for fifty years. Similarly, there are enlightened individuals (*Bodhisattvas*) who reach the cusp of attaining nirvana but choose to forgo salvation in order to assist others toward that goal.

The ethical aspect in Buddhism that focuses on social concerns does not conflict with the quest for personal liberation. Bad behavior leads to the suffering of others and is distracting to oneself. One needs a clear conscience to concentrate on the self-awareness that is necessary for liberation. Developing a strong social conscience is important, as are ethical guidelines, without which communities would descend into chaos. Buddhism requires that each person accept responsibility for everything that everyone else does. All is interconnected in the world. The Buddha preached compassion to be the most crucial moral requirement and exemplified it in his own life. Ultimately, as noted above, all moral considerations are subservient to the goal of relieving suffering. This makes Buddhism far from being an other-worldly religion.

Buddhists put little stock in religious *belief*. As with other thoughts, they come and go. What matters is *action* (meditation is also a form of action). Yet despite the intense concern over the well-being of others, Buddhism also advocates detachment and avoiding over-involvement—in other words, maximum concern with minimum attachment, including attachment to feelings such as guilt.

Dealing with Guilt in Buddhism

Much of what we have said about dealing with guilt in Hinduism also applies to Buddhism. Unlike monotheistic religions, where morality is part of a personal and communal relationship with God, neither Hinduism nor Buddhism requires a similar sense of moral accountability to a deity. Therefore, the experience of guilt in response to transgressions is less intense. Hinduism plays down the experience of guilt and Buddhism actively opposes it.

Buddhism considers feelings of guilt and shame to be *aversions*. As noted earlier, they are forms of hatred directed toward the self. The very idea of "dealing" with guilt is inimical to Buddhist thinking. The Western way of responding to transgressions is by action—"doing something" about them. By contrast, the Buddhist response is to meditate on the wrong done. *Meditation* is especially important in Buddhism (as it is in Hinduism). There are various meditation techniques, but they all basically involve an intense focusing of the mind, assisted by controlled breathing. This allows for insight and understanding to be awakened from within the person. In *mindfulness meditation* distracting thoughts and feelings (including negative emotions like guilt and shame) are observed non-judgmentally and then set aside. The antidote to guilt in Buddhism is to reflect on your responsibility for wrongful actions to ascertain if you were at fault or not; to examine your motivation (actions done with a positive intention and without self-interest are not blameworthy); change the situation when you can, and accept it if you cannot. Remorse may be constructive if it focuses on what can be done here and now and leads to forgiving yourself and others; otherwise, it is not.[38]

Mindfulness allows you to stop ruminating over the past or fretting about the future by focusing instead on the *present*. We should resist obsessively judging our past actions or projecting our thoughts into the future; both are futile since we can neither change the past nor predict the future. The present is the only reality we have and we need to come to terms with it. The Buddhist attitude toward guilt is part of a broader way of responding appropriately to negative emotions. For instance, Western religious traditions allow for righteous anger in response to injustice. By contrast, Buddhists see anger as a negative emotion that causes suffering to others without helping the person experiencing it. Especially when one acts in anger, the result is likely to be damage.[39]

Following a public lecture, the Dalai Lama was asked how one should let go of the feeling of guilt that follows a serious wrongdoing. His Holiness responded:

> In such situations, where there is a danger of feeling guilty and therefore depressed, the Buddhist point of view advises adopting certain ways of thinking and behaving which will enable you to recover your self-confidence. . . . Because such disturbing emotions are adventitious, they can be eliminated. To think of the immense well of potential hidden deep within our being, to understand the nature of the mind is fundamental purity and kindness, and

to meditate on its luminosity, will enable you to develop self-confidence and courage.[40]

Negative feelings like guilt, shame, or regret, even if useful as moral guides, should be discarded once they have served their purpose. The Buddha captured this idea in an apt metaphor. After crossing a river on a raft, he said, abandon it at the other shore. Do not lug the raft into the forest where you no longer need it.

GUILT IN CONFUCIANISM

Confucianism has touched more lives over the past twenty-five centuries than any other religious tradition (albeit mainly in East Asia). It is not clear, however, if Confucianism should be treated as an institutionalized religion, as an ethical philosophy, or as a scholarly tradition that embodies a social and a political ideology.[41]

For the past sixty years, Communist rule has suppressed religion, including Confucian teachings, as manifestations of the "old life" which is elitist and redolent of foreign influence. The deprivations faced by the Chinese people focused their attention on subsistence and survival rather than ethical issues. Nonetheless, Confucianism has remained pervasive at a cultural level. Moreover, for some time now, China has been undergoing a dramatic transformation, including a revival of interest in religion.[42]

The fundamental concern in Confucianism is with learning how to be human within a web of relationships that include the family, the community, the world, and beyond. Chinese thinkers are generally not concerned with precise definitions of ethical terms and concepts. Instead, they expand such concepts to their widest possible range of meanings. This makes them sound ambiguous to Western ears, and the more crucial the idea, the greater is the perceived ambiguity.[43]

We noted earlier the linguistic and cultural problems in finding Chinese equivalents to the Western terms and concepts of guilt and shame. In the Confucian context, the idea of shame appears to be much more prevalent than guilt, at least as it is commonly perceived by Western scholars. Moreover, the Chinese concept of shame is far broader and encompasses the idea of guilt—an issue we will reconsider in its religious context.[44]

In Confucian texts, the Chinese characters that are translated as *shame* are *xiu* (pronounced roughly "syiu") and *chi* (pronounced "chur," as in "church"), which are combined into *xiuchi* in modern Chinese.[45] Recent studies have come up with a more expanded vocabulary based on terms that people currently use to characterize both shame and guilt. However, this wider vocabulary has not yet been integrated with traditional Confucian teachings. While it may seem tedious to go into these linguistic details, the terminology of guilt and shame is a rich source of information.

There are three terms that correspond to various aspects of guilt. *Neijiu* is the feeling that results from a failure in responsibility to those one is obligated to; for instance, it is the feeling that teachers have when they are too busy to respond to a student's request for help. It involves the failure to fulfill a positive duty—something one should and can do. However, *neijiu* may also arise from the lack of ability one wishes one had. A physician who is not trained as a surgeon may feel it when faced with a patient who requires surgery. Since these situations entail no moral wrong, the feeling is more like a sense of regret than guilt.

The second form of guilt is *zui e gan*. It results from doing something morally wrong, such as lying or cheating. It is a violation of personal morality rather than a legal offence. In that sense, it comes closest to the Western idea of "feeling guilty." The Chinese may express this feeling in terms like "my heart is dirty." This feeling prompts the person to act better in the future. The third form of guilt—*fanzui gan*—is associated with breaking the law, such as by being caught stealing. Hence, it constitutes legal culpability but also a failure of social responsibility—in either case, it is guilt as an objective act rather than a feeling.

All three forms of guilt result from failure *to do* what is expected of the individual (rather than harboring forbidden thoughts or feelings). In *neijiu* the responsibility is derived from a *personal* sense of obligation, whereas in *zui e gan* it involves the expectations of *others* with regard to what one ought to do (hence it is part of a shared sense of moral responsibility). In *fanzui gan*, one's obligation is more formally backed by social and legal sanctions to protect the community.

There are four types shame, which are more nuanced than the Western notion of being ashamed. The first—*diulian*—denotes loss of face, and hence suggests embarrassment. However, it may compromise one's social standing in front of others. In that sense, it gets closer to the notion of moral shame than embarrassment. For instance, it may follow getting caught cheating on an exam (rather than the act of cheating as such). At worse, *diulian* could have a devastating effect by leading to social ostracism. By extending personal responsibility to one's family members and friends, *diulian* helps keep everyone on their toes.

The second form of shame—*cankui*—results from failing to meet one's own expectations of oneself (as in failing to meet one's ego ideal in Western terms). It may also be thought of as the shame counterpart of the guilt of *neijiu* since it too carries no moral burden. It may even appear as a form of modesty, for instance in downplaying one's accomplishments. Nonetheless, since the word *kui* means "harm," there is the implication that the failure to achieve one's goals has hurt others, in particular one's family.

In the third form of shame—*xiukui*—there is a more explicit and serious impingement on the person's character and sense of self-esteem. Beyond failing at a particular task, it makes the person feel like a failure (consistent with the current psychological view of shame as an emotion that engulfs the whole person). The Chinese refer to this sort of shame as a "heavy weight" or a "stain on the heart." An even deeper sense of shame is expressed by *xiuchi*, the term typically translated as "shame" in English, with similar manifestations. It results from exposure of the vulnerable self that leads to the desire to hide.

These various forms of shame share some common features, but they also serve particular functions: *diulian* protects one's reputation; *cankui* prompts people to try their best; *xiukui* and *xiuchi* defend the integrity of one's character and deter one from actions that would undermine it. Ultimately, they are all aimed at maintaining social order and harmony.

Confucian notions of shame and guilt laid the ethical foundations of Chinese society, which have evolved through its long history. Confucianism, which began in the sixth century BCE with Confucius himself followed by Mencius, focused more on shame than guilt. During the imperial period under the Han dynasty (starting in 206 BCE) China became a Confucian state and for reasons of government, guilt in the form of legal culpability became more prominent. In the tenth century CE, *Neo-Confucianism* developed in response to the challenge and influence of Buddhism. Consequently, it turned to concepts like the nature of the soul and the place of the individual in the cosmos. Guilt took on a more metaphysical dimension and there was a greater emphasis on its subjective experience.[46] From here on, we will be mainly concerned with the classic texts of Confucius and Mencius that have been primarily responsible for shaping Chinese moral sensibilities, especially of its educated elite.

The Ethics of Confucius

Confucianism has been so inextricably bound with Chinese culture that it is difficult to understand one without the other. In traditional Chinese society, the web of human relationships was modeled after the extended family. Human beings were seen as the parts, like arms and legs, of the larger social body from which they derived their identity. In the West (especially in the modern period), the basic human unit is the autonomous individual who with all other autonomous individuals constitutes society. In China, the individual is seen as defined by relationships and cannot be conceived apart from them. In our earlier discussion of shame and guilt societies, we discussed how personal identity and its relationship to the group help determine whether shame or guilt becomes the dominant emotion. Some of this bears repeating because it is closely tied to Confucian ethics.

The focus on the family is so strong in China that filial piety has been a central moral obligation, extending to even one's ancestors. Violations of this obligation are the single most important reason for which the Chinese have traditionally felt shame or guilt. Whether this is basically a Chinese cultural characteristic or the result of Confucian teachings is hard to tell. Moreover, we cannot assume that Confucian teachings (which is what scholars have studied) reached beyond the literate elite (any more than the writings of Christian monks reached the peasantry in medieval Europe). Therefore, popular ethical traditions have also been greatly influenced by folk religions and customs, but these are much harder to track down.

Distinctions between the sacred and profane, or the religious and secular, which are taken for granted in the West, are alien to Chinese culture. Confucians believe that the meaning of human existence is realized through practical, everyday living. In Confucian ethics the emphasis is on moral practice, not doctrine. Knowledge and action are aimed at promoting harmony and unity within the community. Ethical principles are adapted to changing circumstances. What matters is not abstract moral principle but the impact of one's conduct on other people. There is also a wide appeal to the shared knowledge of well-educated scholars, who embody the cultural heritage. This makes Confucian moral reasoning less explicit and harder for those outside the tradition to understand.[47]

Confucius (Kong Zi, "Master Kong") was born in northern China in 551 BCE to a minor aristocratic family of modest circumstances. Confucius lived during a turbulent period. Following the decline of the Zhou dynasty in the fifth century BCE, the conflict between vassal states plunged the country into the period known as the Warring States. It was during this time that Confucianism arose as a reaction to the chaos of the time.

Confucius became a minor government official but his aspirations for higher political career were never fulfilled. His vision of a government based on the well-being of its people made little impression on the rulers of his time. Although his public career was hardly a spectacular success (nor was his marriage), Confucius established a school to train young men for public service and came to be revered as the "Teacher of Ten Thousand Generations." He considered himself a restorer and transmitter of ancient traditions, rather than an innovator. He claimed to have learned how to behave well only after reaching age seventy (two years before his death).

The idea of virtue (*de*) is central to Confucian ethics. Virtues represent standards of excellence that guide one along life's Way (*Dao*), which in its Confucian sense is like an ethical ideal for leading a good life. The moral example that Confucius held up to his students is the "noble-minded person" (*junzi*). Translated usually as "gentleman," the term may evoke quaint stereotypes of effete aristocrats, but what Confucius had in mind was a person who embodied the virtues of magnanimity, good faith, charity, and human-heartedness.[48] Being a gentleman was a matter of character—not noble birth, wealth, or social position.[49] It meant being high minded, not high born. The cultivation of character is thus a central objective for Confucianism. Within the social context of his times, Confucius's teachings were addressed to men. But in the modern world, we can apply his views to women as well. Therefore, we can think of the cultivation of character as a moral ideal for both sexes.

Confucius makes the capacity for shame a key ethical requirement. When asked, "In order to be called a noble official, what must a person be like?" he replied, "Always conducting himself with a sense of shame," also translated as "remorse."[50] "If you use government to show them the Way and punishment to keep them true, the people will grow evasive and lose all remorse. But if you use Integrity to show them the Way and Ritual to keep them true, they'll cultivate remorse and always see deeply into things."[51]

Ritual (*li*) is a key term that was associated with the ancient worship of gods. Confucius redefined it to refer to the web of social responsibilities that bind the members of a society together. These include all the proper forms of behavior based on one's position. Thus it may range from court protocol to the ways people deal with each other in everyday life to fulfill their personal and social responsibilities.[52]

In providing ethical guidance to others, Confucius never fails to point to one's own conduct. As one of his most prominent students—Zengzi—said,

> Every day, I examine myself on three counts. In what I have undertaken on another's behalf, have I failed to do my best? In my dealings with my friends have I failed to be trustworthy in what I say? Have I passed on to others anything that I have not tried myself?[53]

Confucius was a great believer in self-improvement and human perfectibility; he rejected the notion of human helplessness. The road to become a "gentleman" is open to everyone. However, he was also a realist. There are limits to how much people can be taught; some issues cannot be explained, so there is no point in trying. How can we understand death, he wondered, when we cannot even understand life?

The teachings of Confucius have a very strong family and community focus, reflecting Chinese cultural traditions. Virtue does not stand alone, "it is bound to have neighbors." It all comes down to human relationships. Confucius identified five basic relationships that formed the fabric of social life. The first three of these relationships (parent and child, husband and wife, older and younger brother) are within the family, which constitutes the basic unit of society and the model for the organization of its larger components, like the state.

How you behave is influenced by the company you keep. To the extent that you have a choice, Confucius advised that you pick the right neighborhood to live in, a neighborhood where there is benevolence. The company you keep defines who you are and reflects on your moral standing. It is in relation to them that you feel shame and guilt. You do not have to be liked by everyone. It is important that good people like you, but also that bad people dislike you. The same is true for choosing vocations. Somebody has to make weapons, but it does not have to be you.

When asked by a disciple if there was a single word that could serve as a guide to good conduct, Confucius suggested *shu*—reciprocity: Do not do to others what you do not want them to do to you. (The obverse of the Golden Rule: Do to others what you want them to do to you.)[54]

The sole literary legacy of Confucius consists of the *Analects*—a short book of aphorisms that does not provide sufficient scope to elaborate his ethics. That task fell to Mencius, the most eminent of his followers, who expanded the teachings of the Master into a more coherent ethical model.

Shame / Guilt in the Teachings of Mencius

Mencius was born about a hundred years after Confucius and lived while the political turmoil in China was still going on. He too failed to get much of a hearing from the rulers in China to put his ideas into practice. His sayings were recorded in the *Book of Mencius*, which became the core text of Confucianism.

Mencius locates the central moral agency in the *heart*. We associate the heart with emotions, but for Mencius it has a rational component as well; hence it is more correctly designated as "heart/mind" (*xin*). This moral compass is part of our "heavenly" endowment. The idea of Heaven in Confucianism is quite different from its more common conception. Heaven is not a place where the righteous end up after death. It is more like a natural cosmic entity with ritual as its organizing principle. It is an agency that has expectations, assigns responsibilities, and is the source of political power. Heaven acts as a moral force encouraging society to abide by the *Dao*. Since there is no deity in Confucianism, Heaven is the closest thing to a supernatural being.

The heart/mind functions more like a form of wisdom than a conscience that guides action. This places moral transgressions in the category of mistakes that are the result of immature or faulty judgment rather than a malfunction of a moral agency. Nonetheless, ethical judgments have a critical emotional component that are closely linked to the feeling of shame:

> No man is devoid of a heart sensitive to the suffering of others.... Whoever is devoid of the heart of compassion is not human.... Whoever is devoid of the heart of shame is not human, whoever is devoid of the heart of courtesy and modesty is not human, and whoever is devoid of the heart of right and wrong is not human.[55]

Confucianism makes a sharp distinction between the virtuous person and those who make a show of being virtuous. Mencius has nothing but contempt for the shallow external manifestations of moral rectitude as exemplified by the "village honest person." Though such a person may look like the embodiment of virtue, he is a "thief of virtue" who is just out to gain social approval.

The Confucian ethical objective is the good life, which is to be achieved through the cultivation of four cardinal virtues or *excellences* of the heart/mind. Each of them starts as a potential capacity (like a seed or a sprout) and develops into its mature form. These incipient capacities are innate, but they must be cultivated in order to attain their full potential. These four sprouts/ virtues are: compassion/benevolence; courtesy/ritual propriety; telling right from wrong/wisdom; shame/righteousness.[56]

Benevolence is the core moral virtue. The Chinese character for it (*ren*) combines the characters for "human being" and "two," marking the relationship between two individuals.[57] It reflects compassionate concern for the well-being of others and is expressed as human-heartedness or simply as *humanity*. The key to being a moral person is benevolence—not piety or intelligence. The sprout of benevolence is *compassion*, which manifests itself as pity and sympathy for the suffering of others.

Compassion and benevolence are the quintessential mark of humanity that sets human beings apart from animals and trumps all other moral considerations. However, benevolence is not an all-encompassing charity; it is conditional on your ability to be benevolent. You cannot help those who are not within your reach. Nor does benevolence necessarily entail self-sacrifice. Nonetheless, it extends beyond kith and kin. As Mencius said, "All within the four seas are our brothers and sisters."

Although compassion is usually the first step in acting benevolently, it may also be possible to act benevolently without feeling compassionate. (You do not have to love your neighbors to treat them fairly.) In other words, compassion makes benevolent action more likely but it is not a requirement. Conversely, there is no merit in feeling compassionate if you do not act on it. Feeling guilty over your neighbors being hungry does not put bread in their mouth.

The second virtue is *ritual propriety* (*li*). Ritual encompasses all the traditions and codes of courtesy and protocol (from shaking hands to paying respects to the emperor) that keep social life on an even keel. It restrains us from acting boorishly, overstepping limits, and provoking conflict. It provides legitimate avenues for satisfying our natural desires and negotiating differences. It ennobles us and leads us to achieve cultural refinement and moral excellence.[58] Mencius places the germ of ritual propriety in *modesty and courtesy* manifested by respect and consideration for others, the willingness to yield and to defer to others who are worthy of our respect.

The third virtue is *zhi*. It is the exercise of practical wisdom and sound judgment.[59] Its germ is the capacity to tell *right from wrong*. This does not mean mindless obedience to rules but exercising ethical judgment by assessing events and making choices based on the merits of the situation. Whereas *li* lays out the general rules, *zhi* applies them to particular circumstances.

Since rules cannot anticipate all contingencies, we need a way of dealing with morally ambiguous or unanticipated circumstances. It is *zhi* that guides our actions in these situations, thereby providing Confucian ethics with a large measure of flexibility. (Confucius said, "I have no preconception about the permissible and the impermissible.")[60] Whereas the focus on what is right and wrong underlies ethical standards and guilt in Western morality, the failure of *zhi* does not lead to remorse but to regret for having failed to act intelligently.

Last, and most directly linked to the issue of shame/guilt is the virtue of *righteousness* (*yi*), which may also be understood as dutifulness or obligation. The idea of duty in Confucianism generally refers to the application of the prescriptions of ritual to human conduct, but may also go beyond ritual prescriptions. *Ren* and *yi*—benevolence and righteousness—are thus the twin virtues that constitute the primary basis of moral conduct. When combined as *renyi* they come closest to the idea of morality.

The sprout of righteousness is *shame*. Although shame is not expressed as a full-grown virtue, it is of central importance in Confucian ethics. The monotheistic concept of morality is backed up by the prospect of divine displeasure and retribution. The muscle of Confucian ethics is more secular but no less formidable. To have a heart devoid of shame leads to being ostracized and placed beyond the human pale, a fate that would spell one's doom in tightly knit Chinese society.[61]

The strong emphasis on the importance of shame notwithstanding, it would be simplistic to explain Chinese ethics as merely the product of a shame culture. Shame is clearly a central issue in Confucian thought but we cannot equate it with our more limited notions of what constitutes shame in Western contexts. As cogently argued by Mark Berkson, shame is a far more complex ethical concept in Confucianism that incorporates some of the characteristics of the Western concept of guilt as well. Consequently, to characterize Chinese society as somehow lacking moral depth, and blaming Confucianism for it, is not a tenable proposition.[62]

Dealing with Guilt in Confucianism

As with other Asian religious traditions, Confucianism does not dwell on guilt. Rather, the focus is on shame (which, as we have noted, may contain elements of guilt as understood in the West). Shame is a painful emotion to be avoided. However, the *capacity* for feeling shame is a virtue to be cultivated. In that sense, the problem for the Chinese is not shame but the *absence* of shame. Since the key moral purpose of Confucianism is the cultivation of character imbued with benevolence, moral failing becomes the occasion for self-improvement. This, however, has to be done in ways that are not humiliating to oneself or to others.

Consequently, there are distinctive ways in which the Chinese deal with shame. To begin with, there is a reticence to express negative feelings to others, let alone publicly. When problems arise, they are to be dealt with in private—between husband and wife, parents and children, or within the family. Public exposure and being talked about by others is to be avoided at all cost. This is reinforced by the Confucian emphasis on ritual and propriety; it requires maintaining a stiff upper lip rather than succumbing to emotional outbursts of regret and remorse. The capacity to handle hardship stoically, or to "eat bitterness" (*chi ku*), is highly esteemed. This tendency extends to other emotions as well. For instance, a mother who feels sad should not complain about it but expect her children to be aware of her feelings and respond to them.[63]

The typical expression of regret (or shame or guilt) for a Chinese is to convey the sense that "I have failed you." This can be done verbally or even through a meaningful silence. Offenders must humbly acknowledge responsibility and reaffirm their loyalty to their family, their friends, or the public authority they have offended. One can then make amends and mend one's ways.

Apology is important, but there are limits on who will apologize to whom. For instance, a parent or someone of higher social position will not apologize to someone of lower rank; it would be socially inappropriate to do otherwise, even if the higher-ranking person is clearly at fault. Thus a father will not apologize to his son, or a mother-in-law to her daughter-in-law. A husband who has cheated on his wife may refuse to admit guilt even if doing so will win her forgiveness. He would rather damage the relationship than compromise his self-esteem.

Communism instituted the practice of public self-criticism but its purpose was social control rather than moral instruction. There are no priests or monks in Confucianism to turn to for moral instruction. The principles of how to behave are inculcated by the family and when one needs guidance, one goes to a parent or older relative, teacher, or a trusted friend.

When we probe deeper into the nature of the negative feeling that follows a transgression, the closest emotion elicited is *sadness* or sorrow (*nan guo*, "difficult to cross"). Therefore, whether you lie, hurt someone's feelings, or hurt someone in an accident, what you feel is sad, rather than ashamed or guilty.

If you have broken the law, then you are guilty in a legal sense, but that is a different matter.

An alternative view claims that Confucianism places an especially heavy burden of guilt / shame on individuals by holding them personally responsible for their actions. Since there is no god in Confucianism to bail you out, you are on your own, fully accountable for everything you do and responsible for everything that everybody else does that has anything to do with you.[64]

THIS BRINGS TO AN END our lengthy consideration of guilt from religious perspectives. It may have been an arduous journey but one we had no choice but to undertake. The impact of religion on guilt is so profound and pervasive that one needs to attend to it, or at least be aware of it, whether one adheres to one or another religion or not.

The next chapter will take us in another direction altogether as we move on to the secular perspective of philosophy based on reason rather than on a perspective based on faith or religious tradition. While it makes good sense to view these two perspectives as being fundamentally different, we should avoid making too sharp a distinction between them. Historically, Western philosophy and religions have influenced each other in important ways. So too in Asian traditions, where philosophical ethics and religious morality overlap.

10 GUILT IN THE LIGHT OF REASON

MORAL PHILOSOPHY plays a less prominent role than religious morality in the lives of most people. Many more know about the moral teachings of Jesus than the ethics of Kant. However, even if philosophy may appear forbidding, it is critically important for our understanding of guilt—be it as a complement or as a secular alternative to religious belief and thought.[1]

The philosophical approach to guilt has, actually, quite a bit in common with the religious approach. Both philosophy and religion are concerned with the nature of morality and focus on some of the same ethical issues involving justice and fairness. However, in Western traditions religious morality is ultimately based on *faith*, while moral authority in philosophy is based on *reason*. This is expressed in a letter Friedrich Nietzsche wrote to his sister Elizabeth in 1865:

> Is it really so difficult simply to accept everything that one has been brought up on and that has gradually struck deep roots—what is considered truth in the circle of one's relatives and many good men, and what moreover really comforts and elevates man? Is that more difficult than to strike new paths, fighting the habitual, experiencing the insecurity of independence and the wavering of one's feelings and even one's conscience, proceeding often with-

I have benefited greatly from the lectures by Marsh McCall and Anthony Raubitschek on the classical world, and the lectures on the philosophers discussed in this chapter given to my seminar by Lanier Anderson, Van Harvey, Robert McGinn, René Girard, Robert Harrison, and Julius Moravcsik. I am most grateful to Lanier Anderson and Robert Audi for their critique and help with this chapter.

out consolation, but ever with the eternal goal of the true, the beautiful, and the good? . . .

. . . Do we after all seek rest, peace and pleasure in our inquiries? No, only truth—even if it be most abhorrent and ugly. . . . Faith does not offer the least support for a proof of objective truth. . . .

. . . If you wish to strive for peace of soul and pleasure, then believe; if you wish to be a devotee of truth, then inquire.[2]

The case history for this chapter is the tragedy of Oedipus. It may seem odd to use a literary work for this purpose. The ancient Greeks, however, who bequeathed to the West both philosophy and drama, used both to explore fundamental moral dilemmas. Aristotle wrote extensively on the tragedy of Oedipus in his *Poetics* and considered it to be the greatest of the tragedies.[3] Tragedy served important purposes in Greek society. By relying on ancient myths, it incorporated a religious element. It also served a psychological function by inducing fear and pity in the audience that culminated in an outpouring of emotion (*catharsis*). This purged the soul and replaced the spectator's personal feelings with compassion for the tragic fate of the characters. It raised profound philosophical questions about the nature of free will and moral responsibility. Freud made the tragedy of Oedipus the centerpiece of his theory of conscience, thereby turning the "Oedipus complex" into a household word.[4]

The play *Oedipus the King* by Sophocles was based on an old and well-known tale.[5] Laius, king of Thebes, is warned that his as yet unborn son will slay him. Thus when his queen, Jocasta, gives birth to a boy, the king has him abandoned on a mountainside, to die. However, the shepherd entrusted with the task pities the child and takes him to Corinth where he is adopted by King Polybus.[6]

Oedipus reaches manhood and learns from the oracle of Apollo at Delphi that he is fated to kill his father and marry his mother. Horrified (and unaware of his true parentage), he flees from Corinth for Thebes. On his way, a chance encounter with Laius leads to a quarrel and Oedipus kills the king (his biological father). He then encounters the Sphinx that has been terrorizing the countryside and he slays her. The grateful Thebans place Oedipus on the throne and give him the hand of the widowed queen Jocasta (his birth mother).

Oedipus and Jocasta live happily and have four children. Then a plague descends on the city that is attributed to some pollution that has brought on the wrath of the gods. Oedipus sets out to find the cause, and his inquiries eventually lead to himself as the culprit guilty of parricide and incest. Jocasta learns the truth and commits suicide. Oedipus blinds himself by plunging Jocasta's brooch into his eyes, and goes into exile with his two daughters.

Oedipus is punished for his crimes—but is he guilty? The facts are clear—he killed his father and married his mother; but how could he be accused of parricide and incest when he was not aware of being the son of Laius and Jocasta? Oedipus had no intention of committing these crimes. On the contrary, he fled from his parents' home to prevent the oracle's predictions from coming true. What more could he have done? If he was fated by Apollo to carry out these heinous acts, how could he have circumvented the will of the god? He could have stepped aside and let Laius pass, but, being the heroic character that he was, he could not have acted differently.

Oedipus admits responsibility for his actions but vehemently denies being guilty. He rejects the accusation that there is "something criminal deep inside" him. He places the responsibility for what happened on the gods: He is being punished by the gods for an offence committed by his forebears. He was fated to commit his crimes ("the gods led me on"). He acted in ignorance when he killed his father ("blind to whom I killed") and married his mother ("I knew nothing, she knew nothing"). In exile he cries in despair,

> Come, tell me: If by an oracle of the gods,
> some doom were hanging over my father's head
> that he should die at the hands of his son,
> how, with any justice, could you blame *me*?
> I wasn't born yet, no father implanted me,
> no mother carried me in her womb—
> I didn't exist, not then![7]

Oedipus makes a compelling argument. Nonetheless, he must be punished to save the city that he has polluted. This is not only a matter of legal culpability but also a religious offence whereby he has become "most hateful to the gods." His ignorance of his parentage is not the issue, nor does it matter that he is paying for the sins of his fathers. Parricide and incest allow no exemption or absolution: the offender must pay the debt. When Oedipus blinds himself, he is not expiating for his guilt. It is because his actions have caused such revulsion that he is no longer able to look upon the world. Oedipus admits to a profound sense of shame. Guilt, however, he adamantly rejects:

> ... look hard,
> you'll find no guilt to accuse me of—I am innocent.
>
>   . . .
>
> I'll be not branded guilty, not in that marriage,
> not in the murder of my father. . . . [8]

How can we resolve this dilemma? How can a person be both innocent and guilty of the same crime? Where does human responsibility lie—within the self, or in the unfathomable will of the gods? The ancient Greeks confronted this question but did not resolve it. Each generation has to confront it anew. The Greeks believed human actions were subject to a dual determinism: What happens to human beings is determined by what the gods ordain and what people themselves choose to do. We cannot change our fate; all we can do is to understand it.[9]

The paradox persists to this day. We think of human beings as being endowed with *free will* that allows *moral choice*. In traditional Western religious terms, an omnipotent and omniscient God holds people responsible for what they do even though he knows what is to happen and could prevent it. That, however, would eliminate the human choice that is the basis of morality. In modern terms, we ascribe our behavior to the interaction of biological and cultural factors—the script of our lives is written in our genes and shaped by our social upbringing. Nonetheless, we still believe we must take personal responsibility for our actions, as did the Greeks, by invoking the concept of free will, even if there is no persuasive philosophical or psychological justification for it. If the idea of free will has been created out of social necessity, should we feel guilty just the same for actions over which we have no control, or, like Oedipus, should we protest our innocence?

The dilemma faced by Oedipus is also an apt metaphor for an ethical problem faced by philosophers. Oedipus is a Greek warrior-hero but he thinks like a philosopher when he puts his trust in reason. He has, after all, solved the riddle of the Sphinx and can figure out what is causing the plague. He will go wherever his inquiries take him, irrespective of the consequences. Yet religious tradition and custom trump reason and lead to his doom. Philosophers likewise proclaim that reason should guide our lives, but we often find it difficult to adhere to it. The Greeks were acutely aware of the limitations and dangers of human beings trying to control their own destinies. The defiant reliance on reason was one version of hubris that provoked the wrath of the gods.[10]

The purpose of this chapter is to provide some understanding of philosophical approaches to moral and ethical principles that have a bearing on guilt. "Morality" and "ethics" are commonly used interchangeably. However, *morality* (derived from the Latin word, *moralis*, for custom or manners) more properly refers to the way people should behave toward each other. *Ethics* (Gr., *ethos*) refers to that which is public and secular, and pertains to rationally defensible assertions about right and wrong. Whereas morality applies more to our personal lives (often with reference to sexual conduct), ethics typically pertains to our professional lives. The branch of philosophy that deals with issues of right and wrong is *moral philosophy*, or simply *ethics*.[11] It has two main parts. The first is *normative* or prescriptive ethics, which is concerned with how people should behave. Like most religions, and unlike the social sciences, its primary interest is not in scientific descriptions of *how* people behave, but how they *ought to* behave. By contrast, *metaethics*, or analytic ethics, is concerned with the rational foundations of ethical systems, including its language (for instance, the meaning of the word "good") and its logic. In that sense, it is more of an examination by philosophers of their own discipline. We will be concerned here mainly with normative ethics since it has a more direct bearing on our lives.

There are three major approaches to ethics in Western philosophy. They are based respectively on virtue, duty, and consequence. The first is based on Aristotle's concept of the virtuous character; the second, on Immanuel Kant's ethical philosophy where moral rules are defined by duty; and the third on John Stuart Mill's utilitarian model, with its focus on the consequences of our actions with the aim of insuring the greatest happiness for the greatest number. Finally, we will turn to the philosophy of Nietzsche, which rejects traditional conceptions of morality and guilt altogether.

ETHICS OF VIRTUE

Western philosophy (Greek, *philosophia*, "love of wisdom") originated in ancient Greece where three Athenians—Socrates, Plato, and Aristotle—addressed virtually every basic ethical question that has since preoccupied moral philosophers. The main subjects of philosophical ethics are *goodness* and *right action*. With regard to goodness, Greek philosophers considered the ultimate good to be happiness (*eudaimonia*). What leads to happiness? Is it pleasure, accomplishments, service to others? Epicurus considered the pursuit of pleasure or *hedonism* (from the Greek *hedonismos*) to be the answer, but he did not mean by that the mindless pursuit of physical pleasures through food, drink, or sex; rather, it was pleasure that comes from exercising one's intellect and moral virtues. Plato and Aristotle opted for the pursuit of excellence as the path to happiness. Such considerations have a direct bearing on the experience of guilt in our lives. We often feel guilty for not achieving happiness (by failing either in our careers or in our personal lives), or we feel guilty for the means we have utilized to achieve happiness.

The concept of virtue was central to ancient Greek moral reasoning. We think of virtue as a moral quality but the Greek word for it—*arête*—has the broader meaning of "excellence." The dominant Greek virtues of honor and fame embodied in the Homeric heroes had little to do with altruism. Greek religion itself was based on ritual with little moral content. The task of determining what was moral fell to the philosophers. And the purpose of morality was how to lead a good life—how to be happy on earth—not to inherit eternal life.

Guilt in Plato's Ethics

If Achilles is the quintessential Greek hero of the battlefield, Socrates is the hero who embodies moral courage in life. Socrates left no writings. All that is attributed to him was written by his pupil Plato. Born in 428 BCE into a prominent Athenian family, Plato was destined for a political career but he became disenchanted with public life, particularly after the death of Socrates, his beloved mentor. Socrates was forced to commit suicide after being condemned to death by an Athenian jury. It was a fate he could have avoided by recanting or fleeing the city. But he refused to do either, and instead obeyed the law. He was found guilty not for anything we would consider a crime but for expressing openly and courageously his moral and social criticisms.

At about age forty, Plato established his Academy in Athens, and spent the next four decades teaching and writing. In his dialogues, Plato presents the views of Socrates as well as significantly revising them.[12]

Prior to Plato, there was no clear linkage in Greek thinking between moral responsibility and free will. You did something wrong and got punished (even if the gods made you do it). Plato recognizes that guilt (as culpability) results from the violation of the dictates of an authority that you recognize. However, the moral authority for Plato is neither divinely ordained nor determined by social custom—it is based on *rationality*. Plato shifts the ground under guilt from religion and human convention to ethical ideas.

Reason makes ethical judgments possible by setting the right aims in life and by harmonizing its rational with its spiritual (psychological) aspects. Committing a misdeed means missing the mark (*hamartia*). This may result from starting with the *wrong* aim (like pursuing physical pleasure as the object of life), or by choosing the wrong *means* to achieve your aim (such as currying favor to advance your career). One can also get *distracted* (by, for instance, some emotion, like lust). So guilt in Plato is due to the failure to use reason and the refusal to take responsibility for one's actions. "The gods made me do it" or "Everyone else does it too" do not work. Moreover, failure to act rationally does not work either. That, however, does not make you a bad person; you try harder to do better.

Ethics for Plato was not a purely personal matter. Since human beings live in communities, the personal and the political cannot be separated. Therefore Plato's moral theories have the same basic structure that operates at both the personal and social levels. Since individuals are embedded in their community, their individual ethics are inseparable from the virtues and values of the community; therefore, the community must also have the right aims and the proper means and must stay on the moral path without getting distracted.[13]

In Plato's model of moral education, the point is not cramming knowledge into the minds of children but engendering the right *emotional* responses to help them make the right moral choices through reason. But one also needs emotional receptiveness and the will to do the right thing, not just follow rules. Plato thought ethical behavior was best taught by role models and he often used medical metaphors where ethical failings were treated like illnesses and moral mentors like physicians.

In psychological terms, what we have in Plato is a well integrated ("harmonious") ethical system that brings together the rational and the emotional components of the human psyche. Individuals are embedded in a moral and just community that sustains them and is in turn sustained by them. It is a well-developed (perhaps over-developed) and tightly integrated ethical system that does not rely on guilt in order to function effectively.

Guilt and Aristotle's Ethics

The son of a physician in Macedonia, Aristotle joined Plato's Academy at the age of eighteen (when Plato was sixty) and became its most brilliant student.

Following Plato's death, he went to Macedonia to tutor the young Alexander then returned to Athens to establish his own philosophical school—the Lyceum—which survived for five hundred years. Aristotle was the most influential philosopher in the Western world for almost two thousand years. He profoundly influenced ancient and medieval philosophy and continues to mold our moral consciousness. We will be mainly concerned here with his book, *Ethics*, which became known as *Nicomachean Ethics* (named after his son, Nicomachus, to whom the book was either dictated or dedicated).[14]

Aristotle's practical philosophy addresses issues of both personal ethics and politics. Its purpose is to help individuals lead a good life and attain happiness. His philosophy exemplifies *virtue ethics*, which focuses on the virtuous self rather than ethical rules or the consequences of actions. He assumes that human beings are born with natural ethical tendencies that need to be cultivated through reason. His purpose in writing the *Ethics* is "not to know what virtue is but . . . to become good."[15]

Aristotle refers to virtues of the soul as *excellences of character*. He conceives of virtues and their opposite, vices, as more than passing dispositions or habits—they are more like traits of character that define us as individuals. Emotions do not entail choice, hence moral responsibility—we do not choose to get angry: we do so as a response to provocation. Virtues are dispositions that express our choices for which we are responsible. They embody a kind of excellence that makes a thing perform its function well. However, excellence should involve a function that is deemed good (being a highly skillful thief is not a virtue).

Aristotle conceptualized moral virtues as representing the *mean* (an intermediate point, not just an average) between two extremes that represent *deficiency* and *excess* within a sphere of action. For instance, in the sphere of fear and confidence, courage is a virtue, while cowardice (its deficiency) and rashness (its excess) are vices. The Christian concepts of virtue and vice are antithetical—one is the opposite of the other, with nothing in between. For Aristotle, there is no inherent difference between virtues and vices—they exist on a sliding scale, differentiated by quantity, not quality. However, the virtuous nature of an action is not solely dependent of its being in the right "quantity." An action must be undertaken at the right time, for the right reasons, toward the right persons, for the right motive, and in the right way to qualify as a virtue. Therefore, virtue is not a simplistic quantitative concept but takes into account the motivational and contextual factors that determine our actions.

Aristotle discusses a dozen virtues and vices, but it is the sphere of *shame* that is of particular interest to us.[16] He makes no reference to guilt (but as noted earlier, the idea of shame in ancient Greece incorporated some elements of guilt). He astutely compares shame to fear whereby the fear of disrepute has an effect similar to that produced by the fear of danger. The mean that makes shame a virtue is modesty (*aidos*). Its deficiency is shamelessness (*anaischuntia*); its excess, shyness (*kataplexis*). Actually, modesty does not qualify as an adult virtue since it is useful mainly as a curb on youthful indiscretion; it should have no place in the life of a mature adult (note in particular, the last sentence below):

> The feeling [of shame] is not appropriate to every age: only to youth. We consider that adolescents ought to be modest because, living as they do under sway of their feelings, they often make mistakes, but are restrained by modesty. Also we commend a modest youth, but nobody would commend an older man for being shamefaced, because we think that he ought not to do anything to be ashamed of. . . . It is the bad man who ought to feel shame, because he is the sort of man to do a shameful deed; but it is absurd to think that being so constituted as to feel shame at doing something shameful makes you a good man, because modesty is felt about voluntary actions and the good man will never voluntarily do bad ones. . . .
>
> . . . Although shamelessness, that is, not being ashamed to do what is disgraceful, is a bad thing it does not follow any the more from this that to be ashamed if one behaves disgracefully is a good thing.[17]

The crown of virtues is *magnanimity*. The magnanimous (L., "great-soul") person is endowed with pride and honor rather than modesty and humility. Such people have courage, nobility, and goodness of character. Even if of a high social standing, they are moderately disposed toward, even disdainful of, power and wealth. They generously confer benefits on others, but are ashamed of receiving favors. They can love as well as they can hate, speak the truth, and shun gossip. They make mistakes, but have no reason to feel shame or guilt.[18]

True magnanimity is a rare virtue and can be attained by only a few; however, its corresponding vices are many, and few of us can avoid them entirely. The deficiency of honor is the vice of *pusillanimity*—where diffident persons deprive themselves of the advantages they deserve. The excess of honor takes the form of *conceit*, which is manifested by ignorance of one's limitations, overreaching, and affectations of dress and manner.

Aristotle, who was as much a biologist as he was a philosopher, observed that not all intellectual disciplines can aspire to the same degree of precision. Topics like ethics allow only modest levels of precision. Consequently, he abstained from casting the principle of the mean as an absolute rule. Rather, he set it in terms of what would be appropriate *relative* to each individual under a given set of circumstances. For instance, for someone with a family to support, staying out of the thick of battle may not constitute cowardice.

Aristotle's rejection of unqualified ethical rules should take a huge load of guilt off our shoulders. Instead of unbending rules, there is the possibility of exceptions. If we abuse this flexibility and make a mockery of morality, that would be our, not Aristotle's, fault. However, Aristotle is not a total moral relativist. The principle of the mean should not be applied to feelings or actions that are inherently bad:

> Not every action or feeling admits of a mean; because some have names that directly connote depravity, such as malice, shamelessness and envy, and among actions adultery, theft and murder. All of these, and more like them, are so called as being evil in themselves; it is not excess or deficiency of them that is evil. In their case, then, it is impossible to act rightly; one is always wrong. Nor does acting rightly or wrongly in such cases depend upon circumstances—whether a man commits adultery with the right woman or at the right time or in the right way—because to do anything of that kind is simply wrong.[19]

How do we reconcile these two dimensions of the absolute-versus-relative character of ethical rules? The problem is not specific to Aristotle—other moralists (and all of us) face the same dilemma. We want clear moral directives about what is right or wrong, yet when given such directives, we complain that they leave nothing to discretion or personal choice. Aristotle was aware of this problem and offered practical rules to deal with it. Thus, he advises us to avoid the extreme that is more contrary to the mean. For example, with regard to the virtue of truthfulness, it is better to err on the side of understating facts than exaggerate them by being boastful. If we examine the pattern of our errors, it will reveal our natural tendencies. (One person may be prone to turn wittiness into buffoonery, another to be boorish.) We need to pull ourselves away from the direction that we tend to lean toward (as in straightening a warped piece of wood). We must guard ourselves in particular against pleasure because it clouds our judgment. Thus with respect to temperance, there is a greater danger of licentiousness than prudery. Knowing our moral vulnerabilities helps us from falling into error.[20]

Aristotle holds happiness to be the ultimate aim of life. A successful human being is someone who is happy. Happiness requires an enjoyable life, but not one dedicated solely to physical pleasures (that may be good enough for cows, he says, but not people). Rather, happiness is an activity of the soul in accordance with virtue. How does one achieve that highest happiness? Through *contemplation*, claims Aristotle. However, contemplation (*theoria*) is nothing like the relentless intellectual effort of a scholar lost in books or a mystic mentally roaming through eternity. It is a form of intellectual activity whereby the person who has already acquired knowledge reflects on it. A life of contemplation can readily coexist with the exercise of the other virtues and pleasures as well. Moreover, it is not antithetical to social engagement. As with Plato, so too with Aristotle ethics and politics are linked. The state should make its goal the happiness of its citizens.[21]

Aristotle opened the door to moral relativism that came to dominate so much of modern life. It was, however, not until the Enlightenment that the idea took off. Influential thinkers are currently calling for a return to virtue as a basis of individual and social ethics by reaffirming Aristotle's classical virtues like fortitude (perseverance in the face of adversity), temperance (self-discipline to control unruly passions), prudence (practical wisdom to make right choices), and justice (fairness, honesty, lawfulness, and honoring commitments).[22]

ETHICS OF DUTY

Duty represents a moral obligation to act in a prescribed manner under a given set of circumstances. It is closely tied to the idea of *rules*, hence its designation as *deontological* ethics (Greek, *deon*, "what is required").[23] The ethics of duty have their origins in religious prescriptions, referred to as *divine command theory*. However, moral duties in philosophy are based on reason, not the will of God. To the religious person, reason may not seem like a reliable enough force to guide our actions, but as Freud put it, "the voice of the intellect is a soft one, but it does not rest until it has gained a hearing."[24]

The dominant theory of the ethics of duty is that of Immanuel Kant (1724–1804), arguably the greatest moral philosopher of modern times.[25] Kant was born into a pious Christian family and educated at the University of Königsberg in East Prussia. His spent his career as a professor of logic and metaphysics; his works on ethics did not appear until he was in his sixties. Kant never married, did not enjoy robust health, and led an uneventful life. He was a highly methodical person, but not a dour character—he was an accomplished card player and his students adored him.[26]

Guilt plays a far more prominent role in Kant's ethics than in Aristotle's. Kant's ethical theory is difficult. He is a philosopher's philosopher and uses complex vocabulary to convey his ideas. His ethics are austere and set the moral bar so high as to make it almost impossibly demanding. Nonetheless, one cannot discuss philosophical ethics without reference to Kant.[27]

Good Will and Moral Duty

For Aristotle, goodness consists in activities that lead to happiness. For Kant, the only thing that matters is a *good will*—the unique human ability to act according to moral rules and principles, irrespective of personal inclinations or the consequences of one's actions. If you are endowed with good will, you will do the right thing for the right reason.

A good action as such is not immune to getting compromised. If you save someone from drowning to get a reward, it is no longer a selfless act and lacks moral value. I may be kind to someone because I like the person. Or take good care of myself because I want to live longer. Such actions are good, says Kant, and conform *with duty*, but they fall morally short because they are not undertaken *from duty*:

> To be beneficent where one can is a duty, and besides there are many souls so sympathetically attuned that, without any other motive or vanity or self-interest they find an inner satisfaction in spreading joy around them and can take delight in the satisfaction of others so far as it is their own work. But I assert that in such a case an action of this kind, however it may conform with duty and however amiable it may be, has nevertheless no true moral worth but is on the same footing with other inclinations, for example the inclination to honor, which . . . deserves praise and encouragement but not esteem; for the maxim lacks moral content, namely doing such actions not from inclination but *from duty*.[28]

This is puzzling. As long as what we are doing benefits others, why should we not call it good? Why should it matter why we are doing it? For the person I save from drowning, my motives are irrelevant even if they do have a bearing on the moral quality of my action. Should we then feel guilty not only when we do wrong but even when we do the right thing but it is not motivated by duty? That is a daunting moral challenge.

Kant does not claim that simply because we enjoy doing a good deed that will cancel its moral value; as long as we act from duty, we may enjoy it all we want. Nor does Kant view human beings as heartless machines who justify any act as long as it is done in the line of duty ("I was following orders" is the standard defense of war criminals). In such cases, Kant expects a moral person to disobey orders when they conflict with a higher moral law.

The Categorical Imperative

The *categorical imperative* is Kant's central moral principle. It is the absolute command of the moral law given by pure reason and universally binding on everyone with a rational will. It is unconditional, hence not dependent on circumstances nor subject to exceptions. A course of action may be imperative, or essential, if one is going to achieve a certain outcome. However, there are two sorts of imperatives. For instance, consider the statement, "If you want to lose weight, you have to stop eating ice cream." Statements like this that start with *if* constitute a *hypothetical* imperative—they apply to certain defined conditions only. They are not universally applicable (as would be "Never eat ice cream"). A *categorical* imperative is an absolute, unconditional requirement that asserts its authority under all circumstances, as an end in itself. It is a universal law that governs the *maxims* that are first principles. Maxims, in turn, govern the *rules* for moral actions that obligate us to act in certain ways under given circumstances. The categorical imperative states, "Act as if the maxim of your action were to become through your will a universal law of nature."[29]

This means not to make a moral rule for yourself that you would not want to become a general rule for everyone—you cannot make an exception for yourself. For instance, you cannot claim that your lying is morally justified unless you allow everyone else also to lie under similar circumstances. This translates to the philosophical counterpart of the Golden Rule: Do to others what you want others to do to you; and conversely, do not do to others what you do not want others to do to you.

Kant is setting up an absolute moral system based on reason alone. The propositions of such a system should be logically consistent; they cannot be self-contradictory (like, "A circle is a square"). They are universal and applicable under all circumstances. Nevertheless, Kant does not expect us to appeal to the categorical imperative every time we face a moral decision. Its purpose is to generate maxims, not to regulate actions directly. The maxims themselves do not tell us exactly what moral path to take in a given case. They are not detailed maps of moral action, but a compass that points us in the right direction. Even the moral rules derived from them must be applied using rational judgment. Moreover, simply intellectually accepting the categorical imperative does not make us virtuous. We need the will and the commitment to obey the rules.

Kant concedes that some maxims when universalized could end up being inconsistent or immoral. For instance, assuming that adultery is immoral, I cannot say: I should be free to sleep with my neighbor's wife, and my neighbor is welcome to sleep with mine; and everyone else may likewise sleep with whomever they wish. To that end, Kant promulgated a series of rules—do not steal, do not break promises, and so on. Even then, the categorical imperative may not be able to deal with genuine conflicts between rules reflecting competing interests: What should I do when my telling the truth will lead to the death of an innocent person? Kant addressed such difficulties by allowing qualification of his rules, but once they are in place, he refused to make exceptions. However, if we are going back to having rules, why do we need the categorical imperative?

The difference, Kant argues, is that in accepting the categorical imperative we are accepting a principle whose content is determined by our own reason. We are thus following our own law and exercising *autonomy* as rational beings, not following somebody else's moral directives. Respect for the freedom and autonomy of each individual requires that we abstain from coercion, deception, or any other act that would interfere with another person's self-determination. Consequently, every human being exists as an *end in itself* and should not be used as *a means to an end*. This led Kant to formulate a second universal rule, called the *formula of humanity*: "Act in such a way that you always treat humanity, whether in your own person or in the person of any other, never simply as a means, but always at the same time as an end."[30]

Kant considered the formula of humanity to be as important as the categorical imperative. It is a powerful rule that cuts through a lot of moral verbiage. Most moral prohibitions come down to stopping us from using others as a means to our ends—exploiting them for our own benefit (*objectifying* them: for instance, by reducing them to objects for our sexual gratification). Kant calls the formula of humanity, "the supreme limiting condition of the freedom of action of every human being."[31] This is one moral barrier we cannot cross without incurring guilt.

Guilt and the Tribunal of Conscience

What we have discussed so far provides the moral backdrop to understand the place of guilt in Kant's ethics of duty. The inference from his theory is that guilt arises from the failure to live up to the requirements of duty. In this respect, he addresses the role of conscience as follows:

> Every human being has a conscience and finds himself observed, threatened, and, in general, kept in awe (respect coupled with fear) by an internal judge; and this authority watching over the law in him is not something that he himself (voluntarily) *makes*, but something incorporated in his being. It follows him like his shadow when he plans to escape. He can indeed stun himself or put himself to sleep by pleasures and distractions, but he cannot help . . . waking up from time to time; and when he does, he hears at once its fearful voice. He can at most, in extreme depravity, bring himself to *heed* it no longer, but he still cannot help *hearing* it.[32]

Since the tribunal of conscience operates like a court of law, guilt would imply culpability rather than a subjective experience. Yet, it is hard to imagine that if we were to be found guilty in our own inner court, we would not be filled with remorse. The reason Kant may have avoided dwelling on the subjective aspect of guilt is to maintain his basic premise that morality should be based on reason, not feelings. To introduce guilty feelings would dilute and compromise its rational foundation. Consequently, conscience acts as an aid to morality but it is not the basis of moral conduct. If guilt (or fear of it) is providing the incentive for morality, then the action is not from duty, hence not truly moral. In that sense, the prospect of guilt is relevant but not critical for moral conduct. Whether or not we feel guilty is not a reliable moral guide, even though it may help.

Guilt and Duties of Virtue

Kant differentiates between the operation of *justice*, which relies on externally imposed laws, and the *principle of virtue*, which relies on internal commands aimed at moral ends (as the voice of conscience).[33] Under the principle of virtue, Kant discusses *duties to oneself* and *duties to others*. These applications of moral principles to specific behaviors give us a concrete sense of Kantian ethics.

Some duties to ourselves relate to our biological ("animal") nature. They deal with self-preservation and reproduction. Kant has an absolute prohibition against suicide, which he calls "murdering oneself." He discusses reproduction and sexuality under the heading of "On Defiling Oneself by Lust."[34] Kant makes marital intercourse the moral standard for sexual conduct. He acknowledges that within marriage, sex need not be limited to reproduction and that it is moral for a couple to engage in sex for love and pleasure. By the same token, all forms of sex outside marriage are morally wrong. Kant makes no reference to homosexuality, but he launches into a spirited condemnation of "defiling" oneself through "unnatural lust," where one is aroused not by a real object but by the imagination, contrary to natural purpose (a clear reference to erotic fantasy): "unnatural lust, which is complete abandonment of oneself to animal inclination, makes man not only an object of enjoyment but still further, a thing that is contrary to nature, that is, a *loathsome* object, and deprives him of all respect for himself."[35] Kant does not name this "vice," but it clearly suggests masturbation. His views here are consistent with the misguided, and at times bizarre, medical and religious notions on "self-abuse" that were prevalent in Europe at the time.[36]

Another duty is not to "stupefy oneself by excessive use of food or drink." Kant's objections here are not based on negative health consequences—that would be acting out of prudence, not duty—rather, it is because such indulgences reduce us to the level of animals and compromise our human dignity.

The duties of virtue to others are of two kinds. First come duties toward others as human beings that place them under reciprocal obligations to us (such as lending money to a friend). The second kind of duties to others are owed to them, and hence they incur no reciprocal obligation. These obligatory duties are *love* and *respect*. While they may exist separately (you may respect but not love someone, or vice versa) they are united under one duty.[37]

What Kant is referring to here is altruistic love, not romantic passion or erotic attraction. Its maxim is *benevolence* reflected in loving one's neighbor. Whereas benevolence is the feeling of satisfaction in the well-being of others (which costs nothing), *beneficence* consists of efforts to promote the happiness of others in need, without hoping for something in return (at some cost to ourselves). If we are rich, we must be careful not to burden our beneficiaries with a sense of obligation. If we are not rich, we should not expend our resources in helping others to the point where we will need the beneficence of others.

Kant places a high premium on friendship, which he places ahead of marriage or parenthood as the highest from of human association. (Did being a bachelor color his philosophical views, or did his philosophical views convince him to remain a bachelor?) In its perfect form, friendship is the union of two persons through shared love and respect. Friends should help each other when they can, but mutual assistance should not be the basis of their friendship. Friendship that has a moral foundation (rather than being based solely on feelings) entails the complete confidence of two persons in revealing their innermost feelings and secrets to each other consistent with mutual respect.

Ultimately, Kant had to "make room for faith" in God to give ultimate meaning to his moral vision. He acknowledged that human beings are not adequate judges of their own virtue so as to bring forth the highest good whereby virtue is accompanied by happiness. This meant belief in a personal God "who sees into our hearts and arranges the laws of nature so that happiness will be the reward of virtue; and an immortal life, in which we can achieve the moral perfection which is impossible in this life."[38] Yet, he would not yield entirely to religion as the ultimate source of morality.

Kant remains highly influential among modern philosophers such as John Rawls. Rawls is primarily interested in social justice, and his moral thinking has deep Kantian roots.[39] Rawls challenges the view that guilt plays a prominent role is Kant's moral thinking: he claims instead that Kant considers shame rather than guilt to be the response to failure to act on the moral law. "Those who think of Kant's moral doctrine as one of law and guilt," says Rawls, "badly misunderstand him."[40]

Kant also has his detractors. His eminent contemporary Hegel claimed the categorical imperative to have no moral content. A basic problem is Kant's refusal to take the consequences of one's actions into account in assessing guilt. After all, what should matter more than the impact of what one does in determining moral conduct? It is the impact of one's actions that forms the centerpiece of the philosophical view we turn to next.[41]

ETHICS OF UTILITY

The moral justification that "if no one gets hurt" then we may do as we like is a popular expression of the basic idea underlying the ethics of utility; the idea that an action is considered right or wrong depending on whether its outcome is good or bad. There is a set of theories called *consequentialism* that build on this idea by using the consequences, or outcomes, of actions to ascertain their morality. Stated simplistically, the basic objective is to promote the maximum happiness for the maximum number of people.

As a practical matter, we cannot worry about the impact of anything and everything we do on everyone in the world. The scope of our concern has to be limited, by necessity, to those who are actually affected by what we do in ways that we can ascertain or control. For example, the decision to shift from gas to electricity in an apartment building will impact directly those living there (though the impact is not strictly limited to them). Other decisions, like generating electricity for a city through nuclear power, would involve many more constituencies. In principle, one should be concerned with both—the personal and the public impact—but we tend to be more engaged with what affects those around us more immediately.

The most important consequentialist theory is *utilitarianism.* Utility means usefulness, but in this context it carries more of a sense of ultimate value. Its basic objective is commonly understood as engaging in those acts that would achieve "the greatest good for the greatest number of people."[42]

After the complexities of Kant, the ethics of utilitarianism may seem almost self-evident. Yet, utilitarianism too is a complex and controversial theory about the fundamental nature of morality.

In the eighteenth century, the British philosopher Jeremy Bentham put forth the notion that *pleasure* is the basis of happiness. However, he did not limit pleasure to physical sensations; he also applied it to the acquisition of knowledge and the goodwill of others.[43] However, it is the British philosopher John Stuart Mill who was to become the most prominent exponent of utilitarianism. Mill rejected Bentham's overly schematic and quantitative concept of pleasure and focused on the *quality* of pleasures, and placed greater emphasis on "nobler feelings" that led to intellectual and esthetic fulfillment.[44]

Mill placed great importance on justice and liberty in social policies. It is easy to see why we should be concerned with our own happiness, but why should we care for the happiness of others? Because, Mill claimed, we cannot be truly happy in the midst of unhappy people. Our happiness depends on the happiness of everyone else and vice versa. This makes the principle of happiness more impersonal and less subject to self-serving interpretations of moral principles.[45]

These ideas did not go unchallenged. Mill published his book *Utilitarianism* in 1861 as a defense of the greatest-happiness principle against the rising tide of criticism.[46] This slim volume of eighty pages became the fundamental statement of utilitarian philosophy and has had a large impact on ethics and social thought.[47] In it, guilt plays a crucial role.

The Ultimate Sanction of Remorse

Mill realized that the utility principle alone was too abstract and impersonal to be supported by our natural desires. To perform a good action (like sharing what I have with others) or to refrain from a bad action (taking what belongs to others) is not easy if it goes against our natural inclinations, which are self-ish. To heed my conscience, I must feel *compelled* to listen to its voice. Mill looked for a *psychological* force that would accomplish this and identified it as *remorse*: To avoid the pain of remorse, people would refrain from violating the utility principle. Remorse would act as a "mass of feeling," like a huge wave, that would make it impossible to resist. Remorse had to be elicited by believing that one has violated the utility principle. Otherwise, feeling remorseful as such would serve no moral purpose. We could condition people to feel bad for doing virtually anything, but such an aversion would be just a feeling, and would not qualify as a moral sentiment.

Although Mill does not use the word "guilt," that is clearly what remorse refers to. Moreover, in keeping with his consequentialist position, he was mainly concerned with the *prospective* aspects of guilt. He wanted guilt to *inhibit* people from violating the utilitarian principle, not lead to hand-wringing after the damage had been done. To be useful, the remorse over the wrong I did yesterday had to be converted to the anticipated remorse that would follow my wrong action tomorrow.[48]

Mill claims that in all moral theories remorse is the *ultimate sanction* that enforces morality. However, avoiding the pain of guilt is not enough—it would be like putting on the brakes. We also need a positive incentive—like pressing on the accelerator—to propel us forward on our moral path. This positive incentive comes from the natural *fellow-feeling* we have for others; it is the love of humanity that leads us to obey the voice of our conscience. Where does this fellow-feeling come from? Mill rejects God as its source and assumes it to be part of our nature even if it needs to be more fully developed by education. (There was no evolutionary explanation of altruism yet for Mill to rely on.) Mill's moral vision of utilitarianism is thus ultimately based on "a desire to be in unity with our fellow creatures, which is already a powerful principle in human nature, and happily one of those which tend to become stronger, even without inculcation, from the influences of advancing civilization."[49]

This is a very optimistic view, a noble vision based on high hopes—and it sounds utterly utopian. Moreover, the implanting of these sentiments into the minds and hearts of people raises them to the level of a secular religion:

> If we now suppose this feeling of unity to be taught as a religion, and the whole force of education, of institutions, and of opinion, directed, as it once was in the case of religion, to make every person grow up from infancy surrounded on all sides both by the profession and the practice of it, I think that no one, who can realize this conception, will feel any misgiving about the sufficiency of the ultimate sanction for the Happiness morality.[50]

What are we to do with those who have no fellow-feeling of moral responsibility? Mill confronts this question but he does not have a good answer for it (nor does anyone else a hundred years later). He believes moral feelings are socially cultivated rather than innate, so he puts great emphasis on moral education. If Mill sounds modern to our ears, it is because he was ahead of his time and the way we think about these issues has been greatly influenced by his ideas.

Act and Rule Utilitarianism

Mill started with the premise that one should act so as to bring about the greatest good to all concerned. This principle is easy enough to understand but how do we implement it? Suppose you want to install a sprinkler system for your lawn. That may serve your purposes but would it be good for the neighborhood or the environment as a whole? There are no rules to guide us except the general utility principle. The guiding idea of what is called *act utilitarianism* is: "Everyone should do what will bring about the greatest amount of good over bad for everyone affected by the act."[51]

Limiting moral responsibility to individual actions avoids the problems involved in setting up moral rules (Who should set up them up? Why should we obey them? What do we do if the rules conflict?). Moreover, since the circumstances of our actions vary, we cannot have rules that apply across the board. Consequently, there can be no absolute rules about anything—be it lying, stealing, or killing. There may be circumstances under which such acts could conceivably serve the common good.

This creates its own problems. One difficulty is in determining the actual consequences of our actions: How am I to know in advance the impact on others of what I do? Much of the time, I have to guess, and my guess can be wrong (especially since self-interest is likely to cloud my judgment). Do I

276 GUILT IN THE LIGHT OF REASON

need to conduct a poll of the neighborhood before I can lift a finger? How do I know that my neighbors, in ascertaining the impact of my actions on their lives, will be fair and objective, rather than self-serving? Not only are personal judgments liable to error, but we often lack the facts or the experience to make correct choices. Applying our moral analysis of acts may also lead to some judgments that are hard to accept—like the goodness / rightness of sacrificing one individual for the greater good of the many. Having a rule would make it easier to know what to do, and in setting up rules we can benefit from the collective experience of others. This reasoning led to *rule utilitarianism*, which says, "Everyone should always establish and follow the rule that will bring about the greatest good for all concerned."[52]

Once you accept, "You shall not steal," you do not have to agonize over the prospect of stealing each time the opportunity comes up. Having rules also makes it easier to guide those with less mature consciences. For instance, can we rely on a teenage couple, with a six-pack of beer under their belts, to figure out the consequences of having unprotected sex? Are they not more likely to follow a simple rule such as "Safe sex or no sex"? By the same token, if we do impose rules, how is that different from the ethics of duty? Are we back to Kant? The utilitarian answer is that it is not rules as such but their justification that gives them moral force. That justification for rule utilitarians would depend on the utility principle and not whether or not they conform with duty, as Kant would argue.

However, the setting of rules makes the problem of anticipating consequences even more difficult; we are no longer dealing with the effects of just a single act but the consequences of all acts. It can be argued that the problem of figuring out what to do in a given case is helped by experience and the use of common sense. After all, every time Christians or Jews are confronted with a moral dilemma, they do not scour the Bible looking for answers—they act on the basis of their best judgment informed by their mature conscience.[53]

Utilitarians have been accused of making morality too easy. Subjecting moral judgment to individual's discretion leads to a do-it-yourself morality. Maximizing the general happiness also runs into conflict with personal obligations. Typically, we feel most responsible for the needs of our families, then our friends, and only then others (as in the example of the "expanding circle"). It is when we fail to attend to the needs of those who are closest to us that we feel especially guilty. Mill's idea of doing away with all considerations of kinship and friendship is counterintuitive and sounds like a hopeless proposition.

On the other hand, dying for strangers is not such an odd idea. Soldiers do it all the time. It is one thing, however, to encourage such actions and another thing to *enforce* self-sacrifice. Mill did not condone slavery, but it has been historically justified because it makes life more productive for society as a whole.

The issue of what is *right*—apart from what is *good*—does not get much attention in utilitarianism. The-end-justifies-the-means argument that flows from it leads to a slippery moral slope. Should a physician sacrifice a healthy person and use the organs to save the lives of five others? Should we conduct human experiments that harm the subjects so as to find a cure for a lethal disease? Should we torture suspected terrorists if the national security requires it? Such dilemmas are not limited to utilitarianism. Other moral system when confronted with extreme scenarios yield equally dubious results. Despite these problems, utilitarianism comes closest to an all-purpose ethical theory for others. For instance, social scientists and evolutionary biologists fall back on its ethical underpinning for their theories.

THE ASSAULT ON GUILT: NIETZSCHE'S MORAL PHILOSOPHY

We have assumed so far that we need to act in an ethical manner and that we should feel guilty when we do not. But why should we? What is in it for us? Particularly when we do not have God to fear, these questions become particularly relevant. There have always been people who have bridled at moral constraints, especially when imposed by conservative religious and cultural traditions. There is even a philosophical viewpoint called *ethical egoism* that accepts the centrality of self-interest in human nature and tries to float with the current, so to speak, rather than swim against it. In this view, the fact that people pursue their own interests over those of others does not mean that they have to be enemies.

A popular advocate of this view was the Russian-born American novelist Ayn Rand, who called her doctrine *rational ethical egoism*. Rand was highly popular a few decades ago and she still has her followers. She summed up her egoistic viewpoint in these words: "My philosophy, in essence, is the concept of man as a heroic being, with his own happiness as the moral purpose of his life, with productive achievement as his noblest activity, and reason as his only absolute."[54]

Rand never had much of a standing among academic philosophers or outside the circle of her admirers. The far more renowned critic of traditional

Western morality is Friedrich Nietzsche. Born in Prussia in 1844, Nietzsche was the son and grandson of Protestant ministers. His father became insane and died when Nietzsche was four years old. Without a father, he grew up in a household of five women. Endowed with a brilliant mind, Nietzsche became a professor at the University of Basel at the astounding age of twenty-four.

Trained as a philologist and a classicist, Nietzsche was not a conventional philosopher and his thoughts do not cohere into a systematic ethical theory, like those of Kant and Mill. His writing style is literary, his ideas often paradoxical and expressed in aphorisms ("The man of knowledge must not only love his enemies, he must also be able to hate his friends").[55]

A troubled man in poor health, Nietzsche left the university to lead a lonely life dedicated to intellectual pursuits. He subsisted on his meager pension and never married. He got interested in several women who rejected him; one was Lou Andreas Salomé, a disciple of Freud and an extraordinary woman, who ran away with Nietzsche's friend, Paul Rèe. Nietzsche was also deeply attached to the composer Richard Wagner and his wife, Cosima (the daughter of Franz Liszt), who bore Wagner three children while married to another man. Nietzsche's relationship with the Wagners ended badly, although he remained loyal to Cosima to the end. Nietzsche was particularly close to his older sister, who was a virulent anti-Semite and tampered with his writings, contributing to his reputation being tarred with the same brush. At the age of forty-five, Nietzsche became insane (probably as a result of neurosyphilis) and died a decade later.

Among his many grievances, guilt was Nietzsche's arch enemy. He considered the "bite of conscience" (*Gewissenbiss*) to be one of the baleful legacies of fire-and-brimstone Christianity.[56] It may be tempting to interpret his philosophy in the light of his own personal struggles. However, as his biographer Walter Kaufmann points out,

> The thought of a philosopher may be partly *occasioned* by early experiences, but the conception of strict causality is not applicable here. . . . We must follow the development of his thought—and that is done best separately from the survey of his life, as any joint treatment will almost inevitably suggest a false notion of a causal relationship between life and philosophy.[57]

Nietzsche's acerbic moral philosophy pervades his voluminous writings, much of which are polemical and do not reflect a balanced philosophical viewpoint. He admits that his writings are difficult. ("Usually, one must *condense. . . .* I have to be diluted, liquefied, mixed with water, else one upsets one's digestion.")[58] Nietzsche's sayings are often intended to shock the conventional reader:

> Christianity gave Eros poison to drink—he did not die of it, to be sure, but degenerated into vice.

> It is inhuman to bless where one is cursed.

> One is punished most for one's virtues.

> Even concubinage has been corrupted:—by marriage.[59]

Nietzsche's philosophical posture is to question all beliefs and presuppositions, thereby forcing us to stand back and reconsider our own views. This is a moral philosopher who claims that there is *no* ethical value in ideas like free will, rational ethics, justice as obligation, equality, democracy, human rights, universal rules (like not using people as ends, or loving your neighbor), and no inherent good or evil.[60] In short, he is opposed to virtually everything that passes as morality in its usual sense. Obviously, he has little use for guilt.

Although Nietzsche was vehement in his condemnation of Christian morality, he was actually quite sympathetic to the original message of Jesus; Nietzsche blamed his disciples, like St. Paul, for distorting his message:

> Everyone is a child of God—Jesus definitely claims nothing for himself alone—as a child of God, everyone is equal to everyone else. . . . God gave his Son for the forgiveness of sins, as a *sacrifice*. All of sudden it was all over the Gospel! The *guilt sacrifice*, and furthermore in its most repulsive, barbaric form, the sacrifice of the *innocent one* for the sins of the guilty![61]

Nietzsche considered not only Christianity but Western culture as a whole as being on the verge of collapse. He ascribed the "death of God" to the secularization of Western society (which turned churches into "sepulchers of God"): The moral rules of the church had become empty prescriptions with no teeth; everything people believed in had been revealed to be prejudice, untruth, and deception; divine assurances were nothing more than a means of assuaging a terrifying sense of meaninglessness. Like a tree whose tap root had been cut, European culture was dying even though people did not yet realize it. To prevent total moral collapse and descent into nihilism, there was need for a new morality, which Nietzsche would provide in his role as a "physician of culture."[62]

The Origins of Morality and Guilt

Nietzsche's account of the origins ("genealogy") of morals starts with a class of powerful nobles who celebrated their power and superiority over the powerless "herd" of common folk.[63] Their aristocratic virtues, or *master morality*, was based on egoism, pride, strength, courage, and risk-taking. At the outset, these were free, joyous, and warlike individuals with a triumphant affirmation of life. The *good* man was a warrior. (L., *bonum*, "good," has the same root as *bellum*, which means "war.") The opposite of the good (noble, superior, strong) was the *bad* (common, inferior, weak). When a nobleman (they were all men) did something wrong, he may have felt foolish for making a mistake, but he did not feel guilty because he was not subject to moral judgment.[64]

In due time, this master morality was challenged by the emergence of a *slave morality* of the masses. Its virtues were humility, altruism, meekness, and self-denial. Their terms for *good* (submissive, self-denying) were contrasted with *evil* (dominant, selfish). (Note the shift from *good/bad* to *good/evil*.) Consequently, the lives of people became restrictive, brooding, life-denying, and imbued with *resentment*. (Nietzsche uses the French term *ressentiment*.) This resentment reflected the slave morality's own lust for power—an idea that became central to Nietzsche's moral conception.

Unlike master morality, which was direct and forthright, slave morality was devious, spiteful, rancorous, and repressed. It was this slave morality that gave rise to the *bad conscience* which suppressed the resentment of the slaves over their powerlessness by making them feel *guilty*. This guilt was the outcome of the conflict between the slaves' desire for retribution and the cardinal slave virtues of altruism and forgiveness.

Aristocrats, who were formerly free of guilt, were now reined in and became infected by slave morality—they too developed a bad conscience. What had been their virtues now became vices and instilled in them a sense of guilt, which brought them to heel. Everybody ended up in the same boat, loaded with guilt and captained by conscience.

Nietzsche claimed that slave morality first arose among the Jews, then spread to the oppressed masses and slaves of the Roman empire through Christianity, which later duped the Romans into accepting it as their own, and slave morality became the dominant ethic of the Western world. Through this process, the noble virtues of power, freedom, and dominance were inverted into vice and maligned as arrogant, cruel, sensual, and godless.

Nietzsche did not equate masters and slaves with actual social classes. Rather, they represented character types with particular moral attitudes. Nevertheless, Nietzsche gave his account a historical cast by identifying master morality with Homeric heroes, like Achilles, as the prototype of the ideal noble, followed by the Roman elite, the Vikings, and all the way down to Napoleon.

The full expression of Nietzsche's moral exemplars was to come in the future with the rise of heroic figures Nietzsche called the *Übermensch* (usually translated as Superman or Overman). The *Übermensch* moves "beyond good and evil" and beyond the distorted doctrine of slave morality that sees master morality as evil.[65] He exhorts these superior beings to surpass the pitiable happiness of the greatest number. (So much for John Stuart Mill.)

Guilt and the Bad Conscience

Nietzsche did not damn conscience as such. Instead he differentiated between the bad conscience of slave morality and the good conscience of master morality:

> The proud awareness of the extraordinary privilege of *responsibility*, the consciousness of this rare freedom, this power over oneself and over fate, has in his case penetrated to the profoundest depths and become instinct, the dominating instinct. What will he call this dominating instinct, supposing he feels the need to give it a name? The answer is beyond doubt: this sovereign man calls it his *conscience*.[66]

If that is the good conscience, what is the bad? "Bad conscience" (*schlechtes Gewissen*) means feeling guilty (as in, "I have a bad conscience for lying to you"). Nietzsche, however, uses it to refer to a conscience that is bad in itself and fulminates over how that "somber thing," the consciousness of guilt, came into the world. To repeat, he ascribes it to slave morality subduing the instinct for freedom of the "sovereign man," turning his will to power inward.[67] Man became his own adversary, his own enemy, and guilt the tool of his self-inflicted torture. Through a process of *moralization* the natural (biological) drives (like sex and aggression) are turned into behavior condemned by society and the bad conscience became the whip of guilt to keep us prisoners within its walls.

Nietzsche argues for a *naturalization* of conscience that would sustain our natural instincts instead of contaminating them with guilt. He says we should redirect our guilt to unnatural inclinations espoused by slave morality: Do not let Christianity make you feel guilty—feel guilty for being a Christian! "If one trains one's conscience," says Nietzsche, "it will kiss us as it bites."[68]

Nietzsche also ties guilt with debt. Originally, punishment was for exacting vengeance—it had nothing to do with justice. Slave morality elaborated by Christianity placed a double debt that could never be repaid. It was first incurred through Original Sin, then by God's sacrifice of his Son for the sins of humanity. Christians are thereby doomed to suffer everlasting guilt.

Nietzsche would agree with Kant that when the inner tribunal of conscience finds us guilty, it will have a divisive and debilitating effect of our sense of self. To avoid that, Kant would say, do not do things that make you feel guilty in the tribunal of conscience; Nietzsche would say, get rid of the damned tribunal.

Nietzsche considers the basic human impulse the *will to power*, which craves for self-determination. It leads to the *instinct for freedom*—the essence of life that gives expression to the spontaneous, aggressive, expansive, form-giving forces that give new interpretations and directions to our actions.[69] The will to power is not an end in itself or a mindless quest for power (like the power of money, it can be used for good or ill). Its ultimate aim is *autonomy*: to do with your life as you wish and to have it be what you want—not someone else's idea of what it should be. Nietzsche does not want a one-size-fits-all morality enforced by guilt. Slave morality may have had its uses but it should not be imposed on everyone. It is this vision of personal freedom and autonomy in Nietzsche that appeals to his admirers and followers.[70]

Nietzsche's provocative language makes him look dangerously unconstrained and makes it easy to misunderstand him. Walter Kaufmann cautions us:

> The most common misunderstanding of the book is surely to suppose that Nietzsche considers slave morality, the bad conscience, and ascetic ideals evil; that he suggests that mankind would be better off if only these things never appeared; and that in effect he glorified unconscionable brutes.[71]

> Without acquiring a bad conscience, without learning to be profoundly dissatisfied with ourselves, we cannot envisage higher norms, a new state of being, self-perfection. Without ascetic ideals, without self-control and cruel self-discipline, we cannot attain that self-mastery which Nietzsche ever praises and admires. But to settle down with a nagging bad conscience, to remain an ascetic and to mortify oneself, is to fall short of Nietzsche's "Dionysian" vision.[72]

"The bad conscience is an illness, there is no doubt about that," says Nietzsche, "but an illness as pregnancy is an illness."[73] This puts matters in a new light. Pregnancy can have adverse complications but it is not an illness in itself; it is source of new life. Similarly, perhaps what Nietzsche is damning (despite his rhetoric) is not the Western conscience, but only its bad effects. Like pregnancy, it too may hold the promise of a new life.

PHILOSOPHICAL WAYS OF DEALING WITH GUILT

Unlike clinicians, moral philosophers are not in the business of giving advice to help people deal with their feelings of guilt. Instead, they are interested in providing rational models for leading moral lives. Even at that, they are careful in the advice they may give. Aristotle addressed select individuals, not all Athenians. Kant is a philosopher's philosopher. John Stuart Mill aims to reach a wider audience to promote the common good, but in that sense, he is more of a social activist than a philosopher.

There are two strands in philosophy that are pertinent to the issue of dealing with guilt. The first is exemplified by the Socratic method of self-reflection aimed at attaining understanding. It would point to examining one's thoughts of guilt and analyzing them rationally to ascertain whether they are justified or not. Since, in this view, all wrongdoing is caused by ignorance, a better understanding of one's actions allows one to gain greater control over them. If one discovers that a wrong has been committed, then the resolution more or less follows the standard path of acknowledgment and apology, leading to compensation. This way of resolving guilt is not that different from psychological methods for dealing with guilt.

The second approach goes beyond personal introspection and provides a method of resolving moral conflicts as exemplified by the idea of *reflective equilibrium* as proposed by John Rawls. The reasoning here is that we are often caught between two or more conflicting moral choices, which makes our behavior erratic or leaves us feeling guilty, no matter which way we choose to go. For instance, I know it is wrong to lie, but I also do not want my telling the truth to hurt my friend. So, if his wife asks me if my friend is having an affair (which I know he is), what do I do—lie or tell the truth?

The Socratic method of self-reflection is not going to help me resolve this dilemma. Moreover, there are so many conflicting factors to consider that I need some general principles to guide me through all the relevant considerations (including the rational, intuitive, emotional, and cultural). Reflective equilibrium provides a way of reconciling competing moral directives that are buffeted by various considerations, some more important than others. The point is to reach a determination that is both reflective and stable (at equilibrium).[74] This approach is, of course, aimed at ways that will *avoid* feeling guilty, rather than providing a way of dealing with feelings of guilt after the fact.

Should any of this matter to non-philosophers? Those who belong to a religious tradition may feel they have all the guidance they need (although some of the greatest theologians have also been philosophers). Those who are secular may base their ethical choices on a *commonsense morality* that depends on their intuitive sense of right and wrong rather than clearly articulated ethical principles.

However, even if we assume that we have an innate capacity for moral judgment, we still need to learn the particulars of how to behave. What we think of commonsense morality is likely to rely on tidbits of religious and secular moral precepts that are cobbled together. This may work for some, but more often it does not. If moral choices were so self-evident and easy to figure out, why would there be so much regret, shame, and guilt around us? Thus, morality may not be the sort of music one can play by ear. Moreover, to have the benefits of philosophical reasoning in moral judgments one need not be a professional philosopher. We can use the fruits of moral reasoning without knowing their philosophical roots. For it to be effective, the philosophical point of view we choose should be most responsive to our personal needs and abilities. Moreover, this need not be a lifetime choice, but one that depends on the stage of life we are in. I will have more to say about this in the Epilogue.

Against this background, we now turn to the last perspective on guilt—that of the law. All the perspectives we have considered so far are optional, but the reach of the law is universal; it is binding on all of us. The ethical principles that guide the law are ultimately derived from the religious and philosophical values and cultural traditions that define guilt. However, the law is not wholly derivative and has its own distinctive moral logic and language based on its own principles and practices.

11 GUILT IN THE COURTROOM

WE MAY SCOFF AT psychological theories of guilt and dismiss religious teachings and philosophical speculations. However, we are all subject to the judgment of the law, which determines who is guilty and who is not. We may not quite appreciate the awesome power the law holds over our heads until we get entangled in a legal conflict. No wonder courtroom dramas are so fascinating—as long as we watch them within the safety of our homes.

Fyodor Dostoevsky's novel *Crime and Punishment* provides a compelling account of a man's struggle with guilt and his being brought to heel by the law. This is not an ordinary murder mystery but a fascinating and disturbing account of an idealistic and tormented man coming to terms with his actions. Its central theme hinges on the enigma of guilt even though the word hardly appears in the book.[1] The protagonist, Rodion Raskolnikov, is an impoverished university student in nineteenth-century St. Petersburg who murders an old woman—a miserly and miserable moneylender—and her sister, an unintended victim, who happens to be with her. The ostensible motive is robbery, but Raskolnikov manages to steal only a few trinkets that he makes no use of. The murder is a political statement, an act of defiance by an alienated young man caught up in the radical nihilist ideology of the time. It is an expression of his rejection of and disdain for the corrupt society around him and an assertion of a morality of his own to justify his actions.[2]

I am grateful to Robert Weisberg for his lectures to my class, which introduced me to the legal perspective on guilt, and for his help in the preparation of this chapter. Paul Brest encouraged me to undertake this chapter and provided insightful critiques, as did Steve Toben.

Raskolnikov resolutely rejects all feelings of guilt in the aftermath of his crime. Yet he broods over his actions and is tormented by feelings he does not understand and cannot control. Even when his world is crumbling around him, he refuses to express remorse and tells his sister that his only regret is that he failed to accomplish the purpose of his crime:

> "Crime? What crime?" he suddenly cried out in some unexpected rage. "I killed a vile, pernicious louse, a little old money-lending crone who was of no use to anyone, to kill whom is worth forty sins forgiven, who sucked the life-sap from the poor—is that a crime?"[3]

His beloved sister is horrified and cries out in despair, "Brother, brother, what are you saying! You shed blood!" to which he responds, "Which everyone sheds, . . . which is and always has been shed in torrents in this world, which men spill like champagne. . . . and afterwards [are] called benefactors of mankind."[4]

The crime is so senseless that had Raskolnikov kept his peace, it is unlikely that he would ever have been apprehended. However, his growing turmoil leads him to make overtures to the police and eventually tips off the magistrate Porfiry, who relentlessly presses him to confess.

> "Porfiry Petrovich!" he said loudly and distinctly, though he could barely stand on his trembling legs, "at last I see clearly that you do definitely suspect me of murdering that old woman and her sister Lizaveta. . . . If you believe you have the right to prosecute me legally, then prosecute me; or to arrest me, then arrest me. But to torment me and laugh in my face, that I will not allow."[5]

Then he breaks down:

> Raskolnikov, his lips pale, a fixed look in his eyes, went straight up to the desk, leaned on it with his hand, and tried to say something but could not; only incoherent sounds came out. . . .
>
> Raskolnikov sank down on the chair . . . and said softly . . . , with some pauses, but distinctly:
>
> *"It was I who killed the official's old widow and her sister Lizaveta with an ax and robbed them."*[6]

By this time, Raskolnikov is alienated from his family and friends. His only human link is to Sonya—a saintly teenage prostitute—who has sacrificed herself for his family. When Raskolnikov is sentenced to exile in Siberia,

Sonya goes with him. Even in exile, he refuses to admit his guilt to relieve his torment:

> If only fate had sent him repentance—burning repentance, that breaks the heart, that drives sleep away, such repentance as torments one into dreaming of the noose or the watery deeps! Oh, he would have been glad of it! Torments and tears—that too, was life. But he did not repent of his crime.[7]

Finally, Sonya's love breaks through and enables Raskolnikov to acknowledge his guilt and seek redemption. In this compelling account, Dostoevsky melds legal entanglements of guilt with psychological, religious, and philosophical issues in a masterful manner that has made the novel a classic of Western literature.

The law is primarily concerned with punishing and preventing bad conduct rather than with rewarding good conduct. Its primary focus is on guilt as culpability—*being* guilty rather than *feeling* guilty, even though the offender's mental state also matters a good deal. The basic questions we will address in this chapter are: What are the factors that render a person guilty of a crime? What is culpable conduct and what is a culpable mental state? What constitutes justification and excuse? What determines the punishment for a crime and what are its consequences?

BASIC ELEMENTS OF AMERICAN LAW

The basic tenets of Western jurisprudence reflect Judeo-Christian moral values and Greco-Roman philosophical and legal traditions. At its core are the principles of *justice* and *fairness* in allocating what is due to each individual. Ideas of justice and fairness may appear to be self-evident truths, but basically they mean what society wants them to mean. Typically, laws have reflected the interests of those in power, but democratic societies are relatively egalitarian, and their values are derived from utilitarian principles to protect the interests of the majority, while safeguarding the individual rights of minorities—a delicate balance to maintain.

Although what is considered legal and moral often overlap, they are not always the same; some actions may be legal but not moral (such as consensual adultery) or illegal but moral (such as civil disobedience). The influence of moral considerations is especially prominent when crimes are considered wrong in themselves or "inherently evil" (*mala in se*) as opposed to crimes that are prohibited by law but not inherently evil (*mala prohibita*).

Most major crimes (such as murder and rape) belong to the first group; conduct prohibited by legislation (such as carrying a concealed weapon) may fall into the second group. Some other crimes, including a variety of consensual sexual behaviors between adults, entail "moral turpitude." These crimes often involve no identifiable victims, which makes the determination of guilt problematic.

Adjudication is also difficult when different moral considerations conflict. For instance, abortion pits a woman's right to choose against society's interest in safeguarding human life. The issue may hinge on determining whether or not the unborn fetus / child qualifies as a "person," or "when life begins," questions for which biology and medicine cannot provide precise or generally acceptable answers. In 1973, in *Roe v. Wade*, the Supreme Court of the United States overturned all state and federal laws restricting or prohibiting abortion, on the grounds that such laws violated a constitutional right to privacy. If the Supreme Court overturns *Roe v. Wade*, it may allow states to re-enact laws that would criminalize abortion. The issue here is not if a woman, or a doctor, should feel guilty for having or performing an abortion (which is a personal matter), but whether or not abortion makes them guilty of a legal offence (which is a public concern).

The law is conservative by its nature in order to maintain consistency over time, but it also changes in reaction to shifts in public attitudes. The ancient Greeks developed the idea that laws should reflect the will of the people, hence they should be changed when they cease to do so. Homosexual acts (but not being homosexual as such) were considered to be a crime until the mid-1970s; now state laws protect homosexuals against discrimination. Similarly, until the 1960s, obscenity laws made the production, distribution, and possession of sexually explicit material illegal. Now the First Amendment right to free speech trumps the right not to be exposed to offensive materials and the internet is awash in pornography.

What if I consider a law to be immoral and obeying it would violate my conscience? Should I break the law and suffer the consequences or try to have the law changed? There is no single or simple answer to this question that would cover all contingencies. It is clear, however, that where there is no violation of one's conscience, individual freedoms must be subordinated to the common good. It may be safer for some persons to drive at 80 miles an hour than for some others to drive at 40 miles an hour, but we cannot have speed limits customized for individuals—one size must fit all.

Some legal practices, such as being judged by a jury of one's peers, go back to the ancient Greeks.[8] Roman law evolved in a piecemeal fashion until the Byzantine emperor Justinian systematized it in the seventh century. Ever since, it has been the basis of legal practice in continental Europe (modernized through the Napoleonic Code). English common law followed a different tradition, which based judicial decisions on cases that established precedents.[9] American law was derived from English common law but most American laws are currently statutes enacted by legislatures and governmental agencies.

The American judicial system relies more heavily on the jury system than European (including English) courts, which primarily depend on judges. Actually, most cases are now dealt with through plea bargaining, or mediation, and never come to trial, which is time-consuming and expensive. When they do, they are dealt with more expeditiously by judges except when they involve serious crimes, like murder, which are tried by juries.[10] The validity of laws is ultimately determined by the Supreme Court, which rules on their constitutionality.

European justice systems place greater emphasis on rehabilitation and are administered by career civil servants. The American system stresses individual responsibility and punishment. By some measures, the American justice system is more punitive. For example, the United States has less than 5 percent of the world's population but incarcerates almost a quarter of the world's prisoners. (It has far more prisoners than China.) This is partly because of higher crime rates, but also because some people are sent to jail for offences that do not lead to incarceration in other countries (such as using drugs or writing bad checks). Offenders also serve longer sentences.[11] America is also one of the few countries left in the world that still impose the death penalty and give life sentences to some juvenile offenders.[12]

Laws are classified in two broad categories: *criminal law* and *civil law*. The purpose of criminal law is to protect the public against harm. A crime is not only an offence against an individual but also a violation of a community's code of conduct. Civil laws deal mainly with commercial transactions (like contracts) or torts (harm to persons or property). Thus, damaging someone's car in an accident may constitute a tort, but causing an accident while drunk would be a crime.

Criminal and civil law follow the same basic legal principles. However, criminal offences are more serious and typically entail incarceration; torts require monetary compensation for the victim. Criminal law makes a convicted defendant culpable for the crime; tort law makes one liable for damages. We will be mainly concerned with criminal law because that is where the issue of guilt figures most prominently.

Criminal offences are subdivided into *felonies*, which entail major crimes, and *misdemeanors*, which are less serious offences. A particular offence may be predefined or the determination may be made based on considerations of the severity of the offence and the circumstances under which it was committed.

The severity of American law is mitigated by the fact that a defendant is innocent until proven guilty. The court may find a defendant *guilty* or *not guilty*—but there is no verdict of "innocent." What is at issue here is the ability, or inability, of the prosecution to prove its case beyond reasonable doubt. This may make trials look like a contest of wits between prosecutors and defense attorneys, with the smarter side winning the case. Does this mean that courts do not care about innocence? They certainly do. Actually, the adversarial system places the burden of proof on the prosecutor, whereas to require proof of innocence would place the burden on the defense. Since it is difficult to prove that a person did *not* commit a crime, defendants would be placed in greater jeopardy if they did not have the benefit of the doubt.

For the same reason, the Fifth Amendment allows defendants not to incriminate themselves if they choose not to confess. Forcing the defendant to confess was standard practice in the past and ingenious and brutal methods were used to obtain confessions. Torture is illegal and abhorrent to Americans, but that has not stopped its use by exploiting legal loopholes, hiding behind euphemisms, or having it carried out by proxies. Far more common are psychological tactics used by the police to induce a suspected criminal to confess (a staple of television crime shows), often playing on the defendant's sense of guilt.

What Constitutes Criminal Conduct?

In order for an action to constitute a crime, it must fulfill a set of requirements. To find a defendant guilty, a judge or jury must find, beyond reasonable doubt, that the defendant engaged in a culpable conduct and ascertain the defendant's state of mind at the time the crime was committed. Criminal conduct may consist of engaging in a particular behavior (such as causing harm to someone) or failing to act in a way required by law (such as paying taxes). When there is no culpable act, *or* culpable state of mind, no crime has been committed. The requirement that a culpable *act* be present ensures that people are not punished for their thoughts or feelings. The requirement that a culpable *state of mind* be present ensures that those who cannot be held responsible for their actions are not punished either. Fulfilling these two criteria insures that the requirements of justice and fairness are satisfied.

Culpable conduct (actus reus) Conduct is culpable, or blameworthy, when it results in significant harm to others. Culpable conduct is encapsulated in the verb describing the action: for instance, *killing* another human being.[13] To qualify as a crime, the action must be *voluntary*. This usually means that it is done willingly, by your own choice. It covers anything you do volitionally, irrespective of whether or not you wanted to do it. This may sound contradictory, but consider the following example. Suppose somebody holds a gun to your head and orders you to stab someone. If you carry out the order, your action is voluntary because you could still have refused to do it despite the threat of the gun. However, if the offender literally holds your hand and physically forces you to stab the victim, then the action would no longer count as voluntary, because it would have been physically impossible not to carry it out.

The law makes rare exceptions in accepting some actions as involuntary, hence absolving the person of legal responsibility. These include actions undertaken when asleep (sleepwalking), or while suffering the aftereffects of an epileptic convulsion. So if you hit a pedestrian while driving a car under such conditions, you may not be held criminally liable. Acting when under hypnosis is no longer an admissible defense in many jurisdictions. Moreover, knowing that you are subject to epileptic fits but not getting treatment makes you liable. Under those conditions you should not be driving a car for the same reason that you should not be driving when drunk.

Acts of omission that constitute crimes have a more limited scope than acts of commission. Some actions are required by law, such as responding to legal summons. However, despite moral considerations, we have no legal obligation to help or rescue another person who is in danger. You can watch someone getting stabbed or beaten to death and not intervene without breaking the law. The law, however, does hold one liable when a person has a special responsibility toward another. For instance, parents have a legal obligation to care for their children, and teachers must protect from harm children entrusted to their care. Similarly, employers and service providers must provide safe environments for their staff and clients.

In other instances, responsibility for others is based on contractual obligations (albeit informal ones). For instance, babysitters and caregivers have an obligation to look after the well-being of their charges. A babysitter cannot watch a child in her or his care being exposed to danger and do nothing. The same is true when a person voluntarily assumes responsibility for helping another person. For instance, if I take an accident victim into my car, or tell others that I will call for help but then fail to do so, I may be liable for negligence. Similarly, we are responsible for what happens to others if we put them in danger, as for instance, by driving a snowmobile on thin ice. The one qualification is that we are absolved of legal responsibility if the action required in helping another poses serious harm to ourselves. For instance, no one—not even a parent—is legally required to go into a burning house to rescue someone, including one's own child.

It may be difficult sometimes to distinguish between acts of commission and omission. For instance, if a physician pulls the plug from a patient's life support system (an act of commission), he or she may be liable for the patient's death (irrespective of motives). If the physician decides not to connect such a patient to a life support system (an act of omission), it does not constitute criminal conduct.[14] Yet the end result is the same—the patient dies. This raises questions about the moral basis of such distinctions.[15] Moreover, culpable conduct does not pertain to who you are, only to what you do. For instance, *being* a drug addict is not a crime as such, but the production, possession, and sale of narcotics are.

Culpable mental state (mens rea)   The second element that determines guilt is the state of mind of the defendant at the time of the crime. Harmful acts alone are not enough to constitute a criminal offence. It is the additional presence of a culpable mind that determines if the defendant is guilty and deserves to be punished.[16]

The state of mind that makes one culpable is based on awareness of the act—knowing what you are doing. The more clearly and strongly a crime is linked to this factor, the stronger the guilt and the more severe the punishment. There are other considerations that may also have to be taken into account, such as whether one acts reluctantly or without qualm, or whether one pities the victim or not. However, while such factors may affect the severity of the punishment, they do not in themselves determine legal responsibility for an act.

The definition of *mens rea* has been a thorny problem in American law. The traditional language in common law may no longer mean what it meant in earlier times. Consequently, the Model Penal Code has developed alternative terms whose meaning is clearer.[17] There are four terms that correspond to levels of intent and determine *mens rea*.

Purposely: This is the highest level of intentionality. It characterizes a situation where the defendant has a specific purpose, or intention, to act in a particular way to achieve a preconceived aim. For instance, a husband stalks his wife's lover and shoots him in order to kill him. When the phrase "with intent" is used, it refers to this highest level of intentionality required to substantiate a charge of, for example, premeditated murder.

Knowingly: Suppose that a person fires a gun at a car passing by in order to disable the vehicle, but hits the driver instead. The level of intentionality is lower here because the defendant did not intend to harm the driver. Nonetheless, the defendant should have known that such an outcome was possible, thus should have refrained from firing.

Recklessly: In this case, there is no intention of causing harm, yet the conduct is likely to do so and the person disregards the risk. For instance, one may drive carelessly under hazardous conditions and hit a pedestrian. The fact that the driver did not intend to cause the accident does not make the conduct any less reckless. Reckless behavior may also involve the failure to act. Thus, a parent who realizes that a child is critically ill but fails to get medical help would be acting recklessly.

Negligently: Negligence refers to cases where a person acts without being aware of the risks involved. These are risks, however, that a reasonable person should have known to be present, such as lighting a cigarette when pumping gas. The issue here is not intentionality but the nature of the conduct itself. (In that sense, this situation is different from the other mental states.) Taken together, the level of being blameworthy based on the state of mind decreases in severity, from intention to knowledge, recklessness, and neglect.

The issue of intention also arises in *inchoate crimes*. Inchoate does not mean chaotic but rudimentary, or not fully formed. Hence, an inchoate crime is one where the intention to commit a crime progresses through its planning stages but stops short of its execution. For instance, two burglars may set out to break into a house but back off when they realize that there are people inside. Or a group may conspire to commit treason and place explosives under a public building but not detonate them. In such cases, the prelude to committing the crime becomes a crime in itself. Merely contemplating, or discussing, such prospects without taking concrete steps does not rise to the level of an inchoate crime.

Causation

The concept of causation in the law refers to the connection between the defendant's acts and the ensuing harm (it does not refer to why people become criminals). When the combination of the *actus reus* and *mens rea* results in the execution of a crime, the determination of causation must address two questions:

First: Was the defendant a link in the chain of causation? If the answer is yes, it represents the *actual cause* of the crime. In other words, it responds to the question of whether the crime would have occurred without the defendant's actions (or "but for" the defendant's actions). For example, if an employee had not negligently left the cash register unattended, the money from it would not have been stolen. However, this rule does not apply when there is no crime. For instance, if Judy has an accident for which she is not at fault, and her friend Gail, sitting next to her gets injured, Judy would not be legally liable for Gail's injuries even though she would not have been injured "but for" the fact of being in Judy's car.

Second: Were the defendant's actions a sufficiently direct cause of the harm to warrant imposing criminal liability? The answer to this question is the *legal cause* of the crime.[18] For example, the driver of the getaway car in a bank robbery is part of the robbery, even without actually being in the bank at any time during the commission of the crime.

Justification and Excuse

A defendant charged with a crime is entitled to a vigorous defense. Usually, this consists of arguing that the prosecution has failed to prove the required elements of a crime beyond reasonable doubt. But even when such proof has been presented, the defense may contend that there are valid justifications and excuses for the criminal conduct (called "affirmative defenses") that make the defendant not guilty.

In ordinary speech, justification and excuse are virtually synonymous, but the law differentiates between them. *Justification* defenses recognize that the defendant engaged in conduct that would ordinarily be considered a crime, such as killing someone, but the action was "justified" if it was done, in this example, in self-defense. On the other hand, an *excuse* defense is based on a defendant's not being criminally responsible because of some disability, such as insanity.

Justification   Justification defenses include acting in response to necessity by choosing the lesser of two evils—for instance, one shoots a burglar in self-defense or in defense of one's family, or a police officer clubs a suspected criminal who is resisting arrest.

There are, however, strict limitations on such actions. Economic necessity does not justify theft. The fact that my family is hungry does not permit me to steal food as long as there is an alternative (for instance, I could beg). The circumstances that require the criminal action should not have been anticipated, or created, by the defendant. For example, when a storm is brewing, you should not start on a mountain hike knowing that there is a cabin on the way you can break into; but you can do that in unforeseen emergencies.

Finally, you cannot act against the intent of the law however worthy your motives. For instance, one cannot distribute sterile needles to drug addicts to prevent the transmission of AIDS if the law forbids it. On the other hand, a prisoner can justify escaping from intolerable conditions in jail, but must immediately surrender to the police.

Acting in self-defense is the most compelling justification for conduct that would otherwise be criminal. Virtually all moral and ethical precepts allow individuals to resort to force to protect themselves. So when it comes down to a choice between being killed or killing the person who seriously threatens one's life, choosing the latter is not blameworthy. However, self-defense is not a license to kill. One must have an honest and reasonable fear of death or grave bodily injury; in other words, the threat must be real, not merely possible or suspected. You cannot shoot someone who says "I want to kill you" without producing a weapon that would indicate imminent danger to you.

Under stressful conditions both the level of fear and the perception of threat are likely to be colored by the defendant's psychological state. As Justice Holmes put it, "Detached reflection cannot be demanded in the presence of an uplifted knife."[19] The threat should also be unlawful—you cannot shoot a police officer who is pointing a gun at you to arrest you—and it should be immediate. You cannot act in response to past or future threats. If someone, even with a gun, threatened to kill you last week, you cannot shoot that person next week and claim self-defense.

This issue becomes more complicated in the case of battered spouses. Suppose that the battered wife of an abusive husband lives in fear of her life. He repeatedly beats her up and threatens to kill her. One day he comes home in a foul mood and tells her this is going to be the last day of her life. He then takes out his loaded shotgun, sits down with a beer and falls asleep. Feeling certain she is going to be killed, the wife takes the shotgun and shoots her husband.

In an actual case, the claim of self-defense was denied because the sleeping husband did not pose an immediate threat and the wife could have gotten away by leaving the house.[20]

Actions in self-defense must also be proportional to the threat. You cannot shoot a person who slaps you in the face. That would constitute using excessive force. The Model Penal Code limits the use of deadly force in self-defense to threat of death, serious bodily injury, kidnapping, and rape. These limitations also apply to the police, who must use force reasonably, proportionately, and within the limitations of the law (for instance, police officers cannot club a suspect who is already handcuffed or subdued).

In common law, a threatened person was not obliged to retreat before resorting to deadly force. Various jurisdictions and the Model Penal Code now require that one try to retreat before resorting to deadly force, provided it is possible to retreat safely. If one is threatened in one's own home, there is no obligation to retreat. A person who resorts to force in defense of another is subject to the same limitations that apply to self-defense. The rescuer cannot do anything that the apparent victim would not have been legally entitled to do. For instance, you cannot come to the aid of someone being subdued by the police.

The use of force is justified to protect one's property, particularly one's home. However, the use of deadly force is no longer allowed when only property is at risk. You cannot shoot a burglar unless your life, or someone else's life, is threatened. All these safeguards are intended to save life and to prevent the use of violence unless there are compelling reasons. Police officers may engage in deceptive actions that lead to the arrest of criminals by "sting" operations. They cannot, however, engage in entrapment whereby a defendant is induced to commit a crime by a government agent unless the defendant is predisposed to commit the crime. For instance, an undercover agent may pretend to offer drugs to a suspected dealer but not to someone who is not under suspicion of being a dealer.

Excuse   Excuses are based on some disability on the part of the defendant that provides reasons why the defendant could not help committing the crime. Excuse defenses include acting under coercion, diminished capacity, and insanity.

The first type of excuse relates to conduct that takes place under *duress*, or coercion. Duress must be imposed by another person rather than be the result of impersonal circumstances. Otherwise, many of the elements of self-defense would also apply here (such as imminent threat of death).

More complex questions arise with excuses based on the defendant's mental functioning. This encompasses two situations: diminished capacity and insanity. The underlying idea is that in order for a person to be judged guilty of a criminal act the law requires a certain level of mental capacity to be present at the time the crime is committed.

It has been long recognized that children cannot be held accountable for their actions. The age limit varies but is usually linked to some biological marker such as puberty. Under common law the threshold of responsibility was set at the remarkably low age of seven, then raised to fourteen. Currently, criminal behavior among children is dealt with in the juvenile court system. Under the Model Penal Code, a youth below 16 years of age must be tried in a juvenile court. These courts make allowances in dealing with children and place more emphasis on rehabilitation than punishment. However, with particularly serious crimes, offenders over fourteen may be prosecuted as adults.

Diminished capacity is a more controversial defense and one that has largely fallen out of favor. It reflects the law's understanding that *mens rea* is subject to varying degrees of mental impairment. This allows the defendant to invoke mitigating psychological factors without asserting the more demanding defense of insanity. A successful application of diminished capacity does not clear the defendant of criminal responsibility nor does it necessarily lead to hospitalization instead of incarceration. But it may reduce a charge of first-degree murder to manslaughter, which does not imply premeditation and thus involves a lower level of criminal intent.

An example of how far the diminished capacity argument can be stretched is the "Twinkie defense." In 1979 Dan White, a former San Francisco County supervisor, was tried for the murder of Mayor George Moscone and Supervisor Harvey Milk. His defense lawyers argued, based on psychiatric testimony, that White had been depressed at the time of the crime and that his mood swings had been exacerbated by his addiction to Twinkies (presumably because of their high sugar content). In the end, he was judged incapable of the premeditation required for a murder conviction, and was convicted of voluntary manslaughter instead, a verdict that proved to be highly controversial.

The much-harder-to-prove excuse is the *insanity defense*. The treatment of the mentally ill has been a sorry tale in the Western world until fairly recently. It was not until the eighteenth century that the insane began to be treated as being ill rather than evil. The insanity defense made its first appearance in the mid-nineteenth century in England. Since then, a general rationale has evolved for excusing criminal conduct on the grounds of insanity.

There is a long-standing precedent from ecclesiastical courts in exculpating the insane who commit criminal acts. Punishment in such cases would neither be fair nor serve a deterrent purpose. If the point is to remove the person from doing harm, that can be achieved just as effectively by placing the person in a hospital rather than in prison. More fundamentally, the underlying principle in criminal law is the principle of free will in exercising choice. Those who are mentally disturbed are captives to their illness; they cannot be held responsible for their actions.

In 1843, Daniel M'Naghten, a woodworker from Glasgow, shot and killed Edward Drummond, secretary to the British prime minister, Sir Robert Peel. M'Naghten was under the delusion that Peel and the pope were conspiring against him, so he shot Drummond, confusing him for Peel. The court found M'Naghten not guilty by reason of insanity and had him hospitalized. The ruling caused a public outrage that led the House of Lords to ask judges to establish standards for the defense of insanity. This came to be known as the *M'Naghten Rule*, which states,

> To establish a defense of the ground of insanity, it must be clearly proved that, at the time of committing the act, the party accused was laboring under such a defect of reason, from disease of the mind, as not to know the nature and quality of the act he was doing, or, if he did know it, that he did not know what he was doing was wrong.[21]

The M'Naghten Rule was never enacted into law, but it became the standard grounds for the insanity plea in Britain and the United States. As judges became more aware of how mental illness could affect criminal conduct, the M'Naghten Rule came to be viewed as inadequate because it placed the entire burden on the defendant's mental ability to know the nature of the act and to tell right from wrong with no consideration of the role of emotions and the exercise of the will.

To correct for this cognitive bias, the *irresistible impulse test* was adopted as a supplement to the M'Naghten Rule. It recognized that certain defendants could not control their impulses because of a mental disorder and would have committed the crime even if they knew right from wrong (or had a "policeman at the elbow"). Though this new test broadened the grounds for an insanity plea, it offered no reliable way of differentiating impulses that were uncontrollable from those that could be controlled but were not. This made it easier to fake mental illness in order to plead insanity and led to further iterations of these rules until the American Law Institute proposed the *Model Penal Code Test* in 1962, which states: "A person is not responsible for criminal conduct if at the time of such conduct as a result of mental disease or defect he lacks substantial capacity either to appreciate the criminality of his conduct or to conform his conduct to the requirements of the law."[22]

This code incorporates the key elements of the previous tests while limiting their shortcomings. It preserves the M'Naghten requirement of knowing right from wrong and the lack-of-control element from the irresistible impulse test, while upholding the burden of mental disease without allowing it to be a sufficient condition in itself for an insanity excuse. This rule received wide acceptance, and by 1982 all federal courts and a majority of state courts had accepted it.

All of this changed when John W. Hinckley was acquitted by reason of insanity of the charge of attempting to assassinate President Ronald Reagan. The resulting outrage led to a drastic set of legislative reversals. Several states eliminated the insanity plea altogether. Many others went back to the narrow confines of the M'Naghten Rule. The federal courts shifted from the Model Penal Code to a new law that eliminated the irresistible impulse test and relied solely on the inability of the defendant to appreciate the nature and quality or the wrongfulness of his act because of severe mental illness or defect. The burden of proving insanity now fell on the defense whereas earlier that burden had fallen on the prosecution. Nonetheless, eighteen states still use the Model Penal Code in their definitions of insanity.[23]

Another provision that gained further acceptance was the verdict of *guilty but mentally ill*. This does not exonerate defendants from guilt but merely leads to their hospitalization until such time as they are well enough to serve their sentence in prison. This is where matters stand at present.

It is important to realize that a diagnosis of mental illness does not constitute, as such, an insanity defense. Many career criminals could be shown to have antisocial personality disorders (which are classified by psychiatrists as a form of mental illness). The fact that someone has repeatedly violated the law is itself an important component of the diagnosis; thus to offer it as an excuse would be redundant. The law is interested in the mental state of the defendant at the time of the crime, not the defendant's mental health in general.

The insanity defense continues to be contentious. There is a public sentiment that criminals are "getting away with murder," and the courts are coddling criminals aided and abetted by psychiatrists and psychologists. Consequently, some obviously disturbed offenders are sentenced irrespective of their condition. For instance, Andrea Yates, a mother in Texas, drowned her five young children while suffering from acute postpartum psychosis with paranoid delusions and hallucinations; yet her insanity defense did not prevail. Nonetheless, there is a repugnance for incarcerating individuals who are clearly mentally ill. Despite all the talk of criminals going free by pleading insanity, fewer than 2 percent of defendants who raise the insanity defense are successful, and those who prevail do not walk free but may spend the rest of their lives on a psychiatric ward.[24]

Advances in neuro-imaging that point to brain abnormalities have allowed some defense lawyers to successfully use such images as evidence of diminished capacity even when the defendant has none of the traditional symptoms of mental illness. Thus there is now a growing field of *neurolaw*, which could further transform the legal system's treatment of criminals.[25]

The focus in dealing with criminal behavior is usually on individual offenders. The fact that most violent crimes are committed by young males points to the possibility of underlying biological factors; that many criminals come from a culture of poverty points to social problems (even though most of the poor are not criminals). But does any of this mean they cannot be held accountable for their actions? It is convenient to hold the law responsible for dealing with these difficult questions. But the law does not exist in a social vacuum. Ultimately it is the community that is responsible for the legal system as well as for addressing the social conditions that generate the problems the law must deal with.

CRIME AND PUNISHMENT

We have noted more than once the close association of the idea of debt with guilt. Ancient religious and legal codes, including that of Hammurabi and the Old Testament, recognized that when a person committed an offence against another, the offender incurred a debt that had to be paid in kind:

> And should a man mortally strike down any human being, he is doomed to die. And he who mortally strikes down a beast shall pay for it. . . . And should a man maim his fellow, as he has done so shall it be done to him. A fracture for

a fracture, an eye for an eye, a tooth for a tooth—as he has maimed a human being, so shall he be maimed. (Lev. 24:17–21)[26]

Known as the law of retribution (*lex talionis*), this principle has been a fundamental legal precept. However, people have realized over time that its literal application was not useful. ("An eye for an eye," said Gandhi, "makes the world blind.") The killing of a murderer or a kin of the offender does little for the victim's family, beyond satisfying the impulse for revenge, even if it is cloaked as "justice." Instead, Germanic tribes in the Middle Ages instituted the practice of *Wergild* ("man price") whereby the offender's side had to compensate the victim, or the family, by the payment of money or goods. This gave the idea of guilt as debt a more pragmatic interpretation. The idea persists in phrases like exacting a "pound of flesh" or making offenders "pay" for their crimes.

Punishment is an integral part of criminal law. Justice requires that crime be punished and fairness requires that in the absence of crime there be no punishment. A suspended sentence sets aside the implementation of the penalty but does not negate it. There is some room for forgiveness in the criminal justice system (such as when a governor or the president issues a pardon), but it occurs rarely. Nonetheless, even if the need for punishment seems obvious, there are various questions about the purposes that punishment should serve. These include retribution, restraint, deterrence, and rehabilitation.[27]

Retribution
The traditional justification for punishment is the infliction of pain and suffering on those who have unjustifiably inflicted pain and suffering on others. In addition to its religious roots, retaliation has been justified by some moral philosophers.

Retribution is an end in itself—it requires no justification such as prevention of crimes or rehabilitation. It is expected to bring relief and a sense of closure to victims and their families, and, in crimes like treason, to the nation as a whole. Retribution is seen as "just deserts" based on the notion that certain behaviors *deserve* to be punished. It is a way of redressing the equilibrium through punishing the offender. Offenders must suffer because they deserve it by having engaged in wrongful conduct and broken the law.[28]

Retributive justice may also be justified on the grounds that people would otherwise take the law into their hands and resort to vigilante justice to get satisfaction. However, the basic purpose of retribution is not just to prevent crime but as a merited response to the offender's wrongdoing. As John Rawls states,

> It is true that in a reasonably well-ordered society those who are punished for violating just laws have normally done something wrong. This is because the purpose of the criminal law is to uphold basic natural duties, those which forbid us to injure other persons in their life and limb, or to deprive them of their liberty and property, and punishments are to serve this end. They are not simply a scheme of taxes and burdens designed to put a price on certain forms of conduct and in this way to guide men's conduct for mutual advantage.[29]

The main objection to retributive punishment is that it reeks of vengeance, pure and simple, however it may be dressed to look otherwise. Even Kant admits that to be the case:

> The sweetest form of malice is the *desire for revenge*. Besides, it might even seem that one has the greatest right, and even the obligation (as a desire for justice), to make it one's end to harm others without any advantage to oneself.
>
> Every deed that violates a human being's right deserves punishment, the function of it is to *avenge* a crime on the one who committed it (not merely to make good the harm that was done).[30]

Vengeance is a basic human emotion that needs to be restrained at the personal level. As Kant further points out, "punishment is not an act that the injured party can undertake on his private authority" but it must be administered by a "*supreme authority* over all those subject to it."[31]

Vengeance is problematic, even dangerous, at the societal level. Since retribution serves no demonstrable rehabilitative effect on the defendant, nor deterrent function for others, why should the law endorse it? This issue comes to a head with capital punishment. The U.S. Supreme Court so far does not consider capital punishment to be a form of cruel and unusual punishment (such punishment is prohibited by the Eighth Amendment). Consequently, the United States is the only Western democracy, and one of the few countries in the world, that still has the death penalty (even though fifteen states have eliminated it). It has many proponents, who justify it on various grounds (including providing satisfaction to the families of victims). Its opponents find it repugnant and point out that even if we no longer hang criminals or use the electric chair, the use of lethal injections is hardly more humane. Hence, they consider the execution of criminals to constitute "judicial murder."

Restraint

Society has a duty to protect its members from harm; hence, there is a need to restrain (or "incapacitate," "isolate," or "disable") those who would cause such harm. The idea of restraint is linked to other justifications for punishment, such as deterrence, by locking up offenders and rehabilitating them in prison. All these considerations have combined to make America the country that relies most heavily on the incarceration of offenders. For instance, as noted earlier, the United States has 5 percent of the world's population but almost 25 percent of its prisoners; 756 out of 100,000 Americans are in prison, and one out of every 31 adults is either in jail or on probation. The figures are even higher for African Americans: an African American man has a one-in-three chance of going to jail sometime in his life.[32]

The justification for restraint is self-evident. The problem is in determining how long to detain the person and under what sort of circumstances. Do we lock up criminals and throw away the key or hold them for a reasonable period? And how long might that be? Do we keep them in a dungeon, or a country club with a tall fence, or somewhere in between? We obviously cannot keep every offender in jail for life, but when is it safe to let offenders go: after a predetermined period, or based on their behavior in prison, or based on the testimony of experts that it is safe to release them?

What makes the situation more difficult is that inmates are not simply doing time in prison; many of them are becoming more hardened criminals. This is why prisons are called "schools for crime," especially for younger offenders. Consequently, restraint alone does not provide simple and adequate answers to the question of how and why we should punish criminals.

Deterrence

The idea that punishment deters crime has had many proponents among experts as well as the general public. Yet there is no convincing empirical evidence that it generally works.

Specific deterrence refers to the effect punishment has on offenders themselves in turning them away from a life of crime. *General* deterrence refers to the effect punishing an offender has on others who may be prone to break the law. It is reasonable to assume that the fear of punishment may stop many from doing wrong (think of what you could do if there was no prospect of being caught), but it does not stop many others. Some offenders are particularly unlikely to respond to punishment. For instance, when a person assaults another in a fit of anger, the reaction is specific to a situation and may have been provoked and is not likely to recur (unless the person has psychological problems with controlling anger). The second category consists of career criminals for whom punishment is part of the cost of doing business. While it is true that the higher the cost of committing the crime, the less likely they are to engage in it, even in countries where thieves have their hands cut off, there are still thieves (where they used to chop off a thief's hand, it is now removed surgically in the name of humane treatment).

Rehabilitation

Currently, we have no effective way of changing the behavior of most hardened criminals, a point we considered at length when we discussed psychopaths. Hardened criminals are poor candidates for psychotherapy and are generally resistant to other methods of treatment. It is not even clear if such individuals want to change. If that is the case, is it a matter of choosing a criminal lifestyle, or succumbing to psychological factors over which the person has no control?

Reformers have long advocated the alternative of rehabilitation over punishment, or the use of punishment as a means of rehabilitation. The emphasis on rehabilitation gained momentum until fairly recently and became widely accepted in the penal system, and endorsed by the media, politicians, and ordinary citizens. The tide began to turn in the mid-1960s. Some of the objections came when the latitude it afforded judges led to wide discrepancies in sentencing. There was also a conservative reaction to the social excesses of the time and a return to the "just deserts" mentality. Mostly, however, the disenchantment arose from the perception that rehabilitation was not a good use of scarce public funds.

By the same token, the present way of dealing with offenders in the United States is hardly cost-effective; actually, the cost is staggering. The average cost of maintaining a single inmate in a state prison was about $22,650 per year (or $62 per day) in 2001.[33] That has escalated to the point where the money spent on correctional institutions exceeds the budget for education in a number of states. Get-tough sentencing laws has led to the incarceration of many individuals who do not represent a realistic threat to society, but has provided no tangible benefits. Building more and bigger prisons does not solve the problem.

DEALING WITH GUILT IN THE LAW

Whereas dealing with excessive guilt is the task of psychiatrists and psychologists, it is the courts and correctional institutions that must mostly deal with those with inadequate guilt. Dealing with guilt in the law is not, of course, primarily aimed at helping offenders come to terms with their feelings of guilt. The problems have to do with finding better ways of dealing with criminals, many of whom seem to have a dysfunctional conscience. The general objective of all justice systems is clear: to protect society against criminal conduct (and hopefully prevent it) in ways that are equitable, cost-effective, and effective. While social scientists study criminal conduct and religious and philosophical thinkers ponder its mysteries, the law has to deal with its problems here and now, doing the best it can.

The primary agents who are engaged in the legal determination of guilt and dealing with its consequences are attorneys who act as prosecutors, judges, and defense lawyers. The main task of defense lawyers is to protect the interests of their clients, pitting them in an adversarial system against prosecutors who represent the interests of the public. A defense lawyer does not need to determine if the client is guilty or innocent. Even if the client is guilty, it is still incumbent on the defense lawyer to provide a vigorous defense in court. Lawyers who do not wish to do that may decline to take the case (unless they have been appointed by the court). Lawyers who know their clients to be guilty may try to persuade them to admit their guilt in order to obtain a favorable plea bargain, but they cannot force their clients to do so. Nor can lawyers reveal what they know about the facts of any case without violating lawyer / client confidentiality.

There is general agreement that it is better to resolve legal conflicts through bargaining and settle them by plea bargaining, and increasingly more conflicts are resolved that way, rather than through the much more complex, time-consuming, and expensive process of trial. There are also innovative ways of dealing with the aftermath of crimes through *victim-offender mediation*. In this process, offender and victim meet face to face, together with a trained mediator (and sometimes with family or community members). The objective is to allow both parties to gain a better understanding of what happened and their feelings about it, and to explore ways of repairing both emotional and material damage.

Crime victims benefit from this process by having the opportunity to express their anger, frustrations, and residual fears, thereby obtaining a clearer sense of closure and moving on with their lives. They are also more likely to be treated fairly and receive restitution for their losses. Offenders, in turn, have the opportunity to obtain a better sense of the person they have harmed. The personal encounter, in a non-adversarial setting, makes it easier for offenders to put a human face on the victim they have depersonalized through their crime. This makes it more likely they will take responsibility for the harm they have caused and be more forthcoming in providing restitution. The more offenders benefit through understanding their feelings of guilt, the less likely it is they will repeat their offence.

Victim-offender mediation is part of a larger movement called *restorative justice*, which attempts to deal with legal conflicts in more direct and personal ways by involving all stakeholders and concerned individuals. Such attempts will not replace the formal judiciary, but defining crime as an act against another individual, rather than against the state, makes it easier to deal with it in a more personal and humane fashion. Moreover, this can be used not only between individuals but for wider communities as well.[34]

For most of us, what would seem to matter most with respect to the law is to avoid getting entangled in it. You would not want to be in a courtroom any more than you would want to be in a hospital (unless you are a lawyer or a physician). Nevertheless, the law has a particular significance to all of our lives both at an intellectual as well as at a more practical level. Everything we have discussed about guilt so far comes together in the legal framework. The legal conceptions of guilt and the ways of dealing with it bring together the perspectives of the social sciences, medicine, psychiatry, religion, and philosophy. And as new fields like neuroscience develop new insights into human behavior and misbehavior, they too become incorporated into the matrix of the law. There is no responsible way we can avoid thinking about the law, however we may feel about it.

EPILOGUE

OUR JOURNEY THROUGH THIS BOOK is about to end. We have grappled with the complexities, ambiguities, and uncertainties of what it means to be guilty, to feel guilty, and what to do about it. I pointed out in the Preface why it is difficult to write introductions; it is no easier to bring a book to a close. At the beginning of this book, I promised to keep my own opinions and prejudices out of it, so far as possible. My hope is that the following thoughts of a more personal nature will prompt readers to reflect further themselves on the issues this book has brought out for them. My comments will follow the same order as successive chapters in the book.

Let me start with the issue of what guilt is and how it relates to other self-conscious emotions. I agree with the perception that guilt is a distinctive emotion—and quite separate from shame, embarrassment, and disgust. However, I think the differences among these feelings are overstated in the current psychological literature. Most people experience these emotions of self-assessment as part of a more diffuse sense of "feeling bad" that follows when they have transgressed in one way or another. We do not have a formal word for this general feeling and the distinctions among its components, especially between guilt and shame, are not sharp (as they are, for instance, between anger and fear). Nor are the events that induce these feelings as clearly delineated.

A serious problem in the psychological literature on guilt and shame is the lack of sufficient attention to the cultural context of these emotions, although this problem is now being more widely recognized. The English words "guilt" and "shame" may not have exact equivalents in other languages, particularly

Asian languages, just as the Western concept and content of guilt and shame may not be the same as in other cultures. Consequently, when for instance we consider whether shame or guilt is the more damaging emotion, our conclusions take on a different character if they are placed in their proper cultural perspectives. Anthropologists have pointed this out repeatedly, but we keep looking at the rest of the world as if it were an extension of our own. Even though I grew up in a non-Western culture (albeit one influenced by the West), I was to learn this the hard way in my struggles to understand the concept of guilt in Asian religions, which initially completely baffled me.

I have referred off and on to the tension between the perspectives of scientific and experimental psychology on guilt and shame and those of the clinical and humanistic fields. Temperamentally, and by training, I lean toward the latter cluster. However, this is not to detract from the enormous contributions made by psychologists whose work has put the study of human behavior on a more scientific footing. For me, the scientific and humanistic approaches are complementary, with neither side having a monopoly on the truth. A physicist colleague once told me that any question that cannot be answered scientifically is trivial. Applied to human lives, that would make some of the most basic existential concerns trivial as well since they do not lend themselves to experimentation and quantification. However, without scientific rigor, our investigations will be purely speculative.

Rules and moral codes like the Ten Commandments have stood the test of time, and will continue to do so in their essentials. However, whether of divine origin or of human construction, they should serve people and not have people serve them. Unless God is arbitrary or societies irrational in legislating laws, the restrictions on our freedom should be based on substantive considerations that remain relevant to human lives rather than relics of history. Therefore, we need to reinterpret them in light of changing social circumstances. For instance, the chapter in Exodus that follows the Ten Commandments deals with ordinances concerning slaves, yet we (including those who take the Bible literally) now reject slavery.

Similarly, with regard to traditional sexual morality, it seems plausible to me that the basis for many of its rules was derived from the unpredictable association between sexual intercourse and pregnancy. The consequences of raising a child are such that only a stable institution like marriage could provide for it adequately, at least under the social circumstances of the time. However, the wide availability of reasonably safe and reliable contraceptive methods can now decouple sex from reproduction. Consequently, some of the traditional prohibitions, such as those against premarital sex, need no longer apply (unless other valid considerations are brought to bear on them). On the other hand, nothing should change in our rejection of sexual violence, exploitation, or the abuse of children. The challenge is to steer a reasonable middle course between rigid and immutable moral ordinances and a do-it-yourself rulemaking that makes morality subject to our whims.

It should be clear by now that I have perhaps an inordinate fondness for what may be considered historically antiquated. The Cardinal Sins are a case in point. I find them a fascinating attempt to get to the motivational roots of moral action, ethically as well as psychologically. However, here again, moralists draw too sharp a line between vice and virtue. Perhaps they need to do this to enhance their moral authority, but that is not how human beings feel, think, or behave. As the Victorian novelist Anthony Trollope points out:

> But we are perhaps accustomed in judging for ourselves and of others to draw the lines too sharply, and to say that on this side lie vice, folly, heartlessness, and greed,—and on the other honour, love, truth, and wisdom,—the good and the bad each in its domain. But the good and the bad mix themselves so thoroughly in our thoughts, even in our aspirations.[1]

I fully realize the necessity and unavoidability of feeling guilty when I have done wrong and of dealing with its consequences. However, when it comes to inducing guilt in personal relationships, my gut reaction is that I would rather not have it be a factor in my life. I know it can be effective, and it may be essential under certain circumstances, but the price is too high for me; it is not worth it. I would rather not try to induce guilt in those I truly care about (my wife and children concur), and I resent it when others impose it on me (my wife and children do not do so). Guilt may be useful, as is haggling and bargaining, and I am not above using such tactics if I have to. Nevertheless, I would rather argue and quarrel, if I must, than have guilt taint my close relationships.

Guilt without transgression presents special problems for me. I have not experienced survivor guilt, and I hope I never will. I understand the grief and anger over the loss and misfortune of those we love, but I do not see why we should take on the additional burden of guilt when we have done no wrong. I know this may sound overly rational, and there are situations where it cannot be helped. Collective guilt is another experience that has been foreign to me. I belong to an ethnic group that has been persecuted, hence I do have a problem if perpetrators refuse to accept collective responsibility for their acts. If a group that I identify with is guilty of the same, I hope to have the courage to take on my share of responsibility for it. I am also acutely aware that being a victim does not stop one from victimizing others.

I come from a privileged background, but positive inequity was not something people worried about in the materialistic culture in which I grew up. Over the past two decades I have been associated with the world of philanthropy and become convinced that one can be sensitive and responsive to the plight of others without being prodded by qualms of conscience. The fact that I feel bad does not make the less fortunate feel better. What matters is for me to extend a helping hand. As for existential guilt, I find the idea intriguing but some aspects of it continue to baffle me, such as guilt over the burden of being in the world.

I have had considerable experience in dealing with excessive guilt both personally and as a psychiatrist. I too could have benefited from counseling and therapy as a teenager, but it was not available to me. Consequently, the process of self-healing has been long and arduous. Dealing with patients with excessive guilt has not been easy either. It is more frustrating to try to understand and deal with inadequate guilt. In my work as a consultant to the California Youth Authority, I was fascinated by the young men I encountered in prison (who claimed to feel no guilt over sometimes heinous crimes), but felt at a loss in trying to help them with the tools available to me. Though still young, they seemed frozen in their criminal mind-set. There were others whose criminality seemed tied to their disadvantaged backgrounds and dysfunctional families. But I could do nothing about either.

I ascribe the development of the hyperactive conscience of my younger years to my relationship with my mother. She was the dominant influence in my life and had a stronger hand in shaping my character than any other person; my father was a far more distant figure. My mother was not a typical guilt inducer and far from a harsh disciplinarian. I do not recall her ever reprimanding, let alone punishing me. (My nanny was tougher, but not by much.) Yet my mother had such a grip on my affections that it was unnecessary for her to assert more direct control. The compensation for it was the certainty that she loved me more than anyone else ever could.

When my mother was in her eighties, she wrote her autobiography, where she revealed the story of her tragic love for a young man when she was nineteen. She was an Armenian girl whose father was murdered in a massacre in Turkey when she was an infant; the young man she loved was a Persian Muslim. It was a star-crossed Romeo and Juliet story from beginning to end.[2] Reading the account of her life made it much clearer to me why I felt so different from my father in every conceivable way. I came to realize that my mother had brought me up, albeit unknowingly, to replace her lost love. The Greeks thought gods punished people for what their ancestors did. We may not believe that, but it remains true that the problems we struggle with in our lives continue to take their toll on the lives of our children. I know I paid some of the price for the tragic events in my mother's life in ways she could not have anticipated and would had been distressed to realize.

As a father, whatever influence I have had on my children's moral development has been through example, rather than words. I have resisted the temptation to indoctrinate them in what I believe in order to allow them to develop their own moral sensibilities; yet at the same time I have worried about their growing up in a moral vacuum into which undesirable influences would find their way. Fortunately, that has not happened.

Another formative experience in my life was a serious illness that confined me to bed at the age of nine. It made me come to terms with the prospect of death. That has been a source of strength in my character (if I am not afraid of death, what else is there to fear?). But those early experiences put a melancholy cast on my character (or perhaps colored it with a sense of the tragic nature of life) and planted the seeds of my future predisposition to guilt. During my adolescence, these tendencies took on a religious coloration, further complicating my attempts to deal with them.

Consequently, religion played a crucial role in shaping my moral sensibilities. I have a Christian conscience, even though I cannot identify fully with the moral attitudes of any particular denomination. I envy Catholics their practice of confession, and share in the Protestant freedom of conscience and the more mystical moral vision of the Orthodox church (into which I was baptized although I was brought up as a Protestant). As I have learned more about the perspectives on guilt in other religious traditions, I have come to realize more fully their merits. The prophetic and wisdom traditions of Judaism in particular are an important part of my religious heritage. I grew up among Muslims, but I knew little about Islam. It is only later that I developed a deep respect for its traditions. The unconditional submission of the self to God and the single-minded focus on God's love (particularly in Sufism) have helped clear from my head a lot of theological dead wood. Moreover, the idea of guilt as culpability based on behavior, characteristic of Judaism and Islam, has provided me with breathing room from the Christian sense of guilt induced by sinful thoughts and feelings as well.

From what I know, religious teachings and psychological proclivities interact to shape one's ideas of guilt. Religion provides moral guidance and constructive ways of dealing with a person's psychological conflicts over guilt. However, when the religious view is laden with an excessive consciousness of guilt and its adherents are psychologically predisposed to guilt through their psychological conflicts, the result is a toxic mix that leads to trouble.

I find especially helpful the idea in Hinduism that one may follow the path of one's natural inclinations toward liberation, which for me means the moral ordering of my life. I can therefore attain my life objectives while retaining my basic identity. Buddhism impresses me most by its respect for all forms of life and detachment from the emotional shackles that tie us to the world, including guilt. I understand Confucianism better as an ethical philosophy than a conventional religion. Its key aspects for me are its profound understanding of shame in human relationships and the communitarian basis of its moral judgments.

I came rather late in my career to an appreciation of the importance of the evolutionary perspective in understanding human behavior (thanks to my Stanford colleagues in Human Biology). The glimpse it has provided into the phylogenetic roots of guilt has complemented my understanding of its unconscious origins. Whatever else may or may not be valid about psychoanalytic theory, the idea of an unconscious component of our mind influencing our thoughts and feelings has remained for me a powerful tool in making sense of what is enigmatic in human behavior.

The idea that guilt is hard-wired in my brain provides a firm biological basis for it and connects me with the rest of the natural world. There is something refreshingly "clean" about biological explanations. They stand clear of the haze that often surrounds cultural complexities. On the other hand, I am not a biological determinist who reduces everything to material causes; I am fully cognizant of the role of culture (several of them in my case) in shaping our guilt profile.

The appeal to reason in understanding guilt is not merely the secular counterpart of religious moral judgments. Faith does not preclude, or render unnecessary, the use of moral reasoning. Nor is it necessary to be a philosopher to unravel its mysteries. Many people do quite well by relying on a commonsense morality. What matters is to make sense of what we do by reflecting on why we do it. Problems most often arise not because we cannot tell right from wrong but fail to do what is right. For that, reason helps, but it may not be enough.

For my part, I find the philosophical application of reason to guilt particularly appealing. However, as in connection with religion, I find it hard to wholeheartedly cast my lot entirely with one or another philosophical view. Different approaches seem to have worked for me best at different periods of my life. For example, when I was younger, I needed rules based on an ethics of duty to guide my moral choices. As a more mature adult, when my actions had more impact on others, I found utilitarianism most useful. Now that I am older, and hope (like Confucius) that I have finally learned how to behave, I feel I no longer need so many rules. Since in retirement my actions have less impact on the world of work, I do not have to be as concerned with the consequences of my actions. Consequently, I now find the ethics of virtue most appealing. It is less rigid than Kantian ethics and allows me more flexibility in making moral choices. It provides me with more autonomy than utilitarianism and lets me chart my own path in my waning years, with less worry about where everyone else is going. I find Nietzsche fascinating when he fulminates against real and imagined villains, but I see little that is positive in his views that I could put to good use in my life.

Over four decades ago a bruising experience with the law over a contentious divorce left a bitter taste. I have since been both fascinated and repelled by the law. (I think I would have made a successful lawyer, but it would have brought out the worst in me.) Learning more about the law while writing the last chapter made me far more appreciative of the difficult task the legal system faces in determining guilt and culpability and dealing with its consequences in a fair and humane, yet firm and reasonable, manner. It is easy to criticize the legal system, and for good reason, but that system gets precious little help either from society or for that matter from other fields in its attempts to prevent crime and to rehabilitate criminals.

As I bring this epilogue to an end, I am a bit troubled that these comments might have come across as self-indulgent. I should perhaps not have imposed my personal thoughts on the reader. At least, I hope no one will take my words as a presumptuous attempt to set myself as a model for anyone to emulate. I do not know if my life can be judged as having been good, but as Erik Erikson put it, it has been good enough for me. I wish the same for the readers of this book.

Finally, all considerations of guilt come down for me not in terms of having led an exemplary life but for accepting the burden of moral responsibility for my thoughts, feelings, and actions. There are no clear and definitive rational answers to why or how to be moral, at least none that will satisfy everyone. However we understand it, what matters is that morality be central to our lives, not an appendage, let alone a burden on it. As Albert Einstein said, "The most important human endeavor is the striving for morality in our actions. Our inner balance and even our very existence depend on it. Only morality in our actions can give beauty and dignity to life."[3]

NOTES

Notes to Preface

1. Miguel de Cervantes (1605–15/2003), *Don Quixote*, tr. Edith Grossman, p. 4 (New York: Harper Collins).

2. William Ian Miller (1997), *The Anatomy of Disgust*, p. xii (Cambridge, MA: Harvard University Press). Also, I am fully sympathetic with what Miller says about the contentious issue of gender in language and have adopted his use of "we." As he puts it, "The pronoun I, you, she, he, we, choose(s) to privilege in exposition is now a matter fraught with political and moral implications." Therefore he adopts the "invitational we." This "we," Miller points out, is not "a royal me; it is not me trying to escape responsibility for personal claims or grant my personal claims spurious authority by claiming them the norm. 'We' is the voice of attempted sympathy and imagination." Ibid., p. xiii.

3. The question of why be moral is addressed more specifically by Kai Nielson (1972), "Why Should I Be Moral?" in Paul W. Taylor, ed. (1972), *Problems of Moral Philosophy*, 2nd ed., pp. 539–58 (Belmont, CA: Dickenson).

4. Evelyn Waugh (1945), *Brideshead Revisited*, p. 278 (Boston: Little, Brown), emphasis in the original.

5. I am grateful to John Racy for this observation.

6. Robert Audi, personal communication.

Notes to Chapter 1

1. *Journey Through the Night* (2006), unpublished ms., author's name withheld.

2. The analogy is from "Disgust and Its Neighbors," in William Ian Miller (1997), *The Anatomy of Disgust* (Cambridge, MA: Harvard University Press).

3. I will frequently refer to the roots, or etymology of key words. This may strike some readers as unnecessary or arcane. I realize this is not a book on linguistics but

my intention is to point out the hidden meanings within words that can help us to better understand the concepts they embody.

4. *Affect* is another term for emotions (as in affective disorders). *Passion* is the most intense form of emotion and may imply sexual or romantic love. *Sentiment* is a synonym for feeling, but it may be also associated with an abstract idea (such as a political sentiment) or hint at exaggerated feelings (as in a sentimental poem). Dictionary definitions in this and subsequent chapters are mainly from Elizabeth J. Jewell and Frank R. Abate, eds. (2005), *The New Oxford American Dictionary*, 2nd ed. (Oxford: Oxford University Press); and Christine A. Lindberg, ed. (1999), *Oxford American Thesaurus of Current English* (Oxford: Oxford University Press).

5. Charles Darwin (1872/1998), *The Expression of the Emotions in Man and Animals* (London: Harper). For a general introduction to emotions, see Carroll E. Izard (1991), *The Psychology of Emotions* (New York: Plenum); Jerome Kagan (2007), *What Is Emotion?* (New Haven, CT: Yale University Press). For a sociological perspective, see Jonathan H. Turner and Jan E. Stets (2005), *The Sociology of Emotions* (New York: Cambridge University Press).

6. Dacher Keltner and Jonathan Haidt (1999), "Social Function of Emotions at Four Levels of Analysis," *Cognition and Emotion* 13: 505–21.

7. James R. Averill (1994), "Emotions Are Many Splendored Things," in Paul Ekman and Richard J. Davidson, eds. (1994), *The Nature of Emotion: Fundamental Questions*, pp. 100–101 (New York: Oxford University Press).

8. Antonio R. Damasio (1994), *Descartes' Error: Emotion, Reason, and the Human Brain* (New York: Harper Collins).

9. Guilt and embarrassment activate the medial prefrontal cortex and the left posterior superior temporal sulcus. Embarrassment produces greater activation in the right temporal cortex and bilateral hippocampus. For an overview of this research, see Jennifer S. Beer, "Neural Systems for Self-conscious Emotions and Their Underlying Appraisals," in Jessica L. Tracy, Richard W. Robins, and June Price Tangney, eds. (2007), *The Self-Conscious Emotions: Theory and Research*, pp. 53–67 (New York: Guilford).

10. R. A. Swader et al. (1997), "The 'Big Three' of Morality (Autonomy, Community, and Divinity) and the 'Big Three' Explanation of Suffering," in A. Brandt and P. Rozin, eds., *Morality and Health*, pp. 119–69 (New York: Routledge).

11. June Price Tangney, Jeff Stuewig, and Debra J. Mashek (2007), "What Is Moral about the Self-conscious Emotions?" pp. 21–38 in Tracy, Robins, and Tangney (2007).

12. Joseph J. Campos (2007), "Foreword," pp. x–xii in Tracy, Robins, and Tangney (2007).

13. Jonathan Haidt (2003), "The Moral Emotions," in Richard J. Davidson, Klaus R. Scherer, and H. Hill Goldsmith, eds. (2003), *Handbook of Affective Sciences* (New York: Oxford University Press). "Emotions of self-assessment" is the term used by philosopher Gabrielle Taylor (1985), *Pride, Shame and Guilt: Emotions of*

Self-Assessment (Oxford: Clarendon). The two most extensive sources in psychology on the self-conscious emotions are June P. Tangney and Kurt W. Fischer, eds. (1995), *Self-Conscious Emotions: The Psychology of Shame, Guilt, Embarrassment, and Pride* (New York: Guilford); and Tracy, Robins, and Tangney (2007). For a source aimed at a more general audience, see June Price Tangney and Ronda L. Dearing (2002), *Shame and Guilt* (New York: Guilford).

14. Jessica L. Tracy and Richard W. Robbins (2007a), "The Self in Self-Conscious Emotions," pp. 5–7 in Tracy, Robbins, and Tangney (2007).

15. Janet Landman (1993), *Regret: The Persistence of the Possible* (New York: Oxford University Press); Susan B. Shimanoff (1984), "Commonly Named Emotions in Everyday Conversations," *Perceptual and Motor Skills* 58: 514.

16. John Tierney (2009), "Oversaving, a Burden for Our Times," *New York Times*, Mar. 24, p. D1.

17. Unless attributed otherwise, quotations throughout the book are from about 150 students enrolled in a seminar at Stanford University on multidisciplinary perspectives on guilt and shame that I taught from 1995 to 2003 in the Program in Human Biology. Sixty older adults took a similar course offered by the Stanford Continuing Studies Program. One of the requirements of these courses was for each participant to provide anonymous accounts of one personal experience of guilt and one of shame, which could be then discussed in class.

These surveys were primarily for instructional use rather than for formal research purposes. Since they did not involve random samples of subjects, their findings cannot be generalized to the general population. Similar shortcomings apply to many psychological studies of guilt that are undertaken specifically for research purposes. Their subjects are typically college students, who are hardly representative of the general population. By the same token, ethical considerations constrain experimental studies since investigators cannot have subjects engage in unethical acts in order to study them. These are the limitations under which investigators must work by necessity. The more lengthy accounts and quotations in the book come from literary sources, or from clinical cases. The latter have been modified by changing identifying features and may have been compressed by combining key features of several cases, and in some instances they are fictionalized, to protect the privacy of individuals. The shorter vignettes and quotes (often parenthetical) are from similar sources, or they may be hypothetical statements a person might make under given circumstances.

18. Richard H. Willis (1998), *Human Instincts, Everyday Life, and the Brain*, vol. 1, pp. 234–35 (Charlottetown, Prince Edward Island: Book Emporium).

19. Darwin (1872/1998), p. 334.

20. John Milton (1674/2000), *Paradise Lost*, Book VIII, pp. 620–25 (London: Penguin). I am grateful to Martin Evans for the Milton reference here and in Chapter 8.

21. Darwin (1872/1998), pp. 334, 310, and following pages.

22. I was surprised to see erotic lingerie openly displayed in the windows of clothing stores in Libya. It was explained to me that women bought them to wear at home for their husbands. When my medical school class in infectious diseases was taken to visit the red light district in Beirut, some of the Muslim prostitutes would expose their genitals but not their veiled faces to the public health physician (and presumably did the same with their clients).

23. The role of disgust is discussed in Miller (1997).

24. Philip Zimbardo (1997), *Shyness: What It Is, What To Do about It* (Reading, MA: Addison-Wesley).

25. Rowland Miller (2007), "Is Embarrassment a Blessing or a Curse?" pp. 245–58 in Tracy, Robins, and Tangney (2007).

26. Sandra Petronio (1999), "Embarrassment," in David Levinson, James J. Ponzetti Jr., and Peter F. Jorgenson, eds. (1999), *Encyclopedia of Human Emotions*, vol. 1, pp. 209–14 (New York: Macmillan).

27. Darwin, (1872/1998), pp. 319–20. Darwin also quotes Seneca with respect to Roman actors who hung down their heads and fixed their eyes on the ground to portray shame but could not induce a blush voluntarily (which may be irrelevant since actors typically wore masks).

28. Anita L. Vangelisi and Stacy L. Young (1999), "Shame," pp. 603–11 in Levinson, Ponzetti, and Jorgenson (1999).

29. Bernard Williams (1993), *Shame and Necessity* (Berkeley: University of California Press). I am grateful to Robert Gregg for his help with the Greek terms.

30. Gerhart Piers and Milton B. Singer (1970), *Shame and Guilt* (New York: Norton).

31. For further linguistic considerations pertaining to the self-conscious emotions, see Robin S. Edelstein and Philip R. Shaver (2007), "A Cross-Cultural Examination of Lexical Studies of Self-Conscious Emotions," pp. 194–208 in Tracy, Robbins, and Tangney (2007).

32. For an overview, see Jessica L. Tracy and Richard W. Robins (2007b), "The Nature of Pride," pp. 263–82 in Tracy, Robbins and Tangney (2007).

33. For an outstanding source on disgust, see Miller (1997). The following discussion is mainly based on it.

34. Tamara J. Ferguson (1999), "Guilt," pp. 307–15 in Levinson, Ponzetti, and Jorgenson, vol. 1 (1999).

35. Roy F. Baumeister, Harry T. Reis, and Philippe Delespaul (1995), "Subjective and Experiential Correlates of Guilt in Daily Life," *Personality and Social Psychology Bulletin* 21: 1256–68.

36. Randy Cohen (2002), *The Good, the Bad and the Difference: How to Tell the Right from Wrong in Everyday Situations* (New York: Doubleday).

37. Baumeister, Reis, and Delespaul (1995).

38. Darwin (1872/1998), p. 261.

39. Dacher Keltner and Brenda N. Buswell (1996), "Evidence for the Distinctness of Embarrassment, Shame, and Guilt: A Study of Recalled Antecedents and Facial Expression of Emotion," *Cognition and Emotion* 10(2): 155–71.

40. This new approach informs many of the current publications on the psychology of self-conscious emotions. See in particular the writings of June T. Tangney in Tangney and Fischer (1995) and in Tracy, Robins, Tangney (2007).

41. Tamara J. Ferguson et al. (2007), "Shame and Guilt as Morally Warranted Experiences," p. 330 in Tracy, Robins, and Tangney (2007).

42. The following discussion draws from Tangney and Fischer (1995); Helen Merrell Lynd, (1958), *On Shame and the Search for Identity* (New York: Harcourt, Brace); Jonathan H. Turner and Jan E. Stets (2005), *The Sociology of Emotion* (New York: Cambridge University Press); and Tracy, Robins, and Tangney (2007).

43. Karen C. Barrett (1995), "A Functionalist Approach to Shame and Guilt," pp. 39–56 in Tangney and Fischer (1995); Keltner and Haidt (1999).

44. Tangney and Dearing (2002), p. 18.

45. Ibid. The sources for Lewis are Helen B. Lewis (1971), *Shame and Guilt in Neurosis* (New York: International Universities Press); Helen Block Lewis (1987), *The Role of Shame in Symptom Formation* (Hillsdale, NJ: Lawrence Erlbaum Associates). For the most comprehensive sources on the new perspectives on self-conscious emotions, see Swader et al. (1997). For an overview intended for a more general audience, see Tangney and Dearing (2002).

46. Lynd (1958), pp. 49–56.

47. June Price Tangney, Susan A. Burggraf, and Patricia E. Wagner (1995), "Shame-Proneness, Guilt-Proneness, and Psychological Symptoms," p. 344 in Tangney and Fischer (1995).

48. June Price Tangney, Jeff Stuewig, and Debra J. Mashek (2007), "Moral Emotions and Moral Behavior," *Annual Review of Psychology* 58: 345–72.

49. Campos (2007), p. xii.

50. Richard H. Smith et al. (2002), "The Role of Public Exposure in Moral and Nonmoral Shame and Guilt," *Journal of Personality and Social Psychology* 83: 138–59.

51. Keltner and Buswell (1996).

52. Tangney and Dearing (2002).

Notes to Chapter 2

1. Shakespeare wrote *Macbeth* in 1606 and the play was first published in 1623. The events are set in about the year 1040.

2. Harold Bloom (2004), *Shakespeare's Macbeth*, p. 60 (New York: Riverhead Books).

3. Ibid., p. 65.

4. Ibid., p. 121.

5. Ibid., p. 129.

6. See Harold Bloom's introduction to the play, ibid., pp. 3–37.

7. Sigmund Freud (1916), "Those Wrecked by Success," in James Strachey, ed. and tr. (1953–74), *The Standard Edition of the Complete Psychological Works of Sigmund Freud*, vol. 14, pp. 316–31 (London: Hogarth).

8. The two versions of the Ten Commandments, one in Exodus and the other in Deuteronomy, are essentially identical, except for a few minor differences. For biblical references, I rely primarily on the Revised Standard Version in *The New Oxford Annotated Bible* (1973), Herbert G. May and Bruce M. Metzger, eds. (New York: Oxford University Press). For the Old Testament, I also refer to the Hebrew holy scriptures or the Tanakh (Philadelphia: Jewish Publication Society, 1985), as well as the literary translation of the Torah by Robert Alter (2004), *The Five Books of Moses* (New York: W. W. Norton).

9. God has no gender. The reference to God in the masculine is a problem. Using the feminine form shifts but does not solve the problem. The use of "we" that I addressed in a note in the Preface, does not help in this case. Hence, the use of the traditional masculine form.

10. Alter (2004), p. 432.

11. Nathaniel Hawthorne (1850/2004), *The Scarlet Letter*, p. 267 (Peterborough, Ont.: Broadview).

12. Simon LeVay and Sharon M. Valente (2002), *Human Sexuality*, p. 288 (Sunderland, MA: Sinauer).

13. Ibid., p. 261.

14. Down from about 40 percent in 1972. Ibid., p. 261. The big changes in this regard occurred in the late 1960s and early 1970s. It is estimated that by the 1980s, about 90 percent of men and 75 percent of women were entering marriage as non-virgins. Herant Katchadourian (1989), *Fundamentals of Human Sexuality*, 5th ed., p. 270 (Fort Worth: Harcourt Brace).

15. For a critical view on hooking up, see Laura Sessions Stepp (2007), *Unhooked: How Young Women Pursue Sex, Delay Love, and Lose at Both* (New York: Riverhead Books). The critics of the book say it resurrects the "ugly old notion" that sex is something a female gives a male for good behavior. "A Disconnect on Hooking Up," *New York Times*, Mar. 1, 2007, p. 1.

16. Joel Walkowski (2008), "Let's Not Get to Know Each Other Better," *New York Times*, June 8, p. 6.

17. Robin M. Henig (2006), "Lying," *New York Times Magazine*, Feb. 5, section 6, pp. 47–63.

18. Sissela Bok (1999), *Lying: Moral Choice in Public and Private Life*, 2nd ed., pp. xxvii–xxviii (New York: Random House).

19. Ibid., p. 47.

20. Alter (2004), p. 432, n17.

21. Evagrius of Pontus, a hermit in fourth-century Egypt, and John Cassian in the West listed sins in different orders. They were ultimately categorized by Pope Gregory the Great as the Cardinal Sins.

22. Andrew M. Greeley (1981), "A Note about the Cardinal Sins," in *The Cardinal Sins*, unpaginated (New York: Warner Books). A magisterial literary source for the Cardinal Sins is M. W. Bloomfield (1952), *The Seven Deadly Sins* (East Lansing: Michigan State College Press). Also see Stanford M. Lyman (1978), *The Seven Deadly Sins: Society and Evil* (New York: St. Martin's); Henry Fairlie (1978), *The Seven Deadly Sins Today* (Washington, D.C.: New Republic Books). Lectures organized by the New York Public Library appear in separate volumes: *Pride*, by Michael Eric Dyson; *Envy*, by Joseph Epstein; *Anger*, by Robert A. F. Thurman; *Sloth*, by Wendy Wasserstein; *Greed*, by Phyllis A. Tickle; *Gluttony*, by Francine Prose; and *Lust*, by Simone Blackburn (New York: Oxford University Press, 2001). In a series of articles published in the *New York Times* during June–July of 1993 notable writers addressed each of the Cardinal Sins: Sloth by Thomas Pynchon; Anger by Mary Gordon; Envy by A. S. Byatt; Avarice by Richard Howard; Lust by John Updike; Despair by Joyce Carol Oates.

23. The incorporation of the Cardinal Sins into medieval penitentials added greatly to their currency. They came to be confused in the public mind with the deadly or *mortal sins*. However, the deadly sins are actual transgressions like murder or apostasy that lead to the damnation of the soul, whereas the Cardinal Sins are the motivations behind transgressions. Since the Cardinal Sins reflect natural impulses, they became connected with animals who supposedly exemplify them. Thus, pride is associated with the lion and peacock; envy: the dog, snake, and pig; anger: the wolf and bear; avarice: the fox and camel; sloth: the ass, snail (and of course, sloth); gluttony: the pig and goose; lust: the goat, stag, horse, and monkey. Bloomfield (1952).

24. Dante Alighieri (1308–21/1961), *The Divine Comedy*, tr. John Ciardi (New York: New American Library).

25. Karl Menninger (1973), *Whatever Became of Sin?* (New York: Hawthorn Books).

26. Dante Alighieri (1308–21/1961).

27. This is where Bernard L. Madoff will end up, according to former poet laureate Ralph Blumenthal. *New York Times*, Mar. 15, 2009, Week in Review, p. 2.

28. Lawrence Becker (2001), "Pride," in Lawrence C. Becker and Charlotte B. Becker, eds. (2001), *Encyclopedia of Ethics*, 2nd ed., vol. 1, pp. 1374–77 (New York: Routledge).

29. Lester H. Hunt (2001), "Envy," vol. 1, pp. 471–73 in Becker and Becker (2001).

30. John Rawls (1999), *A Theory of Justice*, 2nd ed. (Cambridge, MA: Harvard University Press).

31. Anger is often equated with aggression, which actually has two meanings: one is energetic and forceful action devoid of anger (as an aggressive game of tennis or the aggressive treatment of a cancer). The other is aggression fueled by hostility that is intended to cause harm.

32. *Homer: The Iliad* (ca. 8th c. BCE/1990), tr. Robert Fagles, p. 84 (New York: Pocket Books).

33. Paul M. Hughes (2001), "Anger," in Becker and Becker (2001), vol. 1, pp. 67–70; Daniel J. Canary and Beth A. Semic (1999), "Anger," in David Levinson, James J. Ponzetti Jr., and Peter F. Yorgenson, eds. (1999), *Encyclopedia of Human Emotions*, vol. 1, pp. 42–49 (New York: Macmillan).

34. William Ian Miller (1997), *The Anatomy of Disgust*, pp. 28–31 (Cambridge, MA: Harvard University Press).

35. Lyman (1978), p. 45.

36. Menninger (1973), p. 151.

37. Max Weber (1904–5/1998), *The Protestant Ethic and the Spirit of Capitalism*, tr. Talcott Parsons (Los Angeles: Roxbury).

38. Petronius (ca. 1st c. CE/1986), *Satyricon*, tr. J. P. Sullivan (New York: Penguin).

39. Ellyn Mantell (2006), "Consumed by Guilt, I Just Stopped Eating," *Newsweek*, June 12, p. 20.

40. Sandra Metts (1999), "Lust," in Levinson, Ponzetti, and Yorgenson (1999), vol. 1., pp. 438–42.

41. Dante Alighieri (1308–21/1982), *The Inferno*, tr. John Ciardi, canto V, p. 57 (New York: New American Library).

42. For a review of books by Charla and Brad Muller and Annie and Douglas Brown, see Ralph Gardner Jr. (2008), "Yes, Dear. Tonight Again," *New York Times*, June 8.

43. E. H. Hare (1962), "Masturbatory Insanity: The History of an Idea," *Journal of Mental Science* 452: 2–25.

44. For an overview of these sexual behaviors, see Katchadourian (1989).

45. Konrad Lorenz (1954), *Civilized Man's Eight Deadly Sins*, tr. Marjorie Kerr Wilson (New York: Harcourt Brace Jovanovich).

46. *Newsweek*, Mar. 24, 2008, p. 27.

47. Roger J. Brooke (1985), "What Is Guilt?" *Journal of Phenomenological Psychology* 16: 31–46.

48. Charles B. Guinon (1999), "Heidegger," pp. 370–73, and William L. McBride (1999), "Existentialism," pp. 296–98, in Robert Audi, ed. (1999), *The Cambridge Dictionary of Philosophy* (Cambridge, UK: Cambridge University Press).

Notes to Chapter 3

1. Roy F. Baumeister, Harry T. Reis, and Phillippe A. E. G. Delespaul (1995), "Subjective and Experiential Correlates of Guilt in Daily Life," *Personality and Social Psychology Bulletin* 21(12): 1256–68.

2. The first major departure in psychiatry from this view was by Harry Stack Sullivan, who established the interpersonal theory of mental illness. See Patrick Mullahy (1975), "Harry Stack Sullivan," in Alfred M. Freedman, Harold I. Kaplan, and Benja-

min Sadock, eds., *Comprehensive Textbook of Psychiatry*, 2nd ed., vol. 1, pp. 598–613 (New York: Williams and Wilkins).

3. Warren Jones, Karen Kugler, and Patricia Adams (1995), "You Always Hurt the One You Love: Guilt and Transgressions against Relationship Partners," in June P. Tangney and Kurt W. Fischer, eds. (1995), *Self-Conscious Emotions: The Psychology of Shame, Guilt, Embarrassment, and Pride*, pp. 114–39 (New York: Guilford).

4. Lawrence Blum (2001), "Personal Relationships," in Lawrence C. Becker and Charlotte B. Becker, eds. (2001), *Encyclopedia of Ethics*, 2nd ed., vol. 3, pp. 1299–1303 (New York: Routledge).

5. Margaret S. Clark and Judson Mills (1979), "Interpersonal Attraction in Exchange and Communal Relationships," *Journal of Personality and Social Psychology* 37: 12–24.

6. Sandra Metts and William R. Cupach (1999), "Relationships," in David Levinson, James J. Ponzetti Jr., and Peter F. Jorgenson, eds. (1999), *Encyclopedia of Human Emotions*, vol. 2, pp. 567–73 (New York: Macmillan).

7. Roy F. Baumeister, Arlene M. Stillwell, and Todd F. Heatherton (1995), "Personal Narratives about Guilt: Role in Action Control and Interpersonal Relationships," *Basic and Applied Social Psychology* 17(1–2): 173–98.

8. For an overview of the interpersonal aspects of guilt, see Roy F. Baumeister, Arlene M. Stillwell, and Todd F. Heatherton (1994), "Guilt: An Interpersonal Approach," *Psychological Bulletin* 115(2): 243–67. Also see by the same authors, "Aspects of Guilt: Evidence from Narrative Studies," pp. 255–73 in Tangney and Fischer (1995). The work of Baumeister and his colleagues is a particularly important source for this chapter.

9. For a more detailed discussion of how these dynamics work in mate selection, see Herant Katchadourian (1989), *Fundamentals of Human Sexuality*, 5th ed., pp. 480–82 (Fort Worth: Harcourt Brace).

10. Tamara J. Ferguson (1999), "Guilt," in Levinson, Ponzetti, and Jorgenson (1999), vol. 1, pp. 307–15.

11. Roy F. Baumeister and S. R. Wotman (1992), *Breaking Hearts: The Two Sides of Unrequited Love* (New York: Guilford).

12. Miguel de Cervantes (1605–15/2003), *Don Quixote*, tr. Edith Grossman, p. 100 (New York: Harper Collins).

13. Baumeister, Stillwell, and Heatherton (1994). Also see June P. Tangney (1992), "Situational Determinants of Shame and Guilt in Young Adulthood," *Personality and Social Psychology Bulletin* 18: 199–206.

14. For a comparison of the association of guilt and shame with empathy, see June P. Tangney (1995), "Shame and Guilt in Interpersonal Relationships," pp. 114–39 in Tangney and Fischer (1995).

15. A. L. Vangelisti, J. A. Daly, and J. R. Rudnick (1991), "Making People Feel Guilty in Conversations: Techniques and Correlates," *Human Communication Research* 18 : 3–39.

16. Reviewed in Baumeister, Stillwell, and Heatherton (1994), pp. 249–50.

17. http://en.wikipedia.org/wiki/Second_Life#Residents.

18. http://today.msnbc.msn.com/id/18139090/page/2/.

19. Benedict Carey (2007), "Denial Makes the World Go Around," *New York Times*, Nov. 30, p. D1.

20. Huston Smith, personal communication.

21. This issue got public attention in connection with the confession of Ruby Rippey-Tourk about her affair with San Francisco mayor Gavin Newsom. *San Francisco Chronicle*, Feb. 2, 2007, p. A17.

22. *Newsweek*, Sept. 27, 2004, p. 52.

23. Baumeister, Stillwell, and Heatherton (1994).

24. Everett Worthington, quoted in *Newsweek*, Sept. 27, 2004, p. 52.

25. Richard H. Willis (1998), *Human Instincts, Everyday Life, and the Brain*, vol. 1, p. 396 (Charlottetown, Prince Edward Island: Book Emporium).

26. For instance, Fred Luskin's book *Forgive For Good* is subtitled *A Proven Prescription for Health and Happiness*. Fred Luskin (2002), *Forgive For Good* (San Francisco: Harper). This book provides specific steps for overcoming anger and achieving forgiveness.

27. Jordana Lewis and Jerry Adler (2004), "Forgive and Let Live," *Newsweek*, Sept. 27, p. 52.

28. Jeffrie G. Murphy (2003), *Getting Even: Forgiveness and Its Limits* (New York: Oxford University Press).

Notes to Chapter 4

1. Aaron Hass, "Survivor Guilt in Holocaust Survivors and Their Children," www.holocaust-trc.org/glbsurv.htm, pp. 1, 4, 5, 7. Original source in J. Lemberger, ed. (1995), *A Global Perspective on Working with Holocaust Survivors and the Second Generation*, pp. 163–83 (Jerusalem: AMCHA/Brookdale).

2. There is an extensive bibliography on Holocaust survivors at www.judymeschel.com/coshpsych.htm. Among the many personal accounts, those of Primo Levi and Elie Wiesel are particularly compelling.

3. In addition to over six million Jews, the Nazis killed large numbers of Gypsies and Soviet prisoners of war, and some 200,000 mentally ill or handicapped Germans. Richard J. Evans (2007), *New York Times Book Review*, June 24, p. 17.

4. Lawrence Langer (1991), *Holocaust Testimonies* (New Haven, CT: Yale University Press).

5. Primo Levi (1988), *The Drowned and the Saved*, p. 57 (London: Michael Joseph). Also see, Elie Wiesel (2006), *Night*, tr. Marion Wiesel (New York: Hill and Wang).

6. Ibid.

7. William Styron (1999), *Sophie's Choice* (New York: Modern Library).

8. Levi (1988), p. 56.

9. Robert J. Lifton (1967), *Death in Life* (New York: Simon and Schuster); Robert J. Lifton and E. Olson (1986), "The Human Meaning of Total Disaster," in R. H. Moos, ed. (1986), *Coping With Life Crises* (New York: Plenum).

10. Lifton (1967), p. 314.

11. Hurricane Katrina, which struck on August 23, 2005, was the costliest and one of the deadliest hurricanes in the history of the United States. A great deal has been written about the disaster, but no systematic account and analysis of survivor guilt have yet appeared to my knowledge.

12. *New Yorker*, June 12, 2006, pp. 127–28.

13. Sanford Gifford, personal communication.

14. R. E. Opp and A. Y. Samson (1989), "Taxonomy of Guilt for Combat Veterans," *Professional Psychology: Research and Practice* 20: 159–65.

15. Ernst Freud (1960), *The Letters of Sigmund Freud*, p. 111 (New York: Basic Books).

16. Quoted in J. Lindsay-Hartz, J. De Rivera, and M. F. Mascolo (1995), "Differentiating Guilt and Shame and Their Effects on Motivation," in June P. Tangney and Kurt W. Fischer, eds. (1995), *Self-Conscious Emotions: The Psychology of Shame, Guilt, Embarrassment, and Pride*, p. 294 (New York: Guilford).

17. I am grateful to David Hamburg for his comments on survivor and collective guilt, and his friendship and support throughout the writing of this book.

18. Daniel J. Goldhagen (1996), *Hitler's Willing Executioners: Ordinary Germans and the Holocaust* (New York: Knopf); Saul Friedlander (2007), *The Years of Extermination: Nazi Germany and the Jews, 1939–1945* (San Francisco: HarperCollins).

19. Amitai Etzioni, *Notes: Personal and Communitarian Reflections*, blog, aeblog@gwu.edu, English translation of an article from *Suddeutsche Zeitung*, Jan. 24, 2005.

20. Richard von Weizsäcker (1986), "Forty Years after the War," in Geoffrey Hartman, ed. (1986), *Bitburg in Moral and Political Perspective* (Bloomington: Indiana University Press). I am grateful to Ulla Morris Carter for bringing this source to my attention.

21. Harlan J. Wechsler (1990), "Collective Guilt and Collective Repentance," in *What's So Bad about Guilt? Learning to Live With It Since We Can't Live Without It*, p. 184 (New York: Simon and Schuster).

22. Howard W. French (1997), "The Ritual Slaves of Ghana: Young and Female," *New York Times*, Jan. 27.

23. www.eoearth.org/article/Exxon-Valdez-oil-spill.

24. For additional views on collective guilt, see Nyla R. Branscombe and Bertjan Doosje (2005), *Collective Guilt: International Perspectives* (Cambridge, UK: Cambridge University Press).

25. Robert S. McNamara and Brian Van DeMark (1996), *In Retrospect: The Tragedy and Lessons of Vietnam*, p. xx (New York: Vintage Books).

26. Jacques P. Thiroux (2004), *Ethics: Theory and Practice*, 8th ed., chs. 13–15 (Upper Saddle River, NJ: Prentice Hall). Also see, Robert Audi (2008), *Business Ethics and Ethical Business* (New York: Oxford University Press).

27. Fred Skolnick, ed. (2007), "Reparations, German," in *Encyclopedia Judaica*, 2nd ed., vol. 17, pp. 220–21 (Detroit: Thomson/Gale). For the negotiations that led to these reparations and their scale and significance, see Nahum Goldmann (1969), *The Autobiography of Nahum Goldmann; Sixty Years of Jewish Life* (New York: Holt, Rinehart and Winston).

28. I am of Armenian background so this is not a neutral topic for me. The view of Armenian and most Western historians is that the exile and extermination of over a million Armenians in Anatolia in 1915 constituted the first genocide of the twentieth century—what the British historian Arnold Toynbee called "the murder of a nation." For further details, see Vahakn N. Dadrian (1995), *The History of the Armenian Genocide: Ethnic Conflict from the Balkans to Anatolia to the Caucasus* (Providence, RI: Berghahn). For an opposing view, see Stanford Shaw and Ezel Kural Shaw (1977), *History of the Ottoman Empire and Modern Turkey* (Cambridge, UK: Cambridge University Press). Parallels between the Armenian genocide and the Holocaust are discussed in Robert F. Melson (1992), *Revolution and Genocide* (Chicago: University of Chicago Press). Acknowledgment of collective responsibility is an important component in the prevention of genocide. See David A. Hamburg (2008), *Preventing Genocide* (Boulder, CO: Paradigm). The Armenian case is discussed in chapter 3.

29. *Armenian Mirror-Spectator*, Jan. 26, 1985, pp. 2, 15.

30. Nügte V. Ortaq (2009), *L'Express*, Jan. 22, p. 33. I would like to thank Marc Bertrand for help with the translation of this text from the French.

31. *New York Times*, May 16, 2006, p. A26. Nonetheless, the Republics of Turkey and Armenia have established a broad accord over the prospect of normalizing ties between the two countries. The issue of recognizing the genocide will in all likelihood be the subject of negotiations. Mary Beth Sheridan (2009), "Turkey, Armenia in Broad Accord," *Washington Post*, Apr. 23.

32. Elazar Barkan (2000), *The Guilt of Nations: Restitution and Negotiating Historical Injustices* (New York: W. W. Norton).

33. *Time*, July 28, 2008, p. 7.

34. Lyn S. Graybill (2002), *Truth and Reconciliation in South Africa: Miracle or Model?* (Boulder, CO: Lynne Rienner).

35. Elaine Walster, G. William Walster, and Ellen Berscheid (1978), *Equity Theory and Research* (Boston: Allyn and Bacon).

36. Kenneth Keniston (1968), *Radical Youth* (New York: Harcourt).

37. Martin Hoffman (1982), "Development of Prosocial Motivation: Empathy and Guilt," in Nancy Eisenberg, ed. (1982), *The Development of Prosocial Behavior*, pp. 302–3 (New York: Academic Press).

38. For negative attitudes toward the wealthy during times of financial crises, see "The Rich Under Attack," *The Economist*, April 4–10, 2009, p. 15.

39. David Brooks (2009), "The Commercial Republic," *New York Times*, Mar. 17, p. A 23.

40. *Time*, Sept. 18, 2006; Joel Osteen (2007), *Become a Better You* (New York: Free Press).

41. Arthur B. Kennickel (2003), *A Rolling Tide: Changes in the Distribution of Wealth in the U.S., 1989–2001*, Nov., table 10 (New York: Levy Economics Institute).

42. The *New York Times Magazine* of March 9, 2008, from which these figures are taken, was entirely devoted to philanthropy.

43. Austin Goolsbee (2007), "Why Do the Richest People Rarely Intend to Give It All Away?" *New York Times*, Mar. 1, p. C3. Philosopher Peter Singer has come up with a formula of how much the superrich—and the rest of us—should donate to meet the needs of the developing world. Peter Singer (2006), "On Giving," *New York Times Magazine*, Dec. 17, pp. 55–80ff.

44. *New York Times Magazine*, Mar. 9, 2008, p. 47.

45. Esther Hewlett, personal communication.

46. Franz Kafka (1925/1992), *The Trial*, tr. Willa and Edwin Muir, p. 220 (New York: Schocken Books).

47. Ibid., p. 220

48. Donald V. Morano (1973), *Existential Guilt: A Phenomenological Study* (Assen, Netherlands: Koninklijke Van Gorum). Also see A. E. Dyson (1987), "Trial by Enigma: Kafka's *The Trial*," in Harold Bloom, ed. (1987), *Franz Kafka's "The Trial,"* pp. 57–72 (New York: Chelsea House); Walter Sokel (1995), "Franz Kafka: Der Prozess," in W. J. Dodd, ed. (1995), *Kafka: The Metamorphosis, The Trial, and The Castle* (New York: Longman); Henry Sussman (1993), *"The Trial": Kafka's Unholy Trinity* (New York: Macmillan).

49. Charles B. Guinon (1999), "Heidegger," pp. 370–73, and William L. McBride (1999), "Existentialism," pp. 296–98, in Robert Audi, ed. (1999), *The Cambridge Dictionary of Philosophy* (Cambridge, UK: Cambridge University Press). Also see www.existentialpsychotherapy.net/#guilt.

50. Morano (1973), p. 41.

51. These concepts of existential guilt are from Rollo May. They are discussed and critiqued in Carroll E. Izard (1991), *The Psychology of Emotions* (New York: Plenum).

52. Martin Buber (1957/1965), "Guilt and Guilt Feelings," in *The Knowledge of Man: A Philosophy of the Interhuman*, tr. Maurice Friedman, pp. 126, 127, 131 (New York: Harper and Row).

Notes to Chapter 5

1. "Mirrors: A Case Study of the Interplay of Guilt, Depression, and Christianity" (1995), unpublished ms., author's name withheld.

2. G. Rattray Taylor (1954), *Sex in History*, p. 44 (New York: Harper and Row). This book expresses a highly critical, if not hostile, view on these matters. For a more extensive and scholarly discussion of the emergence of a Western guilt culture from the thirteenth to the eighteenth centuries, see Jean Delumeau (1990), *Sin and Fear*, tr. Eric Nicholson (New York: St. Martin's).

3. William Ian Miller (1997), *The Anatomy of Disgust*, pp. 158–62 (Cambridge, MA: Harvard University Press).

4. Mortimer Chambers et al. (1979), *The Western Experience*, p. 340 (New York: Knopf). For further discussion of these issues, see Herant Katchadourian (1989), *Fundamentals of Human Sexuality*, 5th ed., ch. 20 (Fort Worth: Harcourt Brace).

5. J. A. Amato (1982), "A New Guilt," in *Guilt and Gratitude: A Study of the Origins of Contemporary Conscience* (London: Greenwood).

6. Hannah Arendt (1963), *Eichmann in Jerusalem: A Report on The Banality of Evil* (New York: Viking).

7. A. C. Grayling (2006), *Among the Dead Cities* (London: Bloomsbury). I am grateful to Sanford Gifford for bringing this matter to my attention.

8. Amato (1982), p. 6.

9. Ibid., p. 13.

10. Sigmund Freud (1929), *Civilization and Its Discontents*, in James Strachey, ed. and tr. (1953–74), *The Standard Edition of the Complete Psychological Works of Sigmund Freud*, vol. 21, pp. 59–145 (London: Hogarth). Freud wanted to call the book "Unhappiness in Culture," but settled for the more cryptic "discontents." It refers to the malaise—the vague feeling of uneasiness—that characterizes life in civilized society.

11. Peter Gay (1988), *Freud: A Life for Our Time* (New York: W. W. Norton).

12. Roger Brooke (1985), "What is Guilt?" *Journal of Phenomenological Psychology* 16(2): 31–46.

13. Theodore Millon, Paul H. Blaney, and Roger D. Davis, eds. (1999), *Oxford Textbook of Psychopathology*, p. 203 (Oxford: Oxford University Press).

14. *Diagnostic and Statistical Manual of Mental Disorders* (DSM-IV-TR) (2000) 4th ed., text revision, pp. 345–428 (Washington, D.C.: American Psychiatric Association).

15. Mood disorders are covered extensively in textbooks of psychiatry and more specialized sources. See Benjamin J. Sadock and Virginia A. Sadock, eds. (2005), *Kaplan and Sadock's Comprehensive Textbook of Psychiatry*, 8th ed., vol. 1, pp. 1559–1707 (Philadelphia: Lippincott Williams & Wilkins); Robert E. Hales and Stuart C. Yudofsky (2003), *Textbook of Clinical Psychiatry*, 4th ed. (Washington, D.C.: American Psychiatric Publishing). The extensive psychoanalytic literature on depression includes Freud's classic paper of 1917, "Mourning and Melancholia." Sigmund Freud (1917), in Strachey (1953–74), vol. 14, pp. 237–60. The work of Melanie Klein is also prominent in the psychoanalytic study of depression.

16. Freud (1917), p. 246.

17. Gerhart Piers and Milton B. Singer (1971), *Shame and Guilt*, pp. 40–43 (New York: W. W. Norton).

18. Otto Fenichel (1945), *The Psychoanalytic Theory of Neurosis*, p. 363 (New York: W. W. Norton).

19. "Obsessive-Compulsive Personality Disorders," DSM-IV-TR (2000), pp. 725–29; "Personality Disorders," in Sadock and Sadock (2005), vol. 2, pp. 2063–2104.

20. Obsessive-compulsive disorders are currently classified under "Anxiety Disorders." See, DSM-IV-TR (2000), pp. 725–29; Sadock and Sadock (2005), vol. 1, pp. 1768–79.

21. George Borrow (1975), *Lavengro*, quoted by John Nemiah, in Alfred M. Freedman, Harold I. Kaplan, and Benjamin J. Sadock (1975), *Comprehensive Textbook of Psychiatry*, 2nd ed., vol. 1, p. 1242 (Baltimore: Williams and Wilkins).

22. Freud wrote extensively about these conditions, including his case study of the "Rat Man," in "Notes upon a Case of Obsessional Neurosis," in Strachey (1953–74), vol. 10, pp. 153–342.

23. Joseph W. Ciarrocchi (1995), *The Doubting Disease: Help for Scrupulosity and Religious Compulsions* (Mahwah, NJ: Paulist Press).

24. Ibid., p. 40.

25. John Bunyan (1666), *Grace Abounding to the Chief of Sinners*, pp. 40–41, in *The Choice Works of John Bunyan* (1811) (Halifax: William Milner), http://books.google.com/books?id=wzkoAAAAYAAJ.

26. J. A. Knight (1968), "Fault and Failures of Conscience," in *Conscience and Guilt*, pp. 126–45 (New York: Appleton-Century-Crofts).

27. Stanley Milgram (1974), *Obedience to Authority: An Experimental View* (New York: Harper and Row); Craig Haney and Philip G. Zimbardo (1977), "The Socialization into Criminality: On Becoming a Criminal and a Guard," in June Louin Tapp and Felice L. Levine, eds. (1977), *Law, Justice and the Individual in Society: Psychological and Legal Issues*, pp. 198–223 (New York: Holt, Rinehart and Winston).

28. "The Human Behavior Experiments," *New York Times*, June 6, 2006.

29. William Golding (1999), *Lord of the Flies* (Philadelphia: Chelsea House).

30. Chris Hedges and Laila Al-Arian (2007), "The Other War: Iraq Vets Bear Witness," *The Nation*, July 30.

31. For an overview of these concepts see, John Seabrook (2008), "Suffering Souls: The Search for the Roots of Psychopathy," *New Yorker*, Nov. 10, pp. 64–73.

32. "Antisocial Personality Disorder," DSM-IV-TR (2000), pp. 701–6.

33. Robert H. Hare (2006), "Psychopathy: A Clinical and Forensic Overview," *Psychiatric Clinics of North America* 29: 709–24. Robert Hare developed a widely used Psychopathy Checklist that has helped standardize the key feature of this condition. Robert Hare (1993), *Without Conscience: The Disturbing World of the Psychopaths among Us* (New York: Guilford).

34. Hare (2006), p. 709.

35. Accounts of rape experiences often focus on the element of guilt. See for instance, Nancy V. Raine (1998), *After Silence: Rape and My Journey Back* (Chicago: American Library Association).

36. For case stories of psychopaths whose reasoning becomes detached from moral emotions, see Hervey Cleckley (1955), *The Mask of Sanity* (St. Louis: C. V. Mosby).

37. Seabrook (2008), p. 70.

38. Stephanie Strom (2009), "Elie Wiesel Levels Scorn at Madoff," *New York Times*, Feb. 27, p. B1.

39. Julie Creswell and London Thomas Jr. (2009), "The Talented Mr. Madoff," *New York Times*, Jan. 25, pp. B1, B8.

40. Ron Chernow (2009), "Madoff and His Models," *New Yorker*, Mar. 23, pp. 28–33.

41. *Time*, Aug. 24, 1998.

42. Antonio R. Damasio (1994), *Descartes' Error: Emotion, Reason, and the Human Brain* (New York: Harper Collins).

43. Jennifer S. Beer, et al. (2003), "The Regulatory Function of Self-Conscious Emotion: Insights from Patients with Orbitofrontal Damage," *Journal of Personality and Social Psychology* 85(4): 594–604.

44. R. J. R. Blair and L. Cipolotti (2000), "Impaired Social Response Reversal," *Brain* 123: 1122–41.

45. Damasio (1994), pp. 124–25, emphasis in the original.

46. Sadock and Sadock (2005), vol. 1, p. 853.

47. June P. Tangney, Jeffrey Stuewig, and Debra J. Mashek (2007), "What's Moral about the Self-Conscious Emotions?" in Tracy, Robins, and Tangney (2007), pp. 26–28. Also see June Price Tangney, Jeff Stuewig, and Debra J. Mashek (2007), "Moral Emotions and Moral Behavior," *Annual Review of Psychology* 58: 345–72.

48. June P. Tangney and Rhonda L. Dearing (2002), *Shame and Guilt*, p. 3 (New York: Guilford).

49. The instruments used to study self-conscious emotions are typically questionnaires, perhaps the best known of which is the Test of Self-Conscious Affect (TOSCA). Such questionnaires present a series of shame and guilt scenarios with responses for subjects to choose from. How the questions are phrased has an important bearing on how they are answered.

50. David W. Harder (1995), "Shame and Guilt Assessment, and Relationships of Shame and Guilt-proneness to Psychopathology," in June P. Tangney and Kurt W. Fischer, eds. (1995), *Self-Conscious Emotions: The Psychology of Shame, Guilt, Embarrassment, and Pride*, p. 382 (New York: Guilford).

51. Tamara J. Ferguson, et al. (2007), "Shame and Guilt as Morally Warranted Experiences," in Tracy, Robins, and Tangney (2007), p. 332. Also see Tamara J. Ferguson

and Hedy Stegge (1998), "Measuring Guilt in Children: A Rose by Any Other Name Still Had Thorns," in Jane Bybee, ed. (1998), *Guilt and Children* (San Diego, CA: Academic Press).

52. John Sabini and Maury Silver (1997), "In Defense of Shame: Shame in the Context of Guilt and Embarrassment," *Journal for the Theory of Social Behavior* 27(1): 2–15.

53. To avoid overreaching from research findings, Helen Lynd cautions us to be aware of "the tendency to think that understanding results from reducing complex phenomena to their simplest elements, or to a single basic principle of explanation," and the tendency to eliminate "surplus meaning" and reduce data to "nothing more" than certain stated empirical observations. She adds, "such explanations are indispensable . . . for understanding certain kinds of phenomena. Phenomena such as shame and identity they may miss, and as exclusive explanations they fall short." Helen M. Lynd (1958), *On Shame and the Search for Identity*, pp. 114–15 (New York: Harcourt Brace).

Notes to Chapter 6

1. Sigmund Freud (1909), "Analysis of a Phobia in a Five-Year-Old Boy," in James Strachey, ed. and tr. (1953–74), *The Standard Edition of the Complete Psychological Works of Sigmund Freud*, vol. 10, pp. 3–149 (London: Hogarth). For a discussion of the case of Little Hans, see Peter Gay (1988), *Freud: A Life for Our Time*, pp. 255–61 (New York: W. W. Norton).

2. Freud (1909), pp. 123–24.

3. Ibid., p. 134.

4. Ibid., p. 45, emphasis in the original.

5. Joseph Anthony Amato (1982), *Guilt and Gratitude: A Study of the Origins of Contemporary Conscience*, p. 49 (Westport, CT: Greenwood).

6. Jayne Hoose (1999), *Conscience in World Religions* (Notre Dame, IN: University of Notre Dame Press).

7. Alan Donagan (2001), "Conscience," in Lawrence C. Becker and Charlotte B. Becker, eds. (2001), *Encyclopedia of Ethics*, vol. 1, pp. 297–99 (New York: Routledge); Michel Despland (2005), "Conscience," in Lindsay Jones, ed. (2005), *Encyclopedia of Religion*, 2nd ed., vol. 3, pp. 1939–46 (Detroit: Gale Thomson).

8. Despland (2005), p. 1940.

9. Peter Brown (1969), *Augustine of Hippo* (Berkeley: University of California Press).

10. Saint Augustine (397/1998), *Confessions*, tr. Henry Chadwick, Book X, ii(2), p. 179 (Oxford: Oxford University Press).

11. The Franciscans construed synderesis as an emotional disposition (you feel the moral law), while the Dominicans placed it in the intellect as a form of cognition (you know the moral law by reason).

12. Robert Audi, ed. (1999), "Butler, Joseph," *The Cambridge Dictionary of Philosophy*, 2nd ed., pp. 109–10 (Cambridge, UK: Cambridge University Press).

13. Ernest Alleva and Gareth Matthews (2001), "Moral Development," in Becker and Becker (2001), vol. 2, pp. 1118–25.

14. Aristotle (ca. 350 BCE/2004), *Nicomachean Ethics*, tr. J. A. K. Thomson (London: Penguin).

15. Despland (2005), p. 1940.

16. Alleva and Matthews (2001), pp. 1119–20.

17. Emile Durkheim (1925/1969), *Moral Education* (New York: Free Press).

18. John Dewey (1932), *Ethics* (New York: Henry Holt).

19. See note 24 to Chapter 10. Thanks to Sanford Gifford.

20. Freud did not discover (or invent) the unconscious. The idea was already present in the work of Nietzsche and others. See Lancelot Law Whyte (1978), *The Unconscious before Freud* (New York: St. Martin's). However, Freud greatly expanded the concept of the unconscious, made it the central organizing principle of psychoanalytic theory, and brought it into the cultural mainstream. For an overview of Freud's life and work, see Gay (1998).

21. George Engel (1962), *Psychological Development in Health and Disease* (Philadelphia: W. B. Saunders).

22. Sigmund Freud (1923), "The Ego and the Id," in Strachey (1953–74), vol. 19, pp. 3–63. Also see Anna Freud (1946), *The Ego and the Mechanisms of Defense* (New York: International Universities Press).

23. Sigmund Freud (1933), "New Introductory Lectures on Psychoanalysis," in Strachey (1953–74), vol. 22, pp. 3–158.

24. David W. Robinson (2005), *Conscience and Jung's Moral Vision: From Id to Thou* (New York: Paulist Press).

25. Robert Coles (1970), *Erik Erikson: The Growth of His Work* (New York: Little Brown).

26. Erik Erikson (1963), *Childhood and Society*, 2nd ed. (New York: Norton).

27. Erik Erikson (1959), "Identity and the Life Cycle," *Psychological Issues* 1(1): 68, 70.

28. Ibid., p. 80, emphasis in the original.

29. John B. Watson (1924/1950), *Behaviorism*, p. 104 (New York: W. W. Norton).

30. B. F. Skinner (1971), *Beyond Freedom and Dignity* (New York: Knopf). The idea is not new. In the seventeenth century, John Locke, the preeminent English philosopher of empiricism, articulated it by comparing the mind at birth to an empty slate (*tabula rasa*) on which one's life script would be written through experience.

31. Albert Bandura (1977), *Social Learning Theory* (Englewood Cliffs, NJ: Prentice-Hall); Albert Bandura (1986), *Social Foundations of Thought and Action: A Social Cognitive Theory* (Englewood Cliffs, NJ: Prentice-Hall); Walter Mischel and Harriet N. Mischel (1976), "A Cognitive Social Learning Approach to Morality and Self-Reg-

ulation," in Thomas Lickona, ed. (1976), *Moral Development and Behavior: Theory, Research and Social Issues*, pp. 84–107 (New York: Holt, Rinehart and Winston).

32. Jean Piaget (1932/1965), *The Moral Judgment of the Child* (New York: Free Press).

33. Lawrence Kohlberg (1984a), *The Psychology of Moral Development*, vol. 1, *Moral Stages and the Life Cycle*, vol. 2, *Essays on Moral Development* (New York: Harper and Row); Lawrence Kohlberg (1984b), *The Psychology of Moral Development: The Nature and Validity of Moral Stages* (New York: Harper and Row).

34. Kohlberg (1984a), *Essays on Moral Development*, pp. 174–76. Subsequently, Kohlberg added a "Metaphoric Stage 7" which addresses mystical, religious, and metaphysical dimensions of moral judgment aimed at ultimate ethical questions like, "Why be just in a universe filled with injustice, pain and death?"

35. James J. Fowler (1981), *Stages of Faith: The Psychology of Human Development and the Quest for Meaning* (New York: Harper and Row). Also see S. Lownsdale (1997), "Faith Development across the Life Span: Fowler's Integrative Work," *Journal of Psychology and Theology* 25(1): 49–63.

36. For a general critique of Kohlberg's work, see Jean G. Miller (1994), "Cultural Diversity in the Morality of Caring: Individually Oriented Versus Duty-Based Interpersonal Moral Codes," *Cross-Cultural Research* 28(1): 3–39; Richard A. Shweder, Manamohan Mahapatra, and Joan Miller (1987), "Culture and Moral Development," in Jerome Kagan and Sharon Lamb, eds. (1987), *The Emergence of Morality in Young Children*, pp. 1–90 (Chicago: University of Chicago Press).

37. Kagan and Lamb (1987).

38. Joan G. Miller (1997), "Theoretical Issues in Cultural Psychology," in John W. Berry, Ype Poortinga, and Janak Pandey, eds. (1997), *Handbook of Cross-Cultural Psychology: Theory and Method*, vol. 1, ch. 3 (Boston: Allyn and Bacon).

39. William Ickes (1999), "Empathy," in David Levinson, James J. Ponzetti Jr., and Peter F. Yorgenson, eds. (1999), *Encyclopedia of Human Emotions*, vol. 1, pp. 243–46 (New York: Macmillan); Candace Clark (1999), "Sympathy," in Levinson, Ponzetti, and Yorgenson (1999), pp. 651–56.

40. Carolyn Zahn-Waxler and Joann Robinson (1995), "Empathy and Guilt: Early Origins of Feelings of Responsibility," in June P. Tangney and Kurt W. Fischer, eds., *Self-Conscious Emotions: The Psychology of Shame, Guilt, Embarrassment, and Pride*, pp. 143–73 (New York: Guilford).

41. A. Sagi and M. L. Hoffman (1976), "Empathic Distress in the Newborn," *Developmental Psychology* 12: 175–76.

42. Martin Hoffman (1982), "Affect and Moral Development," in D. Cicchetti and P. Hesse, eds., *New Directions in Child Development: Emotional Development*, pp. 83–103 (San Francisco: Jossey-Bass); Martin Hoffman (1984), "Empathy, Its Limitations and Its Role in Comprehensive Moral Theory," in William M. Kurtines and Jacob L. Gewirtz, eds. (1984), *Morality, Moral Behavior, and Moral Development* (New York: Wiley).

43. Grazyna Kochanska and Nazan Aksan (2006), "Children's Conscience and Self-Regulation," *Journal of Personality* 74(6): 1587–1617, is the primary source of the following discussion.

44. Jonathan Haidt (2001), "The Emotional Dog and Its Rational Tail: A Social Intuitionist Approach to Moral Judgment," *Psychological Review* 108(4): 814–34.

45. Tomi-Ann Roberts and Jamie L. Goldenberg (2007), "Wrestling with Nature: An Existential Perspective on the Body and Gender in Self-Conscious Emotions," in Jessica L. Tracy, Richard W. Robins, and June Price Tangney, eds., *The Self-Conscious Emotions: Theory and Research*, pp. 395–98 (New York: Guilford).

46. June P. Tangney (1990), "Assessing Individual Differences in Proneness to Shame and Guilt: Development of the Self-Conscious Affect and Attribution Inventory," *Journal of Personality and Social Psychology* 59: 102–11.

47. I am grateful to Estelle Friedman for her lecture to my class on guilt and gender that pointed out some of these issues.

48. Martin Hoffman (1977), "Sex Differences in Empathy and Related Behaviors," *Psychological Bulletin* 84(4): 712–22.

49. Carol Gilligan (1982), *In a Different Voice: Psychological Theory and Women's Development*, p. 139 (Cambridge, MA: Harvard University Press).

50. Grace K. Baruch (1988), "Reflections on Guilt, Women and Gender," Working Paper No. 176 (Wellesley, MA: Wellesley College, Center for Research on Women).

51. I heard statements like this many times in interviews with Stanford graduates ten years out of college. See Herant Katchadourian and John Boli (1994), *Cream of the Crop: The Impact of Elite Education on the Decade After College* (New York: Basic Books).

52. Sources in James Q. Wilson (1993), *The Moral Sense*, p. 181 (New York: Free Press).

53. Miller (1994).

54. I am grateful for Estelle Freedman's lecture on feminist ethics to my seminar.

55. Alison Jaggar (2001), "Feminist Ethics," in Becker and Becker (2001), vol. 2, pp. 528–39.

56. Rosemarie Tong (1999), "Feminist Philosophy," in Audi, ed. (1999), pp. 305–7.

57. Wilson (1993), p. 182.

58. Robert Kliegman et al., eds. (2007), *Nelson Textbook of Pediatrics*, 18th ed., pp. 121–22 (Philadelphia: Saunders).

59. Richard A. Friedman (2008), "Who Are We? Coming of Age on Antidepressants," *New York Times*, Apr. 15, p. D5.

60. Benjamin J. Sadock and Virginia A. Sadock, eds. (2005), *Comprehensive Textbook of Psychiatry*, 8th ed., vol. 2, p. 45 (Philadelphia: Lippincott Williams & Wilkins).

61. For a popular book, see Michel Borba (2001), *Building Moral Intelligence:*

The Seven Essential Virtues That Teach Kids To Do the Right Thing (San Francisco: Jossey-Bass).

62. For a general discussion of these issues, see June P. Tangney and Rhonda L. Dearing (2002), *Shame and Guilt*, pp. 181–94 (New York: Guilford).

Notes to Chapter 7

1. Konrad Z. Lorenz (1954), *Man Meets Dog*, tr. Marjorie Kerr Wilson, pp. 186–87 (London: Methuen).

2. For a good exposition of these issues, see James Q. Wilson (not to be confused with E. O. Wilson of sociobiology fame) (1993), *The Moral Sense* (New York: Free Press).

3. Jerome B. Schneewind (1999), "Natural Law," in Robert Audi, ed. (1999), *The Cambridge Dictionary of Philosophy*, 2nd ed., pp. 599–600 (Cambridge, UK: Cambridge University Press).

4. Quoted in Bertrand Russell (1946/1996), *History of Western Philosophy*, p. 568 (London: Routledge).

5. Quoted in Richard Joyce (2006), *The Evolution of Morality*, p. 3 (Cambridge, MA: MIT Press).

6. Quoted in Bernard Gert (1999), "Hobbes," in Audi (1999), p. 388.

7. Jean-Jacques Rousseau (1762/1979), *Emile*, tr. Allan Bloom (New York: Basic Books).

8. Darwin's (1859/1968) landmark *Origin of the Species* (New York: Penguin), which established the principles of natural selection, had little to say about human evolution. It was followed twelve years later by Darwin (1871/1981), *The Descent of Man and Selection in Relation to Sex* (Princeton, NJ: Princeton University Press), which applied the theory of evolution, including the evolution of moral sentiments, more directly to humans. However, Darwin's followers focused on the biology of evolution for the next hundred years rather than its behavioral aspects.

9. Robert Sapolsky (personal communication) points out that group selection, in a more specialized form, is making a comeback, as part of increased recognition of "multi-level selection." Also see D. S. Wilson and E. O. Wilson (2007), "Rethinking the Theoretical Foundation of Sociobiology," *Quarterly Review of Biology* 82: 327.

10. Edward O. Wilson (1975), *Sociobiology: The New Synthesis* (Cambridge, MA: Harvard University Press). The word was first used by Stuart Altman.

11. Richard Dawkins (1976/1989), *The Selfish Gene* (Oxford: Oxford University Press).

12. See for instance, Robert Wright (1995), *The Moral Animal. Why We Are the Way We Are: The New Science of Evolutionary Psychology* (New York: Random House); Jerome H. Barkow, Leda Cosmides, and John Tooby (1992), *The Adapted Mind: Evolutionary Psychology and the Generation of Culture* (New York: Oxford University Press).

For more recent accounts, see Marc D. Hauser (2006), *Moral Minds: How Nature Designed Our Universal Sense of Right or Wrong* (New York: Harper Collins); Joyce (2006). In their second incarnation, the ideas of sociobiology have received much more public acceptance, despite their having the same limitations.

13. For a discussion of the naturalistic fallacy see, Joyce (2006), pp. 146–56.

14. William Durham, lecture to seminar.

15. The ancestral environment is the period during which most human behavioral patterns were shaped. It stretched over a hundred thousand years, culminating in the Pleistocene epoch, which ended with the last ice age, about 10,000 years ago.

16. Joyce (2006), p. 75, emphasis in the original.

17. Primates include monkeys, apes, and humans. Apes include gorillas and chimpanzees, both of which are highly social; chimpanzees (including bonobos) are our closest evolutionary relatives. Nevertheless, a vast gap separates us from them in many respects, including cognitive functions and use of language. Contrary to common caricatures, humans did not descend from apes—what we share with them is a common ancestor who lived some 25 million years ago and from which these various species evolved. Frans de Waal (1996), *Good Natured: The Origins of Right and Wrong in Humans and Other Animals* (Cambridge, MA: Harvard University Press); Frans de Waal (2006), *Primates and Philosophers: How Morality Evolved* (Princeton, NJ: Princeton University Press).

18. Jason Stanley, "Chomsky." In Audi (1999), pp. 138–9.

19. The linguistic parallel between language and morality is the anchor of Hauser (2006).

20. Whether the basis of these intuitive judgments relies on emotion or reason depends on the particular philosophical point of view we adopt. For a comparison of models based on Kant, Hume, and Rawls, see ibid., p. 45.

21. We get half of our genes from one parent and the other half from the other parent. Identical twins have the same genes; siblings share half of their genes, and so on.

22. Robert L. Trivers (1971), "The Evolution of Reciprocal Altruism," *Quarterly Review of Biology* 46: 35–56.

23. Wright (1995), ch. 9.

24. The element of kin selection confounds this picture. Male baboons leave their natal group at puberty; thus, adult males in a baboon troop are nonrelatives. In contrast, it is the female who leaves the troop among chimps—thus the adult males in a chimp group are relatives or, at least, have known each other their whole lives. Robert Sapolsky, personal communication.

25. It may also be hard to know the impact of one's actions on another person. Occasionally, a former student will tell me, "What you told me twenty ago changed my life." When I ask what that was, the answer often sounds like fortune-cookie wisdom

("Never give up"). I used to make light of it until I realized it hurt the student's feelings. So now I thank the person instead.

26. Arthur C. Brooks (2007), *Wall Street Journal*, Sept. 24. I would like to thank Linda Hoffman for bringing this source to my attention.

27. Leda Cosmides and John Tooby (1992), "Cognitive Adaptations for Social Exchange," in Jerome Barkow, ed. (1992), *The Adapted Mind: Evolutionary Psychology and the Generation of Culture*, pp. 163–228 (New York: Oxford University Press).

28. Robert Sapolsky (personal communication) points out that there is a literature emerging on reciprocal altruism, which includes cheating even in life forms like the amoeba.

29. Trivers (1971), p. 36.

30. Cheater detection is also discussed in Matt Ridley (1994), *The Red Queen: Sex and the Evolution of Human Nature* (New York: Macmillan).

31. Peter Singer (1981), *The Expanding Circle* (New York: Farrar, Straus and Giroux).

32. Quoted in Wright (1995), p. 372.

33. Several philosophers and evolutionary psychologists debate this issue in de Waal (2006). Also see Nicholas Wade (2007), "Scientist Finds the Beginnings of Morality in Primate Behavior," *New York Times*, Mar. 20, p. D3.

34. Jennifer L. Goetz and Dacher Keltner (2007), "Shifting Meanings of Self-Conscious Emotions across Cultures," in Jessica L. Tracy, Richard W. Robins, and June Price Tangney (2007), *The Self-Conscious Emotions: Theory and Research*, pp. 153–73 (New York: Guilford).

35. Sarah I. Johnson, ed. (2004), *Religions of the Ancient World* (Cambridge, MA: Harvard Universtity Press).

36. For general discussions of primal religions, see David S. Noss and John B. Noss (1994), *A History of the World's Religions*, 9th ed. (New York: Macmillan College Publishing Co.); Claude Levi-Strauss (1966), *The Savage Mind* (Chicago: University of Chicago Press); Mircea Eliade (1959), *The Sacred and the Profane* (New York: Harcourt Brace Jovanovich); Sir James G. Frazer (1890/1996), *The Illustrated Golden Bough*, abridged by R. K. G. Temple (New York: Simon and Schuster).

37. Frazer (1890/1996).

38. Taboos persist in modern societies in attenuated forms. For instance, there is the prohibition against eating pork in Judaism and Islam. The protocol for dealing with heads of state and high-ranking religious leaders prohibits touching them except in prescribed ways (you cannot hug Queen Elizabeth or the pope no matter how respectful you may feel toward them).

39. Sigmund Freud (1913), *Totem and Taboo*, in James Strachey, ed. and tr. (1953–74), *The Standard Edition of the Complete Psychological Works of Sigmund Freud*, vol. 13

(London: Hogarth). In *The Future of an Illusion* (1927), Freud extended these speculations to reconstruct the origins of religion. Strachey (1953–74), vol. 21, pp. 3–56. Such
interpretations reduce religion to an elaborate set of superstitions and myths. Current
views among evolutionists on the value of religion range from the hostile to the more
accepting.

40. Freud/Strachey (1953–74). Emphasis in original.

41. Ruth Benedict (1946), *The Chrysanthemum and the Sword* (Boston: Houghton
Mifflin). The symbolism in Benedict's title is based on chrysanthemums being grown
in Japan in a highly scripted manner, with a wire rack holding each petal in its place
(the point is that these flowers are also beautiful naturally without such props and
drastic pruning). Similarly, the sword stands not only for the warrior cult but also for
a more personal code of conduct for a self-responsible person. For a current view, see
Christopher Shannon (1995), "A World Made Safe for Differences: Ruth Benedict's *The
Chrysanthemum and the Sword*," *American Quarterly* 47(4): 659–80.

42. Takie S. Lebra (1983), "Shame and Guilt: A Psycho-cultural View of the Japanese Self," *Ethos* 11: 192–209.

43. Millie R. Creighton (1990), "Revisiting Shame and Guilt Cultures: A Forty-
Year Pilgrimage," *Ethos* 18(3): 279–307.

44. Benedict (1946), pp. 222–24.

45. Joan G. Miller (1994), "Cultural Diversity in the Morality of Caring: Individually Oriented Versus Duty-Based Interpersonal Moral Codes," *Cross-Cultural Research*
28(1): 3–39.

46. Ibid., p. 6.

47. Miller (1994).

48. Olwen Bedford and Kwang-Kuo Hwang (2003), "Guilt and Shame in Chinese
Culture: A Cultural Framework from the Perspective of Morality and Identity," *Journal for the Theory of Social Behavior* 33(2): 127–44.

49. Mark Berkson, "Shame, Guilt and Conceptions of the Self: A Confucian Perspective," unpublished manuscript.

50. Bernard Williams (1993), *Shame and Necessity* (Berkeley: University of California Press). Williams ascribes this misperception to the "progressivist" view that
sees the Western moral consciousness to have evolved by becoming more sophisticated over time. According to this view, the ethical consciousness of Homer was
primitive and unreflective and his heroes childish characters governed by shame.
This had been gradually replaced by guilt by the time of the great philosophers and
tragedians. Yet the full notion of moral guilt, with its implications for freedom
and autonomy, was only attained by the modern Western consciousness. Williams
points out that Homer is full of the need for reparation and compensation, which
are typical components of guilt and essential for justice. While Homeric societies

relied heavily on shame, they did not fail to recognize guilt, even if they did not turn it into the special entity that we have come to recognize as such. This example points, once again, to the futility of making sharp distinctions between guilt and shame, devaluing one over the other, and trying to understand them outside of their cultural contexts.

Notes to Chapter 8

1. Some 30 percent of Americans are considered religious by attending houses of worship at least once a week; 20 percent are secular and never attend; the rest attend sometimes but irregularly. These figures have changed relatively little over the past several decades. *Wall Street Journal*, Sept. 24, 2007, p. A18.

2. Saint Augustine (397/1998), *Confessions*, tr. Henry Chadwick (Oxford: Oxford University Press). For an excellent biography, see Peter Brown (1975), *Augustine of Hippo* (Berkeley: University of California Press). Also see James J. O'Donnell (2005), *Augustine: A New Biography* (San Francisco: Harper Collins).

3. Saint Augustine (397/1998), p. 29.

4. Ibid., p. 24.

5. Ibid., p. 28.

6. Ibid., p. 35.

7. For a brief overview of the relationship of sin to guilt, see André LaCocque (2005), "Sin and Guilt," in Lindsay Jones, ed. (2005), *Encyclopedia of Religion*, vol. 12, pp. 8402–7 (Detroit: Thomson Gale).

8. Ernlé Young, personal communication.

9. For a general introduction to Judaism, see Jacob Neusner (1993), "Judaism," in Arvind Sharma, ed. (1993), *Our Religions*, pp. 293–355 (San Francisco: Harper). There are good introductions to all of the monotheistic religions in Huston Smith (1991), *The World's Religions* (San Francisco: Harper), and David S. Noss and John B. Noss (1994), *A History of the World's Religions*, 9th ed. (New York: Macmillan).

10. Harlan J. Wechsler (1990), *What's So Bad about Guilt? Learning to Live With It Since We Can't Live Without It*, p. 30 (New York: Simon and Schuster).

11. *Mahzor for Rosh Hashanah and Yom Kippur: A Prayer Book for the Days of Awe* (1972), tr. and ed. Jules Harlow (New York: Rabbinical Assembly).

12. Quoted in Neusner (1993), p. 345.

13. For an overview of these divisions within Judaism, see ibid., pp. 309–10.

14. *Tanakh: The Holy Scriptures* (1985) (Philadelphia: Jewish Publication Society). The significance of the Torah for modern American Jews is discussed in Arnold M. Eisen (1996), *Taking Hold of Torah: Jewish Commitment and Community in America* (Bloomington: Indiana University Press). Over a thousand years separate the earliest from the latest compositions in the Hebrew scriptures, which cover a wide variety of

literary styles and subject matters. By contrast, the New Testament was written in less than a century, and the Qur'an in a few decades.

15. J. Lachowski (2003), "Guilt in the Bible," in *New Catholic Encyclopedia*, 2nd ed., vol. 6, pp. 569–72 (Detroit: Thomson Gale).

16. Geoffrey Wigoder, ed. (2002), *The New Encyclopedia of Judaism*, p. 252 (New York: New York University Press).

17. Moshe Sokol (2001), "Jewish Ethics," in Lawrence C. Becker and Charlotte B. Becker, eds. (2001), *Encyclopedia of Ethics*, vol. 2, pp. 909–15 (New York: Routledge).

18. Sokol (2001).

19. I am grateful to Estelle Halevi and Mark Mancall for their help with the Hebrew terminology.

20. E. Y. Kutscher (1969), "Words and Their History," *Ariel* 25: 64–74; also see, David Steinberg, "Body Part Metaphors in Biblical Hebrew," www.adath-shalom.ca/body_metaphors_bib_hebrew.htm.

21. The Revised Standard Version of the Christian Bible translates "reins" as "mind" in the first instance, and the passage reads, "When my soul was embittered, when I was pricked in my heart."

22. Diacritical marks have been largely omitted since those who know the foreign language do not need them and those who do not may not be able to make sense of them.

23. R. J. Zvi Werblowski and Geoffrey Wigoder, eds. (1997), *Oxford Dictionary of the Jewish Religion* (New York: Oxford University Press).

24. *Asham* has the same root as *ashamnu*—"we have trespassed"—which invokes another basic notion connected with guilt involving crossing a line, intruding into someone else's territory (be it your neighbor's house or spouse). One trespasses by stepping out of the moral bounds set by God. (A related term is *'avera*, which means "crossing over.") When guilty of a trespass, offering sacrifice and compensating the victim were not enough. The offender had to make a public confession in front of the community.

25. After sacrifice was no longer practiced in Judaism, one prayed to God for forgiveness (instead of making a sin offering) and gave to charity (instead of making a guilt offering.)

26. Werblowski and Wigoder (1997), p. 742.

27. Daniel Boyarim (1993), *Carnal Israel: Reading Sex in Talmudic Culture* (Berkeley: University of California Press); G. Larue (1983), *Sex in the Bible* (Buffalo, NY: Prometheus). For an overview of sexuality in various religious traditions, see Herant Katchadourian (1989), *Fundamentals of Human Sexuality*, 5th ed. (Fort Worth: Harcourt Brace).

28. Steven Goldsmith, lecture to seminar.

29. Harold S. Kushner (1983), *When Bad Things Happen to Good People* (New York: Avon).

30. Zionism and the state of Israel are secular but Judaism exerts great influence in both Israel as well as the Diaspora.

31. Philip Roth (1994), *Portnoy's Complaint*, p. 124 (New York: Vintage).

32. Martin Buber (1988), "Guilt and Guilt Feelings," in *The Knowledge of Man* (Atlantic Highlands, NJ: Humanities Press).

33. For a general introduction to Christianity, see Harvey Cox (1993), "Christianity," in Sharma (1993), pp. 359–422.

34. Joseph Klausner (1925), *Jesus of Nazareth: His Life, Times, and Teaching*, tr. from the original Hebrew by Herbert Danby (New York: Macmillan).

35. I am grateful to Robert Gregg for his help with the Greek terminology as well as his broader critique of the chapter.

36. The Greek word for shame is *aschemosunen*, meaning indecency. The root for shameful is from "shapeless," in the sense of being without moral form or *schema*.

37. Garry Wills (2006), *What Paul Meant* (New York: Viking).

38. Krister Stendahl (1976), *Paul among Jews and Gentiles* (Philadelphia: Fortress).

39. I am grateful to Robert Gregg for his invaluable help with the teachings of St. Paul and St. Augustine, in particular with respect to the concept of Original Sin. Gregg points out that a curious error in translation may have contributed to Augustine's views. In the Greek original (and in English) Romans 5:12 has the phrase, "because all men sinned," referring to the following of the example of Adam, which resulted in death spreading to humanity. In the Latin translation used by Augustine, the reference to Adam becomes "in whom," whereby sin originates in Adam and is transmitted subsequently to all humans thus making Adam's sin not the *model* but the *cause* of all human sins.

40. John Milton (1674/2000), *Paradise Lost*, Book IV, pp. 744–45 (London: Penguin).

41. Vern L. Bullough and James Brundage (1982), *Sexual Practices and the Medieval Church* (Buffalo, NY: Prometheus, 1982). Also see G. Ratray Taylor (1963), *Sex in History* (New York: Harper and Row).

42. Saint Augustine (397/1998), pp. 61, 145.

43. Bertrand Russell (1945), *A History of Western Philosophy*, p. 365 (New York: Simon and Schuster).

44. Scott Davis (2001), "History of Western Ethics: Early Medieval," in Becker and Becker (2001), vol. 10, pp. 709–14.

45. Jean Delumeau (1983), *Sin and Fear: The Emergence of a Western Guilt Culture*, tr. Eric Nicholson (New York: St. Martin's). The sexually repressive attitudes of the medieval church and the excesses of Christian ascetics are discussed in lurid detail in James Cleugh (1963), *Love Locked Out* (London: Spring Books). Some of these practices arose from psychological disorders, not the teachings of the church.

46. Ralph McInerny (2001), "Thomas Aquinas, St." in Becker and Becker (2001), vol. 3, pp. 1709–11.

47. St. Thomas Aquinas (1264–74/1989), *Summa Theologiae: A Concise Translation*, Timothy McDermott, ed. (Allen, TX: Christian Classics).

48. Katchadourian (1989), p. 585.

49. Kathiann M. Kowalski, "Youth Update 2000," www.americancatholic.org/Newsletter/YU/ayo600.asp.

50. Lewis Spitz, lecture to seminar.

51. Erik Erikson (1958), *Young Man Luther: A Study in Psychoanalysis and History* (New York: W. W. Norton).

52. Walter von Loewenich (1986), *Martin Luther: The Man and His Work*, p. 76 (Minneapolis: Augsburg).

53. Quoted in Erikson (1958), p. 258.

54. The Catholic church eventually came to the same view. See the Encyclical Letter of Pope Paul VI, *Humanae Vitae*, in Katchadourian (1989), p. 655.

55. Joel Osteen (2007), *Become a Better You*, p. 131 (New York: Free Press).

56. Joseph Fletcher (1966), *Situation Ethics: The New Morality* (Philadelphia: Westminster).

57. Katchadourian (1989), ch. 23.

58. Spirit*uality* should not be confused with spirit*ualism*, whose adherents believe that the dead can make contact with the living through a medium.

59. For an overview of spirituality, see Mary MacDonald (2005), "Spirituality," in Jones (2005), vol. 13, pp. 1718–21. There are some highly popular books on this subject, such as Thomas Moore's *The Care of the Soul: A Guide for Cultivating Sacredness in Everyday Life* (New York: Harper, 1992).

60. I am grateful to Nancy McGaraghan for pointing out to me these new currents within Catholicism.

61. Jeffrey Kripal (2007), *Esalen: America and the Religion of No Religion* (Chicago: University of Chicago Press).

62. "American Spirituality: Where 'California' Bubbled Up," *The Economist*, Dec. 22, 2007.

63. Jane Hirshfield, ed. (1994), *Women in Praise of the Sacred: 43 Centuries of Spiritual Poetry by Women*, p. 44 (New York: Harper Collins).

64. For an introduction to her life and work, see Michael A. Sells, ed. (1996), *Early Islamic Mysticism*, ch. 4 (New York: Paulist Press). The fact that Rabi'a could reach such an eminent position in a highly patriarchal society is extraordinary but not without precedent. A'isha, a wife of the Prophet Muhammad, played a formative and critical role in early Islam.

65. Islam is both a religion (with over a billion adherents) as well as a civilization (encompassing more than fourteen centuries). Although Islam is commonly associated with Arabs, most Muslims live in Asia, with Indonesia having the largest number in the world. Arabs account for fewer than 20 percent of Muslims, although most Arabs are

Muslim. The more recent term "Islamist" refers to political or "fundamentalist" Islam (terms that Muslims do not apply to themselves). For a general discussions of Islam, I draw heavily from Seyyed Hossein Nasr (1993), "Islam," in Sharma (1993), pp. 427–532. For a short history, see Karen Armstrong (2002), *Islam* (New York: Modern Library).

66. John Kelsey (2001), "Islamic Ethics," in Becker and Becker (2001), vol. 2, pp. 889–94.

67. *Al-Qur'an* (1984), tr. Ahmed Ali (Princeton, NJ: Princeton University Press); Fazlur Rahman (1980), *Major Themes of the Qur'an* (Minneapolis, MN: Bibliotheca Islamica).

68. I am grateful to Ebrahim Musa and Shahzad Bashir for the clarification of Arabic terms and the concepts they represent.

69. The more inclusive term *ulama* refers to those learned in Islam, including theologians (*mutakallimun*), canon lawyers (*muftis*), judges (*qadis*), and high state religious officials, like the *shaikh ul-Islam*. The *imam* leads the prayer in the mosque (the term has a more special meaning for Shiites).

70. Vartan Gregorian (2003), *Islam: A Mosaic, Not a Monolith* (Washington, D.C.: Brookings Institution).

71. Qur'an 2:190.

72. P. W. Singer (2008), "What Do You Call a Terrorist?" *New York Times*, June 2, p. A21.

73. I am grateful to Ebrahim Musa for the quotations from the Qur'an and the Hadith.

74. Lila Abu-Lughod (1986), *Veiled Sentiments: Honor and Poetry in a Bedouin Society* (Berkeley: University of California Press).

75. For a discussion of major and minor sins in Islam, see Muhammad Qasim Zaman (2006), "Sin, Major and Minor," in Jane Dammen McAuliffe, ed. (2001–6), *Encyclopedia of the Qur'an*, vol. 5, pp. 19–27 (Leiden: Brill).

76. The Prophet was sensitive to how women should be treated sexually. He is said to have admonished his followers that a man should not fall upon his wife as a beast does; there has to be a messenger between them in the form of "kissing and talk." Moreover, men are advised to wait until their partners are satisfied during sex before terminating. For more details, see Devin J. Stewart, "Sex and Sexuality" (2004), in McAuliffe (2001–6), vol. 4, pp. 580–85.

77. Muhammad has been criticized for marrying A'isha when she was still a child. However, A'isha continued to live with her parents and the marriage was not consummated until she had reached puberty. As noted earlier, St. Augustine too was engaged to a child and would have married her after she reached puberty if he had not taken monastic orders. (We need to judge people by the standards of their times even if we now reject those standards.)

78. See Preface by Carl W. Ernst to Sells (1996).

79. I am grateful to Hank Edson for these insights into Sufism. For more details on the Sufi perspective, see Nahid Angha (1991), *Principles of Sufism* (Fremont, CA: Jain).

80. Wechsler (1990), p. 140.

81. Uri Rubin (2004), "Repentance and Penance," in McAuliffe (2001–6), vol. 4, pp. 426–30.

82. Daniel C. Peterson (2002), "Forgiveness," in McAuliffe (2001–6), vol. 2, pp. 244–45.

83. Bahar Dava (2000), "Forgiveness," in Oliver Leaman, ed. (2000), *The Qur'an: An Encyclopedia*, pp. 213–16 (London: Routledge, 2000).

84. J. Jenson (2003), "Redemption in the Bible," in *New Catholic Encyclopedia*, 2nd ed., vol. 11, pp. 963–73 (Detroit: Thomson Gale).

85. *Notes on the Spiritual Exercises of St. Ignatius of Loyola* (1985), ed. David L. Fleming, S.J. (St. Louis: Review for Religious). See in particular, "Consciousness Examen" by George A. Aschenbrenner, S.J., vol. 31, pp. 14–21. I am grateful to Nancy McGaraghan for bringing this source to my attention.

86. For the original version of the Consciousness Examen, see *The Spiritual Exercises of St. Ignatius* (2000), tr. Louis J. Puhl, S.J., p. 44 (New York: Random House).

Notes to Chapter 9

1. Mohandas K. Gandhi (1929/1970), *The Collected Works of Mahatma Gandhi*, vol. 39, chap. 10, pp. 29–30 (Ahmadabad: Ministry of Information and Broadcasting).

2. I am grateful to Mark Mancall for this observation.

3. Erik Erikson (1969), *Gandhi's Truth: On the Origins of Militant Nonviolence*, p. 128 (New York: W. W. Norton).

4. Quoted in ibid., p. 124.

5. Gandhi (1929/1970), p. 23.

6. *The Moral and Political Writings of Mahatma Gandhi* (1986), Raghavan Iyer, ed., vol. 2, p. 131 (New York: Oxford University Press).

7. Tu Wei-ming (1993), "Confucianism," in Arvind Sharma, ed. (1993), *Our Religions*, pp. 141–227 (San Francisco: Harper Collins).

8. I am grateful to Mark Mancall for his invaluable help in connection with the discussion of Hinduism. Among secondary sources I have relied on are Arvind Sharma (1993), "Hinduism," in Sharma (1993); Huston Smith (1991a), "Hinduism," in *The World's Religions*, ch. 1 (San Francisco: Harper); David S. Noss and John Noss (1994), *A History of the World's Religions*, 9th ed., pp. 105–6 (New York: Macmillan).

9. Smith (1991a), p. 60.

10. The Vedas were compiled around 1200 BCE. They come closest to revelations and include devotional hymns (*mantras*), priestly texts, and esoteric philosophical writings. In the post-Vedic period, new religious sentiments found expression in the Upanishads, which came to embody the history, laws, and religious philosophy of

Hinduism. The Puranas, which appeared in the tenth century BCE, are tales about gods and god-like heroes. Their antagonists are demons, but they are not evil beings; Hinduism has only evil acts. Tantras deal with the cultic aspects of Hinduism and some of them use sex as a religious vehicle. The medieval period of Hinduism began to take form after 500 BCE with the Ramayana and the Mahabharata.

11. *The Bhagavad Gita* (2000), tr. Eknath Easwaran (New York: Vintage).

12. Mohandas Gandhi (2000a), *Essential Writings*, selected by John Dear, p. 70 (Maryknoll, NY: Orbis).

13. I am grateful to Raka Ray and Shireen Pasha for their help with the Sanskrit and Urdu terms and for the examples that illustrate them.

14. Frank Reynolds (2001), "Hindu Ethics," in Lawrence C. Becker and Charlotte B. Becker, eds. (2001), *Encyclopedia of Ethics*, vol. 2, pp. 676–83 (New York: Routledge).

15. A number of Hindu concepts and practices, such as yoga and transcendental meditation (popularized by the Beatles), have been adopted in the West. There is also a Western version of Hinduism called *Vedanta* based on a Hindu philosophy. The Hare Krishnas, who take their name from a mantra they chant, became a common sight in American cities in the 1960s.

16. Noss and Noss (1994), p. 106.

17. Mahatma Gandhi (2000b), *The Bhagavat Gita According to Gandhi*, ed. John Stroheimer (Berkeley, CA: Berkeley Books).

18. Ariel Glucklich (2005), "Hindu Dharma," in Lindsay Jones, ed. (2005), *Encyclopedia of Religion*, vol. 3 (Detroit: Thomson Gale).

19. Smith (1991a), pp. 53–54.

20. Mark Mancall, lecture to seminar.

21. Smith (1991a), pp. 26–50.

22. Philip Rawson (1978), *The Art of Tantra* (New York: Oxford University Press).

23. The veneration of the cow in India (so baffling to outsiders) derives from the cow as a symbol of motherhood through the giving of milk, but the cow is neither sacred nor worshipped. The prohibition against the consumption of beef became a dogma in the seventeenth century, probably in imitation of the Islamic prohibition against pork.

24. Robert Gregg, personal communication.

25. Mark Mancall, lecture to seminar.

26. Buddhism developed into three main schools or "Vehicles": Theravada, Mahayana (which includes Zen Buddhism), and Vajrayana Buddhism. Their conceptions of guilt differ somewhat but not fundamentally enough to warrant dealing with them separately here.

27. Many of the core concepts of Buddhism were first brought to my attention by Carl Bielefeldt in his lectures to my seminar. The secondary sources on Buddhism that I have relied on include Masao Abe (1993), "Buddhism," in Sharma (1993), ch. 2; and Huston Smith (1991b), "Buddhism," in *The World's Religions*, ch. 2 (San Francisco: Harper).

28. For instance, there is the "place of excrement," full of intensely hot dung of the bitterest taste that sinners must eat and then be consumed themselves by maggots. Or those who have killed a living creature and eaten it are themselves placed in an iron vat and cooked like beans. Genshin (ca. 985/1974), *The Essentials of Salvation*, tr. Philip B. Yampolsky, microfilm, p. 15 (New York: Columbia University Photographic Service). These hells also appear in Chinese Buddhism.

29. Dennis Hirota (2005), "Karma: Buddhist Concepts," in Jones (2005), vol. 5, pp. 5097–5101.

30. Smith (1991b), pp. 103–12.

31. Hsueh-li Cheng (2001), "Buddhist Ethics," in Becker and Becker (2001), vol. 1, pp. 163–69.

32. Smith (1991b), p. 113.

33. Modified from Donald S. Lopez, Jr. (1988), *The Heart Sutra Explained: Indian and Tibetan Commentaries* (Albany: State University of New York Press).

34. I am grateful to Kendri Smith for the observations in this section, which were communicated to one of my students who then shared them with me.

35. *Dhammapada: The Way of Truth* (2001), tr. Sangharakshita, ch. 18, verses 244–45 (Birmingham, AL: Windhorse).

36. www.mahindarama.com/e-library/hiriotap.html.

37. "The Practices & Vows of Samantabadra Bodhisattva," Avatamsaka Sutra, ch. 40, http://buddhism.kalachakranet.org/guilt.html.

38. http://buddhism.kalachakranet.org/guilt.htm.

39. Venerable Henepola Gunaratana (1992), *Mindfulness in Plain English* (Boston: Wisdom Publications).

40. Transcript of talks given by the Dalai Lama in *Beyond Dogma: The Challenge of the Modern World* (1996), tr. Alison Anderson and Mariarne Dresser (Berkeley, CA: North Atlantic Books). Source provided by Mark Berkson.

41. I am grateful to Mark Berkson and Lee Yearley for their invaluable help with Confucian concepts of shame and guilt.

The primary texts in Confucianism consist of the teachings of Confucius and Mencius. See Confucius (1984), *Analects*, tr. D. C. Lau (New York: Penguin); Mencius (2003), *Mencius*, tr. D. C. Lau, revised ed. (New York: Penguin). The secondary sources I have used include Tu (1993), Smith (1991b), and Noss and Noss (1994).

42. Currently, about 40 percent of the population of China is reported to be nonreligious; 28 percent follow folk religious traditions, and about 9 percent (40 million) are Christian and an equal number are Buddhist. Confucianism is not listed as a religious category. *National Geographic*, May 2008, p. 14.

43. A. C. Cua (2001), "Confucian Ethics," in Becker and Becker (2001), vol. 1, pp. 287–95.

44. Ying Wong and Jeanne Tsai (2007), "Cultural Models of Shame and Guilt," in

Jessica L. Tracy, Richard W. Robbins, and June Price Tangney, eds. (2007), *The Self-Conscious Emotions: Theory and Research* (New York: Guilford).

45. Mark Berkson (n.d.), "Shame, Guilt and Conceptions of the Self: A Confucian Perspective," unpublished manuscript, p. 3.

46. I am grateful to Lee Yearley for pointing out to me these historical elements in the Chinese views on guilt.

47. Tu (1993), p. 206.

48. A gentleman is not quite a sage, who was the ideal human being. Confucius did not consider himself a sage nor had he ever met one personally.

49. David Hinton (1998), Introduction to Confucius, *Analects*, p. xxv (New York: Counterpoint).

50. *Analects* 13:20.

51. *Analects* 2:3.

52. Hinton (1998), pp. 247–48.

53. *Analects* 1:4.

54. *Analects* 15:20.

55. *Mencius*, book 2, part A, p. 38.

56. Modified from handout given to my seminar by Lee Yearley on Mencius's list of virtues.

57. Hinton (1998), p. 247.

58. Cua (2001), p. 292.

59. Not to be confused with *qi* (*ch'i*), which refers to breath, vital energy, the life force (as in *tai ch'i*).

60. Cua (2001), p. 293.

61. Lee Yearley, lecture of seminar.

62. Berkson (n.d.).

63. I am grateful to Jindong Cai and Sheila Melvin for these observations. Sheila Melvin and Rachel Zhu were most helpful with Chinese terms and their illustrative examples.

64. Lee Yearley, personal communication.

Notes to Chapter 10

1. There is a good deal of philosophy that is readily accessible to those who are willing to make some effort. For a good example, see Bertrand Russell (1945), *A History of Western Philosophy* (New York: Simon and Schuster). Some modern philosophers are particularly interested in the psychology of guilt and shame. See for instance, Bernard Williams (1993), *Shame and Necessity* (Berkeley: University of California Press); Gabrielle Taylor (1985), *Pride, Shame and Guilt* (Oxford: Oxford University Press). Guilt is also addressed within the wider context of ethics and justice in John Rawls (1999), *A Theory of Justice*, revised ed. (Cambridge, MA: Harvard University

Press); Peter Singer (1993), *Practical Ethics*, 2nd ed. (Cambridge, UK: Cambridge University Press).

2. Walter Kaufmann (1968), *Nietzsche: Philosopher, Psychologist, Antichrist*, 3rd ed., pp. 23–24 (Princeton, NJ: Princeton University Press).

3. Aristotle (ca. 335 BCE/2002), *On Poetics*, tr. Seth Bernardete and Michael Davis (South Bend, IN: St. Augustine's).

4. In 1940, in *An Outline of Psycho-Analysis*, Freud wrote, "I venture to assert that if psychoanalysis could boast of no other achievement than the discovery of the Oedipus complex, that alone would give it claim to be counted among the precious new acquisitions of mankind." Sigmund Freud (1940/1949), *An Outline of Psycho-Analysis*, p. 97 (New York: Norton). Currently, most behavioral scientists reject the notion that the Oedipus complex is a normative part of human development.

5. Lowell Edmunds (1985), *Oedipus: The Ancient Legend and Its Later Analogues* (Baltimore: Johns Hopkins University Press).

6. Sophocles (ca. 5th c. BCE/1984a), *Oedipus the King*, in *The Three Theban Plays*, tr. Robert Fagles (New York: Penguin). In his introduction, Bernard Know calls the play "the dramatic masterpiece of the Greek theater."

7. Sophocles (ca. 5th c. BCE/1984b), *Oedipus at Colonus*, in *The Three Theban Plays*, lines 1106 and 1112, emphasis in the original.

8. Ibid., lines 1104–5, 1129–30. I am grateful to Marsh McCall and the late Anthony Raubitschek for their discussion of the tragedy of Oedipus in my seminar.

9. The tragedy of Oedipus and its significance continue to attract critical attention. For an overview, see Sarah Boxer (1997), "How Oedipus Is Losing His Complex," *New York Times*, Dec. 6, p. A13.

10. I am grateful to Lanier Anderson for pointing out how Oedipus can serve as a metaphor for philosophical inquiry.

11. John Deigh (1999), "Ethics," in Robert Audi, ed. (1999), *The Cambridge Dictionary of Philosophy*, pp. 284–89 (Cambridge, UK: Cambridge University Press). On moral psychology as a branch of philosophical ethics, see Laurence Thomas (2001), "Moral Psychology," in Lawrence C. Becker and Charlotte B. Becker, eds. (2001), *Encyclopedia of Ethics*, vol. 2, pp. 1145–51 (New York: Routledge); Julia Annas (2001), "Ethics and Morality," in Becker and Becker (2001), pp. 485–87. For a readily accessible and interesting introduction to moral philosophy see, Jacques P. Thiroux (2004), *Ethics: Theory and Practice*, 8th ed. (Upper Saddle River, NJ: Prentice Hall).

12. For a general introduction, see Richard Kraut (1999), "Socrates," pp. 859–60, and "Plato," pp. 709–13, in Audi (1999).

13. Plato (ca. 380 BCE/1992), *The Republic*, tr. G. M. A. Grube and revised by C. D. C. Reeve (Indianapolis: Hackett).

14. Aristotle (ca. 350 BCE/2004), *The Nicomachean Ethics*, tr. J. A. K. Thompson (London: Penguin). In the following discussion I make extensive use of the excellent

introduction by Jonathan Barnes. Aristotle refers to his book as *Ta Ethika*—literally "the ethics." But it means something more like, "matters to do with character." Similarly, *ethike arête*, which is usually translated as "moral virtue," actually means "excellence of character" (introduction, p. xxv).

15. Michael V. Wedin (1999), "Aristotle," pp. 44–51 in Audi (1999) .

16. For a list of virtues and vices, see Aristotle, *Ethics*, appendix 1, pp. 285–86.

17. Ibid., p. 110.

18. Ibid., pp. 93–99.

19. Ibid., p. 42.

20. Ibid., pp. 48–49.

21. Ibid., pp. 44–51.

22. Kenneth L. Woodward (1994), "What Is Virtue?" *Newsweek*, June 13.

23. Thiroux (2004), p. 55.

24. Sigmund Freud (1927), *Future of an Illusion*, James Strachey, ed. and tr. (1953–74), *The Standard Edition of the Complete Psychological Works of Sigmund Freud*, vol. 21, pp. 3–56 (London: Hogarth). I am grateful to Sanford Gifford for bringing this quote to my attention.

25. Roger J. Sullivan (1996), "Introduction," p. vii, in Immanuel Kant, *Metaphysics of Morals* (1797), ed. Mary Gregor (Cambridge, UK: Cambridge University Press).

26. Lanier Anderson's lectures on Kant, John S. Mill, and Friedrich Nietzsche to my seminar introduced me to their philosophies.

27. The main sources for Kant's ethical views are the *Groundwork for the Metaphysics of Morals* (1785), ed. Mary Gregor (1998), (Cambridge, UK: Cambridge University Press); and *The Metaphysics of Morals* (1797), ed. Mary Gregor (1996), (Cambridge, UK: Cambridge University Press). The *Groundwork* (1785) lays out the foundation of Kant's ethical theory by establishing his fundamental points in the search for the "supreme principle of morality." The *Metaphysics* (which was published twelve years later) gives a more detailed explanation of moral duties and their application to a variety of ethical issues, such as suicide. The *Critique of Practical Reason* (1788) acts as a bridge between the two texts. Translated by Mary Gregor (1997), in *Immanuel Kant: Practical Philosophy* (Cambridge, UK: Cambridge University Press). Also see Immanuel Kant (1781/1998), *Critique of Pure Reason*, tr. Paul Guyer and Allen Wood (Cambridge, UK: Cambridge University Press). I have made good use of Christine M. Korsgaard's introduction to the *Groundwork* (1999) and her article on Kant in Becker and Becker (2001), vol. 2, pp 929–39; and the introduction to the *Metaphysics* by Roger J. Sullivan.

28. Kant, *Groundwork*, p. 12, emphasis in the original.

29. Robert Audi (2004), *The Good and the Right: A Theory of Intuition and Intrinsic Value*, p. 90 (Princeton, NJ: Princeton University Press).

30. Ibid., p. 90.

31. Kant, *Groundwork*, p. 39.

32. Kant, *Metaphysics*, p. 189, emphasis in the original.

33. Korsgaard (2001), p. 934.

34. Kant, *Metaphysics*, p. 178.

35. Ibid., p. 179, emphasis in the original.

36. Herant Katchadourian (1989), *Fundamentals of Human Sexuality*, 5th ed., pp. 327–31 (Fort Worth: Harcourt Brace).

37. Kant, *Metaphysics*, pp. 198–217.

38. Korsgaard (2001), p. 933.

39. Rawls (1999).

40. Ibid., p. 225.

41. John Marshall (2001), "Kantian Ethics," in Becker and Becker (2001), vol. 2, pp. 939–43.

42. For a discussion of the ambiguities in this formulation, see Robert Audi (2007), "Can Utilitarianism Be Distributive? Maximization and Distribution as Criteria in Managerial Decisions," *Business Ethics Quarterly* 17(4): 593–612.

43. Richard Brandt (1999), "Jeremy Bentham," in Audi (1999), pp. 79–81. Also see David Lyons (2001), "Utilitarianism," in Becker and Becker (2001), vol. 3, pp. 1737–44.

44. Oskar Piest (1957), introduction to John Stuart Mill, *Utilitarianism* (first published in 1861) (New York: Macmillan).

45. Dan W. Brock (1999), "Utilitarianism," in Audi (1999), pp. 942–44.

46. John Stuart Mill (1861/1957), *Utilitarianism*, tr. Oskar Piest (New York: Macmillan).

47. Piest (1957), p. vii.

48. That Mill should have recourse to such psychological mechanisms to fulfill a moral role is understandable given the increasing prevalence of psychological ideas in the late nineteenth century. The prevalent psychological theory at the time was *associationism*, which considered the association of ideas as the primary basis of learning, intelligent thought, and behavior. This principle is preserved in modern behaviorist models like conditioning. George A. Graham (1999), "Associationism," in Audi (1999), p. 58.

49. Mill, *Utilitarianism*, p. 40.

50. Ibid., p. 42.

51. Thiroux (2004), p. 42.

52. Ibid., p. 44.

53. David Lyons (2001), "Utilitarianism," in Becker and Becker (2001), vol. 3, pp. 1373–1744; Thiroux (2004).

54. Ayn Rand (1992; first published in 1957), *Atlas Shrugged*, appendix (New York: Dutton). Rand's books have sold over 20 million copies and continue to be popular. Though she taught in several major universities, her work has received scant attention from established academic philosophers.

55. Friedrich Nietzsche (1908/1969), *Ecce Homo*, preface, tr. Walter Kaufmann (New York: Vintage).

56. Curtis Cate (2002), *Friedrich Nietzsche*, p. 257 (London: Hutchinson).

57. Kaufmann (1968), p. 21, emphasis in the original.

58. Nietzsche, *Ecce Homo*, appendix two. Nietzsche's ideas are like objects bundled in a lot bubble-wrap: you need to unpack them before they make sense.

59. Friedrich Nietzsche (1886/1973), *Beyond Good and Evil: Prelude to a Philosophy of the Future*, tr. R. J. Hollingdale, pp. 105, 107, 100, 98 (Harmondsworth: Penguin).

60. Van Harvey lecture to seminar.

61. Quoted in Cate (2002), pp. 529, 531; emphasis in the original.

62. Friedrich Nietzsche (1887/1989), "First Essay," *On the Genealogy of Morals*, tr. Walter Kaufmann and R. J. Hollingdale (New York: Vintage).

63. Ibid.

64. The German word *Schlecht*, originally meaning "common," came to mean "bad." Similarly, the English word *villein*, which meant a villager, became villain—a bad person.

65. Nietzsche, *Beyond Good and Evil*.

66. Friedrich Nietzsche (1887/1969), *On the Genealogy of Morals*, pp. 59–60 (New York: Vintage), emphasis in the original.

67. Ibid., p. 85.

68. Nietzsche, *Beyond Good and Evil*, p. 98.

69. Ibid., p. 79.

70. Richard Schacht (2001), "Friedrich Wilhelm Nietzsche," in Becker and Becker (2001), vol. 2, pp. 756–58.

71. Walter Kaufmann, Introduction to the *Genealogy* (1887/1969), p. 10.

72. Ibid.

73. Nietzsche (1887/1969), *Genealogy*, p. 88.

74. Rawls (1999), pp. 42–43.

Notes to Chapter 11

1. Fyodor Dostoevsky (1866/1993), *Crime and Punishment*, tr. Richard Pevear and Larissa Volokhonsky (London: Random House). For critical reviews see, Richard Peace, ed. (2006), *Fyodor Dostoevsky's "Crime and Punishment": A Case Book* (New York: Oxford University Press); Harold Bloom, ed. (2004), *Raskolnikov and Svidrigailov* (Philadelphia: Chelsea House).

2. Nihilism arose in Russia in the mid-1860s engaging the alienated children of the privileged classes influenced by liberal ideas from France and England. They questioned established social norms and fought for the independence of the individual, the equality of women, and other social reforms. While sincere in their beliefs, they came to be seen as political agitators bent on the destruction of the social order.

3. Dostoevsky (1866/1993), p. 518.

4. Ibid., p. 519.

5. Ibid., p. 343.

6. Ibid., p. 531, emphasis in the original.

7. Ibid., p. 544.

8. In Athens, bodies of citizens (which excluded women, foreigners, and slaves) dealt with various offences. The main court was the *Helaia*, which sat in a corner of the agora or the marketplace. It heard all cases other than those concerning offences by state officials and murder. State officials were judged by their peers in the *Boule*, the council of 500 elected citizens. Most cases of murder were tried in the court of the *Areopagus*, with juries numbering in the hundreds. Athenians also had a unique system of ostracism. When it would have been difficult to show in a court of law that an individual was a threat to democracy, he could be banished for ten years by popular vote. The votes were cast by writing the name of the accused on a shard (*ostrakon*), hence the word "ostracism."

9. Legal Information Institute, Cornell Law School, www.law.cornell.edu/wex/index.php/Common_law.

10. The American judicial system has two main branches: a *federal court system* and a *state court system*. Each system has three levels: lower courts (which determine guilt); courts of appeals (which rule on interpretations of law and procedural irregularities); and courts of last resort. The last, in the federal system, is the Supreme Court of the United States, whose primary function is to determine if laws are constitutional or consistent with the American constitution. The judgments of federal courts apply to all of the states; the jurisdictions of the state courts are limited to their particular states only.

11. *New York Times*, Apr. 23, 2008, p. 1.

12. "Prison Nation," editorial, *New York Times*, Mar. 10, 2008, p. A20; Adam Liptak (2007), "Lifers as Teenagers, Now Seeking Second Chance," *New York Times*, Oct. 17, pp. A1, 24. Also see, Bureau of Justice Statistics, www.ojp.usdoj.gov/bjs/prisons.htm.

13. Laurie L. Levenson (2005), *The Glannon Guide to Criminal Law*, p. 1. (New York: Aspen).

14. *Barber v. Superior Court*, 147 Cal. App. 3d 1006 (Cal. Ct. App. 1983); Levenson (2005), p. 22.

15. Richard Joyce (2006), *The Evolution of Morality* (Cambridge, MA: MIT Press).

16. Levenson (2005), p. 25.

17. The American Law Institute (ALI) was established in 1923 by a group of prominent American judges, lawyers, and law school professors to address defects such as the uncertainty and complexity in American law. To promote the clarification and simplification of American common law and its adaptation to changing social needs, the ALI publishes the Model Penal Code. Although courts are not bound by it, the code has proven highly influential in prompting and guiding legal reforms.

18. Levenson (2005), p. 91.

19. Justice Oliver Wendell Holmes in *Brown v. United States*, 256 U.S. 335, 343, (1921).

20. For the particulars of the case, see Levenson (2005), p. 317.

21. Quoted in Michael Gelder et al. (1966), *Oxford Textbook of Psychiatry*, 3rd ed., p. 772 (New York: Oxford University Press).

22. Shirelle Phelps, ed. (2003), *Gale Encyclopedia of Everyday Law*, p. 355 (Detroit: Thomson Gale).

23. Ibid.

24. Levenson (2005), p. 375.

25. Jeffrey Rosen (2007), "The Trials of Neurolaw," *New York Times Magazine*, Mar. 1, pp. 49ff.

26. Robert Alter, tr. (2004), *The Five Books of Moses* (New York: W. W. Norton).

27. C. L. Ten (1987), *Crime, Guilt, and Punishment: A Philosophical Introduction* (Oxford: Clarendon); Herbert Morris (1976), *On Guilt and Innocence: Essays in Legal Philosophy* (Berkeley: University of California Press); Herbert Packer (1968), *The Limits of the Criminal Sanction* (Stanford, CA: Stanford University Press).

28. Joyce (2006), pp. 66–70.

29. John Rawls (1999), *A Theory of Justice*, revised ed., pp. 276–77 (Cambridge, MA: Harvard University Press).

30. Immanuel Kant (1785/1996), *The Metaphysics of Morals*, tr. and ed. Mary Gregor, p. 207 (Cambridge, UK: Cambridge University Press), emphasis in the original.

31. Ibid., emphasis in the original.

32. "A Nation of Jailbirds," *The Economist*, Apr. 4, 2009, p. 40.

33. www.ojp.usdoj.gov/bjs/pub/pdf/spe01.pdf.

34. www.restorativejustice.org/intro/tutorial/processes/vom.

Notes to Epilogue

1. Anthony Trollope (1869/1994), *He Knew He Was Right*, p. 502 (London: Penguin).

2. My wife wrote a book based on my mother's memoirs (which I translated from the Armenian). See Stina Katchadourian (2001), *Efronia: An Armenian Love Story* (Princeton, NJ: Gomidas Institute Press, 2001).

3. Mark Vinocur (1984), *Einstein, a Portrait* (Corte Madera, CA: Pomegranate Artbooks), quoted in Jacques P. Thiroux (2004), *Ethics: Theory and Practice*, 8th ed., p. 26 (Upper Saddle River, NJ: Prentice Hall).

INDEX

Abortion, 38–39, 211, 288

Abstract thinking, 152

Abu Ghraib prison, 126

Achilles, 51

Acquired sociopathy, 134

Acts of commission, 291–92

Acts of omission, 291–92

Actual cause, 294

Act utilitarianism, 275–76

Adam and Eve, 168, 195, 201, 207, 209, 218

Adultery, 39–42

Affect, 316n4

Agca, Mehmet Ali, 81

Aggression, 148, 321n31

Aidos, 17

AIDS, 58–59

Aischune, 17

A'isha, 342n64, 343n77

Alacoque, Saint Margaret Marie, 115

Alcoholics Anonymous, 80

Allen, Woody, 9, 203

Altruism: in animals, 174–75; cheating and, 179–81; evolution of, 175–82; expanding circles and, 181–82; factors promoting, 177–78; and floating pyramid, 182; motivations for, 108, 175–76; reciprocal, 176–81; reparative, 180; resources and, 182

Amato, J. A., 116

Ambrose, Saint, 54

Amends, making, 81

American Law Institute, 299, 352n17

American Psychiatric Association, 58

Amos, 200

Ancestral environment, 172, 336n15

Ancient Greece: and conscience, 145; ethics in, 260–66; and guilt, 257–59, 261–62; legal system in, 352n8; and pride, 48; religion in, 261; and shame, 17, 189–90, 338n50; and sin, 21, 199

Anger, 50–52, 321n31

Animals: altruism in, 174–75; and guilt, 167–68, 172–73, 182; totems, 185

Animism, 184

Antisocial behavior, 125–26

Antisocial personalities, 127–34

Anxiety, existential, 110

Apes, 336n15

Aquinas, Saint Thomas, 44, 46, 144, 169, 210–12; *Summa Theologiae*, 211

Arabs and Arabia, 220, 342n65

Aristotle: Aquinas and, 211; on conscience, 145; ethics of, 263–66; on happiness, 261, 266; *Nicomachean Ethics*, 263, 349n14; and Oedipus, 257; on pride, 48; on shame, 264; on vice, 47

355

development, 158, 160; and Oedipus complex, 141, 146–47, 150, 257, 348n4; on prehistoric societies, 185–86; on reason, 266; and Salomé, 278; on superego, 140, 146–50, 158; and the unconscious, 332n20; on unconscious guilt, 119–20

Friendship, 105, 272

Functionalist approach to emotions, 24–26

Functional magnetic resonance imaging (fMRI), 5–6

Gage, Phineas, 133

Game theory, 177

Gandhi, Mahatma, 227–29, 231, 233, 236, 301

García Márquez, Gabriel, 192

Gates, Bill, 107

Gates Foundation, 107

Gaucherie, 10

Gautama, Siddhartha (Buddha), 238–39

Gender: child development and, 149; and embarrassment, 157; and empathy, 158; and guilt, 157–62; manliness as virtue, 220; moral development and, 160–61; and moral judgment, 130; and shame, 157. *See also* Women

General Examination of Conscience, 224–26

Generosity, 108. *See also* Philanthropy

Genocide, 98, 101–2

Gentleman, in Confucianism, 249–50

Germany, and collective guilt/responsibility, 96–97, 101

Get-tough sentencing laws, 304

Ghana, 97

Gilligan, Carol, 160–61

Girotti, Gianfranco, 60

Gluttony, 54–56

God: and conscience, 143, 144; and free will, 259; and gender, 320n9; and guilt, 34; Hebrew conception of, 198; Hinduism and, 231; human pride as challenge to, 47; Islamic conception of, 216–17, 221; Kant on, 272; name of, 34. *See also* Monotheism

Goethe, Johann Wolfgang von, 146

Golden Rule, 250, 268

Golding, William, *Lord of the Flies*, 126

Good: Nietzsche on, 280; philosophical ethics on, 260

Good Samaritan, 46

Good will, 267–68

Gourmand, 54

Gourmet, 54

Greece. *See* Ancient Greece

Greeley, Andrew, 46

Gregory the Great, Pope, 46, 321n21

Group therapy, 96

Guilt: causes of, 25–26; contemporary significance of, xii–xiii, 22; criminal, 96; cultures oriented toward, 186–87, 189; emotions related to, 3–4, 307; Erikson on, 149; etymology of, 21; excessive, 112–17, 310; existential, 108–11, 310; function of (*see* value/function of); harm/damage from, 23, 67, 76, 134–37 (*see also* Pathology of guilt); hereditary, 96; interdisciplinary study of, x–xi, 27; living with, 86; moral, 96; new perspectives on, 24–26, 135–36; objective state of, 21, 218; origins of, 184–85; overview of, xiii; pathology of, 112–38; personal significance of, 22; political, 96; research on, 317n17; scientific vs. humanistic approaches to, 308; as self-conscious emotion, 7; self in relation to, 19, 24–25, 136–37; shame and, 8, 16–19, 24–26, 134–37, 156, 186–87; subjective feeling of, 21–22, 219; two senses of, 21; value/function of, 4, 23, 66–68, 75, 135, 180–81, 186; virtual, 76–77. *See also* Dealing with guilt

Rwanda, 102

Sabbath, 34–35
Sadness, 254
Sadomasochism, 59
Salomé, Lou Andreas, 278
Sartre, Jean Paul, 108
The Scarlet Letter (Hawthorne), 40
Schadenfreude, 11
Scholastics, 143
School, moral instruction in, 164
Schuld, 21
Scrupulosity, 124–25
Secondary emotions, 5
Second Life (virtual world), 76–77
Secularism: and conscience, 145–46; and guilt, 117; and Jewish guilt, 202–3
Selective serotonin reuptake inhibitors (SSRIs), 138
Self: conscience as, 143; depression and, 121; guilt and, 19, 24–25, 136–37; pride and, 48; shame and, 19, 24–25, 135–37
Self-conscious emotions, 7–8, 330*n*49
Self-defense, 38, 295–96
Self-esteem, 19, 23, 49, 74
Self evaluation, shame and, 16
Self-interest, 178
Self-reflection, 283
Seneca, 318*n*27
Sense of shame, 18
Sentencing, of criminals, 304
Sentiment, 316*n*4
Serbia, 98
Sex and sexuality: adultery, 39–42; Aquinas on, 211; children and, 147; Christianity and, 57, 207–9, 211, 213; contemporary views on, 57, 214, 308–9; Gandhi on, 227–28; Hinduism and, 236; Islam and, 57, 222, 343*n*76; Judaism and, 202; Kant on, 271; lust, 56–59; Luther on, 213; masturbation, 57–58. *See also* Homosexuality
Sexually transmitted diseases, 58–59

Sexual offences, 59
Sexual violence, 59, 128–29
Shakespeare, William: *Macbeth*, 28–31; *Romeo and Juliet*, 12
Shamash, 32
Shame, 15–19; Aristotle on, 264; in Buddhism, 242; causes of, 25–26; in Confucianism, 245–47, 249, 253–55; cultures oriented toward, 186–87, 189, 230; embarrassment and, 14, 15–16; Erikson on, 149; etymology of, 15; exposure and, 15, 19; gender and, 157; guilt and, 8, 16–19, 24–26, 134–37, 156, 186–87; harm/damage from, 134–37; honor and, 18; in Islam, 220–21; moral and non-moral, 16–18; new perspectives on, 24–26, 135–36; pride and, 19; research on, 317*n*7; as self-conscious emotion, 7; and self evaluation, 16; self in relation to, 19, 24–25, 135–37; sense of, 18; sociocultural aspects of, 16–17; survivor guilt and, 91; value/function of, 4, 186
Shamelessness, 264
Shaming, 15
Shariah, 218, 222
Shell shock, 93
Shiite Muslims, 218
Shu, 250
Shyness, 14–15, 74–75, 264
Sierra Leone, 102
Sin: in Christianity, 205–10; in Islam, 217–18; in Judaism, 198–99; in Western religious traditions, 195–96. *See also* Original Sin
Singer, Peter, 18
Situational factors in guilt, 73–74
Situational shyness, 14
Situation ethics, 214
Skinner, B. F., 150
Slapstick comedy, 11–12
Slave morality, 280–82

Slavery, 102
Sloth, 52–53
Social anxiety, 14
Social cognitive theories, 151
Social conscience, 117
Social control, 186
Social Darwinism, 170–71
Social emotions, 7
Social learning models, 150–51
Social order, 173
Sociobiology, 170
Sociopaths, 127. *See also* Psychopaths
Socrates, 129, 261, 283
Sophie's Choice (Styron), 90–91
Sophocles, *Oedipus the King*, 147, 257–59
Soul, Plato's conception of, 46
South Africa, 103
Sovereign immunity, 99
Soviet Union, 103
Spencer, Herbert, 170
Spiritualism, 342n58
Spirituality: Christian, 215; religion vs.,
    215–16; traditional, 215
Spitzer, Eliot, 41
Stages of life, Hindu, 234
Stalin, Joseph, 103
Stealing, 42–43
Sting of conscience. *See* Bite of
    conscience
Sting operations, 296
Stoicism, 145, 168
Strategic embarrassment, 15
Styron, William, *Sophie's Choice*, 90–91
Sudan, 102, 103
Sufism, 222
Suicide, 122, 164, 271
Sunni Muslims, 218
Superego, 18, 140, 146–50, 158. *See also*
    Conscience
Superego lacunae, 126
Supreme Court, 289, 302
Surprise, embarrassment and, 10–11
Survival of the fittest, 170

Survivor guilt, 88–96; accounts of,
    88–89; combat experiences, 93;
    concentration camps, 90–91; dealing
    with, 95–96; individual traumas,
    93–95; natural disasters, 91–92; value/
    function of, 94–95
Sympathy, 74
Synderesis, 143, 331n11

Taboos, 185–86, 337n38
Talmud, 44, 197
Tanakh, 197
Tangney, June Price, 25, 135
Tantric yoga, 236
Tedium vitae, 53
Ten Commandments, xiii, 32–46, 308;
    adultery, 39–42; coveting, 45–46; false
    witness, 44–45; honoring parents,
    35–38; killing, 38–39; Sabbath, 34–35;
    stealing, 42–43
Teresa, Mother, 178–79
Terrorism, 219
Tertullian, 115
Test of Self-Conscious Affect (TOSCA),
    136, 330n49
Theft, 43
Therapy, types of, 95–96
Threat, self-defense and, 295–96
Tibetan Buddhism, 240
Tillich, Paul, 34, 195
Timerman, Jacobo, 94–95
Tit-for-tat, 177
Tolstoy, Leo, *Anna Karenina*, 40
Torah, 33, 197. *See also* Old Testament
TOSCA. *See* Test of Self-Conscious Affect
Totems, 185–86
Tragedy, 257
Transcendental meditation, 236
Transgressionless guilt. *See* Guilt without
    transgression
Trespass, 18, 43, 206, 340n24
The Trial (Kafka), 109–10
Trivers, Robert, 176